Appraising Research in Second Language Learning

## *Language Learning & Language Teaching (LL&LT)*

The LL&LT monograph series publishes monographs, edited volumes and text books on applied and methodological issues in the field of language pedagogy. The focus of the series is on subjects such as classroom discourse and interaction; language diversity in educational settings; bilingual education; language testing and language assessment; teaching methods and teaching performance; learning trajectories in second language acquisition; and written language learning in educational settings.

### Editors

Nina Spada
Ontario Institute for Studies in Education,
University of Toronto

Nelleke Van Deusen-Scholl
Center for Language Study,
Yale University

### Volume 28

Appraising Research in Second Language Learning. A practical approach
to critical analysis of quantitative research. Second edition
by Graeme Keith Porte

# Appraising Research in Second Language Learning

A practical approach to critical analysis
of quantitative research

*Second edition*

Graeme Keith Porte
University of Granada

John Benjamins Publishing Company
Amsterdam / Philadelphia

Library of Congress Cataloging-in-Publication Data

Porte, Graeme Keith.
   Appraising research in second language learning : a practical approach to critical analysis
       of quantitative research / by Graeme Keith Porte. -- 2nd ed.
   p.   cm. (Language Learning & Language Teaching, ISSN 1569-9471 ; v. 28)
   Includes bibliographical references and index.
   1.  Second language acquisition--Research--Methodology. I. Title.
P118.2.P66     2010
418.007'2--dc22                                                     2010022707
ISBN 978 90 272 1991 6   (Hb ; alk. paper)
ISBN 978 90 272 1995 4   (Pb ; alk. paper)
ISBN 978 90 272 8796 0   (Eb)

John Benjamins Publishing Co. · P.O. Box 36224 · 1020 ME Amsterdam · The Netherlands
John Benjamins North America · P.O. Box 27519 · Philadelphia PA 19118-0519 · USA

*To Cristina and Amy, expert appraisers*

# Table of contents

Preface                                                                XI
Notes on the second edition                                          XXIII

Textbook and worked sample appraisals                                    1

CHAPTER 1
**Introduction: The abstract**                                           3
1.1   Worked sample appraisal   4

CHAPTER 2
**Introduction: The problem statement**                                  9
2.1   The background to the problem   11
2.2   The problem statement   12
2.3   Initial indication of variables in the problem statement   13
2.4   Stated contribution to theory and practice   15
Worked sample appraisal   16

CHAPTER 3
**Introduction: The review of the literature**                          20
3.1   Relevance and importance of work cited   22
3.2   Critical address of the literature   24
3.3   Relating the review to the background statement   26
3.4   Time period covered in review   27
3.5   Empirical studies covered in review   28
Worked sample appraisal   29

CHAPTER 4
**Introduction: Research questions and variables**                      36
4.1   Research questions and hypotheses   36
4.2   Nature of the research questions   38
4.3   Nature of the research hypotheses   39
4.4   General appraisal of the research questions/hypotheses   42
4.5   Identification of variables   45
4.6   Variables potentially affecting findings   50
4.7   Operational definitions   52
Worked sample appraisal   56

CHAPTER 5

**Method: Participants and materials**                                                      62

5.1   Descriptive data: Participants   64
5.2   Descriptive data: Groups   68
5.3   Threats to internal validity   72
5.4   Threats to external validity   74
5.5   Descriptive data: Materials   76
5.6   Instruments of measurement: Reliability   78
5.7   Instruments of measurement: Validity   80
5.8   Realisation of main variables   84
Worked sample appraisal   85


CHAPTER 6

**Method: Procedures and research design**                                                  94

6.1   Procedures: Timing of events   96
6.2   Procedures: Test or practice effects   97
6.3   Procedures: Ethical issues and instructions to participants   99
6.4   Procedures: Reactivity   103
6.5   Procedures: Environmental conditions   107
6.6   Research design: Design boxes   110
6.7   Research design: Classifications   116
Worked sample appraisal   128


CHAPTER 7

**Method: Data analysis**                                                                   136

7.1   Data analysis: Description of procedures   136
7.2   Data analysis: Appropriateness of procedures   138
7.3   Data analysis: Statistical assumptions   140
Worked sample appraisal   146


CHAPTER 8

**Results: The nature and presentation of findings**                                        148

8.1   Adequacy of data provided   153
8.2   Graphical displays of results   154
8.3   Descriptive statistics   157
8.4   Statistical procedures   162
        8.4.1   Correlation   164
        8.4.2   Regression   169
        8.4.3   *t*-tests   173
8.5   Explanations of data   176
8.6   Effect size   179

8.7   Other statistical procedures    183
    8.7.1   Analysis of variance    183
    8.7.2   Chi-square    194
8.8   Practical significance and meaningfulness    199
Worked sample appraisal    200

CHAPTER 9
**Discussion and conclusions**    206
9.1   Outcomes in terms of the original research questions/hypotheses    208
9.2   Inferences drawn from outcomes    210
9.3   Outcomes related to literature review    212
9.4   Limitations and future research    213
9.5   Practical implications    215
9.6   Assessment of overall confidence    219
Worked sample appraisal    222

Workbook    231

**Workbook (guided and unguided appraisals)**    233
Abstract 3 (Guided appraisal)    233
Abstract 4 (Unguided appraisal)    235
The background to the problem and the problem
statement 3 (Guided appraisal)    236
The background to the problem and the problem
statement 4 (Unguided appraisal)    238
The review of the literature 3 (Guided appraisal)    240
The review of the literature 4 (Unguided appraisal)    243
Research questions and variables 3 (Guided appraisal)    245
Research questions and variables 4 (Unguided appraisal)    247
Participants and materials 3 (Guided appraisal)    250
Participants and materials 4 (Unguided appraisal)    254
Procedures and research design 3 (Guided appraisal)    256
Procedures and research design 4 (Unguided appraisal)    259
Results: The nature and presentation of findings 3 (Guided appraisal)    261
Results: The nature and presentation of findings 4 (Unguided appraisal)    264
Discussion and conclusions 3 (Guided appraisal)    267
Discussion and conclusions 4 (Unguided appraisal)    270

Glossary of key terms in quantitative research    273

Appendices    291

Further reading    303

Index of main subject entries in textbook    305

# Preface

This book is written to guide student and novice researchers through their critical reading of a research paper in the field of second language (L2) learning. My aim is to help these readers relate the basic knowledge they acquire during introductory courses on investigation in applied linguistics to their own independent reading of research papers. They will be shown ways of approaching the appraisal of the abstract and the introductory section of the study, both of which set the stage by describing the rationale as well as the objective of the work. Similarly, the reader will be given ideas about how to assess the method and procedures section so that he or she can decide, for example, whether the research design was appropriate, and what precautions were taken to guard against threats of validity to the findings. They will become more familiar with, and confident about, interpreting results from commonly-used descriptive or inferential statistical procedures and checking how appropriately these have been presented. Finally, the reader should be in a position to assess his or her overall confidence in the paper and critically to evaluate the researcher's own interpretation of the findings in terms of the extent to which the conclusion is justified, can be generalised, and has limitations.

A knowledgeable reader will also contribute enormously to research practice. Above all, there is the obvious help and experience critical reading gives us towards the better description and presentation of our own studies. Informed criticism of others' work inevitably also helps us to discover new areas of research that have emerged as a direct result of this critical reading. This said, I will *not* be focussing here specifically on designing and conducting a critique of research as direct preparation for carrying out, writing up, and publishing one's own study. Indeed, as will become clear in the text, different journals and other media adopt different policies with regard to the presentation and writing up of research for publication, varying in accordance with the orientation and objectives of the particular medium. Nevertheless, learning to read research appropriately is, indeed, intimately connected with learning to write it effectively, and it is to be hoped that the experience of appraising in this way will help the reader better to present their own work for publication and peer evaluation.

Research in L2 learning[1] contexts takes place in many forms and follows many research traditions, of course. Quantitative research is only one of these approaches, along with others such as ethnographic and survey research, observational techniques

---

1. Except where indicated, "L2" refers to both second language and foreign language learning contexts.

and more introspective methods – all of which have provided us with excellent insights into how second languages are learnt and taught. Within the area of quantitative research much of the focus in this book is on so-called "quasi-experimental" studies using statistical approaches with participants in intact classroom situations. The book helps readers to appraise the most common statistical procedures used in applied linguistics and L2 research such as $t$-tests, correlation, chi-square, and factor analysis. This should not be taken as a recommendation about the "best" way to do research in our field: the real-life world of L2 learning places considerable limits on a researcher being able satisfactorily to select and assign participants and impose conditions on the experiment. Such intact groups imposed by the local administration often mean that it is difficult – on occasions impossible – to meet the many threats to data validity present in such research, in particular those relating to selection of participants, allocation of groups, and experimental procedures. Conversely, for many of us working in the area of L2 learning, undertaking studies with intact groups is the only practical way of conducting research. This is not to belittle the contribution already made – and still to be made – by such studies: our research objectives and appraisal of research will always need to take such unavoidable constraints into account. But this reality means that we should learn not only how to use such familiar designs to our advantage, but also how to appraise what has gone on in other researchers' experiments. In this way, we can search out answers to our research hypotheses and questions, while acknowledging the inevitable limits imposed on the interpretation of results obtained in these research contexts.

## Why do we need to appraise research?

The importance of the book lies in the fact that it responds to a continuing need in the field. Students and potential researchers may have read many academic papers and absorbed considerable theory about research design and how to implement it in their own study. Indeed, more and more universities and teaching colleges are including courses in their degrees aimed at providing students with a basic introductory knowledge of research techniques and practice. This is a particularly timely response to a perceived need for students who will ideally want to contribute to their chosen field of study. However, conducting research is much more than merely knowing how to carry out the investigation. Sound preparation for research also requires the ability to situate and defend our proposed study in the light of existing knowledge. In order to do this, we need to be able to appraise others' work adequately and appropriately enough to help justify the contribution our own work is intended to make to current awareness in the field.

Although my assumption is that all of us work and/or study in the area of L2 learning, our interest in academic papers will inevitably vary according to our own personal line of research. Thus, while the extracts and sample papers the reader is going to study in this book reflect important areas of research, we will inevitably all be approaching a paper from different backgrounds, interests, and needs. Nevertheless, our overall critical approach to the object of our reading will be similar. It will, therefore, always be important for anyone involved in any kind of research in our area to be able to approach the reading of a study both from the point of view of an uncommitted critical reader and/or that of a researcher interested in one focal aspect of that area.

## Who is this book for?

This book is primarily intended as a main course text (or supplementary to a research-techniques book such as those mentioned in the "Further reading" list) and is aimed at classes of both undergraduate and postgraduate students reading for language or applied linguistics degrees who are required to submit work which entails the understanding of the theory and practice of research principally based on quantitative analyses. It also links with the growing number of applied professional courses and should prove of considerable interest to those participating in language teacher-training programmes or degrees, as well as those practising teachers anxious to embark on their own classroom research. Both groups need to be research literate and, as Altman (1988) maintained, "second language teachers have a professional obligation to make sense of research that has a potential impact on their classrooms"[2] – even if they do not wish actively to participate in their own research.

Appraisal of research papers not only requires common sense, but also some degree of literacy in this kind of research. To take full advantage of this text, the reader should already understand the basic principles of research in this field and needs to have some rudimentary knowledge of how the most common inferential and descriptive statistical procedures – as in correlation or comparing means and frequencies – might be used in data analyses. A good number of excellent books are already available which provide an introduction to terminology and the most useful quantitative and qualitative techniques typically used in research in the area of L2 teaching and learning (see "Further reading"). Where descriptive or inferential statistical procedures *are* discussed in this text, the emphasis is on the appropriateness and consequences of their application in the context of what we have read in the paper, rather than on the way these procedures should actually be carried out. Furthermore, a large number of illustrative examples and a "Glossary of key terms in quantitative research" have

---

2.    Foreword to Brown, J. (1991). *Understanding research in second language learning* (p.vii.). Cambridge: Cambridge University Press.

been included to facilitate the critical process. Nevertheless, the book provides only an introduction to key issues in certain statistical matters, such as the advantages and disadvantages of parametric and non-parametric procedures, or the implicit assumptions to be applied when using a particular test, and always strictly in terms of the way such concerns have an impact on the way we appraise any outcomes. Readers who intend to move beyond critique to employing some of these procedures in their own research need to obtain more profound knowledge and are referred to more detailed accounts in the recommended books.

## How is the material to be used?

An important objective of this book is to provide the reader with a suggested methodology that can eventually be applied to his or her own independent appraisal of quantitative research. To this end, the practice of appraisal in this book goes from worked samples, through guided, and finally on to unguided papers.

The appraisal of a research paper requires the ability to be attentive throughout the reading and thereby be able to react recursively to the text based both on what we know and what we have been told. Continually stimulating and channelling such reactions to the reading forms the basis of the learning approach applied in this book. The principal innovative methodology used here to arouse the reader's critical faculties is awareness-raising. The reader is encouraged to react to information at the moment of reading rather than – as usually happens – in a subsequent review of the whole text. Thus, my assumption throughout is that the critical reader approaches their reading in the usual sequential manner. In other words, they will normally evaluate each section as and when they meet it, without looking ahead to other sections of the paper, but recalling what they have already read. I have adopted such a progressive *modus operandi* not only out of practical considerations, but also because it represents a very sound reading strategy when one is learning how to appraise research: it encourages the critical reader to begin to build up a response to what they are reading and eventually gauge their final confidence level based on the accumulation of input. Notwithstanding these assumptions, there will be times within the activities when a reader is encouraged to look ahead to what is said at later stages in the paper for further possible insights.

What this means in practice within a recursive appraisal methodology is that, at various points in the text, I encourage readers to pause in their reading, to summarise and question what has just been read, to ponder over the consequences of a statement, to predict outcomes, to think back to previous parts of the paper and ahead to upcoming sections, or to suggest possible problems or drawbacks in the perceived research design. Obviously, such spontaneous responses are only expressions of our preliminary reactions to something, and they may well be refuted by what subsequent sections of the paper reveal. Consequently, they may or may not need to be modified in the light of that information. However, the exercise of raising our awareness and reacting to the text instinctively in this way is particularly helpful for a reader who is seeking to engage critically with the text. Essentially, it draws us immediately into the research itself and puts us in the role of an inquisitive observer, almost as if we were engaging in a real-time conversation with the author about the study – a scenario I put to practical use in the sample papers when readers are initially encouraged to record their instinctive reactions to what they read as if talking to the researcher face-to-face (see below, *How to use the workbook section*).

Here a word of warning. A popular notion exists that appraising a fellow-researcher's work consists of finding faults in that work. Given what should be the fundamentally supportive role of the critical reader of research, I would like to dissuade you from this notion at once. Appraisal of scientific research can be approached in many different ways but, by definition, will require us to adopt a cautious attitude to what we read and will involve us making judgements about the perceived quality and merit of what has been described. However, such remarks should be seen to have a constructive – rather than *de*constructive – aim both for the author *and* the reader. As scientists and readers of such science it is in the interest of our field that we are sceptical; it is also by asking pertinent questions of the research we read that we ourselves may better shape the course of our *own* future research. We should not expect, as researchers or readers of research, to find a study which provides us with *all* the answers to *all* our questions. However, our reading should at least help put us in a better position to decide whether all the appropriate questions were being asked in the first place. Such appraisal needs to respond appropriately to the most consequential aspects of the study, rather than to some kind of check-list of essential elements of any research paper. Indeed, Gottfredson (1978)[3] identified no less than 83 attributes that many editors/reviewers may use in their appraisals. Given such a large number of elements, it is not surprising that many journal reviewers themselves end up in disagreement about the merits of a paper!

The main idea behind the awareness-raising approach to appraisal encouraged here is that readers see themselves not as judge and jury of a study, but rather as potential consumers of research. As such, we will initially need to evaluate the contribution and importance of the work to our own present interests. In turn, learning how to appraise will enable us to assess the amount of confidence we might reasonably have both in the findings and the interpretations made from these. A well-designed study will provide answers in which we can have confidence and will serve as an example, and perhaps a stimulus, for our own work. In this sense, the overall significance of this

---

3.    Gottfredson, S. (1978). Evaluating psychological research reports. *American Psychologist, 33*, 920–934.

book is that it shows the reader how to learn directly and indirectly from what he or she is reading.

## How to use the textbook section

This book has been written in a combination text- and workbook format. In the textbook section, the reader is introduced to the most typical component parts or sections of a quasi-experimental quantitative research paper in this field. Here a personal perspective on the paper is provided which explains and illustrates ways in which essential information may ideally be communicated to the reader and critically interpreted within that part. There is inevitably a degree of subjectivity involved in one reader appraising certain aspects of L2 research; however, I have tried throughout to provide authoritative advice on appraisal, rather than impose an authoritarian approach.

For the purposes of this approach to appraisal, a research paper is divided into four basic elements (i. Introduction; ii. Method; iii. Results; and iv. Discussion and Conclusions) and a number of subsections within these four. In the Introduction chapters readers will be presented with strategies for appraising the abstract, the background to the problem and the problem statement, the review of the literature, research objectives and variables, and operational definitions. Obviously, an adequate understanding of the value of the whole paper cannot be achieved without appreciating the sum of its parts. The reader is shown how the abstract may provide both context and landmarks: the kind of information which enables the reader to assess the immediate value the paper has for his or her current interests. Subsequently, the reader is taken through the process of locating and evaluating the background to the study and the problem statement and interpreting any variations found during the paper. The reader then decides how far the literature cited provides an adequate theoretical and empirical basis for the subsequent development of the study's hypotheses and/or research questions. Finally, he or she is encouraged to think about the operational descriptions and assignment of variables and constructs in the study. The advice and practice given in this section is aimed at helping the reader be in a better position to handle a posterior evaluation of the Results and Discussion sections of the paper being read, both in the light of the information provided here and the responses made to it.

Once it is established *what* the text tells us about the study and the background to, and nature of, the research question or hypothesis, we might look for a suitable description of *how* the study was carried out. Again, the recursive appraisal process here is one of constant action on the part of the author and reaction on the part of the reader. Thus, what is explained to us in this part of a paper will need continually to be appraised in the light of our reactions to the information in the Introduction. In the Method chapters the following main areas are treated: internal and external validity issues; participant identification, processes of selection and group assignment; procedures; principal research designs; and proposed measurement and analysis. Thus, these chapters deal with the nuts-and-bolts of the research design. Issues which need to be appraised here include how participants have been selected for study and the consequences of such selection for any subsequent interpretation, the conditions in which participants are observed and the limitations imposed by such circumstances, the information and instructions given to the participants and the implications of these for the data obtained, or the way in which research designs with intact groups may differ from true experimental designs. Identifying a study's research design is helpful when evaluating the procedures described by the author. Since research design is not normally described by the authors themselves, it will often be up to the reader to assess the suitability of the procedures used. To this end, the reader is shown the benefits of considering designs graphically, highlighting their advantages and disadvantages using the help given. In this way, the reader is also encouraged to comment on any potential weaknesses in the design and suggest possible improvements.

Throughout, particular attention is paid to the possibility of replicating the research we read. That we might replicate research to confirm results is a condition of the self-correcting nature of scientific inquiry. In order to repeat research in this way we need to have access to the most important details of what went on and, for this reason, I encourage readers to judge the replicability of the research designs we are presented with. If the descriptions we read are vague, they are unlikely to facilitate either a future replication of the study nor allow the reader adequately to evaluate and interpret the information given in the subsequent Results section.[4]

Another of the interesting questions considered here is the appraisal of any proposed data analyses. After an introduction to the most commonly-used statistical analyses of data, the reader is encouraged to appraise with a view to verifying the extent to which the researcher has thought about and checked the assumptions underlying any proposed statistical analyses and/or whether he or she has allowed for the potential effects of violations on subsequent results.

In the Results chapter, the focus shifts to outcomes and their initial interpretation. In many cases, in the kind of study I am concerned with here, the selection of an appropriate analytical procedure will be extremely important to establish confidence in results – both for the author and the reader. That confidence, hopefully gained in previous sections of the paper, will ideally now be reinforced through the nature and presentation of the findings. Readers will need to see how to locate the most important results (i.e., those which have a direct bearing on the proposed problem statement).

---

4.  Further advice about how to carry out a replication study can be found in the journal *Language Teaching, 41(1)*, 1-14.

Consideration for appraisal will include whether these have been stated or presented clearly enough for the reader to interpret them appropriately. To this end, the reader is shown how to make use of any tables or figures provided in the paper, particularly those that provide the basis for checks to be made on claims of relationships, similarities, or differences between variables. The reader is subsequently encouraged to assess the results as a consequence of the research context, the objectives of the study, the participants used, and the choice of instrument used for analysis. Therefore, particular attention is paid here to helping the reader assess what they are being told based on the information given and appraised earlier in the paper. The reader is also encouraged to check on typical but questionable practices, such as doing additional tests when the planned ones did not provide significant results, or using parametric statistical tests without enough evidence of normality in the original database.

Within this section, both statistical and practical significance (or meaningfulness) of results will also be a source of concern. Specifically, readers are shown how they might go about evaluating the significance of findings through any text or tables provided and, if these are reported, to see whether such outcomes actually represent the major question asked or some subsidiary, post-hoc question not really part of the original problem statement. As regards meaningfulness, the aim is to assess whether any apparently significant data reported are, in fact, interesting or important once placed within the context and objectives of the study.

In the final chapter, strategies are suggested to assess the quality of the Discussion and Conclusions. The first focus of appraisal in this section is the extent to which any conclusions drawn are consistent with the results. We will also want to be shown how far these outcomes fit in with what has been discussed in the previous literature review. The more studied interpretations we might expect to encounter in this section of the paper will need to be evaluated in terms of their reasonableness, and any explanations for unexpected outcomes carefully considered. If, for example, an author claims that a particular variable did not affect results in the way predicted, readers may want to judge how far the reason given is acceptable in the circumstances. Similarly, questions of generalisation and practical implications of findings are appraised here. The reader will need to be in a position to assess the justification for any claims that a particular conclusion can be applied to other situations. Finally, in such a practical field as ours, it will be important to weigh up the potential consequences of any outcomes reported for language learning and teaching practice.

At the beginning of each chapter (after the initial appraisal of the abstract), readers are firstly presented with the relevant section to read from the sample paper and are introduced to the initial critical appraisal strategies of summary and annotation of immediate reactions. They are also encouraged at this stage to formulate and attend to a set of initial Observations on any immediate issues noted (see below). At this worked appraisal stage, readers are shown my own approach to the task as an example. Once readers have thereby familiarised themselves with the section of the paper in question, I then go on to discuss a specific appraisal issue in detail, explaining how each can be approached in our critical reading of the text. At the end of each sub-section I return to the sample paper read at the beginning of the chapter to carry out the appraisal itself based on the advice given. Each chapter ends with a second complete worked sample appraisal which readers can use as reinforcement of the theory and practice provided in the chapter just read.

## How to use the workbook section

In the subsequent workbook section the student is encouraged to see how this same approach to appraisal might be used in practice on two complete research papers, before trying it out on their own independent reading. These personal readings of fictitious research papers comprise a guided appraisal, followed by an unguided appraisal for students to work on alone.

The sample papers have been specially written for the book, but have objectives, method, data analysis, results, and conclusions that are based on a number of actual studies. The objective in writing these papers was to present them "warts and all": there has been no attempt to hide weaknesses or limitations in order to present model pieces of research for appraisal. Although the way a researcher expresses him- or herself on the page is a crucial element in communicating to the reader, adequacy of language or style of expression will not be specific objects of appraisal here, except where this reflects directly on the understanding or discussion of the research undertaken.

The worked, guided and unguided appraisals all follow the same procedure: they begin with part of the text of a paper followed by leading questions, all of which are closely linked to the suggestions made in the relevant textbook section and which focus on an awareness-raising approach to critical reading.[5] In the two worked sample appraisals, students can consider my own responses to these leading questions, along-side the ideas expressed in the relevant textbook section. In the subsequent (guided and unguided) papers in the workbook itself, readers should attempt their own responses based on the advice given in the textbook making use, if they wish, of the guidance provided by a number of additional specific prompts and suggestions.

As an initial recommended reading and response strategy for any paper read, and before embarking on these questions, the reader is encouraged to take notes on either

---

5.   This initial pedagogical orientation towards critical reading owes much to the general advice and criteria offered by Bruce Tuckman in his 1994 book *Conducting educational research*. New York: Harcourt Brace College.

side of the text, summarising, where appropriate, what has been read and then record-ing spontaneous reactions to it – much as if he or she were engaged in a dialogue with the researcher. An integral part of the approach to appraisal advocated here is that the reader begins to stimulate their critical faculties through such a stream of conscious-ness on the very first encounter with the text. Clearly, such spontaneous feedback may well need to be revised in the light of what is read elsewhere in the paper; however, both kinds of initial response will stand the reader in good stead as important refer-ences and points of departure for future discussion.

In the book, these spontaneous, initial reactions, and others noted in subsequent readings, are then assembled and formulated as observations (see below) interspersed throughout that text. These will provide suggestions which initially help alert the reader to ambiguous or incomplete information, potential flaws or inconsistencies, weak arguments, or simply points to follow up in the remaining text. The worked example aims to help the student appreciate the nature and degree of critical attention required during a reading and the kind of subsequent questions that might be posed as he or she is reading the rest of the paper. Clearly, both my responses to the leading questions and the observations made are merely suggestions for what could be passing through the mind of a critical reader; doubtless, readers themselves will be able to sup-ply more of their own based on their experience and the textbook procedures.

As these initial activities imply, trying to approach a piece of published research using an awareness-raising strategy is very much about learning to become constantly responsive to what you are being told. This requires a different, more meticulous, approach to reading than you may be used to. I have attempted to convey this need for constant critical receptiveness during appraisal through these preliminary reading strategies and subsequent observations, thereby encouraging the reader regularly to attend to their inner voice during the reading. The objective is to help the students, in their own subsequent independent reading, to raise critical awareness sufficiently to enable them to pause, assimilate something they have just been told in the text, and form the pertinent response – either as a question or, as it were, an aside to oneself for later use. This pause – as one judiciously approaches and responds to a section of the text – is visualised in the workbook samples as a numbered symbol (①,②, etc.) in the text itself. In the worked appraisal after each chapter, these symbols correspond to the kind of response and/or question I found myself asking as I read the text. Subse-quently, in the guided and unguided papers in the workbook, the reader is encouraged to respond independently to the points raised.

In this sense, and in terms of actual class practice, the book lends itself to more than one method of exploitation (see below, *Notes on the second edition*). The approach should appeal to those who seek a way to combine teacher input, student input, and student interaction, and provide for different learning phases during and across classes. The short textbook sections and subsequent worked sample material can be used as the basis for teacher input, group activity, and later discussion. The guided appraisal could be used as self-access material through which a student can work before submitting the responses to individual presentation, peer and/or teacher discussion.

The fact that the textbook chapters are ordered in the way they are is not to be seen as indicative of the way the book must be worked through. Rather, the units follow the format of a typical research paper in this genre. There is no intended progression as regards subject matter or complexity, although readers *are* advised to consider separately the section of the worked sample alongside the relevant textbook pages before attempting their own appraisal of the guided sample and going on to their own independent reading. Doubtless, some readers will want to concentrate on the appraisal of certain sections of a paper more than others, and this is facilitated in the worked samples by constant reference to what was addressed earlier in that particular paper.

## Acknowledgements

Grateful acknowledgement is made to the following sources for permission to reprint material in this book.

*Table* adapted from Brown, J.D. (1992). Statistics as a foreign language: Part 2. *TESOL Quarterly, 26(4)*, 629–664.

*Flow chart* reprinted from Hatch, E., & Lazaraton, A. (1991). *The research manual.* New York: Newbury House Publishers.

All website links mentioned were live at the time of writing (February 2010)

# Notes on the second edition

In the early 2000s, as a frequent referee of research studies submitted to learned journals in our field, and amid the growing interest in practical approaches to carrying out experimental research in L2 learning, I became convinced of the need for a book which guided both novice and experienced researchers in the equally crucial skill of critical appraisal of the final product. Since then, there has been a further increase in the number of practical how-to-do research books (see "Further reading"), but this volume remains the only systematic, instructional manual on how to appraise what we read as we read it. Almost a decade after *Appraising Research in Second Language Learning* first appeared on the scene, the success of the first edition and its current use as a set or recommended textbook on more than a hundred undergraduate and postgraduate courses worldwide has demonstrated that there remains a recognised need for such a book.

This second edition gives me the chance to incorporate a number of additions and amendments, as well as suggestions made by the many reviewers, practitioners, and students who have taken the trouble to write to me. The basic textbook/workbook structure of the book remains the same since the feedback I received indicated this had worked well, but I was also encouraged to review the way in which students encountered the workbook itself after reading each chapter. There were many requests for better integration of the text- and workbook, with the frequent suggestion being made that students be introduced to the practical application of the advice in each textbook chapter sooner than was proposed in the first edition, where the workbook appeared in a separate section at the end of the book and was worked on once the theory chapter had been read. Likewise, the length of some of the chapters meant that readers had, on occasions, to work through daunting amounts of text before being able to see the practice of appraisal at work in the worked samples. A further, related request was that more obvious and closer connection should initially be made between the text and the worked guided appraisals to help readers refer back quickly from these appraisals to the text to see what comments refer to. I have sought to facilitate reading and introduce these suggestions in this edition not only by dividing up the previously rather more extensive chapters such as Introduction and Method into more manageable units, but also by providing section numbers within each chapter corresponding to the practice appraisal questions as well as a set of advance organizers after each section (indicated by the book symbol ▱ ). These encourage readers to stop their reading at this point and look immediately at how the advice in the text is then carried out in practice in one of the two worked sample appraisals now included within each textbook chapter, rather than in the workbook itself. The reader may then choose to work independently through the second sample at the end of each chapter and the further guided and unguided examples in the Workbook.

As I foresaw in the preface to the first edition, testimony to its flexibility of use are the different routes the reader might follow through this book. Much will depend on issues such as whether the reader is using the book alone or as part of a class, whether he or she is a novice or a more experienced researcher, or whether the book is being read in a linear fashion or merely referenced for certain sections. The path I propose above is merely one suggestion for those who – alone or in groups – wish to work through the book from start to finish and want to experience a more immediate application of the ideas in the text to a real appraisal. In this way, the new presentation both helps to divide up the appraised sections into more accessible concepts and also encourages readers to raise their awareness about what is involved in appraising research by immediately seeing how what they have just read can be applied in practice. Other colleagues have suggested alternative routes: for example, I have taken up and extended Christine Goh's (National Institute of Education, Singapore) suggestion in this edition that students might start most chapters by skimming through the corresponding section in the worked sample appraisal first – before reading the text itself – in order to develop greater metacognitive awareness about the appraisal process and be better prepared for the explanations in the subsequent text. Another suggestion, from Reneé Jourdenais (Monterey Institute of International Studies) is that readers might work alternately between the complete chapters and the corresponding sections of practice appraisal. Florencia Franceschina (Lancaster University) described the advantage of using the book also as a tool for writing up one's own research by writing down the list of questions used in each section and then using them as a checklist against which to compare one's own writing.

In the textbook there have also been a number of incorporations following reader recommendations and in the light of the kind of papers I am now seeing presented on a regular basis to learned journals. Firstly, there is more attention given to procedures such as meta-analysis and also to increasingly prominent statistical procedures such as logistic regression as an extension of linear regression and loglinear analysis as an extension of chi-square. The importance of being able to replicate research was emphasized in the first edition of the book. Specific calls for such research have since followed in journals such as *Language Teaching* and *Studies in Second Language Acquisition*, together with increasing interest evidenced in a recent colloquium on the subject at the 2009 *American Association for Applied Linguistics* conference, and a forthcoming book on the subject, have all prompted me to add more detailed and extensive reference to such procedures throughout this edition. Readers are firstly shown how the critique of papers can stimulate replication studies by addressing what to look out for in each separate section: e.g., participants, method, analysis, etc., and then advised as to what studies may lend themselves to useful replication and why. The increasingly important critique of research ethics in L2 acquisition data gathering and research reporting has been addressed in considerably more detail and given a further appraisal question in its own right. The assessment of overall confidence in a paper has also been addressed and a further appraisal question provided. Finally, the references in text, where appropriate, have been revised and the final "Further reading" list completely updated.

In the workbook itself, and again in response to requests, I have included more guided as well as unguided practice material. This material was originally provided as a supplement to the first edition and on my website. It has now been adapted to the new appraisal questions where necessary.

In the preparation of this book, I have received the help and interest of colleagues and friends who have been kind enough to send me feedback on their experiences using the book on a large number of courses. As well as those students and staff who have taken the time to contact me with suggestions and comments, I would particularly like to thank the following for their help and input to this edition:

Rebekha Abbuhl (California State University-Long Beach, USA)
Andrew Cohen (University of Minnesota, USA)
Christine Goh (National Institute of Education, Singapore)
Alison Mackey (University of Georgetown, Washington, USA)
Hossein Nassaji (University of British Columbia, Canada)
Nina Spada (OISE, University of Toronto, Canada)
Aek Phakiti (University of Sydney, Australia)
Kees Vaes (John Benjamins Publishing Company)

I hope students and practitioners alike will continue to find the approach and content of this new edition both stimulating and useful. As always, any feedback and experiences using the book are gratefully received and individually acknowledged.

Graeme Porte
Granada, 2010

# Textbook and worked sample appraisals

# Chapter 1

# Introduction

## The abstract

For the author, the principal aim of the abstract is to summarise the most important points of the paper. This summary, however, will often be the first contact – and sometimes the only contact – that the reader will have with the paper. There are a number of different guidelines to authors about writing this, and other sections, of a research paper in our field. Typically, however, it will provide concise information and all-important indicators to the reader about what to expect in the body of the text.[6] From our point of view as potential consumers of the research, there are two main objectives: (1) We would like to have enough information provided to be in a position to judge if the study is sufficiently relevant to our own current interests to be subsequently read in its entirety *and* (2) where the study *is* going to be of interest, we may want to make a mental note at pertinent points during our reading of the abstract of aspects mentioned about which we would be looking for more details in the main body of the text. We might consider the importance to our research interests of the question asked: does it seem to have the potential to change, or add to, our theoretical understanding of the problem? This should also help us to make a preliminary evaluation of how successfully and appropriately the research has been carried out. Furthermore, we could be in a position to judge its initial merits based on our acquired knowledge of standard procedures in this kind of research. In order to help achieve these objectives, we could be looking to the abstract for some or all of the following:

a.  a statement of the topic and aim of the paper, which may be accompanied by a statement more broadly situating the research.
b.  a concise description of the SAMPLE and materials used.[7]

---

6.  Readers are reminded that the format and presentation of different sections of a research report may vary according to the requirements of the particular publication. Many journal editors in the field direct contributors to the guidelines available in the latest *Publication manual of the American Psychological Association (APA)* (Washington, DC: APA) for specific information on the recommended detailed content of each section. Thus, where relevant, I will also refer to these recommendations in the body of the text.

7.  Terms in small capitals in the text are further explained in the Glossary of key terms in quantitative research (p. 273).

c.    some information about the procedures used and the way DATA were later analysed.
d.    a brief summary of results, or the general trend of these, and what conclusions are to be drawn from these.

## Worked sample appraisal

### Abstract 1

1.    **Read this abstract. When you have read a paragraph, stop and write in the *left-hand column* a few words which summarise the gist of that paragraph, to help you understand and focus on what the researcher is saying. Then, in the *right-hand column* write a few words which record your instinctive reactions to what you have just read as if you were addressing the researcher face-to-face (see below).**

This is your first chance to hear about the study and respond to what you read, so attend closely both to what is read *and* how this is communicated, and record thoughts immediately. Imagine we are being informed about the study in a conversation with the researcher. Feel free to interrupt and say whatever is necessary. Record your agreement, disagreement, doubts, surprise, or even disbelief in the margins of the text. Although our initial reactions may be countered, or opinions necessarily revised as a result of what is read later in the text, the idea here is already to trigger your response in a number of ways, and so immediately begin to involve ourselves in the study. Look out for places where we think the meaning of something is unclear or incomplete, and then formulate a quick question to the researcher establishing what we would like to know to clarify things. Examine how the researcher uses empirical or intuitive knowledge to illustrate or defend something, and jot down a response to the point made. Be prepared to identify possible good or weak arguments or inconsistencies, concentrating particularly on the language used to present such points of view. At early stages in the paper, there will no doubt also be aspects of the procedures used about which we will want to see further details in later sections. Jot these down too, so that they can be referred to later on.

**In this worked example, the columns have been filled in to show you one way of going about this initial reading task.**

| | | |
|---|---|---|
| *Using computer software to understand EFL writing and help teacher correction in large classes. Has a positive effect on production and gives information about errors.* | The purpose of this paper is to study the use of a computer-based instrument to monitor, evaluate, and understand better ① EFL student writing in Country X. Specially-designed software, used together with software commercially available ②, was used initially to alleviate teacher obligation in the correction of written work③ from the large numbers of students in Country X's EFL writing classes. | *What do you mean by "use"? How can one program do all three things?*<br><br>*But can a computer program do the same work as a teacher correcting?* |

| | It is suggested that objective analysis and feedback influence positively and significantly students' production, and also serve to present detailed information about the errors often found in particular writing genres. | Do you mean "significantly" as a result of some statistical test on the data? |
|---|---|---|
| Could help teachers in these classes. Test group errors significantly less than control. | I suggest that this kind of finding might help change the way teachers understand large class sizes in this country. Groups were divided into test and control④ and they completed writing assignments during the first six months of 1995 using the software. T-TEST procedures revealed more statistically significant reductions⑤ in the test groups' errors than in the CONTROL GROUPS. I also describe other data which revealed the precise error types found throughout these writing genres. | I don't see how this finding can bring about such an effect.

So **both** groups used the software? |

2. **Read again the relevant section in the textbook and then study my responses to the following questions:**

a.   Can you see a clear statement of the topic and aim of the paper?
*The topic of this paper appears to be computer-assisted language learning. The aim of the study is less clear: I wonder how software such as this can be used to "monitor" or "evaluate" or "understand better" student writing, all of which would normally seem to require a more subjective judgement.*

b.   Is there a concise description of the sample and materials used?
*No basic information is given as regards the participants used. It appears they might have come from large classes in Country X, but some more information about who participated and the material used would have been useful here for me to judge the study's immediate relevance.*

c.   What details are provided about the procedures used and the way data were later analysed?
*I am told that both groups used the software; how the groups then differed in the procedures used will hopefully be explained later. Data have been analysed using a procedure known as a "t-test". I have made a note here to check in the relevant section to see what the specific test was.*

d.   Is there a brief summary of results, or the general trend of these, and are you told what conclusions are drawn from these?
*There seems to be adequate information here about the results. However, the connection between the t-test results on different amounts of errors and the aims mentioned in the first*

*sentence is not obvious. Similarly, I am not sure how the "other data" described in the last sentence will fit in with the original "purpose" stated. The conclusion given states "It is suggested that objective analysis and feedback influence positively and significantly students' production". I also made a note to check in the body of the text what "feedback" is actually being provided to the student by the software and how its positive influence was measured.*

Observations

① What do you think of this as an objective of the study, and where would you look for more information to see if it was achieved?
*I was not sure how the results of such a study might help us to "understand better EFL student writing". Results might describe the present situation and participants, but I thought it sounded somewhat ambitious to hope for more GENERALISATION or more insight than this – maybe the Discussion or Conclusion sections of the paper will throw more light on this.*

② What information will you want to have about this software, and where would you expect to find it in the paper?
*I got the impression here that two kinds of software "treatment" (i.e., "commercially-available" and "specially-designed") were given to the two groups involved. I will be looking for more details of the software in the Method section of the paper and also to see whether steps were taken, or needed, to measure or separate out the effects of each of the two kinds of software.*

③ What do you think is meant by "alleviate teacher obligation", and how could the software help?
*If the alleviation of "teacher obligation" in correction involves what I currently understand is the correction and evaluation of written work, I cannot see how the objectivity normally found in computer software can hope to replace both these subjective teacher actions. I made a note to look out for, perhaps in the Discussion and conclusions section, how the authors believe "teacher obligation" is being alleviated if the final evaluation still remains in the hands of the teacher.*

④ What else would you be looking to read about this division, and where would you most likely find this information?
*I would be interested to see (in the Method section) how the division was decided upon. Given the comparative aims here, it will also be useful to read there about whether these groups were considered equal to begin with.*

⑤ What do you understand as yet by the term "statistically significant reductions"?
*Presumably, this refers to significant differences in error frequency between the groups. It might have been useful to have included information here about the observed PROBABILITY LEVEL (p). This could give me, as the interested reader, important information to judge whether the cut-off point reached in terms of significance is sufficient to warrant a more detailed reading of the Results section.*

**Abstract 2**

1.  Read this abstract. When you have read a paragraph, stop and write in the *left-hand column* a few words which summarise the gist of that paragraph, to help you understand and focus on what the researcher is saying. Then, in the *right-hand column* write a few words which record your instinctive reactions to what you have just read as if you were addressing the researcher face-to-face.

| | It is generally recognised① that customizing the way we speak helps a non-native speaker comprehend what he or she hears of the target language input②. This is particularly the case when several features of phonology, syntax, and lexis are united in the message. However, to date, little is known about which main and secondary characteristics of this input really do help such a speaker to comprehend. The aim here is to see if, and in which way, adjusting pauses, speed, and syntax helps beginners③ improve their oral comprehension. An initial group of 208 participants④ were assigned to 4 groups⑤, with each group being given one version of the same text. Findings are that firstly, there is a significant⑥ improvement in oral comprehension when syntax is simplified and, secondly, comprehension is enhanced more by including a number of pauses into the text rather than speaking more slowly. | |

2.  Read again the relevant section in the textbook and then attempt to answer these questions. Finally, compare your responses to mine.

    a.  Can you see a clear statement of the topic and aim of the paper?
        *The topic of this paper is L2 listening comprehension. In sentence four we read a clear aim of the study to see if modifying certain elements of the input helps improve listening comprehension.*

    b.  Is there a concise description of the sample and materials used?
        *We only learn of the numbers involved here and the fact that they were assigned to different groups. Few, if any, details are provided about the material used, beyond the fact that each group heard one version of the same text. Obviously, we would be on the lookout for considerably more information in the rest of the paper about the numbers in each group, which group heard what text, whether this selection was RANDOM, and who designed these texts.*

c.  What details are provided about the procedures used and the way data were later analysed?
*Given the nature of the study, it would have been very useful for the reader to have been given some initial idea here as to how the groups were actually presented with these texts, and what they had to do. Since the topic is based on the effect of modified input on L2 listening comprehension, an hypothetical reader would immediately be interested in the method used to modify the text. This information is provided here in a succinct form ("syntax…simplified…, including a number of pauses,…speaking more slowly"), and we presume more exact measurements will be given in the body of the text. No information is given about how the data were analysed.*

d.  Is there a brief summary of results, or the general trend of these, and are you told what conclusions are drawn from these?
*We read of improvements when syntax is simplified and when pauses are included; no conclusions are offered at this point.*

Observations

Look at each observation marked in the text and decide what kind of pertinent reaction could be made at each point. Help is given in the form of short prompts.

①  What would you be looking for in the literature review section of the paper as a result of this statement?
②  How would you be expecting "target language input" to be defined in the study? Can you anticipate any potential problems with describing or measuring what a non-native speaker comprehends of L2 input?
③  What would you need to know about this proficiency level in this context?
④  What information would you be looking for about these participants?
⑤  What information, apart from the numbers involved, would you be interested in reading about with respect to these groups?
⑥  What is a possible reading of "significant" here?

For further practice in appraising this section of the research paper, turn to pages 233–235 in the Workbook.

# Chapter 2

# Introduction

## The problem statement

Before you read this chapter, familiarise yourself again with the paper by reading Abstract 1 (p. 4). Then read the following section of the worked sample appraisal paper and the Observations associated with it.

The background to the problem and the problem statement 1

When you have read a paragraph, stop and write in the *left-hand column* a few words which summarise the gist of that paragraph, to help you understand and focus on what the researcher is saying. Then, in the *right-hand column* write a few words which record your instinctive reactions to what you have just read as if you were talking to the researcher face-to-face.

In this worked example, the columns have been filled in to show you one way of going about this initial reading task.

| | | |
|---|---|---|
| *Origin of problem: large class sizes and exam demands make it difficult to monitor students. Teachers need help.* | What sparked off this research idea is the way foreign language is currently taught in Country X, where there are often very large groups of people in class, and teachers have a lot of work to do to get the students to the level required by external examinations. As a result, it has become difficult to establish the true level of skills each student has arrived at, where their weaknesses lie, and if they are improving to any extent. To make matters worse, teaching takes place in an educational context that places great emphasis on testing and objective skill measurement. Thus, it was felt that teaching staff faced by these kinds of classroom problems in Country X could benefit from some kind of instrument which provides an answer to this situation①. | *Is it difficult because of the class size or the demands of the exam, or both?* <br><br> *How will the instrument solve all these problems?* |
| *Computer-based writing and correction program designed to help teachers save* | The answer was sought in a technological instrument that could help teachers in such a situation②. This is a writing and correction system based on the use of a computer that makes use | |

| *time in their correction but not replace them.* | of currently-available technology and software programs, an example of which is *Grammatik©*, and which are used in conjunction with our own software program③. Our intention was not to invent a foolproof parsing machine or a better expert writing system, but rather an inexpensive instrument which would present no problems of introduction into the classroom for teachers in Country X. Similarly, we were concerned to design something that would not actually replace the teacher nor add to his or her current burdens. Rather, our aim has been to harness what we know about the positive uses of CALL④ to a particular aspect of a normal writing class that often requires too much of the teacher's precious time⑤. | *…so a number of programs are used as part of the software package?*<br><br>*What problems might there have been in this introduction?* |

## Observations

①    Think about how, or whether, this program might realistically "provide an answer" to the situation described.

*I already noted the somewhat ambitious claims in the abstract that the "computer-based instrument" would help to "monitor, evaluate, and understand better EFL writing in Country X". I still wonder how the use of only one technological instrument can help in a situation brought about by decisions made outside the classroom and probably out of the average class teacher's hands (i.e., the massification of classes and the concomitant requirement for individualised information on student progress).*

②    Why do you think the author considered "a technological instrument" would be helpful for these teachers?

*Perhaps the teachers and/or students were already amenable to such technology, or perhaps the authors felt that such technology had intrinsic benefits to alleviate the problems in their current teaching situation.*

③    What would you want to know about the way these programs were used together? Where will you look for this information? How will this be useful in your appraisal of results?

*Since the experimental software is used "in conjunction" with other software, I will look in the upcoming Method section for more detailed information on just how the two programs differed, and, in particular, what specific needs the specially-designed software was designed to address that were not already tackled in the published program.*

*Since the software apparently consisted of a blend of programs, I would eventually be interested in discovering which elements of which program were thought to have had the best effect on results. As it stands, any significant improvement seen may have been the result of any combination of elements from all the software involved, rather than due solely to the authors' own specially-developed program.*

④    Where would you expect to read more about these uses?

*This statement will be best expanded upon and/or justified in the review of the literature to enable me to understand how the authors felt their own study would contribute to the established theoretical and practical advantages already assigned to computers in language learning.*

⑤   To what extent do you think this program might have the potential to save the teacher time? *Little information is provided here about what elements of the writing class are actually taking up so much of the teacher's time and which are intended to be addressed by this program. I still wonder how much is gained eventually in terms of relieving teacher burden if – subsequently – the teacher still has to evaluate the student's writing, perhaps reviewing what has been corrected by the program and/or the way the student has interacted with the information provided by the program.*

## 2.1   The background to the problem

The introduction to the paper traditionally contains a number of sections whose aim is to establish a framework for the research in question so that we are aware of how it fits in with other research. While we should remember that different publishing media may suggest other content for, or sequences of, these sections, there will be a common objective to give the reader a clear idea about what has been done, and why.

**"Is the background to the problem described? If so, what is it?"**

The background to the problem is the section which helps the reader to situate him- or herself in the area in which the problem is found. The section therefore might aim to rationalise the problem and explain why that problem is, in fact, a problem. This element will often be the initial standpoint of many research papers and can take its lead from, or refer directly to, prior published or unpublished work. However, this is not the literature review section of the paper – a subsequent, and comparatively more extensive, analysis of current thought on the problem. The writer might want to use this background section, however, to set the situation for the forthcoming research in as succinct a way as possible and specify where exactly the problem has come from. This orientation is best accomplished by providing the background. One possible way to establish such a frame of reference for the research problem is to quote respected sources. Often, as a result of quoting these sources, the conclusion arrived at is that the problem has not been fully or sufficiently studied or that the present study, in some way, makes a useful contribution.

📖  **Now read this worked appraisal of the sample paper:**
1.   Is the background to the problem described? If so, what is it?
     *The author sets up the need for computer-assisted language learning through a "technological instrument" to aid L2 writing/correction by referring to the current limitations and burdens placed on teachers as a result of the teaching context described.*

## 2.2   The problem statement

**"Is there a problem statement? If so, what is it in your own words?"**

The next step in the introduction is often the problem statement. It is not obligatory to state the problem at such an early stage in the introduction, but one advantage of so doing is that the reader is thereby given a clear perspective from which to assess, firstly, the relevance of the paper to their work and, secondly, the subsequent arguments presented (in particular, during the review of the literature). Even if this has already been mentioned in the abstract, it is useful to see specific identification of the problem here in the main body of the text. One or two sentences in the form of a clear statement might have been chosen to give us the idea. We might be on the look-out for sentences that begin: "Our main aim in this study…" or "The principal objective here…" or "In this paper I will describe/explore/investigate….", and so on. As an additional aid to comprehension of the problem, the problem statement might identify, where necessary, the nature of the principal VARIABLES studied, in particular INDEPENDENT and DEPENDENT VARIABLES, and perhaps suggest possible INTERACTIONS between these. However, no great detail needs to be sought at this point beyond the concept itself, particularly since these variables will probably have yet to be operationalised formally within the study (see below, p. 52).

One useful way of approaching the critique of this section of the paper is, first, to highlight the problem statement in the introduction and then follow its re-appearance throughout the text (including the abstract itself). In other words, the reader should be able to find out the aim of the study and then confirm subsequent mentions as a check on this proposed aim. It should go without saying that, if there are various allusions to the problem statement at different points in the paper, these should all be consistent with, if not equal to, what has already been highlighted as the original problem statement. Any apparent discrepancies will need to be noted down, as they might well affect both the conclusions proposed and our appraisal of them.

Once the problem statement has been located and analysed in the above way, we will need to keep in mind – while we continue our reading – how far that statement, as expressed in the author's or our own words, is a comprehensive statement of what has been studied. For example, as we read through the rest of the paper from this point, we might feel that another slant begins to be taken on the problem, or that data are collected in a different way to that we had anticipated by reading the statement, or even that other variables are being presented for study which do not appear in the problem statement. Yet the problem statement (and, particularly, the subsequent RESEARCH QUESTIONS) should be taken as a comprehensive statement of aims. In other words, once an aim is proposed or problem statement made, the reader is right to assume that what he or she has just been told is going to be "the whole aim and nothing but the whole aim" – anything else could be seen as an afterthought by the researcher and, therefore, might affect our confidence in the comprehensiveness of the statement and, *ipso facto*, in the study itself. For example, it is particularly confusing for a reader interested in learning about the effect of a particular foreign language methodology on listening comprehension SCORES to discover that, although the problem statement promised such a comparison, the research question or HYPOTHESIS then goes on to analyse this INDEPENDENT VARIABLE against a number of *other* dependent variables – as well as listening comprehension scores. The problem with this is that the outcome might be a piece of research that provides a rather more broad, but less profound, study of a number of variables instead of the closer investigation of just the variable the reader was looking for in their reading of the paper.

These considerations about comprehensiveness will also lead us perforce eventually to consider the extent to which the problem was reflected correctly in the original statement. Again, this might sound like a mere question of linguistic accuracy, but it also reflects on the overall confidence we can have in the study itself. For example, if the problem statement claims that "relationships" will be determined between two or more variables, it could both disappoint and frustrate an interested reader to find that what is actually being tested is the separate effect of the two variables named.

Thirdly, and as part of the appraisal, the expression of the problem statement should be seen to be unambiguous. An inability to comprehend what the proposed objective of a paper is at the start does not bode well for subsequent comprehension of the text. One recommended way of checking on the transparency of the statement is to try to put it into our own words and then ask ourselves whether – now in its rewritten form – we understand better the stated problem. As always during appraisal, any doubts created by such analysis need to be considered carefully. The fault is not necessarily on the part of the author, of course. Nevertheless, we will not be in a position adequately to appraise a piece of research if part, or all, of its stated aim is not completely clear to us at the start.

> 📖 **Now read this worked appraisal of the sample paper:**
> 2.  Is there a problem statement? If so, what is it in your own words?
>     *This is not clear in this opening section. Implicitly, I have to assume that the study will describe the positive results obtained from the use of this technological instrument in this educational context. The abstract did provide somewhat more information about "feedback", but aims should also be made clear at this point.*

## 2.3  Initial indication of variables in the problem statement

> **"From the problem statement, do you understand: (a) the variables to be measured and (b) the functions of these variables. If not, what values would you assign from what you have been told so far?"**

The issue of accuracy can also be extended to the correct assignment of the functions of these variables in the problem statement. To be in a position to understand how the variables in a study are supposed to relate to one another, we need to be clear about their proposed function – these functions are inevitably a central aspect of the problem itself and should, in turn, be clearly identified rather than being left to the reader to work out. A sound grasp of the functions of variables in quantitative research is particularly important to help us appraise how far appropriate statistical procedures have been carried out on data. For example, the widely-used descriptive or INFERENTIAL STATISTICAL procedure known as the *t*-test requires a comparison of two LEVELS (or groups) of only one independent variable. Thus, if a problem statement indicates that an independent variable, say, *native language* is to be defined for the purposes of the study as "German" and "French", there are indeed two levels of the independent variable envisaged. However, if the same independent variable were defined as "subject-prominent", "topic prominent", or "mixed", we are being presented in the problem statement with a variable with three levels or groups. The ASSUMPTIONS of the *t*-test, however, mean that only two levels or groups can be compared – no cross-comparing is possible. The reader might already have his or her attention drawn to potentially spurious findings before he or she even gets to the Method section! Similarly, we might want to think ahead and consider whether we will expect the researcher to provide any CONTROL VARIABLES, based on what we have read (or know) about the research aims.

Since the variables have yet to be operationalised at this stage, we would be looking for their identification in a conceptual form only. Thus, the variables could be named, but no description of how they were measured is necessary at this point. However, as part of our awareness-raising approach to reading, we ourselves could begin to think of how the main variables might ideally be measured. Once again, this can help us to be in a better position to assess upcoming sections of the paper. For example, many descriptive or inferential statistical procedures require the variables to be measured in score (INTERVAL or ORDINAL) data form. If the problem statement appears to indicate (even though it does not mention overtly) that one or both variables are "frequencies", "percentages", "tallies", or "RATIOS" and that these data are to be used in their RAW state (i.e., as NOMINAL DATA, without conversion to another form), the reader should already be aware of the possible inappropriateness of the statistical procedure about to be used.

---

📖  **Now read this worked appraisal of the sample paper:**

3.    From the problem statement, do you understand: (a) the variables to be measured? and (b) the functions of these variables? If not, what values would you assign from what you have been told so far?

*(a) and (b): Again, the lack of information within this section means I must return to the abstract to see what is being measured or contrasted here. Apparently, I am reading about a study that will compare two groups (of test and control) and that will demonstrate the advantages of this program. Perhaps the dependent variable here will be something like "frequency of errors". Since both groups, according to the abstract, will use the special software, I am not yet sure what the function of the independent variable will be.*

## 2.4 Stated contribution to theory and practice

### "Is there a contribution claimed to theory and to practice?"

Finally, two further criteria are of great usefulness to our appraisal of the significance of the work about to be described. Judgements will need to be made about both the contribution to theory and the contribution to practice provided by the problem. Contribution to theory addresses the extent to which the outcomes have the potential (i) to add to what we already know, (ii) to help us better understand a particular observable fact, and/or (iii) better evaluate a number of previous explanations or models. Therefore, it is important to remember that the assumed or stated contribution to theory is intended to provide an important link between research and theory and depends to a large extent on prior knowledge in the field. The author will need to make us more aware of this in the literature review, but at this point we might look for references to prior thought or previous theories that help us see where the current study actually fits in with what is already known. For example, if an author sets up an investigation into the effects of a particular methodology on noticing and L2 development, he or she might be advised here initially to place this proposed aim against the past and current arguments about consciousness in L2 learning. In this way, he or she will be able directly to suggest how far their own study's outcomes will throw further light on these arguments – and thereby contribute to current knowledge. If the research you are reading is a replication study, this section should also provide a satisfactory overview of the current situation in the field regarding the object of study and explain the perceived need for, and objectives of, the replication undertaken. Similarly, you might be reading a meta-analysis: comparatively little replication work is carried out as yet and research in our field often produces contradictory results since researchers may use different settings, instruments, data analyses and methodology which ultimately does not facilitate comparison between outcomes. Indeed, we might even find that replication itself may not help to clarify previous doubts. Meta-analyses aim to make sense of it all – they will usually aim to use systematic techniques to analyse a number of results from previous related studies and offer a further contribution to what we know by resolving apparently conflicting findings across related studies and using statistical approaches to explore these relations.

Ironically, such contribution to theory is to be welcomed, even when the stated aim of the paper is "only" to provide findings which are to be directly applied in the classroom. It is, perhaps, all too easy to forget – in today's pursuit of instant methods and quick solutions to classroom problems – that L2 learning and teaching belongs to the field of applied linguistics which, in turn, means that research in that area inevitably aims to contribute to a particular science. It should be part of the professed aim of a piece of research to contribute something to the advancement of that science. Both theory and research are vital and necessary elements of science. Science without controlled, empirical research would consist of only untested ideas and biases. At the same time, science without theory would consist of a selection of disorganised observations and practices rather than meaningful comprehension of the psychological world. Advancement should mean – as far as possible – innovation and contribution at both a theoretical *and* empirical level.

One way of assessing the contribution to practice is from the potential contribution provided by the study to promoting change or other kinds of application at classroom level. At this stage in the paper (i.e., before we read any of the assumed pedagogical implications from the point of view of the researcher), we might try to discover how the researcher predicts the outcomes of their study might have the potential to change the way the L2 is learnt or taught. For example, the author may feel that their findings might provide greater insights into the success of a particular methodology and thereby help identify which elements of that methodology may be more successful in that context. Similarly, we might read about an hypothesised significant effect on language proficiency of a specially-designed language-laboratory programme. The author might then suggest that such results would support the implementation of the programme on a larger scale in classrooms.

As so often in the appraisal of papers, it will be important for the reader to be able to follow the researcher's line of theoretical and practical reasoning leading up to the problem, the research design, and the procedures used. In this way, we can also appreciate how far he or she anticipated certain results, and how far the contribution declared by the researcher in this section was later borne out by the findings obtained, which we will later be reading.

> 📖   **Now read this worked appraisal of the sample paper:**
> 4.   Is there a contribution claimed to theory and to practice?
> *It would appear from these introductory lines that the problem addressed here only has established contribution to practice. However, I assume that data here might also provide us with more information to add to the body of knowledge about computer-assisted language learning and, specifically, in the area of the teaching of L2 writing in such contexts.*
>
> *The contribution to practice is evident: not only does the author see this instrument as providing "help [for teachers] in such a situation", but also an effort has been made to design a product that is inexpensive and easy-to-use, both of which may well be practical merits in such a teaching situation. What I am still unclear about is whether this instrument helps to relieve the teacher in some way directly (as seems to be implied in this section), or only indirectly, by helping the student solve their own problems of correction.*

## Worked sample appraisal

**The background to the problem and the problem statement 2**

1.   **Read Abstract 2 again (p. 7).**
2.   **When you have read a paragraph, stop and write in the *left-hand column* a few words which summarise the gist of that paragraph, to help you understand and focus on**

what the researcher is saying. Then, in the *right-hand column* write a few words which record your instinctive reactions to what you have just read as if you were talking to the researcher face-to-face.

|  | Recent developments in teaching L2 within a communicative methodology have meant that there is an assumed emphasis in spoken output on the importance of interacting and negotiating meaning① with the interlocutor. Not only are both characteristics important, but it is also assumed that interaction must include comprehensible input to enable acquisition to take place. Native speakers are thought to make input more comprehensible because they consciously alter their output when they are addressing non-native speakers②. Such modified input may also be assumed to be present in other L2 learning situations: for example, it may be typical of some classroom situations where L2 teachers are addressing their students. If a speaker modifies the way he or she speaks in such situations to aid comprehension and what the listener comprehends itself aids language acquisition, it follows logically that such modifications may encourage acquisition. My objective here is to use experimental research③ in order to examine how far these conscious language alterations④ affect listening comprehension⑤ and thereby second language acquisition⑥ at beginners' level of language learning⑦. |  |
|---|---|---|

3.   Read again the relevant section in the chapter, and then attempt to answer these questions. Finally, compare your responses to mine.

1.   Is the background to the problem described? If so, what is it?
     *The background to this problem is the way input is consciously modified by speakers to make this more comprehensible.*

2. Is there a problem statement? If so, what is it in your own words?

   *From this background, the researcher implies (it is not explicitly stated here but rather in the abstract) that certain elements within this modified input may be more instrumental than others in enhancing such comprehension at beginners' level language learning. This problem statement is slightly different from the abstract in that the latter predicts a direction for results. I am told there that the study will explore if modification "helps beginners to improve......". The difference might be an important one in terms of the research design and the analysis to be carried out; therefore, I might make a note here to check on the way the final research question is phrased in subsequent sections.*

3. From the problem statement, do you understand: (a) the variables to be measured? and (b) the functions of these variables? If not, what values would you assign from what you have been told so far?

   *From what I read here, the dependent variable, or what is to be measured, will be "listening comprehension" (see Observation 5, below). Since the abstract talked of "significant improvement" in the findings, we might be looking at a score variable measured as interval or ordinal data. The independent variable is the conscious language alterations or modified input which, according to the abstract, appears to be subdivided into aspects of syntax, speed, and pauses – all referring to nominal* CATEGORY *measures.*

4. Is there a contribution claimed to theory and to practice?

   *From the abstract and this section of the paper, I learn that current theory surrounding "communicative methodology" supports the idea that the negotiation of meaning in an interaction depends largely on comprehensible input for its effectiveness. This study will help us better understand how certain modification aims to make input more comprehensible and, therefore, affect oral comprehension. No obvious contribution to practice is mentioned; however, the researcher does suggest that such conscious modifying of input goes on in the teacher's use of language in classrooms and outside in native/non-native interaction. Logically, therefore, if we can find out more about the effects of certain modified input on comprehension, this may provide new insights for teachers and materials writers and help them in their presentation of oral language in the classroom.*

## Observations

Look at each observation marked in the text and decide what kind of pertinent reaction could be made at each point. Help is given in the form of short prompts.

① What do you understand by "interacting and negotiating meaning", and how would you think a study which aimed to research this might usefully go about collecting data?

② Can you think of ways in which you or native speakers might do this? Would the way you do it depend on any particular factors in the interaction? If so, which factors do you think could be of importance?

③   What do you understand by this term, what kind of details would you therefore be looking for, and where would you be looking for them in the paper?

④   What does the word "conscious" suggest, and how would you think these alterations might be adequately reproduced in an experimental situation?

⑤   Before reading any OPERATIONAL DEFINITION by the researcher, what do you understand by L2 "listening comprehension"? Can you think of ways you could adequately measure listening comprehension in an experimental situation?

⑥   What do you think of the implicit link made here between making language alterations to aid listening comprehension and thereby affecting L2 acquisition?

⑦   What constraints might you predict on the kind of data obtained as a result of studying such effects on listening comprehension at this level of language learning?

For further practice in appraising this section of the research paper, turn to pages 236–240 in the Workbook.

# Chapter 3

# Introduction

## The review of the literature

Before you read this chapter, familiarise yourself again with the paper by reading Abstract 1 (p. 4) and The background to the problem and the problem statement 1 (p. 9). Then read this Review of the literature section of the worked sample appraisal paper and the Observations associated with it.

The review of the literature 1

Read this section below, written in 1996. When you have read a paragraph, stop and write in the *left-hand column* a few words which summarise the gist of that paragraph, to help you understand and focus on what the researcher is saying. Then, in the *right-hand column* write a few words which record your instinctive reactions to what you have just read as if you were talking to the researcher face-to-face.

In this worked example, the columns have been filled in to show you how you might go about doing this initial reading task.

| | | |
|---|---|---|
| *Studies with native speakers have produced positive effects with computer-based feedback, but future work needs to concentrate on better design and other POPULATIONS. There are positive effects of this technology in the classroom. Many programs exist to help writing.* | In general, there have been positive results① from studies which have investigated the effect of computer-generated feedback on native English speakers (Researcher 1, 1983; Researcher 2, 1985; Researcher 3, 1987). Researcher 4 (1991) complains about the poor design used in these past studies② and suggests that further research is needed before any firm conclusions can be made about the effects of this feedback. In general, we need better structure in our studies, with particular concentration on aspects of internal/external reliability and validity③; such studies will also need to check on the effect of such feedback on other populations, particularly on ESL/EFL students over longer periods of study④.<br><br>Research has often reported that students are positively disposed towards using computer technology in the classroom and that such use in lessons does have a positive impact⑤ (Researcher 5, 1989; Researcher 6, 1990; Researcher 7, 1986; | *"In general"? What have other studies discovered that was not positive?*<br><br><br>*What has been concluded so far?*<br><br><br><br>*Why do you insist on "longer periods of study"? What specific "use" do you mean?* |

*Whether the teacher or computer helps more is a complex question; how and when are computers efficient? Local research reports generally positive results.*

Researcher 8, 1988; Researcher 9, 1990). There are a large number of computer programs commercially available which make claims such as this: "the easiest way to improve your writing" (found in the instructions to the program Grammatik©). There has also been research carried out by specialists such as Researcher 10 (1989) who have tried to compare the way students write when they work with their tutors to when they work with programs that correct their grammar. It is surely not surprising that those using the computer program did not produce writing with the same quality as that produced by the group working with tutors. Many researchers have emphasised that there is more to the problem than just whether computers are better than teachers. Researcher 11 (1990) wonders how effective computer programs can be and whether their efficiency is the same at all stages of the writing process. Such questions need to be answered by the kind of detailed research recently done by Researcher 12 (1993a; 1993b) who found that using these programs in Country X produced overall improvements in students' attitudes and writing. Researchers 13 (the authors) (1994) report quite positively on the results of their customizing the program Grammatik© (which the authors also customized in the present study⑥) to make it respond better to the particular needs of their students.

*Why is it not surprising? What would you have expected? Why compare the two anyway? Should it not be how computers can supplement, rather than replace the teacher?*

*"quite positively"?: it sounds as if there were problems, too – what were they?*

## Observations

①  What might be understood by the term "in general"?
*This gives me the impression that I am going to be given some idea of both positive and negative findings. Although the target group was "native English speakers", perhaps some information could have been given about some of the conflicting findings hinted at here, if only with which to com-pare results obtained in this study.*

②  What might be the implication of this remark for the present study?
*My reaction here was to assume that the poor construction of previous studies is, in some way, to be improved on in the present study. By embarking upon such improvements, the author is building up part of the contribution to the field from his or her own study. Thus, some critical engagement here with some of the specific weaknesses mentioned would have been useful.*

③    What might this refer to, and where would you expect to read more information?

*Reliability is not normally referred to as "internal or external" although validity is discussed in this way. I made a mental note to look out for more specific information in the upcoming Method section. I assume that such previously-detected problems have been addressed in the present study. However, if other studies did present problems of internal and/or external validity, this could seriously affect the amount of confidence to be placed in their results.*

④    What is your reaction to this remark in the context of the present study?

*The implication is that this study will indeed be "over longer periods". It appears from the abstract that the study will be over a six-month period. However, I still do not know to what extent such a time period will, in fact, be an improvement on these previous studies. I also do not see that a case has been made for the need for work with EFL/ESL students based on the literature reviewed so far.*

⑤    What could be understood here by "positive impact"?

*A large number of studies is cited, and some indication of the nature of this impact could usefully have been given.*

⑥    What more would the reader want to know about the authors' actions?

*Since the use of this program also appears to have been central to the objective of the present study, the reader might benefit from having more information about the kind of modifications (and their outcomes) carried out in other key studies.*

## 3.1    Relevance and importance of work cited

**"Are you satisfied that the review describes the most relevant work done and indicates its relative importance?"**

Although there is no obligatory sequence of elements in the introductory section of a paper, we would now reasonably expect the author to fill in some of the background details previously sketched in through the background to the problem and the problem statement. The aim might be to use previous and current knowledge to continue to explore the problem, now from a variety of appropriate angles and, by so doing, present the pertinent arguments which ultimately herald the study's hypotheses and/or research questions. This section of a research paper is often highly focussed and summarised. The main reason for this is that the author will have looked for key previous studies or relevant work that helps him or her eventually to underline the deficiencies or limitations in the current research area and the need for, and the importance of, the present study. If the research you are reading is a replication study, you would expect to find at this point a thorough review of the original study to be replicated in which, for example, the perceived need for replication was explained with relation to the original outcomes, and previous replications (if any) are discussed. We would also want to appreciate from the review of other related studies that the current literature and research agenda relating to the topic is able to support its continuing relevance to the field. Indeed, you might well be reading a study with a view to deciding upon whether to replicate it yourself. In this case, as you read the review of the literature, you might perhaps be alerted to a body of research on a topic that appears not to have been carried out in multiple settings, or to studies where dissimilar operationalizations of research CONSTRUCTS have led to confusing outcomes across different studies. In the case of a meta-analysis, you might expect to read here a brief outline of the perceived conflict in previous study outcomes and/or the need for the analysis given the amount of work carried out in a particular area and which is now seen to require systematic, critical summary.

A review of the literature should include a critical selection of work that highlights or discusses the same or similar variables to those about to be studied (according to the background to the problem and the problem statement) or suggests hypotheses that are to be tested in this study. The researcher takes on a particular responsibility in summarising relevant work for the reader and trying to make sense of the large amount of literature. Let us assume, for example, that we are reading a paper because we have been attracted to it by what was read in the abstract. Perhaps it promises new insights into a particular construct, a specific methodology, or a relationship of variables we are interested in. However, if every author of research were to start anew within that area, re-defining constructs or methodologies, working out entirely original meanings and definitions of variables, and then positing their own links between them, the resulting mass of knowledge would soon become confusing to the field – chaotic rather than summative knowledge.

Thus, one of the fundamental criteria we could use in our appraisal of this section is the perceived importance of the studies cited. Therefore, as readers, we will need to be attentive to references which, in some way, deal with the central variables or elements in the study and their relationship as declared in the problem statement. It would be logical for the reader to expect more detailed information about the studies which are more directly related to that currently being carried out and/or to the subsequent formulation of hypotheses. In other words, the reader should reasonably expect the review to be considerably more than a list of what has been read up on the subject; papers are not just mentioned in the review for their own sake. Rather, we are looking for a summary of the literature, and past work should be cited for the light it potentially sheds on what is and is not known to the field and, thereby, on the author's *own* study. The advantage gained is that results of the most important work would then ideally be tied together so that their consequences for the present research become immediately clear to the reader. The author is then seen to be genuinely trying to carry on from a certain consensus reached by other researchers, and thereby profitably adding to the current body of knowledge. In this way, he or she builds a case or a context for the present research. Thoughtful organisation of the review of the literature will therefore enable the reader to follow logically, and thereby appraise, the questions emanating from the background to the problem/problem statement and the arguments leading up to the subsequent research questions and/or hypotheses themselves.

It is also useful for the reader to have clarification on the relevance and relative importance of the work cited. Unfortunately, there also exist literature reviews which are little more than disguised bibliographical lists. This is often signalled by padding, or what appears to be the citing of particular researchers or work just for the sake of it. Such a procedure may be a warning to the reader that little relevant or reflective background reading has gone into building up the contribution of previous research to the study. Within this criterion of appraisal, the reader should also be made aware of the comparative importance of any results from the studies reviewed. Inevitably, some results will have more bearing on the current problem than others and the reader needs to be aware of this as he or she digests the previous knowledge available on the subject, thereby to be in a better position to judge where the present study fits in. It is also useful for the reader to try to determine, as far as possible, whether any relevant work has been omitted.

> 📖  **Now read this worked appraisal of the sample paper:**
> 1.  Are you satisfied that the review describes the most relevant work done and indicates its relative importance?
>    *I had earlier assumed that the objective here was to "describe the positive results obtained from the use of this technological instrument in this educational context". Given this supposed objective, I wonder about the immediate relevance of including studies with native English speakers. Similarly, student attitudes to the software – to which a number of references are made in the second paragraph – does not seem to be part of the study. Finally, it would appear that the study wherein changes were made in the Grammatik© program is of far more direct relevance than others mentioned here, and more information about the methodology and/or data analysis may have been useful. I find no obvious indication by the author that certain studies and their results have more bearing than others on the current investigation.*

## 3.2    Critical address of the literature

**"Are you satisfied that the review has sufficient critical address of the literature?"**

Such explanation on the part of the author is not limited merely to summarising what is already known, of course. The critical consumer of this research could reasonably expect the researcher, in turn, to have been suitably discerning and analytical in their reading of this selected literature. It is instructive to read a paper which not only identifies, but also explains and critically addresses issues relevant to a study that have emerged from this reading of the literature. We might usefully see such critical engagement on the part of the author presented in the form of a structured explanation showing what the author has found satisfactory or wanting in an argument or finding – rather than mere unsubstantiated declaration. Progress in our science will very much depend on how researchers review the work of their predecessors and make suggestions about how to improve or change things. Through such description and explanation, the author might be able to produce a concept or build a theoretical structure that may explain facts and the relationships between them. The importance of theory, as we have seen in the previous section, is both to help the researcher summarise previous information *and* guide their future course of action – thereby establishing the contribution to theory provided by the study. Often the formulation of such theory through a critical review of the literature will help indicate missing ideas or links and the kind of additional data to be provided by the study in question.

The nature of this critical address will be another factor in assessing the amount of confidence we may feel able to place in the paper. Much will depend, therefore, on the way the author argues his or her case before us. We will return in Chapter 9 to the way the reader needs to analyse findings put forward in discussion and conclusion sections of published research. Suffice to say here that the reader could hope the author indulged in a similar practice in his or her own reading. Such critical address will probably not need to be applied to each and every study cited in the review, of course. Much of the previous research related to the background of the study, for instance, may require little more than description of the main outcomes, unless we are reading a replication study – in which case sufficient details of the original study will need to be communicated to permit adequate comparisons with the present study. However, we might want to know more about how the author interprets findings or conclusions which have a direct bearing on the problem statement itself. Ethical standards in reporting of research mean that such address should not be dismissive or aggressive towards previously published work: good scholarship requires author (and reader!) to adopt a positive and enquiring attitude to ideas presented by others. Such an attitude has the advantage of transmitting to the reader the idea that the author is able not only to analyse previous arguments and findings in a way that synthesises this work, but also to use this synthesis to generate new ideas and open up research directions. Typically, we might appreciate a stance which shows us both what the author has found acceptable or unacceptable in a particular idea or finding *and* which then also explains why the author has reacted in this way.

It is often useful for the reader, to whom the results of the author's literature search are now being presented, to get into the habit of appraising how authors classify their findings, and how they critically explore and explain relationships between findings. Of particular interest will be the treatment given to potentially conflicting findings and controversies within and across studies: such conflict is quite common in research in our area and, where it is found, we might reasonably expect the author to explain, or seek to provide possible insights into, such deficiencies in our knowledge or discrepancies across studies. There is always a temptation to ignore such differences in the interests of summary; however, these should be of interest to the researcher *and* the reader, as such apparently inconsistent findings can actually provide a rationale for further study. For example, the researcher may subsequently decide to examine the same question from a different point of view, possibly with improved methodology, so as to offer more convincing findings. For the reader, learning about areas of knowledge where findings are unconvincing or in some way incomplete can also help him or her to form their own research agendas based on current needs in the field. Furthermore, the common practice of evening out findings in the literature review will certainly mean that we lose information, and it may also mean the possible complexities of a problem are not fully grasped – or communicated to the reader. The literature review should transmit the idea that the author has studied existing work in the field with analytical insight, leaving us with a balanced picture, albeit necessarily partial, of the current state of knowledge and of major questions yet to be answered in the relevant subject area.

> 📖    **Now read this worked appraisal of the sample paper:**
> 2.    Are you satisfied that the review has sufficient critical address of the literature?
>       *The author has included a relatively large number of references in this review and from a variety of other researchers. However, the review is limited to the description of what were the summarised findings in each case. For example, the second paragraph opens with reference to five studies in order to support the summary statement that the interaction of student and learning context with computer technology has been positive. If this is considered of importance, it would have been useful to have had more critical address of these studies: did success depend on how the teaching was distributed within a lesson, for example, or do these authors recommend ways of improving student predisposition to the programs, which are now to be tested in this present study?*

## 3.3    Relating the review to the background statement

> **"Are you satisfied that the review communicates the main points related both to the background to the problem and the problem statement/independent and dependent variables?"**

Once again, there are no explicit rules about the way a review should communicate the main points to the reader, but its reading and appraisal can be facilitated if there is logical progress within the text itself. The reader's understanding of the situation that led up to the research can be enhanced if there is an evident movement from reviewing general work within the background to the problem towards more specific research which reflects on the eventual statement of the problem itself and any research questions or hypotheses to follow. Within this coherent progression, it would be interesting to read about the kind of methodological approaches or analysis of data used by previous researchers in the area, together with how and why the present author seeks to replicate, or improve on, these. Another useful way of helping the reader appraise how the literature review reflects on the study about to be described is to move from studying the relevant literature on the main independent variable(s), to that done on the dependent variable(s), and finally concentrating on the literature which has related the independent and dependent variable(s).

Other problem statements might suggest a chronological approach to reporting the literature. Whatever the way chosen by the author, the idea behind any of these routes is gradually to focus on the situation in question and pave the way for the research hypotheses or questions. As readers, however, we will want to be able to follow the route chosen throughout the text, and this means continually stopping and asking ourselves if we understand the arguments put forward so far. One way this can be done is by attempting to recap the main points made in each paragraph. If we can do this in our own words, we might assume that the author has successfully communicated what needed to be said. Our own summary obtained should likewise reflect logical progress from the general to the specific.

> 📖   **Now read this worked appraisal of the sample paper:**
> 3.   Are you satisfied that the review communicates the main points related both to the background to the problem and the problem statement/independent and dependent variables?
> *Although the review does take in some studies on writing in the second paragraph, the first ones cited appear to have concentrated on native English "speakers", and it is not clear whether the objective was to study their written output or their overall language learning. There **is** a discernible movement towards the problem statement in that I then begin to read about the effect of specific programs on writing. The second paragraph cites what seems to be a similar case to this in which test and control groups were set up to test the effect of the software. However, little detail is given to enable us to appreciate how the present study makes an advance on what was revealed. The final paragraph further narrows the focus onto the present context in the same country (Researcher 12) and another study which adapted the same computer software (Researcher 13); however, where we would now expect to read more important comparative information from this same teaching context or research area, tantalisingly little is forthcoming.*
>
> *My recap of the paragraphs highlighted a lack of continuity or logical flow in the review. For example, I did not find it easy to follow the internal logic or see the overall aim of the second paragraph, moving as it does from describing reactions to software to how certain software is marketed. Similarly, there would seem to be no obvious connection between the first and second paragraphs. The general impression given me is of a number of somewhat randomly-connected aspects of using computer-generated software eventually rather loosely focussing on the problem statement.*

## 3.4   Time period covered in review

### "Are you satisfied that the review covers an adequate time-span?"

The reader will also want to consider the extent to which the literature read and/or studied satisfactorily reflects current thinking on the subject and covers an adequate time-scale. There is little to be gained by an author including research that has now been superceded and/or contributes little or nothing to the current argument: this may result in mere padding. The problem here is that the reader may not be adequately informed of the research carried out. Nevertheless, we are right to want to be made aware of the latest, and most relevant, information which reflects on what we are about to be told. This does not necessarily mean that the review should include only the most recent work in the area. Indeed, references may be found to many classic studies in the field that are over twenty-five years old. The key here is that we are looking for previous evidence that helps us see how the current problem or situation has come about and thereby clarifies the need for the present work about to be described. Indeed, even if the author claims to be dealing with a relatively virgin area of knowledge, it will be advantageous for us to see how the apparent deficiency in the field has come to light as a result of past and present research. The critical reader might expect at least an explanation of the route by which this new ground was reached. Inevitably, this will mean the author giving information about how and where their study fits into the field and the current body of knowledge and also, *ipso facto*, how this particular study came about.

> 📖    **Now read this worked appraisal of the sample paper:**
> 4.    Are you satisfied that the review covers an adequate time-span?
>    *Given that the paper was written in 1996, I would like to have been informed why work carried out so many years earlier is still considered relevant here (e.g., Researchers 1 and 2 (1983) and (1985) or Researcher 7 (1986)). If this work was to be deemed "classic" in the field, then this could be indicated or highlighted by the author, so that I am aware of the central relevance of such studies, despite their age.*

## 3.5    Empirical studies covered in review

**"Are you satisfied that the review has adequate reference, where necessary, to empirical work?"**

In much of the experimental and QUASI-EXPERIMENTAL research in our area, we will also want to be concerned about how far the work being critically addressed here has not only been directed to similar concerns as the paper in question, but also has used similar empirical methods. This comes down to our assessing how far a fair comparison is being made between like and like. For example, if the author of a paper wishes to convince us of the need to provide more experimental data about the order in which L2 learners acquire their L2 vocabulary, we might logically expect that some or all of the literature addressed includes findings which are based on data gathered with similar aims rather than merely derived from discursive literature about the way these students might acquire their vocabulary.

**"Does the review succeed in convincing you of the need for the study?"**

As a result of our reading, we should be able to comment on how convincing the review is: in other words, has the author succeeded in making a strong enough case for the study in question? In particular, the reader will need to ask him- or herself whether meaningful, significant, and innovative data are likely to be contributed to the body of knowledge as described in the review.

> 📖    **Now read this worked appraisal of the sample paper:**
>
> 5.   Are you satisfied that the review has adequate reference, where necessary, to empirical work? Does the review succeed in convincing you of the need for the study?
>
> *Most of the work here seems to have been empirically based. It would, perhaps, have been useful to have the specific contexts of the empirical work in references to Researchers 10 and 13. This would also enable me to weigh up the relative importance of such previous study to the current work carried out in Country X.*
>
> *On the whole, the literature review does not convince me of the need for this study in the current context. Given the potential importance of the contribution and application of "specially-designed software" to the problem of large classes, I was surprised to find only one fleeting reference (Researcher 12) to relevant work on this application. More critical engagement with the literature cited might have helped to highlight the current gaps in our knowledge that make it necessary or advisable to carry out the present study in this particular context. The fact that other researchers think more research needs to be done may not, in itself, be enough to justify the study.*

## Worked sample appraisal

**The review of the literature 2**

1.   Before you read this review of the literature, familiarise yourself with the paper by reading Abstract 2 (p. 7) and The background to the problem and the problem statement 2 (p. 16).

2.   Read this section below, written in 1997. When you have read a paragraph, stop and write in the *left-hand column* a few words which summarise the gist of that paragraph, to help you understand and focus on what the researcher is saying. Then, in the *right-hand column* write a few words which record your instinctive reactions to what you have just read as if you were talking to the researcher face-to-face.

| | | |
|---|---|---|
| | Research into the effect of modifying input has tended to concentrate on how far introducing pauses helps or hinders comprehension. The practice consists of organising language output sequentially in an experimental setting (Researcher 1, 1990) and is accomplished in one of two ways: either by time modification (adjusting the length and frequency of the pauses), or by RATE modification (artificially speeding up or slowing down the output on the tape-recording). Such procedures are usually measured in terms of rates, such as words per | |

minute. Typically, two methods are used: a tape recording is made to play back at a slower speed than the original recording, or the original speed of output can itself be manipulated using a speech compressor. Use of the compressor is more reliable since any distortion is avoided as pitch is automatically compensated for as the speed changes. One of the first experiments using the L2 by Researcher 2 (1985) was with non-native participants of intermediate level of proficiency①, and concluded that listening comprehension was enhanced by decelerating the amount of speech delivered②. Researcher 3 (1980) had earlier reported no differences between 20 advanced-level participants who heard speech which had been slowed down and others who had received the language at a normal speed.

Although speech compressors have been used successfully in these studies, a number of researchers still believed that output is thereby distorted. Researcher 4 (1979) and Researcher 5 (1980) claim that artificially reducing the speed of articulation only serves to alter the flow of sound; thus, according to these researchers, only the length of pauses should be manipulated, so permitting normal speed and time to process the new information. Researchers who favour using pauses in such experiments into modified input do so because they believe that language perception is not instantaneous, since listeners need time to process what they hear (Researcher 4, 1979). Such an hypothesis might be open to question since surely the main aim will always be to comprehend language delivered – and received – at natural speed. Slower speech might only be heard at the early stages of language study; as the learner's speech proficiency increases, such an alteration in speech output often decreases. Researcher 6 (1990), who also defends modifying pauses, experimented with modifications in speech rate, syntax, and pauses. Initial findings were that neither speech rate nor syntax impinge in any measurable way on listening comprehension. However, a second study revealed that pauses did indeed help L2 listening comprehension. Nevertheless, comparison between groups was made impossible because participants differed considerably both in terms of their dissimilar levels of proficiency and their levels of motivation. It was also unfortunate that the Polish participants used were English majors and were amongst the best students. On the other hand, the other group consisted of Puerto Rican participants, none of whom were English majors and who were obliged to study English. As a result, some outcomes might have been influenced by the participants' language level – and thus their comprehension③.

Syntax was not found to have any significant effect on listening comprehension by Researcher 7 (1990). Researcher 8 (1983), however, suggested a relationship did exist between syntactic complexity and listening comprehension success, arguing that the length and number of transformations will affect sentence comprehension. Researcher 9 (1988) hypothesised that syntax is complicated by increasing the frequency of coordinated sentences, present simple tense verbs, ungrammatical sentence fragments, declarative/statement varieties, and shorter sentences. He further suggested that the formation of shorter sentences is through the adjustment of sentence length for beginner level students (5.8 words per sentence), which is steadily increased as the learners improve in proficiency (10 words per sentence for advanced learners vs. 29 in native-speaker speech). In the present study, Researcher 9's suggestions have been used, and it was also decided to include preservation of SVO structure④, because participants here were English native speakers beginning to learn L2 Spanish, and therefore were not used to non-SVO structures, which are very common in Spanish.

3.  **Read again the relevant section in the chapter and then attempt to answer these questions. Finally, compare your responses to mine.**

    Are you satisfied that the review (a) describes the most relevant work done and indicates its relative importance, (b) has sufficient critical address of the literature, (c) communicates the main points related both to the background to the problem and the problem statement/ independent and dependent variables, (d) covers an adequate time-span, (e) has adequate reference, where necessary, to empirical work? In general, does it convince you of the need for the study?

    a.  *All the work reviewed here appears to be highly relevant to this study, as it reports on the results of modifying input through various means. Furthermore, what is cited seems to have been carried out on L2 (i.e., rather than L1) listening comprehension. Having said that, we learn very few details about the participants, and more importantly, whether these were studies in second or foreign language situations. We might suggest that success in listening comprehension might well be affected by the kind of learning context in which these participants regularly find themselves. In other words, students in L2 situations – wherein the target language is widely used within the participants' country – might be hypothesised to be receiving more comprehensible input as part of their everyday lives. I have not yet been told whether the participants used here were studying Spanish in second or foreign language contexts. However, since context might well be hypothesised as an important* INTERVENING VARIABLE *here, it would have been interesting to have heard about whether any such studies have also revealed significant findings.*

*The reader is also implicitly made aware of the fact that the Researcher 6 and Researcher 9 studies are to be considered of more relative importance to the study at hand. The author engages more critically with both studies, pointing out the "proficiency" limitation in the former study and the modifications suggested in the latter study. With such highlighting of the two studies, I might also be looking for possible reference back to the same studies in the Discussion section of the present paper – suggesting how the present study has managed to advance on information provided there as a result of these adjustments.*

b.   *The abstract to this paper described a study that would investigate the effect on listening comprehension of adjusting "pause, speed, and syntax". Logically, therefore, we might be looking for more critical engagement with those studies that most reflect on that aim. The way the review is presented does indeed echo these concerns, dedicating a paragraph to each variable. In most cases the review is descriptive and explains how past research has tackled the problem of modifying input. Nevertheless, there are a number of points brought up in this description which might merit a more specific focus (see Observations, below). There are, for example, conflicting results from Researchers 2 and 3, for whom comprehension was either enhanced or remained the same after deceleration of output. What, at first, appears to be inconclusive evidence from these studies may be due to the nature of the participants, the material used, the procedures, or other intervening factors. Either way, it would have been interesting to read the researcher's reaction. We know from the abstract and problem statement that the author intends to use 180 "beginners' level" participants, and it may well be that this decision is as a result of reading about Researcher 3's lack of success with advanced-level students and/or the small number of participants this researcher might have used. By suggesting possible reasons for reported findings, the author is helping pave the way for the important advances to be made in the present study.*

*A more critical stance is taken in paragraph three, when discussing the previous work on pauses. The author seeks to challenge the argument put forward by Researcher 4. If such a reply is intended to support a particular stance in his or her own study is not yet clear, but I do remember that participants used here were beginners, and I might make a note to check in the Method section of the paper to see whether this author decided to use spoken output at "natural speed" too, or whether speech was slowed down to allow for participants still "at the early stages of language study". Researcher 6's findings are also addressed specifically by the author and criticised because of weaknesses in participant selection. The logical implication of such comments is that such weaknesses will be addressed in the present study. I might even want to look ahead at this point to the Participants section of the paper and, particularly, questions of participant selection, to see if, or how exactly, the author has sought to improve on the study analysed.*

*In the last paragraph, there is rather more description than critical insight into findings, despite the fact that there continue to be somewhat conflicting outcomes reported. Nevertheless, Researcher 9's observations about sentence length are taken up, presumably in order to set up an operational definition of "shorter sentence" for this study using beginner level participants.*

c.  *The background to the problem here is how consciously modifying input affects L2 listening comprehension. The first paragraph takes the reader into this context by discussing the concept of, and investigations in, one aspect or level of the first independent variable – pauses. The first paragraph might be summarised by saying that investigations wherein attempts were made to insert pauses into the flow of speech received by participants have produced conflicting results. In the second paragraph, the reader is informed that certain modification using speech compressors is thought adversely to affect the sound stream. The third paragraph highlights specific work involving the variables to be used in the present study. The gist is that pauses appear to help L2 listening comprehension but that previous studies may have suffered from a number of flaws or limitations which skewed results. In the final paragraph we are told that, while one investigation found no effect of syntax on listening comprehension, others maintain that complexity and length of sentence elements may be an important factor.*

*This review certainly attempts to guide the reader through work on the background to the problem to the more specific investigations carried out on the variables to be used in the present study. In general, the reader is left with the impression that studies have not revealed convincing conclusions to date and that – implicitly therefore – more information is necessary from studies that pay attention to a number of control variables. As a result, the reader is prepared to read a research question or hypothesis that seeks to provide this information in some way.*

*I have noted that the problem statement refers to the participants as at "beginners' level". This has yet to be defined specifically, but it is not clear in this review why the researcher opted to study this level of proficiency with modified input rather than any other. The criticism already noted of Researcher 6's results would indeed argue for an homogenous proficiency level in the participants, but it would have been interesting to be told why exactly beginners' level students were considered more suitable in the present study. On the face of it, it seems a curious choice for experimental research of this kind: at such initial stages of language learning, it might be difficult to comprehend any input that is **not** modified in some form.*

d.  *Most of the work cited here spans a large period of time, with the key studies coming from the last ten or twelve years. Although the most recent work cited is some seven years before the paper was written, the reader is given a sense of how the current situation has come about.*

e.  *This review includes both discursive-based and data-based research, not only to establish the context of the study and its contribution to theory, but also, in the latter half of the review, to inform the reader of the outcomes of similar work in other research contexts.*

*In general, the reader is presented with a good introduction to the field in question and the state of current knowledge. The initial discussion on the nature of using pauses is also useful to help reinforce the contribution to theory of the study. Perhaps a more convincing case could have been made for the need for further information from other L2 contexts – as in the present study. The author does succeed in critically addressing the need for more information as a result of limitations, or conflicting results, from certain previous studies. Nevertheless, a better case could have been made for the reader on the question of why the author decided to choose beginners as the population, and/or why learning Spanish was considered as potentially contributing meaningful and innovative data to the current question of the effects of modifying input on listening comprehension.*

Observations

Look at each observation marked in this review and decide what kind of pertinent reaction could be made at each point. Help is given in the form of short prompts.

① = What kind of further detail might be useful here? Why might it be useful?
② = How might the nature of these students have affected findings?
③ = Why "and thus..."? Is this such an obvious connection?
④ = Is input data being manipulated therefore? What are the possible effects of this on eventual findings?

> For further practice in appraising this section of the research paper, turn to pages 240–245 in the Workbook.

# Chapter 4

# Introduction

## Research questions and variables

Before you read this chapter, familiarize yourself again with the paper by reading Abstract 1 (p. 4), The background to the problem and the problem statement 1 (p. 7), and The review of the literature 1 section (p. 20). Then read this Research questions and variables section of the worked sample appraisal paper:

Research questions and variables 1

When you have read a paragraph, stop and write in the *left-hand column* a few words which summarise the gist of that paragraph, to help you understand and focus on what the researcher is saying. Then, in the *right-hand column* write a few words which record your instinctive reactions to what you have just read as if you were talking to the researcher face-to-face.

In this worked example, the columns have been filled in to show you how you might go about doing this initial reading task.

| | | |
|---|---|---|
| *Students' skills will improve as a result of using this computer program and error profiles will become available.* | The research hypothesis in this study was that objective measurements and feedback will have a significantly positive effect on students' skills. Furthermore, these measurements and feedback will also enable detailed profiles to be made of the errors common to specific writing genres. | *Why didn't you opt for a* NULL HYPOTHESIS? *What do you mean by "students' skills"? "..will also enable.." – is this also part of the hypothesis?* |

## 4.1 Research questions and hypotheses

Our route through a sound research paper is typically well-signposted by the researcher to ensure that we are accompanying him or her on the same road and that we all understand the direction in which we are going. So far there have been a number of key signposts in the text which have guided us. The abstract should have given a clear idea of the route to be taken, then the problem statement confirmed the main direction of the study. Now – in the light of what has been revealed from the review of the literature – the final signpost can help to refine the problem statement and clarify the objective as research questions or hypotheses.

### "Are research questions or hypotheses formulated? If so, what are they?"

Research questions and research hypotheses are different, and the reader should also be able to appreciate that difference in the method and procedures to be followed in the rest of the study. The research *question* is more typical of descriptive and survey-type research; it does not need to predict any possible outcome as such. The main idea is to look into a particular situation and see what is there. The result may well contribute to generating hypotheses for future testing, but this is not obligatory.

When we have questions, we usually want to know the answers. But this does not mean that we have no idea of what those answers might actually be. After thinking about the question ourselves, reviewing the literature, and studying what others have discovered about the questions we ask, we may come up with suggestions about possible answers. These tentative answers, written formally, are research hypotheses. The research *hypothesis*, most often found in experimental and quasi-experimental studies, does provide a suggested response or expected outcome to the problem described in the problem statement, previously outlined and discussed in the review of the literature. Basically, this is a hunch that the researcher has about the existence of relationships or differences between the variables used and which will be subject to examination through the subsequent investigation. Indeed, the way this relationship or difference is perceived in the hypothesis provides a guide to the researcher (and the reader) as to how the original hunch is to be tested among the participants in the study. Thus, the reader will need to attend closely to the research hypothesis, since what follows will need to be structured in such a way as to enable the stated hypothesis to be tested.

Typically, the research questions or hypothesis would be located after the literature review, wherein logical and empirical support for such statements would hopefully have been found. In a replication study, we would expect the research question or hypothesis to relate directly to that of the original study. Firstly, the original research objective is assumed to be significant and retains the potential to contribute to the body of knowledge supporting the discipline. The review of the original paper (above) would also have established how the researcher came to the conclusion that an exact, approximate or conceptual replication of that original question or hypothesis would be useful to the field. At this point in a meta-analysis we would expect to read about the organizing framework of the analysis – the practical or theoretical questions which have guided the collection of studies to be discussed and their data.

Once read, it is always a good idea to underline the hypothesis or questions to be able to refer back when reading and interpreting the Results section. Since these hypotheses or questions give the study direction and form, our understanding can be enhanced by explicit statements of such questions and/or hypotheses and not mere implicit objectives, which leave the research question or hypothesis and subsequent results open to whatever interpretation. Particularly in the case of DIRECTIONAL HYPOTHESES (see below), look for explicitness and confidence through expressions such as "Results were expected to confirm that…..", or "Data collected should support the notion that…..", and so on. It should be clear from the above that the research questions and/or hypotheses (in whatever form they are introduced) represent a key element for a reader trying to understand the connection between the perceived problem and the way the author has chosen to go about responding to it.

## 4.2   Nature of the research questions

### "Are the research questions exploratory, descriptive, or explanatory?"

Very often the researcher's prior study of the field and review of the literature will have exposed a need to explore, describe, or explain further a particular phenomenon through research questions, *before* arriving at possible hypotheses. It will be useful for the reader to predict the nature of the study suggested by the particular research question as part of the valuable practice of progressively building up a critical response to what he or she is being told. In this way, we can begin to envisage outcomes and perhaps already consider possible problems or drawbacks in the research design. Exploration will see a research question in which the researcher aims to find out what is happening, to seek new insight, to pose new questions, or to attempt to assess the phenomenon in a new light. In other words, the study structures the research rather than the other way round and the research may thereby become one of hypothesis building rather than HYPOTHESIS TESTING. Descriptive research questions will attempt to portray an accurate profile of people, events, or situations. Finally, explanatory questions will seek an explanation of a situation or problem, often in the form of CAUSAL RELATIONSHIPS. A particular study may be concerned with a combination of all three tendencies, but we should be able to highlight one principal trend through our initial reading of the research questions(s).

> 📖   Now read this worked appraisal of the sample paper:
> 1.   Are research questions or research hypotheses formulated? If so, what are they?
> 2.   Are the research questions exploratory, descriptive, or explanatory?
>    1.   *A research hypothesis is described which, as it stands, indicates that two variables (i.e., "objective measurements" and "feedback") will affect "students' skills" and also give detailed information about specific student errors. It is not clear to me whether the latter is meant to be part of the hypothesis or, in fact, an additional research question.*
>    2.   *Not applicable here*

## 4.3   Nature of the research hypotheses

**"Are the hypotheses offered directional and do they predict differences or relationships between variables?"**

As one might expect when a hunch is at the centre of the argument, the hypothesis itself is often couched in language of prediction, which sounds as if the author is making a bet with the reader (e.g., "The number of errors made by elementary German-as-a-foreign-language students is related to the kind of methodology they receive" or "The ability to discriminate between minimal pairs in L2 Portuguese increases with age and educational level"). The hypothesis should ideally present the following information to the reader: firstly, there should be some statement concerning assumed relationships (or lack of them) between the variables, or the presumed influence of one (or more) of the variables on the other. Secondly, we can expect to read an hypothesis which really can be tested: that is, it looks to us as though it will become possible to assign operational definitions to the constructs or variables described and thereby produce useful data which can then be analysed.

When a researcher presents an hypothesis, this will traditionally be written in either a positive, directional, or a null form. The choice of presentation is important for the critical reader too, for it has repercussions both on the way we will expect subsequent data to be statistically analysed and on the way findings should be interpreted. Any hypothesis will represent a written form of the hunch that the researcher has about the outcome of the study. A *positive* hypothesis might declare that there will be differences found as a result of the interaction between the variables but does not specify whether these will be positive or negative outcomes. A *directional* hypothesis goes one step further by informing the reader about the specific trend of the difference or relationship. For example, we might read that instruction in certain reading comprehension strategies is hypothesised to result in *fewer* errors of comprehension and/or *better* acquisition of vocabulary. These hypotheses go beyond merely saying something will happen and state exactly what will happen (i.e., there will be *less* of something and *more* of something else). However, such direction cannot be an arbitrary decision. Direction in an hypothesis should ideally be understood by the reader to proceed logically from the data provided in the previous review of the literature. In other words, other researchers may have already revealed or suggested a particular direction using these variables in other contexts. On the basis of previous research in the field or previous theoretical discussion, the researcher is thereby prepared to predict that a relationship will exist between the current variables *and* that such prior knowledge also permits him or her to predict the direction of such a relationship.

We will need to reflect back on what we have read in the literature review as we take in such an hypothesis. However intuitively acceptable a directional hypothesis may sound, if it is not soundly based on previous outcomes or theory, such an hypothesis may become impossibly vague. In our example of comprehension strategies above, for instance, fewer comprehension errors may indeed be an effect of the teaching; nonetheless, a number of other explanations for such outcomes may also be possible. It may be something to do with the speed with which the participants read, or the difficulty of the passage used, or any number of variables. When previous research gives us a clue to what might happen, however, the researcher has considerably more empirical evidence to back up any such claim.

In the field of L2 learning, with its many differing teaching and learning contexts, methodologies, objectives, and students themselves, it is always going to be difficult to support directional hypotheses beyond reasonable doubt. Much previous literature may indeed exist, and other prior studies may have experimented with, and confirmed, similar outcomes using these variables. Conversely, it is more often the case that relatively little replication is done in our field and the researcher may often have few valid equivalent studies to support their own findings. Given such a situation, it is hardly surprising that many experimental and quasi-experimental studies in our field opt for presentation of the hypothesis in its *null* form: in our example, the null version would read "There is no effect of instruction in certain reading comprehension strategies on improvement in comprehension or vocabulary acquisition". If this null hypothesis is supported, then instruction will have no effect on comprehension or vocabulary acquisition – hardly what the serious L2 teacher would be hoping for! If the null hypothesis proves to be incorrect, then such instruction might prove useful. In this case, the researcher may be using DESCRIPTIVE or inferential statistical procedures (see Chapters 7 and 8) which help him or her to reject the null hypothesis in favour of the logical alternative. Use of the null hypothesis has become traditional in experimental and quasi-experimental research in our field because it allows the researcher working in what are such heterogeneous language-learning contexts to be conservative in their initial hunch and more cautious in the conclusions he or she draws from the data. Indeed, analysis of the caution expressed in extracting conclusions from results based on such hypotheses will be one of the elements in our appraisal of the discussion and conclusions of such a paper.

The problem is that hypotheses can be dangerous things if used carelessly. As cautious readers of research, we will need to be attentive to what is read into any possible outcomes. Firstly, and in order to carry out any test of an experimental or quasi-experimental hypothesis, it must in principle be possible for the predicted effects either to occur or *not* occur. Therefore, to return to our example above, it must be possible for the reading comprehension strategy instruction either to bring about improvement in comprehension or vocabulary acquisition or not to. This is a basic tenet of experimental research. If there is no chance that a particular experiment will not go the way the researcher predicts, then there may be little point in doing the experiment. This is another reason why the null hypothesis has acquired its traditional use: this states that the researcher will *not* find the results he or she expects.[8]

Secondly, we may often come across a piece of research which attempts to use the results from a directional hypothesis or a rejected null hypothesis to suggest that a particular effect of, or relationship between, variables is thereby proven. As readers of research in L2 learning, it is worth recalling that most study in our field is perforce exploratory in nature. It is unlikely – and to a certain extent, undesirable – that a study starts out to *prove* that an hypothesis is or is not correct. Although certain research designs and inferential statistical procedures will give a researcher the possibility to generalise from their findings to other contexts (see Chapter 7 and 8), the process should be interpreted by the researcher as one in which support (rather than outright proof) is sought and found for their hypotheses. The reader will need to remember this as he or she later reflects on the findings and discussion presented. Confirmation or rejection of the original hypothesis is unlikely to lead to any firm conclusion or provide definitive answers to the original problem statement. Much more desirable is that what comes out of the research is destined to become another element in the current body of knowledge. This element, in turn, will be used to refine a prior theory, provide additional evidence for a phenomenon, or open up further research directions. As we have indicated above, this is also one way in which replication studies help the field to move on, as each outcome contributes to the information previous studies have provided, helping to make science a self-correcting system.

A further useful exercise for the reader at this point would be independently to consider any alternative relationships between variables not stated but implied in the previous review of the literature and the problem statement. The researcher may have decided to limit the study to only one aspect of the problem and presented only this in the research questions or hypothesis. Nevertheless, the reader might also have appreciated during their reading other possible relationships between the variables that could be used to shed light on certain findings in the study. It will always be useful to note down somewhere any such perceived alternative relationships or explanations in order to approach the Results and Discussion sections with a more critical eye and also to

---

**8.**    You may come across different terminology when referring to the outcomes of addressing the null hypothesis. Some scholars have argued for outcomes which see the null hypothesis as "supported" or "not supported". Cohen et al. (2007) claim "Rejecting a null hypothesis is not the same as….not supporting that null hypothesis, rejection implying an absolute…state which the research will probably not be able to demonstrate" (p. 515). See "Further reading".

consider how far the author has successfully, convincingly, and completely explained the findings obtained.

---

📖   **Now read this worked appraisal of the sample paper:**

3.   Are the hypotheses offered directional and do they predict differences or relationships between variables?

*The tone of "..will have a significantly positive effect on".. indicates a directional hypothesis that looks towards some measurable difference between the groups and improvement in these skills. As was mentioned in the textbook, directional hypotheses should ideally be seen to proceed logically from what we have been told about previous studies in the literature review section of the paper. In this case, I noted that the first part of the review did indeed highlight positive outcomes of computer-generated feedback, despite some perceived research design faults. However, I was told such positive results and attitudes had been obtained with "native English speakers" rather than the present population. On the other hand, we are later told of previous studies in Country X that "produced overall improvements in students' attitudes and writing". Although I will need to understand what the "skills" mentioned actually are, this would seem – in theory at least – an hypothesis that can be tested.*

*As regards alternative relationships possible here, I suggest the relationship between using a software program offering feedback and seeing improvement could be more complex (and less easily observed and measured) than it initially appears in the hypothesis. It might be argued that success might also come as a consequence of the way one chooses to work with the software, rather than the software as such. As the literature review indicated, improvement may also be associated with an individual's attitude towards the technology. Perhaps improvement could also come about as a result of a more subtle – and less observable - combination of software content, familiarity with using computers to write assignments, and the ease with which the effect of the software can be integrated into the individual writing process.*

---

## 4.4   General appraisal of the research questions/hypotheses

**"Are the research questions/hypotheses unambiguous, consistent with the problem statement, feasible, and supported by the review of the literature?"**

Once we have located and established a research hypothesis or question, the reader might usefully make a judicious pause in their reading in order to form an initial response to this defined aim of the study with the use of a specific set of criteria. This break will ideally allow us to ponder the potential consequences – as we see them – for the forthcoming method and procedures of this expressed aim. It will further help guide our reading of upcoming sections of the paper and, once again, prove an important element in establishing our confidence in the study itself.

In the previous section I mentioned how, ideally, the literature review should guide the reader through the background to the problem and dovetail into the research questions or hypothesis by way of the critical engagement with prior studies or with current knowledge (or lack of it) in the field. Thus, the reader should then be able to use the research question or hypothesis, as the researcher does, to focus the study, to give it direction, and to make it easier to follow. As such, the hypothesis or research questions should ideally be unambiguously stated in the body of the text. Although hypotheses are abstract and ultimately concerned with theories and concepts, this does not mean that the research hypothesis itself should be reported in abstract *language*. Once again, it is useful to have the hypothesis (or research question) re-stated in the reader's own words. Such rephrasing can often help us to make note of key concepts or constructs that suggest the need for adequate definition and/or further explanation, perhaps as a consequence of the imprecise language used by the author. It should be clear to us what is being hypothesised to relate to what or which variable is thought to affect another.

Consistency can be ascertained by checking whether the hypothesis (or research question) presents us with the kind of likely outcomes that will provide adequate responses to what has previously been posited in the problem statement and subsequently analysed in the review of the literature. The review of the literature will ideally have already provided the basis for previous support for the hypothesis or research question, thereby convincing the reader that this is based on substantially more than mere intuition on the part of the author (or, worse, one made up after the researcher had seen the results!).

It would also be wise for us to start thinking about a number of factors with respect to the perceived feasibility of the study as we understand it so far. If no time interval is mentioned as yet, we might want to consider how far the researcher could reasonably accomplish the aims in the question or hypothesis as regards the time and access to participants apparently needed. For example, if a researcher's expressed aim is to describe the language development of a group of "bilingual" children (because their mothers talk to them in one language and their fathers in another), we might suggest it would take years (if not a lifetime) adequately to complete the study. If the researcher defines the time period involved, we might think about the advantages and disadvantages of this and any constraints on possible outcomes. We then need to envisage the extent to which the researcher might reasonably have sufficient contact or access to a large enough sample of participants or, indeed, whether that access will be of sufficient value to permit useful data to be obtained. We might also look carefully at the number of variables involved or the complexity of the relationships expressed to consider how initially workable it all looks as a research design. In short, thinking about feasibility will help the reader to reflect on how far he or she considers the research question or hypothesis manageable given the circumstances described so far and, therefore, what kind of constructive outcomes may be possible. It may well be that further reading of the upcoming Method sections will help clear up any doubts we have on these points; nevertheless, forming our own opinions now will help us to be in a better position to appraise results and discussions later on.

A research question or an hypothesis is likely to have been justified or supported in one, or both, of two possible ways. Firstly, there is the route via logic. A theory will allow for a large number of potential associations between its component parts. The author may have described and/or analysed such a theory and its constituent elements. Any number of possible relationships to be tested will have been revealed and from which outcomes will – in sum – provide a testing ground for validating (or rejecting) that theory. On the other hand, empirical justification requires reference to previous studies and findings. We would have expected the researcher to have conducted a review of the relevant literature, appropriately reporting on, and summarising, the significant prior published studies that reflect on the supposed description or link between variables and that support this logically and/or empirically.

Whichever route was chosen, the researcher would want to have provided the reader with enough justification or support for each hypothesis or research question to assure us of its reasonableness and soundness. Published research may be encountered wherein the author has assumed too much on the part of the reader or taken for granted the fact that their arguments have led logically to the research questions or hypothesis. If there is no underlying reason for, or background to, a research question or hypothesis, the reader is being left to work out from whence that question or hypothesis came. A normal reaction might then be, at best, perplexity (the reader is not able to appreciate what led up to such a statement in the first place) or, at worst, scepticism (the reader cannot appreciate how variables can ever have been thought to be related in this way). The wary or confused reader may even decide to dismiss the study's findings completely because he or she feels that the author has simply fitted the data into a post-conceived hypothesis or research question, according to the results found.

---

📖   **Now read this worked appraisal of the sample paper:**

4.   Are the research questions/hypotheses unambiguous, consistent with the problem statement, feasible, and supported by the review of the literature?

*I was faced with having to read between the lines in what is a somewhat imprecise hypothesis. In my own words, the researcher thinks that "independent evaluative data and feedback will help to improve students' skills and that these will also help to give us exact descriptions of the kind of typical errors made when these students write in a particular style".*

*Firstly, I am not sure which of the two variables (or the two jointly) is being seen as predicted to bring about the desired effect. Secondly, I could not see how something like "objective measurements" can effect changes in skills. Thirdly, such a variable may well be manipulated and expected to affect student skills, but it would not be considered a normal direct property of such a variable also to "enable detailed profiles to be made of the errors".*

*As regards consistency, the problem statement left me in doubt about the real purpose of the study – whether it would be a descriptive study of the "technological instrument" or a comparative study looking at the effects of the instrument using control groups – although the abstract had spoken of "test and control.. groups" (page 5). Also, I remember that the problem statement talked of developing a "writing and correction system". There might be some inconsistency here, as I felt that providing "feedback" on skills requires something more than merely "correcting" that production.*

*With regard to the feasibility of time engagement here, the researcher had already warned in the literature review section of the paper about the need for more attention to "longer periods of study" in research studies investigating computer-generated feedback. I felt that participants will need to be in regular (and perhaps prolonged) contact with the software for any "significantly positive effects" on student production to be reliably registered. I will be interested to see how improvement is measured, and how much is considered relevant: a long-enough period with any new learning device will usually conclude with **some** positive effects on learning being seen.*

*Since the review of the literature in this paper was seen to provide a certain amount of positive support for the use of computer-generated feedback (albeit mainly from L1 studies), it seems logical that an hypothesis that basically posits the same outcome is supported to a certain extent. On the other hand, there would appear to have been no support – beyond intuition – for the second part of the hypothesis that states such computer-generated activity will provide detailed information about student errors.*

## 4.5   Identification of variables

**"Can you identify the principal variables of the study, and are these to be measured as nominal, ordinal, or interval scales? Comment on the perceived appropriateness of these scales. Are moderator or control variables evident?"**

It is important that the reader be able clearly to identify which variables are which in the study, to understand the roles these variables will play in the research, and, ideally, how these variables are to be operationally observed. This is useful because it will help us later to determine how far the data have been correctly analysed and interpreted – and therefore how much confidence we can place in the conclusions themselves. Obviously, if the research hypothesis or question is not stated clearly enough in this respect, the reader will have little basis for subsequent judgement. Independent and dependent variables should be obvious although, in certain studies (see below), such classification is of lesser importance.

In the kind of empirical research we are concerned with here, it is helpful to be able to appreciate what the independent and dependent variable is, together with any moderating, control, or possible intervening variables. Summarising, the *independent* variable is the element that the researcher believes may in some way relate to, or influence, the dependent variable. The *dependent* variable is the major variable that will be measured or observed to determine how, and if, it is affected by the presence of the independent variable. We expect performance on this variable to be influenced by the other variables in the study. In other words, what the researcher may be suggesting in his or her hypothesis or research question is "My hunch is that data from my dependent variable will be related to or affected by the way my independent variable is used". While here I refer to single dependent and independent variables, it is important to remember that studies can deal with many variables, which may be further independent/dependent or MODERATOR/control variables. The key, however, to understanding what the researcher is attempting to do is to perceive the link between the variables. A research hypothesis may suggest that a change brought about on the dependent variable will have its origin in the independent variable or the way that variable is used or manipulated during the study. It follows that a researcher may manipulate the independent variable as well as measure it, but the dependent variable itself will only be measured – it should not be manipulated.[9]

In other studies, we will understand from the hypothesis that the researcher is less interested in predicting differences as a result of manipulating the independent variable, but rather in investigating the extent to which the variables are related. For example, the researcher might want to know whether one group of students score similarly on one kind of listening comprehension test, (e.g., listening to a tape recording in class) as on another (e.g., listening to, and watching, a video recording). On this occasion, neither of the variables need be denominated independent or dependent; both will be measured (rather than one of them manipulated) in order to see whether students who score highly on one test perform similarly on the other test. For the reader, the difference is another important one to establish, as statistical tests vary for testing differences and testing relationships. Furthermore, since neither of the variables is being manipulated, it will be impossible for the researcher to predict or suggest which variable is having an effect on another. All he or she will be able to state is that a relationship does or does not exist; any number of explanations for that relationship could be ventured (and, later, tested), but are not consequences of this particular experiment.

It is also worthwhile, when reading the research question and/or hypothesis, distinguishing between variables themselves and levels of these variables. For example, we might want to know how well L2 students are able to do a listening comprehension test, comparing when they hear it read on a tape and when they hear it read by a native speaker in class. The variable here is "L2 student", but that variable could then be divided into *levels* for the purposes of the study. If the participants were of different nationalities, for example, a participant might be sub-classified as "German",

---

9.    For a useful explanation of intervening and moderator variable differences, see Mitchell, M., & Jolley, J. (2009). *Research design explained* (pp. 74–85). Belmont, CA: Wadsworth.

"French", or "Spanish", so that posterior comparisons could be made between "levels of L2 student". The original variable now has three levels. Such a distinction between variables and levels of a variable is rarely made explicit, and so the reader may have to work this out. It is, however, important to do so at this point in the reading, since the function and measurement of variables will determine, for example, exactly what kinds of statistical test will be appropriate when analysing the data.

The *moderator* variable describes a particular type of independent variable that is thought to mediate or moderate the link between the main independent and dependent variables. Thus, the question being asked here is something like "I want to see what will happen to my dependent variable when it is affected by my independent variable, but I suspect that that relationship is also affected in some way by the presence of another factor – the moderator variable". As we might imagine in our field of L2 learning, the cause and effect relationships between an independent and dependent variable are relatively complex. A number of factors might mediate between the two to produce the outcomes described. Often the link between the two remains ambiguous until such a moderator variable is identified. Such identification will often be made by the researcher after reading findings from previous studies, as a result of which he or she wishes to study the effect of such a variable on the main independent-dependent relationship.

Similarly, the researcher – perhaps as a result of reading previous studies – may be interested in reducing or counteracting the effect of certain elements in a study to make sure they do not have a moderating effect on the relationship to be studied. *Control* variables are factors which the researcher deliberately decides to control in order to cancel out any possible effects on the main relationship studied. Thus, the researcher will not actually be studying such variables (unlike the study which *is* made of the moderator variables); the effects of control variables are merely offset.

In such circumstances, however, it will be important to consider the care perceived to have been taken in such control. We will very often only discover which variables have been deliberately controlled for in the Method section of the paper. So, and not for the first time, it is wise to think ahead and make a mental note of any reasons which we may have thought of during our reading of the paper so far for controlling one or other factor. We should then be in a better position – come the subsequent section – to decide on the appropriateness of the researcher's own decisions. Such assessments on our part and on that of the researcher allow us to perceive patterns in the data. Learn to become aware of the importance of variables such as age, sex, intelligence, previous knowledge, language ability, or dropout rate, each of which may or may not have been controlled for – with the resulting consequences for any findings revealed.

Without controls, patterns in data are often less easy to perceive. Nevertheless, we will need to recall that – however expedient controlling certain elements may be for the research design itself – such a procedure imposes its own "control" on the interpretation of findings. Depending on the kind of control exercised, the researcher will not be able to generalise very far (if at all) in the conclusions or discussion beyond the current context and the controls imposed therein. Indeed, the use of controls in studies lends itself to further study – whatever the results – as future researchers gradually release any previous controls in order to perceive the outcome. This is something to look for as we read the Further Research section often found towards the end of a paper: the present researcher (or we ourselves) might suggest which controls could be dropped or eased in the future with a view to improving the generalisability of findings. This contributes to further discovery by allowing researchers to find out which controls most influence outcomes.

Identification and function of variables are not the only pieces of information the reader will need to look for in this section of the text. Equally important is to be informed of the way the main variables are to be measured and to begin to think about the appropriateness of such measurements. Although more detailed information will invariably be presented in the Method section of most papers, initial indications of measurement are often found here in the operational definitions of variables (see below). If no information is offered at this point, it is still a worthwhile exercise for the reader to envisage how each variable might reasonably be measured. This helps us raise our critical awareness enough to be in a better position to evaluate the appropriateness of the kind of analysis suggested here by the hypothesis or research question and later described in subsequent sections of the paper. A nominal scale gives a name or category to something. Measurement involves classifying the data according to the presence or absence of that attribute – it might be sex, nationality, proficiency level, and so on. When we begin to tally how many objects or people or participants have this attribute, we end up with a FREQUENCY measurement. It is important for the critical reader to appreciate the limitations of such data for posterior analysis. They can be very useful if we want to know, say, how many men and how many women took an exam or how many of these were intermediate level, advanced level, and so on (assuming, of course, that "intermediate" and "advanced" were operationally defined). On the other hand, if we want to do any real comparison between group performances involving mathematical manipulation, unconverted NOMINAL DATA are of limited use.

An *ordinal* scale puts the data in order or RANKS. Very often we will come across such data measurement in papers where opinions or attitudes are collected in terms of increasing or decreasing numbers or definitions on a scale: 1 through to 5 or "totally in agreement", "partially in agreement", "neither in agreement nor disagreement" through to "totally in disagreement". For the reader, it is again important to assess the value of such data for analysis. Although we do end up with important information about rank order, and this order has useful arithmetic worth, the value assigned is not precise. Thus, it does not follow, for example, that there is an equal mathematical unit or interval between the judgements of "totally in agreement" and "partially in agreement" or between this and "neither in agreement nor disagreement". This problem can be got round by increasing the number of alternatives from which to choose from five to, say, seven. The researcher then treats such interval differences as equal because the increased number of options is said to encourage the respondent to think in equal-interval terms. As I explain below, readers will have to make up their minds on the appropriateness of this kind of procedure.

Finally, *interval* data not only order or rank, but do so by also reflecting that rank as points on a scale. Furthermore, each interval is assumed to have the same value so that units can be added or subtracted and also subjected to other kinds of mathematical analysis. Indeed, very often, interval data like these are drawn from some kind of test or exam score, but we will still have to think about the extent to which the test itself encourages equal-interval data. For example, in equal-interval data, the difference between obtaining scores of between 1% and 3% in a reading comprehension test might be thought to be the same as that between 98% and 100%. Both differences amount to two percentage points, of course, but we might wonder whether students scoring such high scores on a test do so because they are obtaining their points by getting rather more difficult answers right than those who score between 1% and 3%. If, after reading about the kind of test involved, it is felt that the interval data collected may be seriously affected by the reliability or validity of the instrument of testing itself (see Chapter 5), it might be suggested that the researcher would have been more justified in using ordinal data analysis.

These mathematical and logical constraints often placed on data measurement mean that we may also come across research wherein data are overtly or covertly converted from one type of measurement to another, presumably to allow for better, or more insightful, analysis to be carried out. If such conversion is suggested either at this point or in later sections of the paper, the reader might want to consider (or be told) how appropriate such a conversion is and the reasons for it. The idea is to think about what information might be lost in converting interval to ordinal data or what information may actually be distorted by converting, say, ranked scores on a listening test into four (nominally-designated) groups of "excellent", "good", "fair", and "poor" performers. The argument is that we still end up looking at the same data, but from different directions. However, in the latter case, a consequence of the conversion is that we find ourselves comparing four grouped performances rather than individual rankings between students. This will inevitably affect the kind of conclusions to be drawn from the data, and the reader will need to be aware of this as he or she reads those conclusions.

📖    **Now read this worked appraisal of the sample paper:**

5.   Can you identify the principal variables of the study, and are these to be measured as nominal, ordinal, or interval scales? Comment on the perceived appropriateness of these scales. Are moderator or control variables evident?

*This would appear to be a study wherein effect is anticipated on a dependent variable.*

*Reading directly from the hypothesis, the dependent variable here appears to be "students' skills". The paper so far seems to indicate that what is being investigated are students' skills in correcting their written errors rather than all or any other skills. The abstract did mention use of "a test group....and a control group" and "reductions in the test group's errors", so I assumed that some measurement will be made of these "errors" at some time to permit such a comparison. The independent variable will be used to effect this comparison, but I am still not sure what is being manipulated here. There is no evidence here of any explicit moderator or control variables. No indication has so far been given whether participants are to be sub-categorised into, say, levels of proficiency for the purposes of the study.*

*There is as yet no indication of the proposed measurement of the variables. However, I read in the abstract that "t-test procedures" were carried out, and I assumed that* CONTINUOUS *(most probably, interval) data are going to be forthcoming from the variable "students' skills".*

## 4.6    Variables potentially affecting findings

**"Can you predict any intervening variables or contributory factors – if not stated here – that might affect findings?"**

Independent, moderator, and control variables can all be manipulated by the researcher and the effects on the dependent variable of such manipulation can be observed and/ or measured. Thus, these variables can all be identified prior to the study itself and form an integral part of the research design. However, sometimes the researcher will obtain data from the original hypothesis wherein the effects of the independent and/ or moderator variable are not clear. We often hope to establish some sort of direct link between independent and dependent variables in a study. In planning their research, ideally the researcher would have been able to identify all the important variables (or control for them). However, sometimes this is impossible. An *intervening* variable is a factor that – in the light of findings – has now been judged to have affected the original hypothesised relationship. How, and to what extent, it affects the original link between the variables may only be revealed by future detailed study of the effects of the "main" independent and moderator variables on the dependent variable. In essence, the moderator and intervening variable look at similar things; the difference is that the latter is not directly observable and therefore has not been or cannot be identified precisely for inclusion or control in the original research.

This is not a fault on the part of the researcher of course, but it does have important consequences for the reader of the paper. It means that we must be aware during our reading that the author may not have been able to identify all the important variables for us and, perhaps, control for them. Indeed, in our research field, this may frequently be the case, for we are often studying internal mental processes that we may or may not be able to measure accurately. Factors such as intelligence or test-taking ability may not be directly observable or measurable but may affect research outcomes considerably. For the reader appraising the paper, however, it is important to begin to think about what may contribute to an observed effect/relationship or lack of it *before* being presented with the actual findings. Such a prediction can often be made by reading through the hypothesis and thinking "Is there anything which forms part of that (independent) variable as it is described here which might affect the hypothesised results?". In other words, look closely at the (independent) variable and try to work out what process (inside the participants, as it were) might be going on to explain the notional outcomes.

Beginning to think about possible intervening variables or indeed other, more detectable, factors that might affect outcomes is far from being a pointless exercise for the critical reader. As so often throughout our appraisal, we are trying to make an active contribution to the text we are reading, as we are reading it. Identifying potential problems such as these can set us off thinking about why a certain outcome may occur and help us identify further research areas or studies which may provide more answers by using this information as their starting point. Moreover, if the researcher has not been able to identify all the important variables or contributory factors in a supposed relationship, we will need to remember in our evaluation of the results that there may be inherent sources of "error" in these data. For example, in a cause-effect relationship, this may be because only a certain number of the outcomes described in the dependent variable were due to the MAIN EFFECT of the independent variable.

If there is no explicit identification of variables in the problem statement, research question, or hypothesis – and particularly if it is the kind of study where these *should* be identified – the reader might look forward to the method or analysis section of the paper to glean further information. Thus, for example, particular statistical analyses presuppose certain denominations of variables. The commonly used *t*-test, for example, investigates the effect of two levels of one independent variable on one dependent variable. In the procedure known as ONE-WAY ANOVA there should have been only one dependent variable and only one independent variable with three or more levels. Names of variables can often be discovered by looking at results tables or from tables of MEANS and STANDARD DEVIATIONS in the Results section.

Although the identification of variables by the reader is an analytic procedure, rather than an evaluative one, it is a process which helps us understand what a study is about. On certain occasions, however, it can help to reveal additional insights into the data offered later and/or to weigh up any findings. One of the most serious cases is when CONFOUNDED RESEARCH DESIGNS are suspected. Here, the design of the study has made it impossible for the real effects of the independent variable to be measured across groups, since elements of one variable are present in more than one of the groups examined (see Chapter 6).

 **Now read this worked appraisal of the sample paper:**

6.  Can you predict any intervening variables or contributory factors – if not stated here – that might affect findings?
    *I hypothesised a number of factors that might intervene in any direct cause-effect link between the independent and dependent variables in this study. Attitudes (towards using the computer and writing), ability (to use the computer), or familiarity (with the machine) may not be directly measurable, yet may well play some role in affecting expected research outcomes. Similarly, sex and language proficiency level of participants might also affect outcomes, although no work is cited in the literature review.*

## 4.7  Operational definitions

> **"What were the constructs used and have these been adequately delineated to permit operational definition? How have these constructs then been defined operationally, where necessary, and is this description acceptable in its present form?"**

Researching in the area of L2 learning inevitably means working in such well-established and defined areas as "bilingualism", "motivation", "language proficiency", and so on. Such areas or constructs are, however, very broad, and previous researchers would normally have facilitated the present researcher's work by narrowing them down in certain ways and making them much more precise or specific. Thus, for example, "motivation" is a construct which has been focussed down to "intrinsic", "extrinsic", "instrumental", "integrative", and so on. "Language proficiency" has been further defined in terms such as "advanced", "upper-intermediate", or "intermediate". However, during the process of examining a research question, and testing an hypothesis, the researcher will need to move even further from this, as yet theoretical and abstract level, to the concrete, practical, and real world – where the research is actually taking place! In narrowing a construct in this way, the researcher must also think about providing a definition of the new concept that limits this to its strictly practical, testable, observable, and measurable application in the present study and thereby also enables other researchers more adequately to replicate the investigation using the same conditions and definition applied by the original researcher. For this reason, the reader should not ignore such considerations, but rather look very carefully at the way a researcher has operationally defined a particular construct in the form of the variable. After all, if we feel such a definition is deficient in some way or otherwise unacceptable, logic should warn us that the variable selected to define the pertinent construct may now no longer represent (or measure) what it is supposed to represent or measure.

The reader is encouraged critically to address these operationally-defined constructs precisely because so many of those we use in our field have acquired an acknowledged, unchallenged meaning as a consequence of their frequency in the literature. This, in turn, has given them an acquired credibility or denotation. The inherent danger is that we may then all too easily set aside any objections we may instinctively have to the accuracy with which a key construct has been operationally defined. Many of us working in the field of applied linguistics regularly refer to constructs such as "grammatical knowledge", "language acquisition", or "communicative competence" and think we all share a basic, similar understanding of what they are; however, such shared definitions will inevitably be influenced by personal circumstances and experience, and it follows that there might be as many operational definitions as there are people using them! For the researcher trying to discover something about a particular construct and then trying to communicate this to others working in different circumstances and with different participants, such a potentially chaotic situation will conflict with the basic requirement that empirical research should aim to deal with precise, measurable data and be grounded in reality. Everyday communication – even among researchers! – may involve an implied acceptance of an undefined construct on both the speaker and the listener's part. On the other hand, we should expect the author to convey meanings with sufficient precision for a reader from any background to understand exactly what is being said, and in sufficient detail to permit subsequent replication. After all, totally different results might be obtained if the reader carried out similar research using, say, a different definition of *bilingualism*.

An operational definition is a clear statement of how the researcher judged or identified a construct in their research through the variable. Although the question of replication and precision are important, the reader also uses these definitions to confirm that a particular construct has been defined consistently throughout the research process. As consumers of research, we need always to keep in mind any operational definition offered at this point in the paper. All such definitions will be used within a particular procedure and/or measurement in the following Method section. For example, if the construct *language level* has been operationally defined by the author as the mark obtained on a multiple-choice test of French grammar, and we find this definition – or even the test itself – in some way deficient or unacceptable, such objections will need to be recalled when we later decide on the confidence to be placed in the author's method, results, and analysis of findings.

However, these very observations also highlight some of the recurring criticisms made of this approach to definition. It has been pointed out that operational definitions may be hopelessly content-specific.[10] That is, if one reader does not like a

---

10.    See Shaughnessy, J., Zechmeister, E., & Zechmeister, J. (2005). *Research methods in psychology* (Chap. 1). Boston: McGraw Hill.

particular definition of, say, "language proficiency" there is nothing stopping him or her providing another. Also, definitions may not always be meaningful to all readers: defining "advanced language proficiency" in terms of the number of languages someone can speak – but not write – may not be readily acceptable to many. Despite these limitations, however, it would appear the field currently feels that the clarity of communication provided by operational definitions offsets any possible drawbacks in their use.

Just how feasible it will be to answer the research questions or test the hypothesis as proposed by the researcher will largely depend on whether suitable operational definitions have been provided through the variables. In other words, operational definitions are part of the instruments with which the research question can be explored or the hypothesis tested. Assume, for example, that the researcher has told us that he or she wishes to test the hypothesis that "L2 (Italian) students who have been taught by native-speaker Italian teachers make greater improvements than those taught by non-natives". The onus is now on the researcher to provide us with acceptable definitions, not only of "greater improvements", but also of "native-speaker teachers" and "non-native speaker teachers". By "acceptable" I wish to indicate that the cautious reader of the research might also usefully already be reacting to the way in which the researcher is operationally defining their constructs in the variables described. As I mentioned above, this will enable us better to evaluate the information provided as a result of applying these definitions. Thus, if "greater improvements" were then operationally defined as the difference between two proficiency test scores measured at the beginning and end of a six-month teaching period, the reader might want to argue that the outcome of a test is not the improvement itself but only a reflection of the construct. Since other forces come into play in test-taking (and marking), we inevitably are being presented with a somewhat inadequate representation of "improvement".

Our reading of this part of the paper, therefore, will need to be guided primarily by questions of accuracy. Firstly, we will need to consider if the constructs have been sufficiently narrowed down or focused to start with. Then we will need to evaluate whether the operational definition of the variable is an acceptable description of this delimited construct. In many of the papers we read, formal operational definitions may not be provided – at least not in this introductory section. In such cases, we may well need to flick ahead to the Method section, as the determination of operational definitions may be based implicitly or explicitly on information given there. However, by now it should appreciated that such definitions are of prime importance to the research questions and/or hypotheses, which *are* part of this present section. It is, therefore, helpful for the reader to have an early idea of what each variable is taken to mean. Once a suitable definition has been located, we will need to consider carefully how acceptable this is in the present context. In the above example, for instance, the reader would have to decide whether the difference in two test scores is a satisfactory measurement or description of improvement in language learning. There are other contentious points here, too: within this operational definition of the construct "improvement" there is an implicit assumption that the test itself (its content and the way it was carried out) sufficiently allowed for participants to show improvement in the first place. We might make a mental note to be on the lookout for such information in the upcoming Method section. If, for example, the tests contained listening comprehension elements wherein the participants had to hear native speakers conversing, it could be argued that the groups who had been taught regularly by such teachers had had a theoretical advantage; therefore, the tests were biased towards this group. Our confidence in the findings from such a study may be weakened since the variables themselves have not been adequately defined at the outset.

Therefore, we see that the main purpose of the operational definition in a study is to define concepts or constructs in a sufficiently detailed and concrete way to permit them to be studied, examined, measured, and replicated in future work. They are, therefore, crucial statements of intent from the researcher to the interested reader. However, defining is not an easy task for the researcher because it requires him or her to juggle concepts of inclusiveness and exclusiveness. On one hand, the researcher must aim to identify a *finite* group of observable, measurable characteristics associated with the variable. The more detail is used in this definition, the more restricted is the variable defined and the more possible it becomes to specify its exact nature. Ironically, this may place restrictions on the generalisability of any results obtained using this definition. In other words, the author will not be able to generalise beyond this strictly-defined variable – and generalisation can also be a very desirable objective in empirical investigation in our field.

Let us go back to the case of "improvement" itself, as an L2 construct to be defined operationally. We have read that an author chooses to define this, logically, as the percentage points increase in tests of proficiency at the beginning and at the end of the experimental period. However, we could argue that this definition would not be very exclusive because some students may have improved their L2 ability but not have been able to show it in the test devised. The definition could then be broadened to include those students who, in the opinion of their teachers, were also showing improvement in their class work. However, this would admit a large element of subjective – and not easily measurable – opinion from the class teacher. Again, the operational definition would be of limited usefulness. We would be looking for a better definition that succeeds, as far as possible, in providing some observable – and, preferably, measurable – characteristic that helps us clearly differentiate between those participants who improve in the L2 from those who do not, or who do so to a lesser degree. There is no solution to such a situation for the author beyond their attempting to marry both needs as far as possible; however, as critical readers of this research, we will need to be aware of the consequences of such decisions as we read them.

> 📖    **Now read this worked appraisal of the sample paper:**
>
> 7.    What were the constructs used and have these been adequately delineated to permit operational definition? How have these constructs then been defined operationally, where necessary, and is this description acceptable in its present form?
>
> *There are no operational definitions provided as yet for "students' skills" or for "objective measurements and feedback". I also do not understand what "significantly positive effect" will mean. Also, as it stands, "errors" could be understood at best as any category, or quality, of errors. This may not be exclusive enough to permit the kind of specificity mentioned as desirable in the textbook section. I made a note to look for more details in the following Method section.*

## Worked sample appraisal

**Research questions and variables 2**

1.    Before you read this section of the paper, familiarise yourself again with the paper by reading Abstract 2 (p. 7), The background to the problem and the problem statement 2 (p. 16), and The review of the literature 2 (p. 29).
2.    When you have read a paragraph, stop and write in the *left-hand column* a few words which summarise the gist of that paragraph, to help you understand and focus on what the researcher is saying. Then, in the *right-hand column* write a few words which record your instinctive reactions to what you have just read as if you were talking to the researcher face-to-face.

| | |
|---|---|
| | The main research questions are the following:<br><br>1.  Is listening comprehension affected when input includes more and longer① pauses?<br>2.  Is listening comprehension affected when the speed of the input is diminished?<br>3.  Is listening comprehension affected when the syntax of the input is made simpler?<br>4.  Is there any significantly greater influence of one of these modified input elements on comprehension than another?<br><br>[*From Method section* ......... the standard variety of Spanish was used for these modifications........<br><br>Participants were studying Spanish as a foreign language in their second semester② at University C.... Listening comprehension was measured as a result of participant recall, whereby participants were told to recall as much information about what they had heard as they could.] | |

**3. Read again the relevant section in the chapter, and then attempt to answer these questions. Finally, compare your responses to mine.**

1. (a) Are research questions or research hypotheses formulated? If so, what are they? (b) Are the research questions exploratory, descriptive, or explanatory? (c) Are the hypotheses offered directional, and do they predict differences or relationships between variables? (d) Are the research questions/hypotheses unambiguous, consistent with the problem statement, feasible, and supported by the review of the literature?

   a. *The research questions we are provided with are clearly expressed. Summarising, each of the first three questions posits a potential influence of one element of modified input on listening comprehension. The final question studies the comparative influence on comprehension of the three variables.*

   b. *All these research questions seek to find out more information about the effect of modifying L2 input on listening comprehension. No predictions are made, and the general tone of the questions is exploratory.*

   c. *Does not apply.*

   d. *The research questions are clearly expressed, but it is always a worthwhile exercise to try to simplify them as much as possible in our minds so that the research design becomes clearer. Firstly, the researcher asks whether L2 listening comprehension improves, worsens, or remains the same as a result of inserting more pauses and/or longer pauses in the text. The second and third questions ask similar questions about listening comprehension based on when the input is artificially slowed down and when the syntax of the input is simplified. The fourth question asks if one of these three factors brings about a greater influence on comprehension than the others.*

   *This reformulation highlights the fact that the effects studied on comprehension are declared to be of interest be they of better or worse consequence for comprehension. In other words, the reader will be expecting descriptive evidence of the effect of these variables on comprehension, both negative **and** positive (the abstract, however, seemed to hypothesise only a positive direction). Secondly, words like "slowed down......more...... longer" and so on will obviously need further definition, but their ambiguity does highlight part of the problem with studying these variables and one already touched on in the literature review (see my comments on the feasibility of the study, below).*

   *The questions seem generally to suggest the kind of data required from the problem statement itself. I did note there that the researcher makes reference to "conscious language alterations" to describe the kind of modifications experimented with in the study. However, the abstract makes it clear that the "experiment" will consist of 4 groups hearing different (presumably modified) versions of the text. I find myself wondering how "conscious" modifications can be accurately predicted in a group experiment, using "artificial" means such as tape-recorders or speech compressors to modify that input. How far is the relationship between input and comprehension in a native speaker/non-native speaker context based on unpredictable, momentary turns in the interaction itself? Problems of comprehension will not be the same for all the members of a group hearing the same text. Some will benefit from more, or longer, pauses; others will not need them. Some will need syntax to be simplified; others not.*

*Is not comprehension something that is negotiated between the immediate interlocutors as the need arises in the interaction? In other words, can any experiment be set up that can realistically hope to reproduce this kind of variable relationship and describe its effects?*

*A further point mentioned as part of the objectives of the study in the problem statement, but not recalled in this section, is the assumption that these modifications indirectly will be further examined to see how far they "thereby affect... L2 acquisition". No studies cited in the review threw any further light on this objective either, but it would seem unlikely that the data to be obtained as a result of these research questions could be shown directly to enhance or diminish L2 acquisition.*

*As with much of the investigation in educational fields, there always exists the awkward problem of just how much engagement is necessary with the participants in order to present convincing data which demonstrates positive or negative outcomes. We are, after all, dealing with listening comprehension, a skill of language learning which is not – even in the native language – something acquired in a day. We might suggest that participants (even beginners) would need to be monitored (and, preferably, individually so) over quite long periods of time before some kind of improvement or deterioration curve can be accurately perceived in their listening comprehension capabilities. The same thing might be said with respect to the aims of the fourth research question: if we are to establish with any accuracy which, if any, of these three input modifications has the greater effect on comprehension, we would probably need data from **all** the participants interacting with **all** the texts (and, therefore, all the input modifications), and across a sufficient time-span. It also follows from this argument that the researcher would need to be able to get results from a large enough group of participants to obtain representative data on the effects of modified input and – if inferential aims are involved – that these participants are selected appropriately to represent the population to which he or she wishes to generalise. As yet, I only know from the abstract that 180 participants were involved, and so I might make a note here to check up on such specifications in subsequent sections.*

*Manipulating pauses, speed, or other modifiable elements of L2 input to see how far each affects comprehension is potentially an endless task. One could, for example, vary speeds of delivery by seconds each time and see the outcomes, or one could gradually increase the pauses between syllables, words, or phrases ad infinitum. Indeed, the conflicting evidence as regards the efficacy of these measures was very evident in the literature review, and I might even conjecture that such potentially open-ended variables such as adjusting speed, pauses, and syntax are so language-, context-, and person-dependent that it would be difficult to report conclusive data, whatever the manipulation. Furthermore, as I mention below, modifying input and its effect on comprehension may be such an individual process that, arguably, the kind of group experiment envisaged in the abstract (i.e., each group presumably getting one version of the text, modified by either syntax, pauses, or speed) may never be able adequately to reflect the true complex nature of the relationship involved.*

*My previous comments indicate that we are dealing with research objectives that are adequately supported in the review of the literature. I also suggested that an argument was being put forward for a study that aimed to throw more light on apparently confusing and conflicting findings so far in the field of study. It would appear at first sight that the researcher does indeed intend to provide some of the kind of information apparently lacking in previous studies, particularly with regard to homogeneous proficiency levels and academic status.*

2.  Can you identify the principal variables of the study, and are these to be measured as nominal, ordinal, or interval scales? Comment on the perceived appropriateness of these scales. Are moderator or control variables evident?

    *We seem to have a study wherein the researcher is looking at the hypothesised influence of one variable on another without any consideration of treatment. On the other hand, while participants will not be submitted to any treatment, the independent variable will be manipulated by the researcher. This nominal independent variable is more accurately referred to in the literature review as "modified input" and has three levels: "more and longer pauses", "diminished speed", and "simplified syntax". The dependent variable, or what is being observed here, is the effect on "listening comprehension". As I have indicated in the observation, little or no information is given here, but this effect will presumably have to be measured in some way that I will need to read about in the following Method section. The assumption would be that this variable is of a continuous, score nature – it will tell us how much of the variable is present. It remains to be seen – in the following, or the Results, section – if the scores are to be interval or ordinal based. As I mentioned in question 1d, a number of potential limitations to previous findings were highlighted by the researcher in the review of the literature; the implication was that such drawbacks would be taken into account in the present study, presumably through participant selection, variable control, and/or analysis of data. However, it might be worth checking at this point to see whether such aspects are addressed in the variables themselves. For example, although there are no specific control variables identified here, the extract from the upcoming Method section reveals that certain decisions were made, the objective of which might have been to control for certain variables in the study. Specifically, we are told that the "standard variety of Spanish" was used for input. No reason is given, but presumably this was kept constant in order to provide the same conditions for all groups and/or to control for the possibility that participants were used to hearing any other varieties. This latter reason, on the face of it, seems doubtful given the nature (i.e., all beginner-level) of the participants. The review of the literature also informed us that the researcher decided to preserve the SVO structure of input in view of the nature of these participants' L1 (i.e., English). However inherently reasonable this might be in the circumstances, I will need to bear in mind such control of the input because, inevitably, it will have a bearing on the generalisability of any findings.*

3.  Can you predict any intervening variables or contributory factors – if not stated here – that might affect findings?

    *I have emphasised throughout how important it is for the reader to learn the value of pausing regularly in his or her reading, both in order to take stock of what he or she has been told so far, but also to think ahead to the possible outcomes of the research. At this point in particular it was recommended that the reader reflect on the independent variable(s) so that he or she can begin to think about what might mediate between it and – in this case – what is comprehended from this input. Firstly, it would seem fair to suggest that the subject matter of the input might affect outcomes. This might be particularly important in the case of beginner students, who might be expected to have a rather limited vocabulary in the target language. It would be as wise to check on how far this was taken into account in the description of the Materials. A further question arising from the beginner-level status of these participants might be how far they use or need the reduced speed, longer pauses, etc., not so much to comprehend more (and, therefore, affect results here), but rather to store and effect a first surface recognition of the language itself, rather than the content. This would be hard to measure, of course, but it could mediate in any direct link between the extent of listening comprehension measured and the way the modified input is given. In other words, the researcher knows and controls how input is given (i.e., by introducing longer pauses, reduced speed, etc.,) but cannot control (nor measure accurately) the way that input is received or used by the participants.*

*I would also be looking to confirm in subsequent sections that these beginners – in their classes – were also used to hearing exactly this variety of Spanish from their teacher(s). Obviously, if this is not the case, there could be an added obstacle to comprehension for these beginner students. Another point to be clarified is the origin of this input; if this turns out to be recorded text of native Spanish speakers, I would need to know how far the medium itself also placed possible obstacles in the way of comprehension for these students.*

*Most of the above observations stem from what has been previously commented upon in question 1d. The way input affects L2 comprehension must surely be very context-specific. In real communication between a native and a non-native speaker (i.e., outside this experimental context), we might imagine that the decision to modify some or all of the independent variable used here will depend on the nature of the discourse and on the way both protagonists perceive the necessity for more or less comprehension. In a sense, the intervening variable is the nature of the interaction itself. If this is the case, accurate measurement of the effects of modifying this input can only reasonably be applied to describing **this** experimental situation, but not beyond it.*

4.   What were the constructs used and have these been adequately delineated to permit operational definition? How have these constructs then been defined operationally, where necessary, and is this description acceptable in its present form?

*The "conscious language alterations" mentioned in the problem statement has been delimited to "modified input" and more detailed information will be needed in the Method section about the criteria for inserting or lengthening pauses, together with the way speed was diminished, or syntax simplified, all of which will be required to permit possible replications of the study. "Listening comprehension" is as yet defined rather too loosely on the basis of how much information is recalled (see question 5, below).*

*The operational definition provided for "listening comprehension" as it stands raises certain doubts in my mind as regards its exclusivity. I wonder whether successful listening comprehension of a text is not considerably more complex than the sum of the number of information units recalled afterwards. Is not the quality of that information recalled of equal, if not more, importance? After all, we might successfully comprehend a text we hear with very little information recalled afterwards, simply because the little that we did recall was enough to complete our comprehension. Conversely, the fact that we recall a lot of information units after hearing a text does not necessarily mean that – even with all that information – we successfully understand the text. Just what the researcher means by "recalls" will need to be further explained, but I will need to keep in mind the apparent score nature of the variable and my doubts about the validity of the definition in later parts of the paper. Furthermore, "the number of recalls" measured in "as much information about what they had heard as they could" might presumably also mean that participants could recall (and, therefore, have counted in their score) elements in the input that are superfluous to comprehension.*

Observations

Look at each observation marked in this text and decide what kind of pertinent reaction could be made at each point. Help is given in the form of short prompts.

① Is there any potential confusion here?
② What more are you going to want to know about this study?

For further practice in appraising this section of the research paper, turn to pages 245–249 in the Workbook.

# Chapter 5

# Method

## Participants and materials*

Before you read this chapter, familiarise yourself again with the paper by reading Abstract 1 (p. 4), The background to the problem and the problem statement 1 (p. 7), The review of the literature 1 (p. 20), and the Research questions and variables 1 (p. 36). Then read this Participants and materials section of the worked sample appraisal and the Observations associated with it:

Participants and materials 1

As you are reading, in the *right-hand column*, write a few words which record your instinctive reactions to what you have just read as if you were talking to the researcher face-to-face.[11] In this worked example, the column has been filled in to show you how you might go about doing this initial reading task.

| | |
|---|---|
| Over three months① during the autumn term of 1994, eight classes were chosen to take part in the study. The total number of participants involved was 374 students, all of whom came from two higher education establishments② in Country X. Of these eight classes, six were final-year students at the Country's only Institute of Business Studies and were in the EEC Business and International Accounting Departments. The remaining two classes consisted of second-year students from the main university of the capital, who were reading Business Studies. | *"chosen": who did the choosing, and based on what criteria?*<br><br><br><br>*So they were all studying Business Studies? What would be the implications for any eventual generalisation of results? Were they comparable in other senses?* |

---

*I intend "participants" to refer only to the people whose characteristics, processes, texts, etc, were examined, rather than including other participants in the research such as researchers, scorers, or coders.

11.    Since this, and the following "Results" section typically present summarised details of procedures or findings, it is not considered necessary for readers further to summarise what they read here.

The participants had to write a series of detailed business letters③ with the help④ of my specially-designed software. This software formed part of a larger package and had been especially adapted to the needs of my students⑤. The program functions as a text editor and provides advice for the students as they are working on how to write business letters. The program also has the advantage of being able to store the errors made during its use and to form databases of the types of errors made during each letter-writing task. Participants were told at the start of each session the kind of letter to be written and the context of the same. Five different types of letter were required: an application, an inquiry, a response, a sales letter, and an offer.

*Were they used to doing this? And with this software?*

*"My"? Which students? These present or previous ones? It might make a difference.*

*I'd want to know more about how this advice works on screen…*

Observations

① Why do you think three months were needed?

*It is not clear why selection should take place over such a relatively long period. If this corresponds to some specific selection procedure or any difficulties encountered, I would have been interested to learn about it for replication purposes. For example, it could be that this time was needed to contact and solicit the agreement of institutions and/or participants or to choose between a number of different classes, based on some kind of criterion.*

② What more information would you be looking for about these institutions, and why?

*Both for replication purposes and for questions of data validity, I would be interested to know why only two institutions were used, if these were also "chosen", and whether these institutions are representative of similar large-class institutions in Country X. Similarly, it would be useful to have some information about the kinds of courses and L2/EFL teaching they undertake.*

③ Why would it be important to learn about the participants' experience writing in these genres?

*If students are not familiar with this kind of writing in their own institutions, it might be argued that the task itself presented certain difficulties for these participants, and that therefore results are also affected by this, rather than just as a direct outcome of the treatment (or lack of it).*

④ What might you want to know about this "help"?

*Some sentences below I also read of "advice" provided by the software: I would be interested to read whether such help or advice was with reference only to the errors made by the partici-pant or – as it seems from this paragraph – consisted of more wide-ranging information about writing, such as content, style, and so on. If this were the case, it would be useful to know how this actually worked in practice with the participant writing at the computer. Similarly, are errors automatically corrected by the computer program, or is merely advice given without any sugges-tions for correction possibilities? If the former, how far would the end result then be a valid repre-sentation of the "students' skills" as such, and how far a result based on the combined efforts of the student and the advice from the computer?*

⑤ What do you understand by "my students" in this context?

*I am not sure whether the researcher is referring to the fact that the software was designed for his or her own students (i.e., previous to the study) or to these present participants. If the former is the case, one wonders how far the present participants (and the class sizes involved) represent the same population – with the same needs – for whom the software was originally "specially-designed". If they do not, there might be a question about the intrinsic value of data from participants for whom the software was not actually intended.*

## 5.1   Descriptive data: Participants

If the Introduction to the study can be said to be "what" the research is about and "why" it is being carried out, we can look to this next section of the paper to tell us "how" everything happened. Here we should find the nuts-and-bolts of the whole operation. The researcher, in describing what went on, will want to address two supposed conditions in the hypothetical reader: he or she can assume that the reader of the present study is an interested consumer of this research and, potentially, a person who might eventually be interested in carrying out the same or a comparable experiment in a similar context. The APA *Publication Manual* suggests two main aims of this section: firstly, enabling the reader to evaluate both the appropriateness of methods and the reliability and validity of results and, secondly, enabling interested readers to replicate the study. For this reason, in our appraisal of this section of a paper, we will be concerned to see how far the information the researcher provides us with theoretically enables us to repeat the study in our own contexts and also if this same information allows us to have enough confidence in the validity of the data to suggest satisfactory description and interpretation of any findings will follow.

Replication is – or should be – the basis of much of the research undertaken in our field. Foreign and L2 learning goes on in many different contexts, under many vastly different conditions, involving many different kinds of teachers and teaching, themselves using much diverse material with many different learners. It follows that it will be extremely difficult ever to discover the definitive response to a research question or hypothesis found in one particular study and carried out in just one of these contexts, and which then permits us to generalise those findings to fit exactly another context of language learning. This means that much of the experimental and quasi-experimental research in our field will benefit from being replicated in many different contexts and circumstances before any tentative generalisations can reasonably begin to be made. For a number of reasons, currently there seem to be relatively few replication studies published in L2 learning research journals. Despite this, the crucial thing to remember here is that the critical reader – be he or she primarily interested in replicating the present study or not – needs continually to consider the degree to which the study as described could reasonably be repeated by another researcher in the same or a different context. In other words, the reader is looking for the kind and amount of information that will permit another interested researcher to carry out the study and thereby for the reader to be in a better position to assess the reliability and the generalisability of the original findings. If we are reading a study with a view to replicating it in some way – and even if we are not – it is from this point on in the paper where we would expect to be reading enough details as to make the study replicable. The amount of detail you might reasonably expect an author to provide is up for debate. Many journals in our field stipulate that contributors should include enough information to permit replication but do not elaborate on what "enough" actually means. A reader who is not necessarily interested in replicating the study might, arguably, require only enough information to be able to appraise what has been done satisfactorily, but the researcher intent on replication will want to be given as much information on the set-up, procedures, method and analysis as possible so that informed decisions can be made on how a replication of the study might test the reliability and generalisability of the results obtained. Either way, it should be easy to access that information, either directly on the page or by contacting the journal itself, some of which even provide web access to data which could not be printed through lack of space.[12]

I have already emphasised elsewhere how the end result of our appraisal depends to a large extent on the confidence we are able to have in the study. We want to read about research that has been carried out in a manner that allows us to feel confidence in the outcomes of that research. Confidence is something that is built up cumulatively throughout our critical reading. At every step, the researcher will need not only to describe what went on, but also convince us that the way he or she searched for and found answers to the question or support for the hypothesis was both reliable and valid. Particularly close study of the text will be necessary, for the reader will need to be alert to the large and diverse number of elements of the method and procedures that are susceptible to threats to its validity. Often, the way in which the researcher has devised the study itself means that certain key components of the research are not valid. As a consequence, we can neither place our confidence in the use to which these components are put, nor in the findings obtained as a result of that use. For example, he or she would want to have avoided bias in any choice of co-researcher, member of the research team or those charged with collecting and assessing the data received. In the use of data which uses returned questionnaire protocols we would expect the researcher to have taken steps to ensure the non-return of these questionnaires was kept to a minimum. In interviews, we would expect subtle aspects of interviewer/interviewee interaction to have been addressed – personality, age differences, dress or the researcher's non-verbal communication.

The field continues to debate the relative importance of certain aspects of validity. There are so many potential threats to validity within a study that it can become

---

12.    The Cambridge University Press periodical *Language Teaching* is one such journal.

virtually impossible for a researcher to control for them all.[13] Realistically, the most he or she might be able to do is show an awareness of the possible threats and plan accordingly. Part of our task as we appraise this section, therefore, will be to ascertain how far the researcher has foreseen, and dealt with, specific threats to validity, and how far any remaining questions of validity are likely seriously to compromise outcomes, and thereby our confidence in the study itself.

Internal validity refers to the extent to which any findings obtained are exclusively the result of the variables being studied here or are potentially affected by other factors that are not part of the original relationship studied. These factors may derive from any number of aspects related to the study, but mostly arise from the research design and/or the procedures used (see below). Just as there are factors which affect internal validity, there are others which compromise external validity. However, it is important to bear in mind that if a study does not have internal validity, it cannot have external validity. This is because external validity allows the researcher to generalise beyond the present data to other contexts. Logically, if the outcomes described are already seen to be jeopardised by questions of internal validity, we can have little confidence when we attempt to infer from them to other contexts beyond this present study. However, this does not mean that one kind of validity is a direct consequence of another. Much of the research we read will be well controlled and designed, so that there are no serious objections to internal validity. In this case, the researcher (and the reader) will be able to have reasonable confidence in the description of any outcomes obtained.

However, trade-offs will inevitably need to have been made by the researcher: the very control or restrictions placed on components (which was needed to achieve such internal validity) may, in turn, mean that the study becomes so far distanced from the reality of other L2 learning contexts as to have no external validity (cf., the argument in the previous chapter concerning the accuracy of operational definitions). In appraising the many quasi-experimental studies with INTACT GROUPS in our field, consideration of threats to internal validity will be paramount. If any major threats are found in the setting up of the study, the acceptability of any description of data may be seriously compromised. Where TRUE EXPERIMENTS have been undertaken, we will need to pay particular attention to the way the researcher specifically overcomes any relevant threats to external validity presented by the participants and procedures used, so that we are then in a position to evaluate generalisations or inferences based on findings (see below).

**"What basic identification data are provided about the participants, and are these data sufficient to permit replication?"**

---

13.    For a fuller description of this question the reader is referred to, for example, Mackey, A., & Gass, S. (2005). *Second language research: Methodology and design* (Chap. 4). Mahwah, NJ: Lawrence Erlbaum Associates.

The presentation of the section in the paper known as the Method will vary according to the type of study being read. Typically, however, a section will be provided wherein the source of the data to be collected is described. In the studies we are concerned with in this book, we will often find language learners and their characteristics as the main source of data. However, it is as well to remember that data can come from many sources, such as pieces of text, specially-selected or randomly-selected words from a corpus, or utterances from one case-study participant. Similar considerations to those that follow will need to be made in the appraisal of such sources. So, for example, if the source of data turned out to be a transcript of speeches made at an L2 teaching congress, and we were interested in using the same data in our own replication, that data would need to be readily-available for consultation. Similarly, if data were anonymous responses to a test, these would usefully be supplied by the researcher in an appendix or available on request. In a meta-analysis, our sample will most likely be the collection of data from the studies that have met the specified criteria for inclusion indicated in the previous section. Such analyses are, typically, comprehensive surveys of the sample data from all the relevant studies.

The kind of information about learners and their characteristics which the interested reader would need to replicate the study is what we might call basic identification data. Firstly, who were the participants, and how many were involved both prior to and during the research itself? As regards the "who" were involved, the researcher would want to supply sufficient information to make replication feasible. There are no strict rules about what information should be conveyed; it inevitably depends on the study itself and our own knowledge of the field. For example, gender might need to be known, as it has often been shown to be an important variable in our field. Age has been similarly shown to be a central factor in some aspects of language-learning. The participants' previous academic (language-learning and other) experience may play an important part in outcomes. Doubtless, we can imagine how these and other basic factors such as nationality, the native language of participants, current course and place of study, or their attested level of L2 proficiency may all be of central importance in certain studies of L2 learning. However, other, more subtle, characteristics may also impinge on the way participants act and react in an L2 learning situation. Knowledge of another (i.e., third) foreign language can often be a help or a burden. Moreover, many studies have indicated that ability and desire to learn an L2 may not be enough when the socio-economic background of these participants does not permit them to compete on equal terms with other students who are more easily able to access such resources as internet, exchange visits, or satellite television.

The researcher will also have decided – according to his or her reading of the circumstances – whether individual, group, or average data are given in such basic identification categories. Much will depend on the way results are to be presented and what is to be read into these findings. Just what, and how much, detail is supplied will depend on the researcher's judgement – which the reader will then need to appraise. Our understanding of what happened is not necessarily enhanced by describing the participants and the context in minute detail. Indeed, there will be many occasions when superfluous detail about the participants and the context of the study only succeeds in confusing matters. In practice, the reader should read the basic identification data provided in this section, think about what he or she has been told so far in the study, and make note of any apparent deficiencies. Once again, however, whether any highly relevant information about participants is lacking here may only become apparent as we read on in the paper. Hence, I emphasise the renewed need for the critical reader constantly to be aware and to note down anything he or she will want to follow up as a result of subsequent findings.

> 📖  **Now read this worked appraisal of the sample paper:**
> 1. What basic identification data are provided about the participants, and are these data sufficient to permit replication?
>   *Participants are identified as coming from the local university and business institute; I learn of their respective courses and their current year of study. In terms of replication, however, much more needs to be known and much of this could affect my understanding of the eventual findings. Participant age and L2 proficiency level might well be seen as important factors in a study that is implicitly looking at the way participants respond to computer-assisted language learning. This information is supplied only indirectly here: I can only guess at the age of "final-year" and "second-year" students based on my own experience, which may or may not reflect the situation in Country X. Adequate replication of this study would require some basic information about L2 abilities. If I assume there were some basic differences by virtue of academic year and/or institution, I would need to treat any generalised findings with considerable caution. After all, to what L2 proficiency levels can we apply any outcomes? Finally, in order to provide for adequate replication, a study of student/computer interaction should surely have provided information about the kind of computer experience participants have both on a personal and class basis. Indeed, in my comments on the research hypothesis, I suggested that participants might stand a greater chance of obtaining better results with new computer programs if they were already familiar with their operation and, secondly, if they were already used to managing computers in their L1 and/or L2 writing.*

## 5.2  Descriptive data: Groups

> "a. What are your initial reactions to the numbers involved or any grouping envisaged?
>   b. Do these groups reflect the original pre-group sample in terms of their basic characteristics and is any justification provided for the eventual group size?"

Although we will probably not yet know the kind of research design envisaged or the analysis to be carried out on the data, the kind of conclusions we can draw from findings will often depend – amongst other considerations – on the numbers of participants involved and whether these numbers remained constant during the period of data-gathering (see below). Here it would be as well to pause and make an initial response to the logic of the method so far described. In other words, given what we know about the aims of the study gleaned from previous sections, do the numbers of participants involved appear to suggest that useful data will be collected? For example, in a study where the research question aimed to gather information about typical classroom L2 learning strategies, one might wonder whether three groups described as each consisting of four participants might provide sufficient data to be adequately studied. Finally, another useful awareness-raising exercise during our reading of this section is to think about what data might *not* be obtained as a result of such numbers of participants. For example, while large numbers of participants from several classes may well provide the researcher with considerable support for any collective responses observed, we will learn nothing about the individual processes involved in forming such group reactions. This is not a fault of the research, of course, nor the researcher, who was interested in other things. But such reflection does have the advantage of helping us set our own minds thinking about other explanations for any outcomes described and, perhaps, helps us form ideas for our own future research agendas.

Crucial factors such as which participants are selected, and how, can affect the internal validity of a study and will need to be appraised carefully. We would be interested to see how the researcher planned to control any sources of possible bias in the participants. The most obvious component of participant selection for the researcher to have validated is that they all actually match any description made of the group – in other words, that any groups eventually to be compared are on equal terms to start off with. Thus, if the researcher has decided that only female students, of between 15 to 20 years old and with intermediate level English are to participate in the study, the researcher would want to have taken the necessary steps to ensure that all participants actually fit that profile. Bias might unwittingly be built into studies where the original sample is subsequently divided into groups. If we read of an initial sample of participants who – according to the abstract – were then divided into four groups, we might want to consider whether these groups still reflected the initial balance in the sample in terms of gender, proficiency level, age, and so on. The reader needs to read about the initial sample characteristics and – if the objective so demanded – understand how far the sub-groups formed still reflected these characteristics, and then consider the extent to which any deviation might seriously affect any outcomes.[14] Imagine, for example, that a researcher tells us that he or she started off with an original sample of

---

14.    A more detailed discussion of sampling techniques can be found in McCready, W. Applying sampling procedures, in F. Leong, & J. Austin (Eds.). (2005). *The psychology research handbook* (pp. 98–112). Thousand Oaks: Sage Publications.

50 participants, 35 of whom were in an advanced-level class, the remaining 15 lower-intermediate level. If we then understand from the abstract that one control group (sometimes also referred to as a "comparison group") and one experimental group were subsequently formed with 25 participants each, we would need to be alert to the possible consequences of such implicit imbalance.

A researcher may choose groups on the basis of the highest and lowest scores on a PRE-TEST, thereby trying to achieve one group of weak and one group of strong participants. A similar situation can be brought about by the common practice of selecting a group in need of special treatment, such as a class of poor language learners who the researcher guesses will (and do) perform poorly on the pre-test. Statistical analyses have shown that chance factors very often play a key role in high or low scores and that these factors are unlikely to reappear on a second or POST-TEST. Therefore, what is likely to happen with our chosen groups on a second or post-test is that more of the original higher and lower scorers get results which move more towards the average (known as "regression to the mean"). In other words, a difference would have been noted between the groups on this measure, even if there had been no treatment in between the two tests. Any findings resulting from such a procedure would then be of doubtful validity.

Selection bias of this kind can be an acute problem in many of the quasi-experimental studies in our field because we are so often obliged to carry out research with intact classes (i.e., classes to which the students have been assigned prior to the study itself). There may be an implicit assumption that such classes already reflect random assignment of groups because they are somehow a suitable mix of students. The study then proceeds with analyses and research designs that are suitable only for truly randomised groups of participants. However, even where students are placed in different classes at the same level of proficiency, the way they are assigned to those classes is usually not random and corresponds to other considerations, such as scores on tests, alphabetical order, or timetable considerations. Students might even have self-selected a class on the basis of the teacher or the time of the class. Likewise, teachers might even select who participates in which class because they wish to have more homogeneity in the group they are teaching. Working with such intact groups does not preclude studies involving control, experimental groups, and a particular treatment. What can be done in these cases is to use findings to present support for some kind of effect of, or relationship between, the variables described. Such findings, however, will need to be read and interpreted with care and few, if any, conclusions about similar results in other contexts could be drawn without replication studies with many other similar classes.

This said, basic designs using intact groups can be improved upon (see below, Chapter 6), and our confidence in the validity of the relationship data can be increased by observing how a researcher sought to control or reduce any potential selection bias. For example, it is relatively easy to flick a coin and randomly assign the control and experimental groups, although random assignment of these intact groups to such groups will not be sufficient to balance any systematic differences among the intact groups. The researcher might also decide to restrict the original population from which the classes are drawn (e.g., only beginners' level of language proficiency) and thereby keep in check any selection bias introduced by using the first classes that come to hand. The problem that the reader will still need to evaluate is how far this restriction limits any conclusions drawn only to this specially-limited group of individuals.

The size of participant groups will also be a cause for concern in many studies. While there are few fixed rules for ideal numbers of participants required for the majority of analyses used in L2 learning research, recommendations do exist and will need to be considered when appraising research design.[15] We may be faced with a description of the numbers in each group, but little more. However, the determination of group size should ideally respond to some principle, particularly in the case of studies that will later involve some descriptive or inferential statistical analysis of the data. In this case, for example, a researcher may decide to increase the size of a group of participants with an eye to increasing the POWER of the study (see below). Thus, NON-PARAMETRIC STATISTICAL TESTS are often used in our field because they carry fewer crucial assumptions about participant selection than PARAMETRIC TESTS. One recommended way of increasing the power of such tests (and, thereby, the confidence to be placed in the results) is by increasing the number of participants.

The fewer participants used, the more likely it is that sufficient bias will be introduced into the sample potentially to distort the data provided. The reason for this is that each member in a small group will perforce bring about a greater effect on the overall group performance than would have been the case in a larger group. In our appraisal of this component, we will want to weigh up the requirements of any group statistical analysis foreseen, since excessively low numbers of participants in each group may well have the effect of distorting key measurements such as the mean or MEDIAN and central measurements of VARIABILITY, such as the VARIANCE or standard deviation. On the other hand, group size will be of lesser importance where the research is basically concerned with individual variability, such as in the case of describing the way in which a select group of L2 students use certain communicative functions, and where inferential statistical analysis is not to be an issue.

---

15.    See, for example, Sapsford, R., & Jupp, V. (Eds.). (2006). *Data collection and analysis* (Chap. 2). Thousand Oaks: Sage Publications.

**Now read this worked appraisal of the sample paper:**

2.  a.  What are your initial reactions to the numbers involved or any grouping envisaged?

    b.  Do these groups reflect the original pre-group sample in terms of their basic characteristics and is any justification provided for the eventual group size?

    *I read that 374 participants are to form the sample, although I do not know whether a larger sample was initially used to arrive at this final total after further selection. Since eight classes are involved, this would represent an average of over 45 participants per class. Each reader would have their own understanding of whether this is a large number of students in class. Furthermore, whether this is a representative large class size of the population to which the findings are directed can only be assumed here, as I am not given any further information. Representativeness would also include the composition of the groups in terms of gender and nationality. I assume that all group members were nationals of Country X. As regards gender, there are no details and – again – I do not know whether the final sample reflects what is normally found in large classes in Country X. More seriously, perhaps, only the total size of the final group is given; it is impossible to work out whether, for example, individual classes in one institution consisted of greater numbers than in the other institution. It seems the business studies institute contributed considerably more participants to the study than did the university. There is no reason given for this.*

    *I have yet to read about how the control and experimental groups described in the abstract are to be set up. However, I would need to be looking for clear criteria for grouping, not least because the initial sample seems to be so large and heterogeneous. Similarly, I do not have enough information to know how far the control and experimental groups will reflect the original pre-group sample. The few details of basic identification provided and the imbalance built into the initial selection of intact classes suggest this may be difficult to obtain.*

## 5.3    Threats to internal validity

**"Can you see any potential threats to internal validity of the data from attrition, history, or maturation factors?"**

We will also need to think about the potential for attrition (also known as "mortality") in the participant sample. Once again, we are referring to possibly troublesome variation within the sample selected, but this time the problem is that participants drop out of the group during the study. This is a particular problem in LONGITUDINAL STUDIES since the researcher obviously does not know in advance who will not continue, and the absence of certain members from groups may seriously affect outcomes and/or the interpretation of these. Those participants that remain in the group may present different characteristics from those that have left. Furthermore, if all the dropouts come from one group, they may then present data which have been directly affected by this imbalance, rather than as a direct result of the variables being observed. Consequently, any comparison between groups will be seriously undermined and the validity of any comparative data brought into question. The reader will need to be alert – particularly in longitudinal studies – to the information given about dropout rates and consider whether sufficient explanation has been given for participants' withdrawal and whether this has been adequately accounted for in any posterior analysis.

History and maturation are two threats to validity which often need to be considered, in particular when we are reading about studies carried out over relatively long periods. Although papers may give the impression that participants have temporarily dedicated their academic lives to the study, many other things could be happening to them – or to their L2 language input – while this is going on! Such history factors are often to be expected in longitudinal studies, particularly when research is taking place in contexts where the target language is already spoken as an L2 outside the "laboratory". We might imagine, for example, that participants are communicating to some extent in that language in their everyday lives and hearing the target language around them. Such uncontrolled input will doubtless have some sort of effect on any data gathered about learning within the L2 classroom. This is less of a problem in foreign language learning contexts but, even so, we might reasonably expect the researcher at least to check up on (even if he or she is unable to control) any possible sources of interference or distortion in the data gathered. One might conceive of a situation, for example, wherein a researcher is testing the effect of a new set of reading and writing materials and is unaware that, concurrent with the research, a number of participants are in regular L2 correspondence with pen-friends or take part in frequent computer chats or e-mail exchanges in that language.

Admittedly, for the reader, we are likely to remain unaware of these factors, but there are language-learning contexts that are used for research in which we can hazard a good guess about what outside influences might potentially be seriously affecting the study. Either way, it would be a sound strategy on the part of the researcher to anticipate such observations and provide us (as far as he or she can) with details about how any potential influence was sought to be controlled. One of a number of ways around the problem would be to provide a control group who are thought to be experiencing the same or similar history factors as those in the experimental group. It should go without saying that the researcher ought to have ensured that any experimental and control groups experience the same history events as part of the research design: both groups to be compared should be experiencing the same teaching, learning, and/or testing conditions, apart from the variables currently being examined (see below, Procedures). The effect of the teacher, for example, might be controlled by having the same teacher teach both groups. Classroom conditions should be similar: if the reader feels, for instance, that the control group are at a disadvantage because, unlike the experimental group, they had their class in the late evening, this history factor might be discussed as a possible threat to internal validity.

Maturation is also related to time and affects internal validity when we suspect growth, change, or development in the participants related to the treatment studied in the research. Once again, this is a particular problem in studies over longer periods of time. We know that young people of a certain age, for example, experience considerably more cognitive development over similar periods of time than adults. Thus, we might not be surprised to find changes in L2 learning ability in such participants caused by factors other than those currently under study. The developing ability to use short-term memory to greater effect may be a particular feature of a child's cognitive ability that could affect results. In addition to actually getting older, maturation might also refer to coexisting elements of long-term classroom experience, including tiredness and boredom. Likewise, care would also need to be taken when comparison is made between groups comprising different age-groups. Adults, with more maturity and greater experience in the classroom, might be hypothesised as better able to handle certain methodologies and specific evaluation measures than younger participants. Once again, the reader will be looking for some acknowledgment that maturation could have occurred (it is difficult to control, of course) and suggestions as to how some of these interfering experiences were confronted in practice.

---

📖   **Now read this worked appraisal of the sample paper:**

3.  Can you see any potential threats to internal validity of the data from attrition, history, or maturation factors?

    *I know from the abstract that the study took place over "six months". There is a large number of participants from different classes and courses, and different colleges. It is not, as yet, clear how the researcher actually managed such numbers throughout the six-month period, but it is reasonable to suppose that there is potential for attrition in this sample; this could, for example, potentially affect any subsequent statistical comparison if there was considerable attrition in one of the eight classes involved.*

    *I found myself wondering about how to manage so many students in different contexts throughout the period of treatment and ensure that the only, or main, feedback on written errors was indeed coming from the computer software. In particular, I wondered how far these participants' own institutions were also concurrently providing/demanding EFL writing practice as part of their specific courses. Indeed, given the nature of these, such writing might well have consisted of the very kind of business letter-writing required in the present study.*

---

## 5.4   Threats to external validity

> **"What information is presented concerning the way participants were selected and/or group membership assigned? What do you see as the consequences of this as regards eventual generalisation of findings?"**

As far as our appraisal of true experimental (as opposed to quasi-experimental) research is concerned, the key point to look for will once again be in the way participants are selected for the study. The question we need to ask when generalisations are intended is whether the participants and the context in the study are representative of the participants and context to which the researcher apparently wants to apply the findings. Thus, for example, we would rightly question whether findings about the abilities of a group of teenage beginner L2 language learners can be generalised to adult beginners. Similarly, it is of doubtful external validity to generalise improvements in L2 proficiency after using an experimental language laboratory program with university students to groups of parents learning the L2 at night-school, where context, participant characteristics, interests, and motivation may be very different.

However, before such generalisations are ventured (usually in the Discussion and conclusions section of the paper), there are a number of elements to look for in the way the researcher goes about forming groups. True experimental designs may look to achieve a representative sample of the population by using random selection, such as allocating numbers to participants and then choosing them out of a hat. One of the unfortunate consequences of such a method is that the researcher might then end up with rather more male than female, more proficient than less proficient, or more immigrant than foreign participants in the final sample. In other words, we should initially regard such evidence of randomisation as rather simple and potentially of limited use for eventual inferential conclusions. More confidence should be placed in grouping that results from previous STRATIFIED RANDOMISATION using selection within specified strata, such sex, age, or region. This suggests a more precise search for data on the part of the researcher: specific previously-identified characteristics are to be represented in the randomised sample and that sample reflects the true characteristics of the population to which generalisation will be made. In such cases, the reader might benefit from being told what these characteristics actually were and on what basis these were identified as being important in the present study. However, we might also want to bear in mind that the more characteristics built into the description, the more difficult the SAMPLING becomes and the larger we might expect it to be since more participants will need to be drawn in to include enough representatives of the wider population.[16]

We would then need to read about how participants, once selected, were subsequently assigned to any groups. As mentioned above, and in the interests of obtaining sound internal and external validity, group membership might also be assigned randomly. At this point we might also need to know whether participants are then to be MATCHED, with an eye to subsequent statistical procedures, and what the basis is for this matching.

The method used to select participants and assign these to groups will be crucial for any posterior analysis and discussion of data, and the reader will need to appraise how far the main threats to external validity have been met. On the one hand, the researcher may decide to use STATISTICS only to describe data and to assure us of the validity of that description. For the description to be perceived by us as accurate, we would need to confirm that all major threats to the internal validity of the data have been met. On the other hand, the same statistical procedures might be foreseen

---

16.    For a detailed description of different sampling strategies, see Cohen et al. (2007), pp. 110–117.

by the researcher to permit generalisation from these data. The critical reader would then want to be sure, at least, that a detailed description of the target population is provided and, secondly, that random selection has been appropriately used. Finally, all other major threats to internal and external validity (i.e., including those in sections below) should be seen to have been adequately met. Whatever the method chosen to select participants, we would expect it to have responded to the criteria of need and fitness for purpose, whereby the method respects not only the aim of the study but also aspects such as the time allotted for data collection and any locally-imposed restrictions on participant selection.

> 📖   **Now read this worked appraisal of the sample paper:**
> 4.   What information is presented concerning the way participants were selected and/or group membership assigned? What do you see as the consequences of this as regards eventual generalisation of findings?
>
> *Previous appraisal did note a tendency in this paper to wish to generalise any findings here to the wider context of Country X. The first thing I notice here is that intact classes have been used; indeed, the researcher uses the word "chosen", which may indicate some other specific and un-stated criterion behind the selection. I am not told so far of any attempt to randomise the group assignments in order to reduce this initial selection bias. Secondly, participants are all chosen from one main study area: Business Studies. Logically, therefore, any findings would only be generalisable to such groups. I have yet to see any conclusions in this regard, but this would already seem to clash with the wider objective put forward in the abstract: "to help to monitor, evaluate, and understand better EFL writing in Country X".*

## 5.5   Descriptive data: Materials

> **"Has any material or instrument of testing/measurement been satisfactorily described and/or samples provided? Where appropriate, has its development/ design and scoring been adequately discussed?"**

Once again, the key to replication is the detail provided by the researcher. Typically, limited space is assigned to published papers in our field, so there will be few chances of our being provided with complete copies of materials or instruments of testing used together with the published study. Given these constraints, the reader would still benefit from seeing some key examples of what participants saw and used, perhaps together with more detailed samples in the appendix, and/or more information as to where the complete materials or instruments can be accessed, if these are not already well-known in the field. Detail includes not only the description of the data-gathering instrument itself but also, where appropriate, thorough informative discussion of its design development, items, scales, and scoring.[17] Therefore, for example, if a questionnaire to participants has been created or an existing one redesigned, it would be useful to be told in general terms how and why the researcher set about designing or redesigning the questions, and what kind of information was sought through these actions. Likewise, learning about how individual responses were weighted as scores will then put the reader in a better position to appraise the way results were obtained and what they mean. In such a way, we can begin to make up our minds whether the questionnaire itself was a valid instrument as such (see below, internal validity) and/or use the information for replicating or adapting the questionnaire using the same criteria as in the present paper, but with our own participants.

Similar considerations need to be made as regards any technology used in the study. Increasingly, one comes across studies wherein use has been made of such things as overhead projectors, tape-recorders, video cameras, or computers. Like other materials, these are all important vehicles through which treatments may be administered. Thus, the researcher must be concerned to describe this apparatus and the use to which it was put in enough detail to permit a similar experiment to be carried out again.

---

📖   **Now read this worked appraisal of the sample paper:**

5.  Has any material or instrument of testing/measurement been satisfactorily described and/or samples provided? Where appropriate, has its development/design and scoring been adequately discussed?

*Despite the central role played by the software in this study, little information is as yet provided about it and the way it is used. From the description given, it seems only to function very much like a normal word-processing program ("a text editor") which incorporates an error-correction complement. What inherent qualities show it has been "specially-designed" for the particular "needs of my students" is not clear, although I note that it has a capacity to record errors made. No details are provided about how these errors are to be scored.*

*I made a note in the analysis of the abstract of the paper to check here for more information about how this software might "alleviate teacher obligation in the correction of written work". However, how it is able to provide "detailed information about errors", give help to teachers, and give "advice for the students" on their writing is not clarified. I also noted in the abstract that this software was to be used "together with software commercially available" – later described as the program "Grammatik©" in the literature review. Although this is indeed a commercially-available program, some basic identifying information would have been useful here for those not familiar with the program itself and interested in using it in their own studies.*

---

17.   "Data-gathering instruments" include tests, observations, or any other formal means of obtaining data. References to "tests" may include any of these means of data collection.

## 5.6    Instruments of measurement: Reliability

**"For any instrument of testing or measurement used (including observation), what evidence of reliability was given and how acceptable is this evidence?"**

To be valid in a specific data-gathering context, materials used must truly be designed to reflect what they are supposed to describe. It is vital, therefore, that whatever procedure is used for collecting the data has both acceptable validity and reliability. Both factors will need to be addressed by the researcher and critically examined by the reader. For example, if we read that a researcher intends to use an existing instrument of testing or measurement, we would expect to read of, and assess, the established reliability and validity of items and scales on this instrument. Moreover, we expect soon to read of the way data were analysed in the study: for such an analysis to be selected and carried out appropriately, the researcher is implicitly accepting that the data are both reliable *and* valid. As we shall see, each statistical test has specific assumptions related to it, but all begin with the one assumption that the data being fed in to any formula respond to this basic requirement.[18]

Reliability may be judged informally by the reader as the extent to which we believe (or we are told) the data-gathering instrument might produce consistent and accurate results when it is given under similar conditions elsewhere. Reliability may be formally reflected in agreement between observers or scorers of a particular phenomenon or, in the case of instruments of testing, in consistency coefficients (see below). In the absence of, or in addition to, such official verification there are a number of less formal factors that we might want to consider in appraising the reliability of any material in a study. Firstly, we might wonder whether the way the instrument is constructed looks as if it promises accurate data-collection: perhaps the samples or test questions themselves seem to be ambiguous when we read them and/or we think they could not be answered accurately or honestly by these students. To reassure us, we might usefully read what steps were taken to pilot the instrument and report back on what items proved reliable and which did not. Similarly, it would be interesting to be told with whom this field testing was undertaken (ideally, a very similar sample to the final target group), and what, if any, provision was made to gather their opinions on the instrument.

Secondly, we need to ponder whether the conditions in which participants use the instrument might reflect on the reliability of data gathered from its use. Perhaps

---

18.    Judging reliability need not always be so rigid. Where the research interest is in individual scores and performance, unreliable instruments will be a serious flaw. Yet if the researcher is interested in average results for posterior group comparison, a certain amount of deficiency in reliability might be tolerable.

we might think participants could easily get fatigued because it is so long and/or complicated, or perhaps there is an over strenuous time-limit on responses that we imagine might have induced unnecessary tension in the respondents. Thirdly, there is an argument that participants need to have some initial familiarity with the specific data-collection instrument to produce reliable results: we might imagine how initially difficult it can be for participants who have never had to face a questionnaire with LIKERT-SCALE responses (i.e., 1-*strongly agree*, 2-*partially agree*, 3-*agree*, etc.) to decide on their answers. Data obtained in this way may be compromised, not only by the previous effect of a variable, but also the participants' lack of familiarity with such a questionnaire format. Finally, in using a test-retest or a pretest-posttest method it would be important to ensure that, between the two samples, the time period did not impinge on the reliability of the instrument in question. Thus, for example, there may be local factors such as class times or composition or teaching method that change between the two samples, or the time lapse between both samples may be considered short enough for participants possibly to have remembered items from the first test while taking the second one.

As we saw in the treatment of threats to validity, it is rarely possible to meet all threats of reliability. Indeed, it might not always be a good idea to strive for such an aim: a more stringent control on reliability might result in a less desirable trade-off with realism. However, once again, our confidence in the readings made of data can be strengthened by seeing the ways in which a researcher has sought to recognise and meet some of these threats. There are a small number of ways in which a researcher can estimate more formally the reliability of any test instrument. These are useful reporting devices to increase reader confidence in the instrument being used. The reader might look out for the reporting of RELIABILITY COEFFICIENTS, with 1.0 indicating a perfectly reliable test.[19] Amongst the many we may come across in this section of the paper are internal consistency reliability coefficients derived from tests such as the KUDER-RICHARDSON or SPLIT-HALF tests (which calculate the coefficient based on dividing the test data into two similar parts) or test-retest reliability coefficients (where the reliability is tested over time and as a CORRELATION between test and retest scores). We might also come across references in L2 learning studies to INTER-RATER/ OBSERVER RELIABILITY, wherein two or more raters' scores using a particular instrument are compared in an effort to establish reliability for the instrument of testing and the raters themselves. Even when a researcher is using an instrument that has already

---

19.    Estimates of what constitutes an acceptable coefficient vary and much depends on the purpose of the instrument in question. More detailed information on suggested acceptable coefficient levels in different types of research can be found in Traub, R. (1994). *Reliability for the social sciences: Theory and applications*. Beverly Hills, CA: Sage and in Pedhazur, E., & Schmelkin, L. (1991). *Measurement, design, and analysis: An integrated approach*. Hillsdale, NJ: Lawrence Erlbaum Associates.

been shown (and suitably reported) to be reliable and valid in previous studies, the researcher (and the reader) would want to be assured of its reliability and validity in the present study. One previously acceptable coefficient in one context is no guarantee of future acceptability in another.

Whatever the route chosen to obtain the reliability coefficient of an instrument of testing, we should consider both the measure and the coefficient obtained with caution: the figure tells us just how reliable a major component of the study has been shown to be, and any low reliability reported will need to be adequately addressed by the researcher. Our confidence in the outcomes should again be suitably bolstered or undermined as a result.[20]

> 📖 **Now read this worked appraisal of the sample paper:**
> 6. For any instrument of testing or measurement used (including observation), what evidence of reliability was given, and how acceptable is this evidence?
>    *Although not, strictly speaking, a test instrument, there is still no specific evidence produced for the reliability of the software used. Some informal support in this regard could have been provided (although it provides no direct proof of reliability) by describing in more detail the development and previous use of similar programs in Country X mentioned in the literature review.*

## 5.7   Instruments of measurement: Validity

> **"For any instrument of testing or measurement used, what evidence of validity was given and how acceptable is this evidence? If none is given, what do you consider to be possible threats to validity here?"**

Once reliability has been acceptably established, the reader would want to see how far the researcher has then considered the validity of the instrument being used. In other words, to what extent is the researcher convinced that the instrument succeeds in obtaining data about what has already been operationally defined as the variable in question, and not something else? There are different kinds of validity, but four are fundamental for work in our field. FACE VALIDITY will be particularly important in our appraisal of data-collection, as it refers to the researcher's (and, in our present context, the reader's) subjective appraisal of what the instrument is measuring. We should ideally be able to read the items, or a representative sample of these, and conclude whether they do, or do not, *appear* to be measuring the construct the researcher

---

20.   An excellent overview of sources of unreliability in tests and examinations can be found in Cohen et al. (2007), pp. 159–164.

intended or the variable to be measured. It is, therefore, an informal judgement (unlike CONTENT VALIDITY, see below) that should be made. Such intuitive judgements about validity can be extended also to other questions: we might ask ourselves whether the length of the instrument appears to be appropriate for the proposed use or whether it seems to require too much or too little time to complete in order to obtain adequate data. Similarly, we might want to know whether the wording in, or readability of, the instrument (particularly if it was presented in the target language) could in any way have inhibited responses from these participants.

Content validity is a more objective and formal evaluation of the instrument. It describes how far the contents represent a demonstrative sub-set of what the whole instrument is supposed to evaluate. It involves clearly defining the construct being considered, selecting a sub-set of this construct for the instrument, and finally operationalising these as items in the instrument. Obviously, operational definitions already established will be important here: if a researcher purports to use the materials to produce data about proficiency in L2 grammar, we would need to decide (or be told) whether a representative and complete sample of such grammar had been chosen for the instrument of testing. If we see from a sample of the test, or a report of its contents, that such a test comprises only multiple-choice type questions on verb forms, we would be right to doubt the content validity of the instrument for L2 grammar. Since there is no specific descriptive or inferential statistical analysis available for content validity, our appraisal of this element will need to be based on the accuracy of previous operational definitions, on samples, and on common sense. The researcher, however, in attempting to establish content validity should previously be seen to have attempted other formal means: for example, the researcher could have submitted the questions to a group of professionals beforehand and asked them to rate the representativeness and comprehensiveness of the content. However, the reader would then need to have enough information about this particular group to accept that they were sufficiently unbiased themselves to provide acceptable judgements on this content!

PREDICTIVE VALIDITY, as the name suggests, describes how valid the instrument is for the prediction of future outcomes. So, we are being asked to accept that a poor result on our L2 grammar test will be a good predictor of equally poor outcomes in other non-test contexts. The assumption here is that the instrument is robust and valid enough to predict results beyond its present confines. Logically, validation would need to include some kind of CORRELATION COEFFICIENT based on the original instrument and the non-test context.

CONSTRUCT VALIDITY has been an underlying feature of much of our appraisal work so far and is a particularly difficult construct to validate, given that there are so many concepts in our field which lack obvious methods of measurement. It is a critical validity to establish for any quantification process because a construct is the perception the researcher has of what he or she is actually quantifying. Indeed, some writers in the field go so far as to suggest that the other types of validity revolve around construct validity or are even included in construct validity.[21] It is established by demonstrating that a particular instrument succeeds in measuring a specific construct. If a researcher claimed to be measuring the construct "advanced level L2 reading comprehension" with their instrument, he or she could find one group of participants who are L2 intermediate level and one group who are advanced L2 students and try to validate the construct validity of the instrument by showing that the advanced students scored higher on the test than the intermediate students. However, the result from one such test and one such sample should not succeed in convincing the critical reader of the construct validity. A number of other variables might interfere with the soundness of results from one test in one situation. A test to show L2 aptitude might have been devised which consistently gives high results to confirm construct validity with EFL students but produces much lower results with ESL students: construct validity of the test is weakened. Much would depend on the use the researcher then wishes to make of construct validity in their study, but we should remain sceptical of the establishment of such validity based on limited testing of the instrument in too exclusive a context. Furthermore, other scholars have pointed out that unforeseen results from these tests (i.e., apparently demonstrating the invalidity of the instrument) might actually be providing evidence of the erroneous *theoretical* viewpoint previously held about a particular construct rather than showing the invalid *measurement* of that construct in this instance. In other words, establishing construct validity for a test or other quantification instrument does not necessarily question the concept of the original theoretical construct itself, where we may or may not agree with the author.

CONSEQUENTIAL VALIDITY is related to construct validity in that it reviews the social consequences of the research study, in particular validating the extent to which the data outcomes of a study are used in the way they were claimed to be used and not beyond such a claim. Imagine the case of a testing or assessment instrument where the researcher was trying to show that the feedback provided on performance helped participants to improve on a subsequent test; however, in your appraisal of procedures you feel that the nature or frequency of the feedback given does not encourage improvement in those participants. For you, the assessment instrument would have little consequential validity. Not every problem with the data outcomes of a study are validity problems within the study itself: some problems arise as a result of the use to which such data is made by agents outside the research, perhaps poor decisions made by those interpreting test results (or research results), not inherent flaws in the design of the tests (or research methods). Such threats to validity also

---

21.    See Pedhazur & Schmelkin (1991): Footnote 20.

impinge on ethical aspects of the research, of course: we would hope results are used ethically in the treatment of all those involved in the research.

In recent years, researchers have posited other aspects of validity which should particularly concern us in our field. CULTURAL VALIDITY acknowledges the importance of socio-cultural influences in a particular research content. As you might imagine, the appraisal of such influences becomes of crucial concern in the kind of cross-cultural and intercultural contexts much research we read is set. We would hope that the research is sympathetic to this context, in that the researcher has shown him or herself to be sensitive to the cultural values of those involved – a particular concern, of course, if the researcher and his or her participants are from different cultures. How, for example, were interviews handled when the interviewer asks a question in English and expects his or her non-native respondents also to reply in this language, and was code-switching allowed? Did the researcher consider the potential effect of this in interpreting the results? Similarly, if the non-native researcher did use L1 data, it would be useful to have that data reviewed by a native speaker to check interpretations of what was said (or written). Cultural sensitivity will have been evident throughout the study. For example, in terms of the background to the study, we would want to know that the theory or theories the research is based on are appropriate for the target culture. The operational definitions of constructs would also need to be verified for that particular culture: a learning strategy, for example, may well have been taught to a group of students prior to the study, but how far is the concept of such an approach to learning inherently unfamiliar or even alien to the culture in question anyway? It will also extend to the instruments used in the methodology: we would expect the researcher to have understood possible specific cultural attitudes to the research in question. Some cultures do not encourage learners to reflect critically on their own learning or on the teaching they receive and many would be wary about doing so openly to someone they do not know.

Apart from those mentioned in passing above, there are a number of other specific threats to validity of materials that the reader will do well to consider as he or she appraises this section. In most cases, these are questions of logic, but we may well find that they are not sufficiently addressed in the text and that more specific information is now required. Firstly, in the case of materials used in previous studies, it is good practice to read carefully any description of the source of such material and subsequent adaptations of this with a view to determining how valid this present application of the material may be. So, for example, we may be told that English-as-a-foreign-language participants' compositions are to be evaluated using an un-adapted version of a marking scheme designed for use in English-as-a-second-language contexts. We would need to decide (from prior knowledge of the instruments involved or detailed examples of the same) how far the scheme is valid for these present purposes or groups, given the EFL group's different learning context, needs, and objectives.

Similarly, the content of any material used will need to be appraised for its appropriateness to the present participants. What needs to be considered here is whether these participants are able to show their real competence given the design of the procedure. We might read of a listening comprehension passage that is being used as a post-treatment test of an innovative classroom methodology; however, as we read through the details, we note that the subject-matter of one of the passages is specifically concerned with economic science. As a result, the vocabulary used could be of a rather too specific nature for these participants. Arguably, therefore, the content is no longer valid for this population as a test of listening comprehension.

---

📖   **Now read this worked appraisal of the sample paper:**

7.   For any instrument of testing or measurement used, what evidence of validity was given, and how acceptable is this evidence? If none is given, what do you consider to be possible threats to validity here?

*Too little information is provided here accurately to judge questions of validity. I did read in the abstract, however, that the aim of the study was to "study the use of a computer-based instrument to monitor, evaluate, and understand better **EFL student writing** (my emphasis)". I find myself wondering how valid data will be in this case, since the software is being used here with students studying English for a specific purpose (i.e., business), and who are being asked to write what we are told are "..detailed business letters".*

---

## 5.8   Realisation of main variables

**"How have the main independent and dependent variables been realised within the method itself, and how satisfactory do you find this?"**

Once the materials to be used in the study have been appropriately described and justified, we can now attempt to link up what we know so far of the "how" of the study with what we have already read of the "what" and "why". It is, once again, another place in our appraisal of the paper where we are advised to stop reading for a few minutes, digest what we have been told so far, and think about the consequences. In the interests of space, published articles rarely dedicate a specific section to the way the main variables are realised in the method itself. However, for the reader, thinking about such concerns is invaluable to help us follow the logic of the study. Specifically, the reader should be in a position to see how the measurement and observation of the variables previously described in the problem statement and research question/hypothesis have now been directly related to the materials used. If the relationship is not made evident by the researcher, the reader should try to confirm the appropriateness of the assignment of variables in the method. Once again, we should be primarily concerned with consistency between sections of the paper, based on what we have read and reacted to in previous sections. Check particularly to see if all this coincides with what had been expected from the description provided in the research question or hypothesis, and confirm if any doubts felt at that point have now been explained satisfactorily or increased as a result of our reading of the method so far. We might also usefully confirm how any levels of the variable predicted in the previous section have been realised in the method.

> 📖 **Now read this worked appraisal of the sample paper:**
> 8.  How have the main independent and dependent variables been realised within the method itself, and how satisfactory do you find this?
>     *Variable assignment has been uncertain throughout this paper so far. I previously described the dependent variable here as "students' skills", which had been elsewhere understood to refer to the outcomes registered through their writing. Data for this variable now appear to be coming from the five different letters the participants will produce and the number and type of errors registered by the program. The independent variable has been realised as the use of the specially-designed software package; I am still not sure how groups will differ on this. There is still no explicit identification of any control or moderating variables, and no information has been forthcoming concerning the possible influence of the intervening variables or other factors I suggested in the previous analysis (such as computer experience or L2 proficiency).*

## Worked sample appraisal

### Participants and materials 2

1.  Before you read this section of the paper, familiarise yourself again with the paper by reading Abstract 2 (p. 7), The background to the problem and the problem statement 2 (p. 16), The review of the literature 2 (p. 29), and the Research questions and variables 2 (p. 56) sections of the worked sample appraisal paper.
2.  As you are reading, in the *right-hand column*, write a few words which record your instinctive reactions to what you have just read as if you were talking to the researcher face-to-face.

---

Participants in this study came from fifteen classes at University C in the United States of America, all of whom were studying Spanish as a foreign language. At the time of selection, they were beginning their second semester of Spanish language study at university. The total number of students involved in the initial data-gathering totalled 208. A listening comprehension test was set up as a control to make sure that all four groups were of equal level in listening① comprehension. The test consisted of two separate exercises wherein participants had to listen and then answer multiple-choice questions about what they heard and follow instructions heard on the tape to fill in a diagram. These tests were the same for all groups and administered over a number of days in the same conditions for all groups②.

The study began some three days after the control tests were completed. The original story, which was later altered in accordance with the research questions, was a fairly long text③ in standard variety of Spanish, which was based on an imaginary telephone call between two Spanish friends who study at University C, and are planning what to do to celebrate Halloween.

Different versions of the text were heard by these participants: three classes were given the text with no modifications as a control, four classes heard the version where speed was diminished, another four classes were given the version with pauses inserted, and, finally, four other classes listened to the text with the syntax made simpler. After data were collected from all these students, it was decided that data would be limited to those participants who regularly only heard English spoken in their homes④ and those who had scored between 35% and 75% on the listening comprehension control test administered to all participants before the study started⑤. Once these controls had been entered, the final sample was 180, with equal numbers of participants in all four conditions (n=45). The version of the text in which the speed was diminished was devised in the following way: verbalization was slowed down but pauses were not modified at all so that the study could investigate separately the effects of pauses and of speed modification. As a result, the modified version lasted for 50 seconds longer than the original version (4 minutes). The version of the text where pauses were inserted was set up by putting more and longer pauses into the original version. These introductions were made wherever there appeared to be boundaries between sets of phrases⑥. There were no further lexical, syntactical or linguistic alterations made to the text. As a result of these alterations, this version slowed down the original by 57 seconds. Finally, the version with modified syntax was composed by reforming any originally long sentences to make them shorter. Furthermore, there was a deliberate attempt to decrease subordinating clauses, increase the use of the present tense and preserve the SVO structure. These adjustments succeeded in slowing down the original version by 20 seconds. Listening comprehension was measured as a result of subject recall, whereby participants were told to recall as much information about what they had heard as they could.

**3.**   **Read again the relevant section in the chapter, and then attempt to answer these questions. Finally, compare your responses to mine.**

1.   What basic identification data are provided about the participants, and are these data sufficient to permit replication?

   *The researcher chooses to provide group, rather than individual data, which seems logical given the numbers involved and the nature of the study (i.e., the description of group listening comprehension outcomes). I am informed of the original sample size, the results of a posterior control on the numbers involved, and of the numbers of participants eventually hearing each version. I am also informed about the educational context of the sample (i.e., four classes in University C) and about the course they were studying (i.e., second semester of Spanish as a foreign language).*

   *As I have emphasised throughout this section, we need to put ourselves in the position of an interested researcher, and ask ourselves if this information is enough to permit replication of the participant sample. Once again, this judgement must be made in relation to the aims and background of the study itself. Here we are dealing with a study that looks at the effect on beginner-level students' listening comprehension of modifying certain aspects of L2 input. As regards the basic identification details of who were involved, I am not told anything directly about gender, age, or nationality. The review of the literature did not mention any studies where gender had been an issue in this kind of study. On the other hand, there is a case for providing specific information about age in an L2 learning research context in the interests of replication. Possibly, the author felt this was implicit as a result of the nature of the classes involved, but a reader from outside this context may not be familiar with the university system in the country. Indeed, it is not immediately clear from the description that ages would necessarily be uniform across the classes: these are participants studying their "second semester of Spanish language", but when do they undertake this course at University C? Maybe Spanish is taken up in the first year at this university, or possibly left to much later. Perhaps it is an optional subject that can be started in any year of the university course. If this is the case, it might mean that – out of the 180 participants – there is a RANGE of, say, four to five years (age and experience) in the sample. Such a range might well be hypothesised to affect outcomes here and would need to be satisfactorily described for possible replication.*

   *Nationality and native language of the participants seem not have been considered a problem here – at least, not at first. I was told (in the literature review) that participants were "English native speakers". However, it would seem – after initial data gathering – that the researcher felt he or she had to control for those who might have been hearing other languages on a regular basis at home. The reader might infer from this that listening comprehension data obtained were seen to have been affected, and the researcher sensibly decided to eliminate these participants' results from the sample. We might be wondering, however, how these participants got in to the original sample in the first place. Returning to the problem of when such Spanish courses are normally taken in University C, I am also not given any information about what these participants' majors were. If Spanish could be studied by all at University C, it is conceivable that – although technically beginners in this L2 – there might also be students with other FL (foreign language) backgrounds,*

*which might have helped or hindered their eventual Spanish language listening com-
prehension. I might remember, in passing, that the researcher also highlighted a study
in the review of the literature in which the nationality of participants and their majors
was thought seriously to have affected the validity of data obtained. Finally, we should
also note that participants come from a large number of classes (n = 15) in which, one
presumes, a number of faculty participate. While they are all theoretically at the same
stage in their Spanish language learning, and also perhaps following the same syllabus
in their classes, I am not told the kind of listening comprehension teaching and exercises
they are used to receiving in these classes. Obviously, I would want to be assured that participants – particularly at the early stages of L2 learning – were already familiar with the
kind of task demanded of them in the study itself and that the nature of this task would
not unduly affect outcomes (see below, question 6.). Again, we could remind ourselves to
read carefully subsequent sections about procedures for any pre-study training that was
thought necessary in this respect.*

2.  a.  What are your initial reactions to the numbers involved or any grouping envisaged?
    b.  Do these groups reflect the original pre-group sample in terms of their basic char-
        acteristics, and is any justification provided for the eventual group size?

    a.  *A large sample size of 180 participants should – in theory – be able to provide the
        researcher with sufficient data to permit acceptable descriptions of outcomes –
        assuming, of course, that other threats to validity are suitably countered. I will
        need to check up in the Procedures section to see how the actual listening com-
        prehension task itself was physically undertaken with such large numbers. I know
        so far that participants had to listen to a tape and follow instructions and that
        conditions for all groups during the sessions were the same. Presumably, how-
        ever, with such large numbers involved, care had to be taken that listening and
        response conditions were the best possible. The last thing the researcher would
        have wanted here was for the link between comprehension and modified input
        itself to have been modified by the conditions of the experiment!*

        *Of course, the other side of the coin is that large group data of this nature will
        not reveal the individual ways students go about trying to comprehend some-
        thing in the L2. As I commented in the appraisal of the research questions, the
        connection between what is comprehended in the target language and how the
        protagonist chooses to "customise" this output to facilitate comprehension may
        be a much more complex and pragmatic issue than that envisaged here. Further-
        more, what strategies do individual students use to make use of this modified
        input, and are these strategies themselves of equal, or more, assistance in com-
        prehension than the actual modified input?*

        *It seems that efforts have been made to ensure that all groups are on equal
        terms to start off with: all are at the same stage of L2 learning, and control has
        been built into the study as a result of initial data-gathering (see above) to ensure
        that history factors do not threaten data (see below, question 3), nor extremely
        high or low listening comprehension levels affect group data.*

b.   *The initially large sample has not been subdivided in a way which leads me to think that the original balance of the sample has been seriously affected. Large intact classes seemed to have remained so throughout the study; however, the number of participants did decrease somewhat as a result of the control measures applied, and it would be important to confirm that this did not adversely affect the original balance in the group. For example, although I am told that 28 participants were removed in this way, I remain uninformed about how many were lost to each of the conditions and, perhaps more importantly, whether one or more of the classes were particularly affected.*

   *I read of no specific reason why, for example, four classes heard one experimental version of the text and three classes heard the control version. Furthermore, I have yet to read of the specific descriptive or inferential statistical procedure that will be used to demonstrate the "significant improvement" mentioned in the abstract, but I might remember to look in the relevant section to see whether any assumptions as regards group size have been met.*

3.  Can you see any potential threats to internal validity of the data from attrition, history, or maturation factors?
    *This study appears to be cross-sectional and to have been completed in a short period of time. Although we cannot – as yet – be sure of the age groups involved, it would not seem that age ranges would likely threaten the soundness of findings here. Under the circumstances, it seems improbable that attrition or maturation factors would have threatened data validity here. On the other hand, the researcher has already had cause to note a history factor potentially interfering with data: some participants were hearing, and possibly communicating, in another language at home.*

    *We might also consider the potential for similar threats due to the context of the study. Spanish is a language that can be heard with increasing frequency in the United States, and it is conceivable that some participants could have been taking advantage of the extra practice available outside their L2 classrooms. This would have been difficult to control for in participant selection, as there are so many possible threats – from Spanish language television channels to Spanish newspapers and internet web pages. The problem, of course, is that there would appear to be little way of knowing to what measurable extent any of these factors (including those controlled for) actually affected ability in listening comprehension. Either way, the problem may have become more serious had we been looking at a longitudinal study of these participants.*

4.  What information is presented concerning the way participants were selected and/or group membership assigned? What do you see as the consequences of this as regards eventual generalisation of findings?
    *Fifteen intact university classes have been used as the basis for study here. There has been no attempt, therefore, to achieve a representative sample through random selection – a basic requirement for any eventual generalisation from data here. On the other hand, groups have been formed that are to receive the distinct versions of the text. There seems to*

*have been no obvious basis for the selection of which group received which version of the modified input or the original (control) text. Presumably, since all the participating groups were considered equal, the researcher saw no reason for any selection criteria.*

*Interestingly, however, a more subtle selection has gone on as a result of the control test results. I have already commented on the control for languages heard at home; now a further control has been used to de-select a number of participants. I am not told how many of these were also eliminated by virtue of the other control measure. However, elimination of extreme scores in the group has to be justified, as it may mean that one is left with a group that is no longer representative of the original sample; therefore, the validity of any descriptive data discussed here may be adversely affected. Again, it would have been useful to read how many were de-selected as a result of this measure so that the reader could better judge the real effect on data. If, for example, 22 of the 28 eliminated for study were as a direct result of this measure, it would tend to imply that either the listening comprehension control test was too easy or too difficult for nearly ten per cent of the participants or that there were large differences in the original sample to start off with. Either explanation would potentially throw doubt on the validity of any outcomes in the study.*

*A further, more worrying, aspect of this de-selection is that the control test represented a different concept of listening comprehension than the experimental test. Whereas the latter was measured through information recall, this control test seemed to be a more typical test of comprehension, with questions testing understanding and with instructions the participants had to follow. The practical problem created by this dissimilarity between the two tests is that those who have been subsequently de-selected are the worst and best performers – in theory, those that have the very worst or the very best listening comprehension skills. The difficulty is that those that now remain to face the experimental test are not going to be tested on the same skills of listening comprehension as in the control test. In other words, the previous results are now no longer valid for having de-selected the best and worst performers from the experimental group. Therefore, there may still remain participants who, although they are not excellent in listening comprehension, are able to recall a lot of information when asked to remember.*

5. Has any material or instrument of testing/measurement been satisfactorily described and/or samples provided? Where appropriate, has its development/design and scoring been adequately discussed?

*The original passage used for modification has not been provided, nor have any examples of the modifications; however, there is a summary of the content and a full description of how modifications were carried out, and these would probably suffice for an approximate replication of the study. Although there is no clear explanation of the development of this instrument for testing listening comprehension, there has clearly been a conscious attempt here to separate distinct types of modifications in the different versions. In other words, each of the three experimental versions aimed to modify only one particular aspect of the output: speed, pauses, or syntax.*

*I have already read in the research questions that scoring will be based on the number of recalls recorded. At that point, I also expressed my doubts about such a procedure but, as yet, no further information is forthcoming about what was scored as a recall, how, and by whom. I might also be on the lookout for descriptions of any technology used in the experiment. In the case of the prior control test, I am told that participants listened to a tape and followed instructions, and I assume that the study itself was carried out in a similar way. It would be important – both for replication purposes and for posterior interpretation of data – to know how technology was used in this case. For example, since texts were modified in a way that might have made them sound somewhat strange to beginner students' ears, it would be important to know how this material was presented to enable participants to give of their best in the experiment. One might imagine, for example, that a tape-recorder at the front of a class full of twenty or thirty students might have made for less easy comprehension than, say, individual listening facilities in a language laboratory.*

6.  For any instrument of testing or measurement used (including observation), what evidence of reliability was given, and how acceptable is this evidence?

    *There is no evidence of piloting or reliability quoted here for either the test instrument or the control listening comprehension test. Again, we would be wise to begin to think about our own informal impressions of reliability. How consistently do you think this test instrument would perform across other contexts and other participants? Although I do not know yet what formal procedures or conditions were involved here, I might want to consider whether other beginners' level Spanish-as-a-foreign-language students might provide similar data, given what I have been told so far. Since measurement is said to have been through the amount of information recalled by each student, it is conceivable that this instrument would prove equally reliable with other participants. What may not, of course, be so consistent across populations are the participants themselves, and I have already conjectured elsewhere (p. 57) that the way each person goes about trying to comprehend a particular text may be very unpredictable. Each of us may have our own preferences or strategies for concentrating on a different aspect of the text in order to comprehend, and the modification of one or more elements in that text may or may not be the facilitator of that enhanced comprehension. Thus, while the instrument's content and construction might informally pass the test of reliability, I would be unsure how far it would promise accurate data-collection elsewhere because of the nature of the listening experience itself.*

    *Our concerns might also be extended to the content and delivery of the passage itself. No information is given about what led up to the test design as such, but the researcher may have felt that beginners' listening comprehension should be tested through a passage in which the situation and vocabulary used were familiar or, at least, described a situation with which they could identify. I might make a mental note to check in the upcoming Procedures section to see whether there was any pre-test briefing to the participants about the situation they were about to hear. It could also be argued, of course, that this very familiarity with a particular situation or context is an essential element in priming our comprehension faculties. Therefore, with other participants in learning contexts less familiar with this kind of situation, the content chosen for the test might not trigger the same level of recognition and stimuli to aid comprehension. I read that the passage was delivered in "standard variety* *of Spanish" and the timings of the various modifications are given. I also wondered how far the speed of the original text represented the norm for the native speakers on the tape or the normal speed for these beginner-level students. In other words, if the passage was already slowed down (i.e., in its original (control) version) to respond to the level of these beginners, there has already been manipulation of the basic material for testing **before** other modifications were introduced. Again, I might wonder how accurate any subsequent data would be on the effects on listening comprehension of reducing speed when the original material was already delivered at a slower pace than normal.*

7.  For any instrument of testing or measurement used, what evidence of validity was given, and how acceptable is this evidence? If none is given, what do you consider to be possible threats to validity here?
    *Face and content validity would be considered acceptable here if we agreed that recalling information units after hearing an L2 passage once constituted a representative and comprehensive example of listening comprehension. Throughout our appraisal of this paper, I have been alerted to the somewhat problematical operational definition of this dependent variable (see p. 60, Question 4.). I now know that comprehension will be measured by recalling information units, which is a different skill from actually understanding what one hears. The practical question now presented here, therefore, is the extent to which this instrument of data-gathering can be said to be an acceptable (i.e., representative and complete) example of what it is supposed to test (i.e., listening comprehension). It could be argued that recalling information units is an essential first step in listening comprehension, but much more is needed, of course, fully to comprehend what is heard. Recalling information in the L2, in fact, may be much more a test of memory for words and phrases than of comprehension. It is conceivable that the problem is merely one of poor definition and that listening comprehension is understood by all involved at this early stage in the Spanish-as-a-foreign-language classes in University C as recall of information. If this is the case, the reader would need to be told, since serious doubts may be thrown on the validity of any outcomes purporting to reflect accurate levels of listening comprehension.*

    *Since I am given no information about the content and methodology in typical classes of Spanish listening comprehension for these participants, I am left to surmise that this experimental test was appropriate to them. A number of doubts have been raised in this section so far as regards the nature of the language used, the speed of delivery, and the content of the passage. I will also need to read attentively any subsequent information about the procedures involved in gathering individual data on comprehension to make sure that participants were afforded sufficient opportunity to demonstrate their true competence.*

8.  How have the main independent and dependent variables been realised within the method itself, and how satisfactory do you find this?
    *The nominal independent variable "modified input" is realised here with its three levels of operation as three different deliveries of the same story. In the section reviewing the research questions, I conjectured that the dependent variable "listening comprehension" might be measured as an interval or ordinal score. There is still no firm indication of the way this will be measured, although the details about recall tend to indicate that it will be quantity, rather than quality of content, that will be measured here.*

Observations

Look at each observation marked in this text and decide what kind of pertinent reaction could be made at each point. Help is given in the form of short prompts.

①   Might this have alerted participants in any way?
②   Do you think information about the study could have leaked to the other groups? What possible effect might this have had on data?
③   Can you think of any possible effects of the length of the passage on comprehension at this level?
④   Why do you think this was necessary? Would all other languages heard at home have presented a similar problem?
⑤   Why do you think this range was chosen, and based on what criteria?
⑥   I am not told how long these pauses were or how many there were in the end; how might these artificial pauses have helped or hindered comprehension, do you think, for these beginner-level participants?

For further practice in appraising this section of the research paper, turn to pages 250–256 in the Workbook.

# Chapter 6

# Method
## Procedures and research design

Before you read this chapter, familiarise yourself again with the paper by reading Participants and materials 1 (p. 62) of the worked sample appraisal paper. Then read this Procedures and research design section and the Observations associated with it:

**Procedures and research design 1**

As you are reading, in the *right-hand column*, write a few words which record your instinctive reactions to what you have just read as if you were talking to the researcher face-to-face. In this worked example, the column has been filled in to show you how you might go about doing this initial reading task.

| | |
|---|---|
| The letters, once written, were given to the teachers as hard copy and on diskette. The hard copy versions were evaluated in the usual fashion, but the computer versions were passed through the special software program to reveal specific errors. The program is designed to monitor a total of 45 error types drawn from a data-base of the most common errors of EFL intermediate-level①② students in Country X when writing.③ The list of errors noted was then given to the student responsible for the writing. | *When were they handed in? Immediately? Might this not have affected their corrections? And what do you mean by "usual fashion"? How did the program "monitor" the errors? …but then what was he/she supposed to do with it?* |
| Grading for both groups took into account the errors found by the program in the sense that the more errors that were revealed, the lower the final grade awarded. However, only the participants in the experimental groups were permitted to see the specific errors in their returned writing since they received the computer error printouts together with the personal feedback from the teacher. The control groups only received the latter feedback. | *"took into account"? So it was the only criterion used? How was this scored? – did it only depend on the frequency of errors?* |
| Comprehensive descriptions of participants' errors were obtained during the six months of the study④ using the specially-designed software and combining its use⑤ with Grammatik as the parsing tool. In order to evaluate the extent to which feedback generated by the computer impacted on the specific errors, two control groups were chosen from those studying final year at the Institute of Business Studies. One group was formed from the participants in the Business department and the other from the International Accounting department. | *What did these "descriptions" consist of? Do you mean "records"?* |

| All groups were using the same computer equipment; this was decided in order to control for any effects that might have been due to the positive feelings these participants had towards using the computer rather than due to the software itself. The experiment was designed in such a way as to ensure that the majority of factors would be consistent across all the groups. Again, it would thereby be clearer that any differences between the groups would have been caused by use of the software program. | *What equipment did they use, and did you check for their computer skills beforehand?*<br><br>*What factors do you mean?*<br><br>*Isn't "caused" rather strong?* |

### Observations

① What might you want to know about the scoring procedures for these types?

*I will be interested to see an itemisation of these types so that some idea can be formed about the kind of error, or absence of error, that was scored in each observation. I read elsewhere that the more errors made, the lower was the score awarded. I wondered what scale was used to decide on the final score, what happened when an error was repeated throughout a letter, and whether this was scored as one or more errors in this grade. Equally, did the program consider all 45 errors of equal gravity for the final score? For example, it could be argued that errors of punctuation or capitalisation are of less import in this business-letter-writing context than, say, spelling or tone of address and that this should be reflected in the scoring procedures.*

② How appropriate is this particular database here, considering the proficiency levels involved?

*The problem here is one of comparing like with like. My question is how far this instrument can be considered valid with these participants; they do all come from Country X as far as I know, but I have been given no information about their EFL proficiency levels and, therefore, whether these error types can be expected adequately to reflect the kind of mistakes the present participants typically make.*

③ How appropriate might this particular database be when used with this kind of writing?

*The above observation leads me to wonder how far an EFL-based instrument like this might appropriately be applied to what, after all, appears to be ESP-based writing. Again, I would need to have been told more about the kind of writing carried out to build the database, but typical EFL students would almost certainly be undertaking different kinds of writing to the present participants with their business studies backgrounds.*

④ How might the length of time of the study affect results of using the software?

*I am not sure whether the six-month period was imposed by the context of the research, or whether this was deliberately chosen by the researcher as a period within which some kind of effect was to be noted. The literature review did suggest that research "over longer periods of study" was needed, but no reasons were given for this. The amount of time with which participants are actively involved with the software (or its feedback) could prove crucial to its effectiveness.*

⑤   Comment on the possible consequences of combining two programs in the treatment.
*I still wonder whether the researcher can point with confidence to any positive effects on error cor-*
*rection as being a direct result of the specially-designed software (feedback) only. There might be*
*a rather more subtle combination of factors at work, such as the ease with which the participant*
*copes with the task itself, the interaction of the participant with the computer, his or her ability to*
*spot and correct error on the screen and, now, the **combined** effect of both these software pro-*
*grams used.*

## 6.1   Procedures: Timing of events

Now that we have read about the participants and instruments involved, we need to be told how the two interacted. In other words, we will now appraise what is arguably the most critical component of the Method section. We now expect to be told what happened to the participants from the beginning to the end of sessions in which they were involved. Once again, possible replication is facilitated if what the participants did and what happened to them is recounted in step-by-step chronological order. This will also give the reader the chance to consider how the context of the investigation might have been changing for these participants throughout the study. Since many studies in the field involve the assignment of participants to groups, it is also worthwhile trying to follow how each group was treated separately throughout the procedure. Our understanding of what went on can be aided if we are provided with separate descriptions of each group procedure or a summary description of all the groups involved followed by details of the distinguishing features of each.

> **"What is your appraisal of the timing of events, and is this information
> sufficient to permit replication?"**

Apart from looking for the kind of detail in the description that permits adequate replication of the study, the critical reader will also need to be attending to possible further threats to internal and external validity of the data. Firstly, we might usefully think about the consequences of the timing of events as they are described: for example, is it felt that the time allowed for different procedures was sufficient given the nature of the experiment and/or the L2 ability of the participants? Or perhaps we read that the period of time elapsing between the pre-test and the post-test is short and, as a consequence, we feel that the threat exists that participants remembered items from the pre-test which then affected their results on the same post-test content. Likewise, we might want to consider the period of time between any treatment and a post-test to evaluate how hypothesised changes were monitored, and how much confidence to place in these observations. For example, we might well be wary of any reported improvements in L2 performance shortly after the treatment period: it would be quite usual to discover a sudden and transitory improvement in participants' motivation, and thereby perhaps language performance, as a result of recent innovatory methods in the classroom during the treatment. Lasting changes in language performance, however, are usually the result of much more subtle processes that require closer and more prolonged observation of participants. We often read that studies are set within a specific time period, "during an academic year", "for two months in the spring term", or "over a semester". What needs to be borne in mind, however, as we consider these events is that – unless previous studies have indicated specific time periods – it is often impossible for the researcher to suggest beforehand a fixed time within which improvement ought be noted as a result of the treatment. Certain research designs can help increase our confidence in any claims made by the researcher in this regard (see below), but there are no specific rules available to follow. The researcher (and the reader) will need to consider the evidence for change in the light of the time periods within and after the treatment, the context of the data-collection, and the appropriateness of the data-collecting instrument itself (see below).

> 📖 Now read this worked appraisal of the sample paper:
>
> 1. What is your appraisal of the timing of events, and is this information sufficient to permit replication?
>
>    *I noted previously the longitudinal nature of this study and questioned how improvement was to be measured across the research period. In this kind of study, where the cumulative effects on L2 error correction of interaction with specific software appear to be a focus of attention, it is going to be of interest to the reader to understand how the nature of this interaction might have affected results throughout the six months of study. However, I am not informed about the period of time elapsing between each of the five letter-writing sessions. Equally crucial is information about how these individual writing sessions were divided up: how long were participants given to plan their work?; did they then have to begin writing immediately?; was this against the clock?; were participants given specific time to check their work, and could the test group see the computer feedback on their previous letters when they were writing?; and when did these participants get the printed feedback?*

## 6.2    Procedures: Test or practice effects

### "Are there any potential threats to internal validity as a result of test or practice effect?"

The period of time elapsing between tests is not the only potential threat to internal validity arising from the way data-gathering is carried out. Being exposed to some kind of test often has an effect on any posterior test, particularly – but not only – if it is the same one. Research into short- and long-term memory has shown that while memory for the *form* of the questions may fade relatively rapidly, memory for content is more long-lasting. There is often a familiarity with the test procedure obtained as well as a knowledge of one's mistakes and, indirectly, an acquired insight into what the researcher is testing in the instrument in question. Having taken the pre-test, the assiduous participant in the control or experimental group might have been made aware of their weaknesses, want to try to improve their performance, go off and bone up on what will in fact constitute the treatment, and return to obtain a better performance on the post-test as a result of these efforts!

Performance in the post-test might, therefore, be enhanced as a result of such test or practice effect, rather than the treatment itself. Another, more subtle threat we need to be alert to as a result of pre-test procedures is when the latter aim to collect data about students' affective characteristics, such as attitudes or feelings. The aim of such pre-tests, of course, is precisely to probe deeply-held opinions or postures and assess them. Unfortunately, what may also happen as a result of this test is that participants end up becoming more aware of their own attitudes and thereby are alerted to how they may develop as a result of the treatment. If the post-test examines the same attitudes, the responses obtained may no longer reflect the effect of the treatment so much as the effect of each participant's reflections on his or her attitudes as exposed through the pre-test. We would also need to be particularly attentive to the time periods between each data sampling. In longitudinal and/or REPEATED-MEASURES studies, where the same participants might be tested a number of times on the same measure, we should remember that participants are also simultaneously practising that task, and we must expect to see change in them – even if a control group is involved and all the testing is done under the same conditions. Thus, we might see experimental participants improve because of the treatment they receive, and control group participants get better (although to a lesser extent) because of the practice they are getting anyway. Conversely, the control group might get worse because of factors such as boredom, frustration, or tiredness.

As with any potential threat to validity, and with a view to increasing our confidence in the procedures used, the reader might be interested to see the extent to which the researcher acknowledges (rather than ignores) the existence of such threats and attempts to counter or allay them. For example, there are research designs (see below) that meet some of these threats by avoiding the pre-test altogether or attempting to get hold of the required data indirectly. Other researchers might opt for the more complicated route of having a number of equivalent pre-tests to use on the different groups (known as counter-balancing).

---

📖 **Now read this worked appraisal of the sample paper:**

2.  Are there any potential threats to internal validity as a result of test or practice effect?

    *Although no formal pre- or post-tests as such are carried out with the participants, I wonder how far the cumulative practice obtained as a result of the five letter-writing sessions and subsequent feedback affects the results obtained. In other words, the experimental group can be hypothesised constantly to have had the advantage, not only of the software and the feedback itself, but also of the continuous use of this.*

## 6.3    Procedures: Ethical issues and instructions to participants

**"What is your assessment of any prior information about the study given the participants and the instructions they received?"**

Another important aspect to be appraised in reading about "what happened to the participants" concerns any prior information they were given about what was going to happen and any key instructions they received. In the interests of replication, of course, precise instructions should ideally be reported verbatim or summarised accurately. In the interests of assessing the potential threat to internal validity, however, any directions given participants would need to have been appropriately checked themselves, normally as part of a previous piloting procedure. An oft overlooked aspect of internal validity, this can be a particularly acute problem when instructions are given to language learners, even more so when those instructions are given in the target language itself! Instructions – in whatever language or medium they are presented – need to be fully and correctly understood by all the participants for subsequent outcomes to be valid. Ideally, we should be able to read through a transcript of what was said to them or what they read before data-gathering commenced. Our attention could be drawn to potentially confusing or ambiguous elements here, particularly when created as a result of lengthy directions.

Similarly, we should include here our assessment of the ethical principles followed before, during and after the study. While we might assume that the research we read has been carried out in accordance with accepted ethical principles for the field, the evaluation of our overall confidence in a study requires us to appraise a number of factors which would hopefully have been addressed by the researcher. Since we are reading about the learning and actions of human beings, we must accept that the research itself will likely impinge on their lives in some way. A number of international overarching organizations have devised guidelines for researchers working with human participants[22], however, the increasing concern for such principles in our own field has become much more evident in recent years through a number of specific recommendations from applied linguistics/L2 acquisition associations, universities and umbrella organizations.[23] They

---

22.    See, for example, *Ethical principles of psychologists and code of conduct* (www.apa.org), *Ethical principles for conducting research with human participants* (www.bps.org.uk) or *Revised ethical guidelines for educational research* (www.bera.ac.uk).

23.    See, for example, *Recommendations on good practice in applied linguistics* (www.baal.org.uk), *Statement of good practice* (http://www.latrobe.edu.au/alaa/goodprac.html), *EALTA guidelines for good practice in language testing and assessment* (www.ealta.eu.org), *Tri-Council policy statement: Ethical conduct for research involving humans* (http://www.pre.ethics.gc.ca/eng/policy-politique/tcps-eptc/), or *Good practice in research* (University of Reading, Department of Applied Linguistics).

are, of course, just that: recommendations, not obligations on the part of the researcher. However, the common emphasis in these documents is clearly on "good practice" and the implication is that those who work in our field have expressed a formal desire to see basic ethical principles of research followed in the studies we carry out, and it is just as wise for us to familiarise ourselves with them before we appraise a study.

In some countries, such as the USA or Canada, for example, research with human participants is more tightly regulated and specific approval is required prior to carrying out an investigation. Research proposals are required to be approved by local university committees, often referred to as Institutional Review Boards (IRBs or, in Canada, Research Ethics Boards), who are charged with the task of seeing that the researcher upholds or intends to uphold the current ethical standards or principles in their research protocols and "protect the rights and welfare of human research participants recruited to participate in research activities" (http://www.hhs.gov/ohrp/irb/irb_chapter1.htm).[24]

While it may be both impractical and unnecessary for you to check whether each and every recommendation made is adequately addressed in the research you read (and much research we read will have already obtained some kind of Research Ethics committee approval), I would suggest a number of key considerations in research with human participants should have been accounted for and should have some weight in our overall appraisal of confidence in the paper.

Firstly, we would want to make sure that participants have been given the right not to take part in the study and that non-participation does not have negative consequences for them. This might seem obvious but, at the very least, they need to be aware of what they are letting themselves in for! Take, for example, a situation where we read "Two similar classes were selected. One acted as the experimental group and the other as the control group". As a summary of part of the procedure it is fine, but it suggests also a number of questions here. Firstly, if all the students in a class were "selected" as part of the class unit, were each of them also given the chance to opt out of the study or not? We would want also to weigh up the validity or reliability of data obtained from participants who had been offered any incentive in terms of differentiating rewards for participating, while those who opted out had perhaps been singled out for overt or covert penalties. If children were involved here, was consent sort and obtained from parents or guardians?

Together with the actual task instructions given the participants, we would also expect that prior information about the aims and objectives of the study – together with any formal aspects of written consent – had been given in the native language and not

---

the L2. One of the reasons for this is to make sure that participants agree to take part in the full knowledge of what the objectives of the study are. Although there are caveats here (see below), it is questionable practice deliberately to misinform participants about the real aims of a study in an attempt to assure participation or a particular kind of response. Where any kind of more covert research is undertaken, we would want to know that the supervising authorities were made aware of this and the reasons for it.

Confidentiality and anonymity are also key elements about which to be informed. It needs to be made clear that data used in the reporting of the outcomes is kept confidential – at the very least through the non-appearance of names. Imagine, for example, that participants have been told (as we would have hoped) that all data would be treated in confidence and that personal identifying details were not relevant to the questionnaire they are about to answer. If then, we – and the participants – see that they are asked for their names, class designations, or other identifying information, we might suggest that certain data are potentially compromised since participants may now be more wary about the responses they give. We might rightly expect to read somewhere in the paper – particularly in studies where potentially sensitive information is to be obtained – that the researcher has been explicit in informing participants about the limits of confidentiality he or she will maintain. In group data reporting, such anonymity is usually respected as scores obtained from individuals is pooled. However, one would assume participants have been informed of this fact too, and have been told that they are merely in a group as the researcher wants to study the population of which they are considered representative. Similarly, names of those in responsibility in an educational establishment such as "The Head of English" or "The classroom teacher" are just as immediately recognisable locally as participant names themselves. In individual interview data, of course, we would expect at the least that data be treated with confidentiality, even if anonymity may sometimes be undesirable. Confidentiality in a classroom study may be more problematical, too: protocols, test outcomes, and questionnaires may well be pooled into group data in a research report but it would be important for participants to know that such data will be collected by number and not name, that all data outcomes were to be destroyed once gathered, and that teaching staff were not to be directly (by he or she collecting the data in class, for example) or indirectly informed of individual results (for example, by receiving the individual questionnaires from the researcher to be then handed back in class).

Working with children also presents problems of another kind and we must be alert to them as we read the text. Apart from the obvious question of obtaining consent, the researcher should also have considered the potential disruption (emotional or practical) to class lessons involved in any long-term research or that involving different teaching methods (or teachers) from those the pupils are used to. The study method used must also be appropriate for children: for example, the interviewing of children requires both experience and sensitivity, particularly if conducted in the L2. We would also wish to be assured in our appraisal of particularly long interventions that sufficient monitoring had been undertaken to ensure the children involved remained willing participants in the study.

In our appraisal it will also be equally important to consider how far the objectives of the study justified a researcher claiming to be more circumspect in the application of the above principles. For example, while it might be sensible to interview children in the L1 rather than the L2 and with the class teacher present, this in turn may well affect the kind of data obtained. Then again, confidentiality may not always be appropriate. If a student has done particularly well working with a new methodology or responding to a new teaching method, should not he or she be rewarded for it, and would not the class teacher want to know who responded well and who did not? In other words, what responsibility do we expect the researcher to have for the knowledge gained from the study data? A researcher may equally have good reason for thinking that divulging too much about the aims of a study might affect the behaviour demonstrated – but not informing them of the aims means you have removed their right not to take part in it. There are also a fair number of research issues that we may feel cannot reasonably be undertaken without limiting the knowledge participants are given about the objectives of the research and many argue that – as long as nobody is thereby adversely affected – the ends might justify the means. These are complex questions for which there are no rules as such; however, in appraising the study, we would at least expect the researcher to have thought through the consequences in each situation and defended the reasons behind any decisions of this nature.

> 📖 **Now read this worked appraisal of the sample paper:**
> 3.  What is your assessment of any prior information about the study given the participants and the instructions they received?
>     *In the Participants section we read that classes (rather than participants) were "chosen" to take part, and I wonder therefore how far a choice was also given individual class members to opt out if desired. In the same section we are told that participants have to write letters which are – we now learn – given to the teachers. It is not made clear whether any attempt was made to make these anonymous; we then read students' writing was returned to them individually so I wonder whether this was done through named manuscripts. In the first of the two sections of the Method reviewed, there was some implied summary of formal instructions, although I was not told the form (i.e., written or oral) or the language in which these were presented. I presume these would have needed to have been quite specific on the day, however, since participants in both groups would have had to know not only what they had to write, but also how much time they had to write, how this might be divided up, how many words were required, and so on. It might be argued that the ability to correct written mistakes on the computer may be related as much to such demands of the immediate writing context as to the software itself. Since these compositions were later evaluated and returned to participants, I also presume that these were told to identify themselves on their texts. I wondered whether participants, instructed to identify themselves and conscious of the fact that their writing is subject to posterior evaluation, might not be more attentive to the surface correctness of that writing than they might be in other anonymous situations.*

## 6.4    Procedures: Reactivity

**"What potential threats of reactivity do you see with respect to (i) observer/
scorer effects and participant expectancies, and (ii) observer/scorer bias?"**

In this section of the paper, we read that participants "had something done" to them. This might be a special treatment, a new methodology, a data-collecting test, an observation of their behaviour, a probing of their attitudes and habits, and so on. The researcher hopes that his or her participants will react in some way to the instrument, method, or observation. However, this very reaction can often extend beyond the strict confines of the immediate objective and affect the very relationship between the observer/scorer and the observed. Such potential for reactivity threats will need to be considered by the reader, both in terms of possible observer/scorer effects and participant expectancies, and observer/scorer bias.

With respect to the first set of threats, research has shown that participants may change their behaviour when they know they are being observed or assessed, and such behaviour may then no longer be typical of how they would normally behave. We might also imagine that, when the person doing the observing is also the person doing the evaluating, such changes may become even more apparent. Indeed, the reader might be even more cautious when he or she is told that observer, evaluator, researcher, and class teacher coincide in one and the same person! After all, our own experience might tell us that few class members would choose to react in a way that their teacher did not apparently approve of. Although these reactions are of interest as socio-psychological phenomena, they represent threats to the validity of data obtained through such observations, and the researcher would, at least, need to have been aware of them and, ideally, to have prepared for them in some way. The reader needs once again to be alert to the potential for this kind of threat to internal validity and weigh up the consequences accordingly. After all, by behaving in a way they think is suitable, participants may unwittingly end up making a particular teaching method, instrument, or other variable look more effective than it really is.

The reader, in turn, needs to think about the way in which participants might be reacting to the research situation. They become aware that they are participating in an investigation, want to do their best, and be a good contributor – all of which can translate into their behaving in the way they think the observer/scorer wants them to behave. Similarly, in a phenomenon known as the HAWTHORNE EFFECT, they react in a way that is related to their pleasure at being included in a study rather than to any treatment involved. We might be particularly attentive to situations wherein intact classes are used, and one group is chosen (and is aware of the fact) to receive a new or special treatment or methodology while their companions in a similar (control) class continue with the normal input. We should also be conscious of the latent possibility for contamination as a result of such a situation. In the latter case, the danger would be that members of the control group with friends in the treatment group may use the information acquired to change their own behaviour – and thereby the data collected from them. One obvious way of meeting this particular threat would be to use groups who are unlikely to inter-communicate, such as those in different educational institutions. As a direct consequence of the physical proximity of groups involved (i.e., within the same building), there is scope for communication of information about the study between groups of participants. Some of the potentially confounding consequences we should bear in mind in such contexts are that there might be a certain resentment on the part of the control group or rivalry set up between the groups (which may affect comparison data between them). Reactions of this type inevitably affect both the internal validity of what is being described and also the external validity of the same, since participants would be behaving in a manner which is atypical of how they would normally react outside the experimental context. Likewise, such reactivity can also make a variable under discussion look more influential than it actually is.[25]

In our appraisal of the possible threats present, we might usefully focus on what we are told (or not told) about participants' knowledge of the study itself and their roles within it. The argument would be that, by limiting participants' knowledge about the aims of a study, more typical behaviour will subsequently be observed. Conversely, there is a fine line to be drawn between keeping participants unaware of the objectives of observation and raising ethical objections by deliberately misinforming them about what is going on. There are, however, a number of other steps that a researcher might take that could increase our confidence in the way these threats were being met in the study. Firstly, he or she might use less obvious means of observation: in practice, this might mean the observer/scorer being outside the direct sight of the participants or microphones and video cameras being made less obtrusive (but see below, Section 6.5). Secondly, participants can be trained before the study commences to adapt to the observer/scorer's presence. The assumption here is that, given enough time, participants will get used to this person and begin to behave in a more typical way in their presence. Finally, the researcher might think about using other indirect means of observation to supplement (rather than replace) direct observations and thereby help confirm such data: these can include homework, school reports, teacher's comments, individual learning diaries, and so on.

At the other end of the reactivity relationship, we will need to assess the possibilities for observer/scorer bias. This comes about when this person – it might be the researcher

---

**25.**    The reader is referred to the excellent discussion of contamination as a threat to internal validity in Cook, T., & Campbell, D. (1979). *Quasi-experimentation: Design and analysis issues for field settings.* Chicago: Rand McNally.

or any of their fellow-observers – has certain expectations about the behaviour they are about to observe or record. This then leads to errors or bias in the correct identification and recording of this behaviour. Similarly, this observer/scorer may consciously or otherwise select the behaviour to be recorded. Logically, the observer or scorer who might therefore be said to be most at risk is the researcher. He or she is only too aware of the hypotheses or research questions at issue in the study and may have their observation biased by such knowledge. Moreover, other observers may also have become aware of the aim of the study in conversation or training with the researcher. We will, therefore, need to assess two possible sources of observer/scorer bias in particular in the kind of studies in our field: that resulting from the observation itself and that resulting from the recording of the observation.

All perceptual processes involving observation, and its subsequent processing, will be subject to bias. It follows that observer/scorer bias cannot be eliminated, only moderated in some way. Some research contexts, however, are more vulnerable than others to this threat. The problem for the researcher and the critical reader to decide is how far data in the study in question are potentially or seriously threatened. Much will depend here on the instructions or training given the observer/scorer. Attention is normally selective in nature and is related to our present interests, experience, and expectations. Unless trained otherwise, observers are unlikely to make a conscious effort to distribute their attention widely and evenly. Readers might also pay attention to the amount of time said to have elapsed between observation and recording of data: the longer the delay after the event, the more likely it is that the recording will suffer in terms of precision and comprehensiveness. We might want to check on the instrument provided the observers to see how far it allows for on-the-spot recording.

A rather more subtle relationship may evolve between the observer/scorer and the instrument used to observe or score. Again, our attention as critical readers will need to be on the period of time during which the observer uses the instrument. Tiredness, boredom, or lack of attention are to be considered normal consequences of such observation. As we read through questionnaire responses, listen to and categorise answers given in an interview, or evaluate compositions from large groups of participants, our judgements inevitably become less focused, and the behaviour we are observing begins to standardise before our eyes. As a result, however, our judgements might become invalid: suddenly a specific response from a participant might cue a different reaction from the observer, an error previously considered serious is ignored or scored less punitively, or a particular behaviour is categorised differently than it was half-an-hour before. Such "observer drift" can be combated by introducing periodic inter-observer agreement checks, particularly since such drift is more likely as not to be an idiosyncratic process. We might be also looking out for the introduction of breaks in evaluation or the use of more than one observer/scorer to combat these kinds of threats.

Further guarantees might need to be built in to studies where observers/scorers are informed about the objectives of the study and are aware of the assignment of experimental and control groups. Again, judgements might be affected when an observer/scorer is conscious of the fact that he or she is being asked to assess someone who has benefited from a special treatment. We should be looking to see how far the researcher sought to offset this bias by, perhaps, limiting the amount of information provided them about the study. The researcher might try to use observers/scorers who are unconnected to the present study and do not know the participants personally or academically. Furthermore, in a process often referred to as the "double-blind" technique, they could try to ensure that neither participants nor scorers are aware of who is receiving the treatment. Unfortunately, the reality in the kind of typical small-scale study undertaken in our field is that such guarantees are difficult to fulfil. Once again, therefore, the reader will need to weigh up carefully the possible threat to data represented by this kind of bias.

📖 **Now read this worked appraisal of the sample paper:**

4.  What potential threats of reactivity do you see with respect to (i) observer/scorer effects and participant expectancies, and (ii) observer/scorer bias?

    i.  *Since I am not told what information about the study was in the hands of the participants, it is impossible to judge whether experimental group members might have been reacting to the investigation rather than the treatment itself. I note, however, that six of the eight groups chosen were studying in intact classes at the Business Studies Institute and that two control groups were chosen from amongst them. It is possible, therefore, that the experimental groups in the same Institute were aware of their special status (or became so, after receiving the special feedback) and that this could have given them an extra impetus to do well. Even if we assume that information would not have leaked about the study's objectives or the differences in feedback afforded both groups, it might well have become clear to either group from the evaluations that "the more errors that were revealed, the lower the final grade awarded" (p. 94); as a result, both groups might have become additionally motivated to check for errors carefully. I wonder if this potential contamination could have been avoided by allocating control status to the two remaining classes studying at the main university.*

    ii. *Although scoring is done mechanically, human bias may be introduced through the "personal...teacher feedback" afforded both groups. I am not told how many teachers were involved in the marking, whether these were the teachers normally responsible for the classes, nor whether they were aware of the study and/or the groups to which each student belonged. What is now clear is that this feedback was additional to that provided by the computer in the case of the experimental group. Although not directly reflected in the score awarded, it is conceivable that this too played its part in any subsequent improvement. The lack of information about the evaluation instrument and the instructions given the teachers also means that I do not know how far this feedback might have been affected by the tiredness and boredom potentially induced by marking so many compositions. The nature of teacher feedback would need to have been coordinated beforehand to ensure that certain participants did not have an unfair advantage in their feedback as a result of any particular detail obtained therein.*

## 6.5    Procedures: Environmental conditions

**"(i.) What details are provided about the environmental conditions of the study and could these have affected outcomes? (ii.) What observations about external validity can be made in the light of these details?"**

A final set of factors affecting internal validity of procedures would have the reader con-centrating on the environmental conditions of the study. In particular, careful thought needs to be paid to the physical arrangements for the study to see whether any natural conditions could possibly have impinged on outcomes. Again, it is doubtful that the researcher will describe such phenomena; the reader will need to consider the poten-tial for such influence and any likely consequences for the study, particularly in the light of possible subsequent replications. Such threats are of particular importance where studies are carried out in classrooms, and where conditions both for teaching and observation can be expected to vary greatly from one context to another. Although not, strictly speaking, vital data for replication purposes, information about the con-ditions in the "laboratory" help the reader picture the proceedings and think about whether any naturally-occurring phenomena might normally accompany such a set-ting. Much of this appraisal will need to be based on common sense and on our own experience of similar environments. Imagine, for example, that a comparison of listen-ing comprehension abilities was set up between two groups after a period of treat-ment. Participants were to hear a taped conversation between two individuals and subsequently answer questions on what they heard. Naturally enough, we would want to be assured that both groups were able to do the exercise in the same conditions. However, we would be especially interested in what those conditions were, since the validity of any data from the instrument itself (i.e., the tape recording and subsequent questions) would be particularly susceptible in this case to environmental phenomena such as outside noise, poor acoustic conditions as a result of the classroom design, or unfavourable seating arrangements (e.g., perhaps some participants were too far away from the loudspeakers to hear adequately).

Similarly, we might want to consider for appraisal here other factors that may form part of the local set up for the research. How far do we feel the content and context of any passage read or heard might be familiar enough to the participants to enable them easily to recognise what is going on? The reader might also want to know about any arrangements that impinge on the environment of participant response on the meas-ure. These do not have to be only those which are naturally-occurring. For example, do the requirements of the task mean that participants have to react atypically – perhaps having to stop and consider a number of options instead of replying immediately? Do they have to read or hear text in the L2 but react in the L1? Does the task require par-ticipants to do two or more things at once that would normally require special train-ing? Once again, our attention might be drawn to any factors that might reasonably affect or explain outcomes in the research other than the variables involved.

eed, these very classroom conditions can create a context which also threat-
ɘrnal validity in the study. Remember that externally valid data might allow the
her to generalise beyond the immediate context of the study. In order to do this,
rse, he or she needs to be satisfied that conditions within the study are similar,
equal, to conditions that could be expected outside the study. The question then
l is "How real or artificial are the experimental conditions in the study?". This is a
cularly knotty problem in the field of research in L2 learning. After all, how authen-
situation is practising a second or foreign language in the classroom? If we read
a researcher aims to describe participants' L2 writing processes by having them
ɪk aloud as they write, we might ask how far data obtained in this way really suc-
:d in probing the authentic experience of writing in another language. Either way,
: might want the researcher to tell us how he or she prepared the best possible condi-
ɔns and what conditions were actually like in the event. Secondly, we should return to the
ʋuestion of how time was used within the study. With regard now to external, rather than
internal, validity, we need to consider how far the time periods set up within the study
can be generalised to the outside context. The reader needs to judge here whether outcomes from a study in which time has been artificially restricted by the limits of the
experimental period or the conditions of treatment can reasonably be externalised to a
situation where such constraints may no longer apply. Second or foreign languages, for
example, are not learnt in a day. Language learning is usually seen as a process in which
we can only hope for lasting results after a considerable period of study. Although many
teachers are happy to see that their students no longer commit a specific error after a
lesson specifically directed at correcting this, few would argue that the real test comes
much later when the students are working independently and speaking or writing in a
less controlled situation. Once again, our interest should be drawn to research designs
where improvement is claimed in an experimental group as a result of some particular
treatment they received which the control group did not. The question to be asked is how
far this perceived improvement could be a direct result of the short time period which
elapsed since the treatment was administered and, more importantly, how far this evidence of learning might then be sustained beyond the end of the study period.

Unfortunately, the list of potential threats to internal and external validity are
many, and there are few simple solutions. Rather than our expecting to find control for
every aspect of validity, it is sufficient that the research we are reading demonstrates an
awareness on the part of the researcher that certain validity factors may have affected
results and that subsequent interpretations of outcomes reflect this caution. In the end,
the researcher will need to trade-off certain less-controllable factors for the control
of others in the search for more valid – if less generalisable – results. For the reader,
however, it is often harder to appraise the threats to external validity than to internal
validity since the descriptions provided may cover internal conditions of the study to
a far greater extent than external ones. In the end, the onus will once again be on the
reader to consider *all* such potential threats and weigh up their consequences for the

research design and data analysis, as well as their influence on the confidence we can have in any reported outcomes.

---

📖 **Now read this worked appraisal of the sample paper:**

5.  i.  What details are provided about the environmental conditions of the study and could these have affected outcomes?

 ii.  What observations about external validity can be made in the light of these details?

> *i.  I am not informed about the conditions in which the writing was undertaken, nor whether this was the same for all the participants involved. However, I note that all groups used the same computer equipment. It is not clear from this how far everyone was actually used to writing in this way and in these conditions in their normal classes. Writing at the computer might not yet be a typical L2 writing experience for many outside this environment and this would need to be taken into account in the interpretation of any results here. That is, how far is what we see in this study a direct consequence of the specific writing conditions, rather than the software feedback (or lack of it) itself?*
>
> *ii.  The considerations in (i) above will obviously mean that the reader would need to consider the extent to which such conditions for L2 writing in this experiment are likely to be similar throughout Country X. Similarly, the lack of information about how time was divided up in the sessions makes it impossible to judge the external validity of any time limits.*

In the light of what you have read in this section, do you wish to amend, or add to, your previous comments on group assignment, materials, and the potential threats to internal validity of the data from attrition, history, or maturation?

*That generalisation will not be advisable in this study has now been further emphasised by the assignment of control/experimental group status: I am told that both control groups were "chosen", rather than randomly assigned. No reasons are given for this choice and the apparent imbalance it creates between the two sets of groups (cf., question 4(i.)). Also, no further evidence has been provided to demonstrate that the groups were equal before any treatment was given and comparison made. Indeed, we read that "the experiment was designed in such a way as to ensure that **the majority of factors** would be consistent across all the groups" (my emphasis). In the light of such an observation, I might need to question the validity of any comparisons between groups after treatment.*

*I remain unaware of the instructions given the participants, and it is also not clear how the experimental material (i.e., the computer feedback) was to be used here. There seems to be potential for the experimental group to be using the feedback however they wish. This may eventually present me (and the researcher) with a problem of interpretation: how do we know if success is down to the software itself or to the way the individual has interacted with this? I do read that this program monitors for up to 45 "common errors" and, presumably, identifies these in the feedback. However, no further information is provided to respond to my previous question about scoring: how are the letters to be scored, given the fact that t-tests were to be applied to what should be continuous score data?*

*No information on attrition is provided, and I assume that all 374 participants continued on through the six-month period of the study. There is no further light thrown on the question of whether the researcher considered parallel college class activities as potentially impinging on outcomes here.*

## 6.6   Research design: Design boxes

**"Identify the basic type of design employed here and draw the design box. What immediate observations can you make about this design and its consequences for the study?"**

As a result of what we have learned about the study in this and previous sections, we should now be better equipped to picture the research design employed therein. In many of the research papers read, where space is at a premium, we should not expect to be given great detail concerning the research design used. Indeed, advice about what should, or what should not, be included in this section (and most others) is often dictated by journal editors. However, much of what we need to know should already have been made clear in previous sections. Being able to identify and then visualise a research design is a useful exercise for the critical reader for it will help us to clarify the appropriateness of the procedures carried out so far and put us in a better position to judge the suitability of any subsequent data analysis chosen.

What should firstly have become evident from the reading of the paper so far is the basic type of design. The identification of type will help the reader to ascertain the appropriateness of any proposed comparisons to be made between groups. PRE-EXPERIMENTAL DESIGNS are simple and inexpensive to implement and exploratory in nature, but lack control groups to compare with the experimental group. They are often used in preliminary research to provide direction and focus for further research using experimental designs, or when circumstances exclude more controlled research design. In quasi-experimental designs, both control and experimental groups are used in the study, but participants have not normally been randomly selected nor randomly assigned to these groups. In PURE EXPERIMENTAL DESIGNS there would have been prior random selection of participants and random assignment to groups. In EX POST FACTO DESIGNS the researcher studies the hypothesised link between two variables, but he or she is not interested in what went on before the study, and no special treatment is applied to the participants.

Our previous understanding of the functions of the variables involved will help us now to make further important distinctions within the design identified. Thus, we will need to consider whether the study uses different participants assigned to different (independent) groups (BETWEEN-GROUP DESIGNS) or uses the same participants but in more than one treatment or taking samples at more than one time interval (REPEATED MEASURES DESIGN). FACTORIAL DESIGNS are used when the researcher wants to cross-compare, by crossing the levels of one treatment with all the levels of another. These designs try to separate out effects: they assess the main effect of each treatment and then the INTERACTION EFFECTS of different treatments.

With this information, we can begin to draw a design box, which graphically represents the essential components of the design described so far. Although it may take time to do, by visualising the basic components of the study in this way, representing its exact particulars using the notation provided,[26] the critical reader will be able to spot possible weaknesses or anomalies in the design and consider workable improvements. The information so provided will also help us begin to see whether any proposed descriptive or inferential statistical procedures will or will not be suitable. First of all, write down the basic functional information we have been provided with about the independent and dependent variables, as in the following fictitious example:

> You are a foreign language teaching assistant giving classes of L2 French conversation at a monolingual secondary school and a bi-lingual international school in Country F. These conversation classes are used as preparation for a section in the university entrance examination, which these participants will be taking at the end of your six-month teaching period. You devise a questionnaire based on the proposed content of your course and its relationship to the examination. The aim is to collect participants' opinions through questionnaire responses about how suitable or useful they think the course is going to be.

Independent variable: *Students of L2 French preparing for a university entrance examination.*

Level 1: *Secondary school*
Level 2: *International school*
Dependent variable: *Questionnaire responses*

Research question: "What do these participants think about the suitability and usefulness of the proposed course of study with regard to the university entrance examination?"

Now draw a box with the details of the dependent variable filling that box and the information about the independent variable at the bottom:

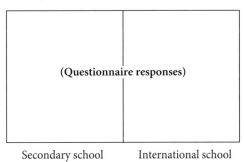

**(Questionnaire responses)**

Secondary school        International school

---

26.    The drawing of design boxes is based on advice originally provided by Hatch, E. & Lazaraton, A. (1991). *The research manual.* New York: Newbury House Publishers, now out of print. For the subsequent diagrammatic versions of research designs, I have used the classic notation suggested by Campbell, D. & Stanley, J. (1966). *Experimental and quasi-experimental designs for research on teaching.* Chicago: Rand McNally College Publishing.

At this stage, we are going to be reading about two sets of responses which might, or might not, be compared (the research question does not clarify this). Furthermore, this is a between-group design, since two independent groups from two different schools are involved. We assume that members of the secondary school will not also be providing data in the cell wherein we find questionnaire data from the international school. Let us now imagine that we want to see if students continue with the same opinions at the end of our course. We administer the same questionnaire again to the same students and then compare what is found. Now the design changes somewhat: we have two samples taken at two different times and from two different schools.

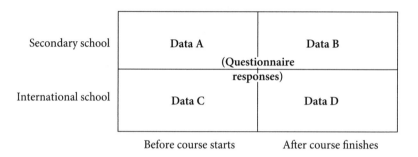

This has now become a repeated-measures design: a sample of data (Data A) will be taken from the secondary school before the course starts and a second sample from the same participants at the same school on the same measure, but at the end of the course (Data B). The same goes for Data C and D from the international school. Repeated-measures designs are very common in research in our field, presumably because of their immediate attraction in terms of procedures and selection. The participants undergoing the treatments – or whatever happens in the experiment – have the same background, environment, age, gender, personality, and so on. However, what we also need to recall in our reading of the procedure is that the same individual has more than one involvement in the study: in cases where the same participants receive more than one treatment, there will be a theoretical effect of order on any measurements. Thus, whatever the participant experiences first will affect what happens next: this could present itself as a practice or carry-over effect from one treatment to the next (see p. 97).

Our appraisal can also show us the potential in a design for further study: the box helps us to see the theoretical possibility (i.e., depending on other features of the design, including selection and threats to internal and external validity) for a comparison between the groups' questionnaire responses: in other words, we might go on to compare the secondary school responses before the study (Data A) with those of the international school (Data C) and so on. If such a design were feasible, the reader would need to be alert to the two kinds of statistical analyses being carried out (i.e., between-groups and repeated-measures) since both require slightly different operations which, if carried out wrongly, can lead to what is known as a TYPE 1 or TYPE 2 error.

Visualising designs in this way is also useful in appraisal since it helps us to spot inherent anomalies which could end up confounding that design and, therefore, invalidating any outcomes. Let's go back to our hard-working foreign language assistant:

As you are preparing both sets of participants for the same examination, you decide to try out, and compare, a new teaching approach to the examination. You decide there is no possibility for contamination or communication between the groups because of the physical distance between the two and you think the two groups would be similar in terms of age and L2 proficiency levels. You toss a coin to decide which of the two groups will receive the new approach (consisting of structured debates in pairs, which are recorded and discussed in tutorials between the pairs and the teacher). As a result, the international school participants are assigned to the new approach, while those at the secondary school get the recommended teaching approach (consisting of class discussions and individual projects delivered orally before the whole class). You give both classes the same test at the end of the six-month period to see if there is any difference in results.

Now let us draw the new box with the following information about the variables and the research question:

Independent variable 1: *Students of L2 French preparing for a university entrance examination.*
Level 1: *Secondary school*
Level 2: *International school*

Independent variable 2: *Teaching method*
Level 1: *Traditional*
Level 2: *Experimental*

Dependent variable: *Post-teaching test results*

Research question: "Is there any difference in test results between participants who have received the new teaching method and those who received the traditional method of teaching?"

The text seems to indicate a simple comparison between groups, which will establish whether one treatment brings about a difference in outcomes. Setting aside the many possible threats to internal validity here for a moment, let us draw a box with the details of the dependent variable filling that box and the information we have been given here about the independent variable and its levels:

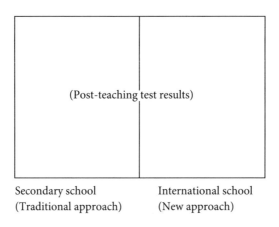

Secondary school
(Traditional approach)

International school
(New approach)

Once the assistant collected the data, he or she could then compare the treatments and prepare to achieve instant fame if their new approach is shown to be successful. However, the design box drawing reveals a much more serious problem. There are two independent variables present. Any differences between the groups might well be due to the teaching approach received; however, they might also be due to the educational institution variable (i.e., secondary school teaching context versus international school teaching context). Hence, the design box drawing succeeds in bringing to light a confounded research design. Confounding is possible when a researcher allows two potentially effective variables to co-vary simultaneously. While some interesting insights might be revealed as a result of *describing* what happened in each institution here, the assistant will not be able to attribute differences in test results at the end of the teaching period to either the teaching approach or, for that matter, the educational institution involved.

Although we may read of more complicated (or complicated-sounding) designs, it is always a useful test of appraisal to try to draw the basic design. Apart from revealing possible confounding, the exercise might also expose other potential relationships that the researcher may not have seen, or may not have considered interesting for their purposes, but which we find noteworthy for our own future research. Imagine, for example, that our reading of a similar paper produces the following box diagram, which represents a factorial research design:

| Institution | Teaching method | |
| --- | --- | --- |
| | Traditional | Experimental |
| Secondary school | (Data A) | (Data B) |
| | (Post-teaching test results) | |
| International school | (Data C) | (Data D) |

We are presented with two independent variables. The researcher, let us say, still claims to be interested in seeing whether participants taught using the experimental method do better than those who receive the traditional method. We again read that the dependent variable is the post-teaching test results. The first independent variable is "Teaching method", and there are two methods involved here. The researcher also wonders, however, whether participants from the two institutions might perform in a different way on the test. There is no longer any confounding inherent in this box design (there are four classes involved), so we can proceed to discuss its implications. This 2 x 2 matrix or factorial design sees the comparison of two methods and two schools. Consequently, four basic comparisons would be open to the researcher, who may or may not pursue all of them. He or she could compare all the participants in the secondary school with all those in the international school (Data A and B vs. Data C and D). We then read on further in the paper and discover that the researcher also wants to compare all the participants receiving the traditional method with all those receiving the experimental method (Data A and C vs. Data B and D). The researcher decides to stop there, but other combinations within this design could be studied and, we might suggest in our appraisal, *should* have been studied at the same time for the light they might throw on the interaction effects of the different variables. It is possible, for example, that a specific teaching method may help participants more in one institution than in another; in other words, one or other group may profit more from one approach than another (Data A vs. B vs. C vs. D).

The advantage of these designs for the reader, and of drawing their visual representation, is that a number of interactions can be set up and investigated or suggested for future research. Here, for example, we might read in the hypothesis that the researcher suggests participants in the secondary and international schools will normally perform in the same way and that the only differences come from the experimental teaching approach itself. Nevertheless, the reader would be looking for data from the researcher which confirmed that no other unforeseen interactions were taking place that weakened the above hypothesis. For example, participants receiving the traditional method in the international school (Data C) might have done better than those receiving that method in the secondary school (Data A). If these data were not forthcoming, our appraisal of the paper might include the need for replication of the study with a different focus for analysis.

📖   **Now read this worked appraisal of the sample paper:**
6.    Identify the basic type of design employed here and draw the design box. What immediate observations can you make about this design and its consequences for the study?

*There are eight groups, two of which have been assigned control status and the rest, apparently, experimental status. There has been no random selection of participants (intact classes are used) nor random assignment to these groups. Furthermore, there has been no attempt to pre-test the groups for initial equality before applying the treatment. This is the kind of design described on p. 119, which straddles a pre- and a quasi-experimental procedure.*

*This seems to be a* MIXED DESIGN *with respect to participant comparisons, since independent groups are involved (eight different classes), but these same participants are to be assessed and followed across five different letter-writing assignments, making this also (potentially, at least) a repeated-measures design. Any information yet to be confirmed has been designated with a question mark to remind myself to re-consider this, when appraising the appropriateness of the design for any posterior data analysis:*

Main research hypothesis: "Objective measurements and feedback will have a significantly positive effect on students' skills"

Independent variable: Writing Group
Level 1: + software feedback (Experimental)
Level 2: − software feedback (Control)
Dependent variable: Scores on letters (?)

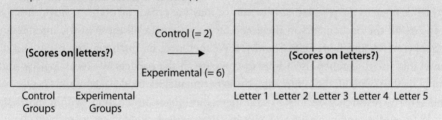

| (Scores on letters?) | | Control (= 2) ⟶ Experimental (= 6) | (Scores on letters?) | | | | |
|---|---|---|---|---|---|---|---|
| Control Groups | Experimental Groups | | Letter 1 | Letter 2 | Letter 3 | Letter 4 | Letter 5 |

## 6.7    Research design: Classifications

> **"Attempt visually to classify the data-collection procedure, and comment on the perceived consequences of this for any eventual findings. Where necessary, suggest how this might have been improved, and why."**

Once the basic design of the study has been established, it is then a useful exercise to try visually to classify the proposed procedure into one of the recognised design classifications for this kind of research. A number of such classifications exist for experimental and quasi-experimental research, and for each classification there are potential threats to reliability and validity to be considered. As with so much in our appraisal of others' work, we must assume it will be the responsibility of the researcher to justify the classification he or she has opted for and acceptably address any such weaknesses. In practice, however, for reasons of editorial policy, space, or perceived priorities, he or she might not be explicit in this regard, and it is again left to the reader to decide on the adequacy and appropriateness of the classification in the present context. The opportunity should not be wasted, since drawing and classifying the research design will again help us to evaluate a key element of the study and will allow us, firstly, to comment on the degree to which this contributes to or detracts from the confidence we can place in any eventual outcomes and, secondly, to suggest possible future improvements to the design.

Before we embark upon classifying the design, the reader needs to check on a number of basic elements of the design so far. Firstly, a check should be made to see whether a pre-test was administered. Then, we should be interested in whether random assignment was used to assign participants to groups, whether intact classes were used, or, indeed, whether one class was used and received a period of treatment followed by lack of treatment (see below, Time-series designs). At this point we will have the information required to confirm the design classification and whether this is going to be basically a pre-experimental, quasi-experimental, pure (true) experimental or *ex post facto* design. Finally, it will be useful to check on whether a factorial design is being used by establishing the number and nature of any independent variables. Using the accepted notation, we should now be in a position to draw a representation of the study as it has been described.

It is beyond the scope of this book to illustrate and discuss all the possible design classifications and their respective modifications associated with each of the above design types, and the reader is referred to the specific books and manuals in the "Further reading" list. However, in order to make an adequate appraisal, it is useful to understand the basic principles of classification, learn how to apply the notation to the more widely-used design classifications in our field, and examine how appropriately the studies we read correspond to such designs. To this end, what follows is intended both as a summary of the most salient points in some of the principal designs, and also an aid to addressing the appropriateness of the steps the researcher has chosen to take in setting up the study.

The recommended notation is as follows:

X means that a group was given or exposed to some experimental event, the effects of which will be measured.

O represents an observation or formal test measurement. A number in brackets afterwards indicates the number of observations made.

X and O in a particular row apply to the same participants, while vertically presented means that they were applied concurrently.

The order of events is described through the left-to-right direction of an arrowed line.

R means that participants were previously randomly assigned to the groups.

Pre-experimental designs

We have already highlighted the fact that much of the research in our field is shaped by the context in which we find the participants we must use. So often only intact classes are available for study, and the researcher must accept and allow for the inevitable restrictions – many of which have been described in the course of this book – these participating classes place on the interpretation of any data obtained. This does not mean that such research designs (and the findings that emerge from them) are somehow inferior to true experimental research.[27] Rather, little can be read into any outcomes. Thus, they will demand considerable replication, but through that replication the field might begin to discern tendencies. By systematically analysing such tendencies across replication studies, a picture will eventually emerge about what is really happening in a specific link between variables, and quasi- or pure experimental designs can then be set up to investigate these further. However, the reader and his or her projected research can still benefit from the immediate exercise of identifying the type of restrictions such designs place on data, and suggesting possible improvements with a view to improving any subsequent replications. In what follows, a number of suggestions are made to help us go about doing this.

The most basic design classification is one in which participants are given a test on something that they have seen or received earlier: $X \rightarrow O$. The appraisal of such a design would need to concentrate on what it does *not* tell us, rather than on what it does. While the researcher might adequately describe the participants, the research context, and the variables involved, there is no information about the control of any possible extraneous variables. Scientific evidence for links between treatment and an observation is based on processing comparisons, not on isolated instances. We know nothing about the group's characteristics before the treatment was given; as a result, it will be almost impossible to infer any kind of effect. In other words, the researcher will not be able to conclude that $X$ *caused* $O$. On the positive side, we would agree with the researcher providing a description of the data obtained; however, we would also be looking for a firm acknowledgement that there are serious enough threats to validity and reliability to recommend extreme caution in interpreting any results. The two obvious suggestions in our appraisal for improvement would be to include some element of pre-testing and/or a control group (i.e., a group that does not receive the treatment):

O(1)  X  O(2)

---

27.    Other scholars can be more critical of these designs, highlighting the inadequate nature of their validity (e.g., Tuckman, B. (1994). *Conducting educational research*. New York: Harcourt Brace College and Robson, C. (2002). *Real world research*. London: Wiley).

By introducing a pre-test we do gain some information about the sample. The researcher would then be able to assure the reader that the students did not already know the material tested on the post-test, for example. A control group would not be needed as the group would classify as its own control. There remain, however, a number of disadvantages to the design which would need to be taken into account in any subsequent appraisal. It fails to control for threats from history or maturation factors. Could not other events have taken place between O(1) and O(2), apart from X, to produce the effect or relationship observed?[28] We would be thinking of events that affected the whole group, of course. Indeed, the longer the time lapse between O(1) and O(2), the more plausible such history factors might become. We might be interested to read about what the normal class procedures and content were during the study for these classes. It is, after all, possible that they would have improved anyway given this normality and the time period involved. Furthermore, the illustration also warns us about the possible effects of timing of events: we would need to read the procedures carefully to see if the time elapsing between the pre-test and the post-test was particularly short, or if the pre-test content and questions inadvertently warned participants about the subsequent treatment and post-test. We might also consider any evidence that these in-between periods of time or parallel events led to those observing or evaluating somehow changing (i.e., the people themselves or their way of observing/evaluating) by the final observation/measurement.

Quasi-experimental designs

The great disadvantage in the above designs, therefore, is that they do not manage satisfactorily to eliminate alternative explanations of outcomes. Fortunately, in the majority of cases, we have seen that a little thought before designing the research can produce much more valid designs and outcomes in which the reader can have more confidence.

$$X \longrightarrow O(1)$$
$$\overline{\phantom{X} \longrightarrow O(2)}$$

Quasi-experimental designs are often used in our field since – while we are able to introduce certain elements of experimental design into many of our studies – we often lack full control over various aspects of the procedures. In the above classification, a control

---

28.   Robson (op. cit.) points out that – under certain, highly controlled, circumstances – such a design can become more interpretable. For example, the researcher might have been able to isolate the group from outside influences or to have demonstrated the absence of any pre-treatment tendencies.

group has been introduced, which consists of another class. However, randomisation has not been used to assign classes to experimental or control status. This design is one that we may encounter quite frequently in research carried out in educational institutions, and may be thought to straddle a pre-experimental and a quasi-experimental design. There is a definite improvement on the above designs, since a second, control class has been added. Its principal attraction in such a context is the fact that it makes use of available groups and can establish a comparison group without disruption of the school organization and/or re-assignment of participants to other classes than those in which they were originally placed. According to the design, a treatment is given one group, and then its results are compared to a second group who have not received the treatment. It would appear that threats from history and maturation factors could be controlled somewhat by the use of the control group. If a coincidental event within the school procedure affected one group, it would probably affect the other as well.

Faced with this kind of design, the reader would again need to have their attention drawn to the serious limitations in the interpretation of any results. We know nothing about the similarity of the two groups *before* the treatment started; any improvement noticed in the experimental group might also be down to a number of co-existing extraneous variables as well as to the treatment itself (e.g., dissimilar L2 proficiency level, different time of classes during the day, different teachers involved, or participant gender). Recommendations for future improvements might include the random assignment to groups and/or the introduction of pre-testing since, as it stands, it is impossible to discover if the two classes really were comparable to start with. Some more validity might be also gained by recommending that future replications begin by matching participants between the two groups for key characteristics such as gender or assessed language proficiency scores. When randomised design is not feasible, matching participants will go some way to permitting increased comparability between the two groups (although the reader will still need to consider the possibilities for "regression to the mean" (see p. 70)).

Faced by the difficulties in obtaining random selection and assignment of participants in many educational establishments, together with the evident drawbacks of pre-experimental designs, a possible solution would follow a single group over a period of time. Again, intact classes would be used, but this time the class continually serves as it own control:

$$O(1)\text{-}O(2)\text{-}O(3)\text{-}O(4)\text{-}X\text{-}O(5)\text{-}O(6)\text{-}O(7)\text{-}O(8) \longrightarrow$$

The advantage for the researcher here over the second pre-experimental classification above is that, now, several pre- and post-tests are administered prior to and subsequent to the treatment itself. Furthermore, only one class is involved, and there is no necessity to find matching participants in another control group – all of which makes for considerable convenience in many research contexts. Our confidence in any outcomes should also be reinforced by the fact that the researcher meets threats to history by taking a number of samples throughout the study. Once a particular pattern of behaviour has emerged before the treatment, the latter can be applied with confidence and the subsequent samples examined for any change. The design gives the researcher the chance to detect change at various points after the treatment, such as immediately following the treatment ($O(5)$) or at successive samples. In general, any possible threats from unconnected events in everyday class (or home) procedures should be seen across all the observations and might then be adequately accounted for across the whole study.

Faced with data from such a study, the critical reader would still need to look carefully at a number of aspects. Firstly, careful consideration is needed of the number of observations or samples obtained so that we consider the evidence of growth trends or change after the treatment. With more points of data collection, the researcher would be in a stronger position to assess the nature of the trend. The reader, however, should be alert to whether the trend post-treatment contains any apparent anomalies. Perhaps, instead of increasing immediately after the treatment, no increase is noted until observation 7. This would indicate a trend we would want to see addressed by the researcher. The same would be true in the case of a non-linear trend that increased immediately after the treatment, but then decreased suddenly, or subsequently revealed much smaller increases. Furthermore, careful attention needs to be paid to any reported gradual, rather than abrupt, changes after treatment, since the possibility exists that these are merely normal fluctuations over time.

A second important aspect to consider here would be the kind of data used to obtain the pre-treatment observations. For example, a researcher may look to available school assessment results. In this case, such material will need to have received adequate scrutiny on the part of the researcher to establish its reliability, validity, and general appropriateness to the study at hand. After all, we would hardly want to accept assessment of listening comprehension proficiency as adequate measurement of overall L2 proficiency in such a time-series design. Indeed, this is true for any freely-available pre-experiment data offered the researcher and then used in the study. Generally, such data will have been obtained for totally different purposes, which may mean that it is systematically biased or has been collected according to different criteria at different times and by different people.

The time period itself might usefully form a subject of discussion: we might want to check on the length of time the group was studied and think about any parallel activities in which they were thought to participate and which might have affected results. Longitudinal studies such as these typically extend over time periods that involve seasonal change, variations in timetables or work-loads, all of which can potentially be confused with change (or lack of change) resulting from a particular treatment. Further recommendations for improvement might include the setting up of a comparable control group who are observed at the same time and the same way, but who do not receive the treatment. The main advantage here is that this group would then further test for any "history" threats. Secondly, we might suggest that such threats could be countered by using the group as its own control, and taking observations on a second dependent variable which should not be affected by the treatment.

This same design would also prove an adequate basis for any single-participant experimental design, although it has the potential problem that the researcher cannot then compare any trends across other participants.

Another commonly-encountered classification in our field is one which builds up on, and strengthens, a previous pre-experimental procedure. Once again, a control group may have been found by using another class from the same section. While participants have not been randomly selected for the course, nor randomly assigned to their respective sections, the researcher still has the chance randomly to assign the experimental and control groups on the toss of a coin:

$$
\begin{array}{l}
\mathrm{O}(1) \longrightarrow \mathrm{X} \longrightarrow \mathrm{O}(2) \\
\overline{\mathrm{O}(3) \longrightarrow \mathrm{O}(4)}
\end{array}
$$

The improvements brought in to this design should enable us to have more confidence in any eventual findings. There is a control group, pre- and post-test measures for both groups. In the case of non-randomisation, pre-tests are essential, unlike in the pure experimental version (see below), to assess the group similarity on the dependent measure. The reader, however, will still want to examine the details of such pre-testing carefully. As we suggested above, by adding a comparison group that is truly comparable and has similar experiences to the experimental group (apart from the treatment), the researcher is theoretically able to answer most possible threats to history, maturation, testing effect, and instrumentation. We might assume that both groups change naturally at the same pace, experience the same effect of testing, or are exposed to similar external events. Assuming these events *are* experienced in the same way by both groups, they will not intervene on any post-test measurements.

Despite these increased safeguards, however, this will not obviate the reader's need to stop and consider any pattern of results reported from such classifications. Let us take the example reviewed above. Imagine that we read of a six-month study in which the researcher has, indeed, set up an experimental and comparison group (intact classes), pre-tested both in the way suggested, provided the treatment to just one group, and finally post-tested the two groups. We read that pre-testing revealed the experimental group to be slightly higher on an important measure than the control group. On the post-test, there is an increase "as expected" in the experimental group; however, the same test reveals a much smaller increase in the comparison group. What might we consider here? It appears that the control group might be changing; a question we would want to see answered is whether the experimental group with the pre-test advantage is changing (maturing) at a faster rate regardless of the treatment received.

The cautious reader will still need to be alert to the characteristics of each component in the design classification of a study, so that he or she can judge whether any intentional or unintentional modifications to this design place undesirable threats on the eventual outcomes. For example, while general history bias threats might be countered here, we would need to be particularly attentive to designs wherein the experimental and control groups go through the same experiences but in *different* centres: problems of local history become more acute as the number of controllable group locations increases. Also, an adverse interaction might take place when, as a result of the treatment, participants in one group grow considerably more experienced at a faster rate than the other group. When the experimental group consists of participants who are brighter or more competent than those in the control group, differences in maturation may confound data. Similarly, the reader might wish to know whether those in the experimental group were self-selected (i.e., volunteers for the experiment). The motivational characteristics of volunteers are not typical of all participants. In other words, comparing a group of volunteers to a group of non-volunteers does not control for internal validity because of the different inherent nature of each group.

With the central importance attached to pre-testing in this classification, the reader may think it useful to know exactly what this consisted of, and who did the examining. Firstly, we need to recognise that, even when pre-test measurements profess the similarity between the two groups, we cannot assume that the two groups are necessarily equivalent. For example, by looking at the details of the pre-test, the reader should be able to confirm whether or not participants have been tested on one or two measures of L2 proficiency only (for example, their writing ability and/or their ability to correct spoken or written mistakes). The fact that these participants are similar on one or two such measures does not mean that they are equally similar on other measurements that may be just as relevant to the study at hand (for example, their ability to plan their writing or to attend to spoken production in order to spot mistakes). Secondly, we might again want to look for information about whether the pre-tests (and post-tests) of both groups were evaluated by the researcher and/or people who were aware of the nature of the two groups. Presumably, such awareness or training on behalf of those who do the measuring could affect the kind of measurements made.

## Pure/True experimental designs

It has been my contention in this book that pure experimental studies are rare in our field because of the nature and context of much of our work. Such designs provide completely acceptable controls for all sources of internal validity. External validity – generalisability to the real world – is much easier to achieve outside the "laboratory" in a setting that corresponds to that of real life. Such studies will use control groups, they will measure and, if necessary, control for differences before the treatment. Random selection of participants will be possible and random assignment to groups carried out. Which group receives the experimental treatment and which becomes the control will also be based on a random decision and the possibilities for cross-contamination between these groups will have been considerably reduced. Given the comparative rarity of such classifications in our field, we will only look briefly at two typical designs here, both of which develop logically from their quasi-experimental and pre-experimental equivalents.[29]

$$\begin{array}{l} R \underline{\quad\quad X \longrightarrow O(1)} \\ R \quad\quad\quad\longrightarrow O(2) \end{array}$$

This design improves considerably on the first quasi-experimental design described above. Grouping is done on a random basis, which basically controls for selection bias. Statistical analyses are used to determine the PROBABILITY that the observed link between variables occurred by chance alone. If that probability is sufficiently low, the conclusion is made that it was the treatment, rather than pure chance, that caused the difference.

An obvious improvement will be the addition of a pre-test:

$$\begin{array}{l} R\,O(1) \underline{\quad\quad X \longrightarrow O(2)} \\ R\,O(3) \quad\quad\quad\longrightarrow O(4) \end{array}$$

The pre-test gives the researcher the interesting option of matching individuals based on their pre-test scores or other criteria and then comparing the pair's performance after the treatment. Also, he or she could compare participants' gain scores, rather than the final test scores, by simply subtracting the pre-test from the final test scores. This provides a useful means of taking into account individual differences and can therefore offer a more precise indication of treatment effects. However, caution is warranted with the use of gain scores, particularly when they are presented to us as indications of progress. For example, a one-point increase in progress starting from a high-level score may have more perceived importance than the same interval score from a lower level. The reliability of gain scores as a sole indicator of progress continues to be the subject of debate. Finally, if as a result of the pre-test the two groups prove not to be

---

29.    For a detailed explanation of the relative advantages and disadvantages of these designs see, for example, Campbell, D., & Stanley, J. (1966). *Experimental and quasi-experimental designs for research*. Chicago: Rand McNally and Mitchell, M., & Jolley, J. (2006). *Research design explained*. Belmont: Wadsworth Publishing Co.

equivalent, it is possible to use a statistical adjustment to the pre-test measurements (such as ANCOVA) that may give a fairer picture of the treatment effect although such an adjustment will help reduce error variance  but not solve those initial differences. Such procedures will all serve to strengthen the reader's confidence in the study by adequately meeting threats to internal and external validity. The reader will again need to consider details of the pre-testing very carefully. According to what it contains and when it was administered, a pre-test might sensitise the participants in a way that their eventual post-test scores are affected.

### *Ex post facto* designs

These designs are included in this brief tour of inspection because they are also very commonly used in our field. It is often too difficult to meet the many threats to internal and external validity and, therefore, it becomes highly inadvisable to make claims of cause and effect as a result of our research. *Ex post facto* designs enable the researcher to study the hypothesised link between two variables, but he or she is not interested in what went on before the study, and no special treatment is applied to the participants. The popularity of this kind of design in our field is easy to understand. Our knowledge of the process of L2 acquisition has increased greatly over the last three decades. However, there is still much more for us to learn and such discovery will be based primarily on finding out what is actually happening in the process, rather than intruding on that process. When we have built up enough information concerning what is actually going on in L2 acquisition, we will be in a better position to begin to see how to improve things by intervention and experiment in that process. Hence, there is a continuing need for studies from different learning contexts that tell us what is currently going on in the L2 learning process. This will provide a useful opportunity for the researcher to describe some data and study how these change (or do not) across different contexts, participants, and tasks. They are particularly useful in our field as the independent variable or variables may not be in the power of the researcher to control: an investigation, perhaps, into the relationship between intelligence and L2 ability or a study comparing teacher characteristics.

The important thing for the reader to remember when presented with such a design is that the researcher is not interested in seeing the effect of a treatment as such, but rather in studying the hypothesised effect of an independent variable on another after that effect has occurred (such as whether gender has any effect on motivation in L2 learning).

Although this kind of research may not always be visualised differently from the other designs in this chapter, the main distinction is that any treatment is already present by nature rather than created or manipulated by the researcher.

O(1)      O(2)

Here the researcher will obtain two (or more) sets of data from participants with the aim of describing the link between those data. The research is not attempting to show that performance has improved as a result of some instruction or other, nor is cause and effect being studied, no group assignment is organised or needed, and no variables are being manipulated to bring about a change.

In appraising results produced from such a study, the reader should be alert to the interpretation of any observed relationships between observations or measurements. There is a temptation to interpret this design as quasi-experimental and then suggest that the variable measured by O(1) has in some way brought about the changes observed in the variable that O(2) has measured. Such designs have an intrinsic weakness: there is no control over the independent or dependent variable. It therefore also becomes impossible to work out with any confidence which are the critical ones. We cannot ascertain even if a potential contributory factor has even been included in the design or whether, indeed, more than one factor has been instrumental in bringing about the outcome. A number of possible causes of outcomes can be posited: firstly, O(1) may indeed have brought about what happened in O(2); secondly, it is also possible that the variable O(2) is measuring had caused O(1); finally, some other, unspecified and unidentified, variable has caused both the outcomes at O(1) and O(2). We should remember that no manipulation of variables has gone on here and no treatment is administered, which means that none of the above explanations is confirmed. A suggestion – nothing more – of a relationship exists. Furthermore, we would not want to see the researcher drawing conclusions from such a study based on an over-limited set of events or small sample. The logical call from the researcher would be for further replication of their study to confirm the suggestion, and/or perhaps an experimental or quasi-experimental study which applies a suitable treatment.

Another type of design is applied when description is needed and the researcher is able to contrast one group of participants who are said – or observed – to possess the characteristics under discussion with another group who have the "opposite" characteristics. This criterion group design can be used to establish how this behaviour came about. For example, how do students who are said to be good language learners get to become that way? What experiences have they had, and what training did they receive? Again, the reader will need to bear in mind that causal accounts of this experience or training will not be acceptable as an explanation of what is observed. The best that can be hoped for are indications of links, which will then need to be subjected to more rigorous study. Similarly, the same design classification might be used to describe the way members of different criterion groups (e.g., poor L2 listeners and good L2 listeners) behave in a similar language-learning situation (e.g., do the latter criterion group make more use of paralinguistic clues when they have to understand and participate in an L2 conversation in a busy street?). Again, the design will not permit conclusions about cause and effect because factors other than listening skills as such might be bringing about any differences observed. However, a valuable platform will have been created for future study of the association between variables, in this case listening ability and paralinguistic clues.

Factorial designs

These designs have much in common with true experimental designs. Essentially, they can make use of the basic elements found therein (such as randomising selection and group assignment, pre- and post-tests) but with the modification that the effects of a number of independent variables (realised as moderator variables) are being measured. Thus, within the factorial design, more than one variable can be manipulated and studied.

As we noticed in the basic design box above (p. 115), the factorial design can involve all possible combinations of the levels of the different independent variables. Thus, a fairly simple factorial design with three independent variables, one having two levels, one having three levels, and the other five would have a theoretical set of thirty (i.e., 2 x 3 x 5) combinations! Conceptually, there is an unlimited number of complex designs, because any number of independent variables can be studied and each one can have any number of levels. As we shall see in subsequent sections when the actual analysis is carried out, this very multi-level characteristic can easily get out of control, with data being reported on any and every combination available, be it of interest to the research hypothesis or not.

The most straightforward design involves (as we saw in the design box) two independent variables, each of which is manipulated at two levels. As a result of these groupings, a number of combinations emerge for potential study. It will be possible to assess the separate effect of each independent variable (known as the "main effect") as well as whether the effect of one variable differs from one level to the other of the second variable (known as "interaction effects"). In this way, a study can report on the fact that one of these variables actually moderates another to achieve a certain effect. A total of four groups are involved in this example. The factorial design helps the researcher to cover more ground, as it were, in one study: there is an assessment made of the effects of two variables, and also of whether they interact.

Analysis procedures for appraising the STATISTICAL SIGNIFICANCE of main effects will be described below and in the Results section, but suffice to note here that the interpretation of the main effects is totally dependent on whether an interaction is or is not present. In general, main effects will need to be interpreted with great caution whenever an interaction is reported in the study. When no such interaction is evident, the main effects of each independent variable can be interpreted as though they had been manipulated in two separate studies, each involving only one independent variable.

📖 **Now read this worked appraisal of the sample paper:**

7.   Attempt visually to classify the data-collection procedure, and comment on the perceived consequences of this for any eventual findings. Where necessary, suggest how this might have been improved, and why.

*No pre-testing was undertaken with the two groups. Intact classes are used ("chosen"), but I am not told whether or not they were equal to start off with. However, at this point, a number of the questions already raised about the present design of the study hinder my ability to classify the procedure more accurately. For example, while a treatment as such is involved, it has not been made clear how this is expected to be used, or how it is expected to reflect on posterior measurements of writing. The basic idea seems to be the following:*

$$O(1) \xrightarrow{\;?\;} X(1) \longrightarrow ?\, O(2)$$
$$\overline{\phantom{O(1) \xrightarrow{\;?\;} X(0) \longrightarrow ?\, O(2)}} \quad \text{etc. up to } O(5)$$
$$O(1) \xrightarrow{\;?\;} X(0) \longrightarrow ?\, O(2)$$

*I have also noted the problem of interpretation presented by the fact that the control group are also receiving (teacher) feedback of an unspecified nature (X(0)). Since the idea may be to compare the groups at each letter-writing session (O), the design indicates that appropriate concurrent measurement will not be straightforward. Look, for example, at letter number two (O(2)): participants in both groups would presumably have received their particular feedback (X 0/1) from letter number one at some time before this measurement, and this is hypothesised as showing (or not) an effect now in this letter. However, I do not know how long the teacher or computer feedback has been in the hands of the respective groups, what they are told to do with this, nor the time periods between each measurement. In this scenario, if both groups are measured at the same time, it might indeed tell us whether either group is ostensibly getting better or worse in their written outcomes, but will probably tell us little about the true comparative effect of the feedback as such. Testing for differences only at the end of the five-letter writing period might be equally inconclusive.*

*Improvements could be suggested, firstly, by random allocation of groups, as well as some kind of pre-test. Some consideration could also be given to matching students across groups as a result of this test, to enable a more precise comparison of treatment effect to be made.*

*Another interesting alternative would have been some type of time-series design (see p. 120). A group from only one institution could be followed over the six-month period: the treatment (X) would be applied once a number of pre-tests were made and over a longer period and then the normal behaviour of the group established. This would solve one of the big problems in the present design: we do not know how the groups differ at the start. Furthermore, we might add a similar control group across the same time period and compare the two:*

$$O(1) - O(2) - O(3) - O(4) - X - O(5) - O(6) - O(7) - O(8)$$
$$O(1) - O(2) - O(3) - O(4) - O(5) - O(6) - O(7) - O(8)$$

## Worked sample appraisal

### Procedures and research design 2

1.   Before working through this section of the paper, you should re-read the corresponding Participants and materials 2 text and appraisal (p. 85).

2.   As you are reading, in the right-hand column, write a few words which record your instinctive reactions to what you have just read as if you were talking to the researcher face-to-face.

This researcher administered all the tests of listening comprehension within the normal timetable of the participants' classes. The information given them about the study was that the test was part of research being carried out by the local education authorities and that the aim was to test out a new listening comprehension examination to be used in the future in University C①. At no time were the participants made aware of the real object of study. Versions of the text were allocated randomly to the respective group and one version was given and tested each day for four days. Participants only heard the tape once②. After they had heard the tape, participants were told to write down in English any single thing they could remember from the tape. They were told that this need not be in order and it was emphasised that quantity of information was the most important thing in the test.

Each text had been previously classified into units of ideas③. The snippets of information remembered by the participants were then given a score based on the amount of correct units of ideas found therein④. This was carried out by this researcher and two of the teachers who taught the classes. Analysis was done on all the scripts by all three scorers and any disagreements were discussed until everyone was agreed. The definition of an idea unit used was one which did not have to be recalled verbatim, but the scorer had to be satisfied that the participant had actually understood the particular idea unit.

3. **Read again the relevant section in the chapter, and then attempt to answer these questions. Finally, compare your responses to mine.**

1. What is your appraisal of the timing of events, and is this information sufficient to permit replication?
   *As in the previous study, participants are not being subjected to a treatment here, nor are their reactions to be judged across a number of measures or a period of time. The study aims to describe the state of affairs at one particular moment in time. Our focus in the appraisal will need to be on what we are told about the order of events, as well as on the timing used in the listening comprehension exercise itself.*

   *The fact that both control and recall tests followed so quickly one after another (see below, question 2) might also have helped meet any other history threats posed by the fact that these participants were probably receiving classes at the same time as the experiment. In other words, had more time elapsed between the control test and the recall test itself, there would have existed the possibility that some or all of the classes were receiving extra listening practice in the interim period – with the consequent distortion of results.*

   *Time was, of course, of crucial interest in this particular data-collection instrument. As a result of the modifications of the text, the speed of delivery was artificially slowed down in all but the control version. I do not need to repeat my previous reservations about the possible consequences of this for any outcomes here. Rather, I might concentrate on what more I am told now concerning the test itself. First of all, I read that "one version was given and tested each day for four days". This was, presumably, because a number of classes were involved (up to four per version) and that "the normal timetable" meant that classes were spread out across these days. It is unclear if we are thereby to understand that one version (of the four) was administered every day for four days, or one version was repeated over the four days until every class involved had heard it. Either way, the question that arises is how far such a procedure may have allowed participants in one class to communicate to other class-members what was in store for them in the listening test (see below, question 4). Since the basic text content was the same in all four versions, and the object of the exercise was to remember details, any such communication about content might have contaminated subsequent results.*

*Secondly, I understand that participants only heard the text once and then had time to complete the task. Although this tends to emphasise the memory-testing (rather than listening-comprehension testing) facet of the exercise remarked on earlier, it might reflect what L2 listening would be like for these participants in real life. The question still remains, however, as to the difficulty of this task (and the time within which it was carried out) for these particular beginner language learners. Nothing more is learnt here about the kind of listening comprehension normally practised by these participants, and I can only conjecture as to the possible effects on the amount of information recalled. It would also have been useful to know – particularly for the purposes of replication – just how long after hearing the tape that participants were told to write down what they remembered. One presumes that the memory trace would have been more accessible as soon as possible after the event. There is also no information about the amount of time available post-listening for participants to write down what they remembered. The argument is that some might have recalled more (and more idea units) than they actually wrote down but were unable to do so because of the time limits imposed. As I have mentioned throughout the appraisal of this paper, what is thereby revealed is not a true measure of comprehension as such, but rather whatever one is able to write down (including the translation of Spanish to English) in the time allowed.*

*Finally, I have already commented in earlier sections about the measurement of effect here. Although there is no question of a treatment being administered and tested here, the abstract did talk of "significant improvement in oral comprehension" as a result of some of these modifications to input. The study looks at the effect of intervention at one moment in time. The reader will need to consider carefully any claims in subsequent sections that such modifications bring **long-term** improvement in listening comprehension. Ideally, perhaps, any positive findings here would justify calls from the researcher for more prolonged observation of participants using such input modification.*

2.  Are there any potential threats to internal validity as a result of test or practice effect?

    *As I observed in the previous paper, in this kind of descriptive research, I would not expect to find any threats to data validity from such effects. We were told in the previous section that the control test for group equality was administered three days before the actual experiment itself, and I wondered at that point what effect this might have had on the participants. Although both this control test and the actual experiment were focusing on listening comprehension, I have already remarked that different concepts of the L2 listening experience were tested and that procedures were very different. It would seem unlikely that this sequence of events would have adversely affected performance on the experimental measure itself.*

3.  What is your assessment of any prior information about the study given the participants and the instructions they received?

    *Earlier, I read only that participants were selected and presume that some allowance was made for those who did not wish to participate. There is a question arising, however, from the stipulation that "at no time were the participants made aware of the real object of study". Although this may be justified sometimes when we feel behaviour may alter as a result of participants knowing the real aim of the research, I wonder why this was felt necessary or justified in this case. Furthermore, it might be argued that the fact that the aim divulged involved citing the "local education authorities" as the source of interest in outcomes may have made some participants unnecessarily anxious. Finally, despite the fact that student scripts were anonymous, I wonder how far using two of the class teachers to score work was altogether satisfactory.*

*In question 1, I wondered how far any time limits imposed on the recall of (translated) content might have affected results. Obviously, the instructions participants received about what and how they were to recall are equally important. I learn that they were told to write down anything they remembered. Presumably, the researcher thought that participants at this level in L2 proficiency would have found it difficult to recall whole idea units and translate these adequately. One wonders, however, what they were told to do if they recalled something in Spanish but were unable satisfactorily to translate it into English. If no instructions were given, a normal reaction (especially if time was at a premium) might have been to omit such a scoring opportunity in favour of something that he or she felt they **could** translate into English.*

*The onus is thereby put on the scorers to decide – from whatever has been written – whether an idea unit can be scored or not. This also means, of course, that L2 comprehension is then seen as a function of the number of previously-determined idea units scored, and many would want to argue with such an interpretation. Interestingly, participants were also informed that the quantity (rather than the quality) of information was being rewarded. One wonders how far such an instruction sends out an implicit message that what they should try to do is remember words rather than try to comprehend what they hear. It follows, therefore, that the scorers are those that are evaluating whether comprehension has taken place, rather than the participants themselves. The only way of knowing what the participants really grasped of the text would have been to conduct post-test interviews.*

*In the appraisal of the previous section, I also reminded myself to check here about whether any pre-test information was given the participants about the content of the test, arguing that this priming is an essential part of the listening experience. It is now confirmed that no such information was given. I can only conjecture as to how far this might have affected the amount recalled with beginner language students, but these doubts will need to be considered along with any subsequent discussion of results.*

4.  What potential threats of reactivity do you see with respect to (i) observer/scorer effects and participant expectancies, and (ii) observer/scorer bias?

   i.  *There would seem to be little reason why we should expect serious reactivity threats from this angle in the study. Although two of the class teachers took part in the data analysis, participants would probably have been unaware of their participation. I have mentioned that the large number of classes selected from the same institution and section might have led to some communication of information between groups (and versions heard) across classes and on the days these were administered. On the other hand, it is unlikely that this would have unduly affected the kind of data sought here. After all, participants might have told others about the aim of the test but are unlikely to have communicated the kind of details about the story that would eventually have skewed scores on the number of idea units recalled.*

   *We should also note that participants are informed about certain aims of the study, but that these are untrue and do not inform the participants of their true role in the study. Indeed, the researcher seems keen to emphasise the fact that participants were not "made aware of the real object of study". It is not clear why he or she thought this so crucial. While the researcher might thereby manage to distract their attention from the real aim of the research (and, hopefully, obtain more typical reactions), it could be argued that there are moral objections to such a practice.*

ii.  *I read that the scorers involved here were the researcher and two of the class teachers. It has become clear in this section that comprehension will be measured on the basis of the successful recall of an idea unit. Bias would seem to have been avoided by providing each scorer with a list of the idea units to be scored and encouraging debate where any doubtful cases occurred. I am not told what, if any, training went on before scoring but might imagine that the task itself was quite a complex and tiring one and would have required a considerable amount of time (and debate) to decide whether or not an idea unit had been satisfactorily recalled across the scripts of 180 students. Furthermore, I read that analysis was done "on all the scripts by all three scorers"; under such circumstances, some kind of reliability value could have been reported.*

*It is also not made clear how far the teacher scorers were informed of the real objectives of the study. Nevertheless, there is no reason to believe this would have affected judgements here, unless these teachers also thought that their classes were under inspection from "the local education authorities"! I do not know whether these teachers were aware of the identity (and, therefore, class association) of those they evaluated, but there would seem no reason to think they would seek to benefit their own students by scoring them higher than others. Furthermore, little would be achieved thereby if all three scorers then saw and evaluated all the scripts.*

5.  i.  What details are provided about the environmental conditions of the study and could these have affected outcomes?
   ii.  What observations about external validity can be made in the light of these details?

   i.  *The researcher informs us that tests were carried out within the normal timetable of these participants, but no specific information is provided about environmental conditions. Information about the acoustic arrangements for hearing the dialogues would have helped the reader decide, for example, how far participants were physically able to provide realistic examples of their comprehension. In the absence of further details, we might usefully think about the possible consequences for such listening comprehension testing in what might be considered normal classroom conditions. Three aspects might be considered: the familiarity of content in the story, the conditions for hearing the dialogue, and for recording what was heard. As regards content, I suggested in the previous section that a dialogue "between two Spanish friends who study at University C...planning what to do to celebrate Halloween" would seem to be a situation that would be readily recognised by these students and, perhaps, hold useful contextual clues for idea recognition. I have no way of knowing the size of the classrooms in which the test was administered, but might well feel that students at this early level of L2 learning need the best acoustic conditions available – particularly bearing in mind that they were only to hear the passage once. I have already noted that participants had to record their responses in the L1 and, possibly, within a limited period of time. Having to write down hurriedly what they recall of a conversation and simultaneously translate these thoughts into the L1 is unlikely to be the normal way we would call upon students to show their comprehension of a foreign language. Such potential inherent difficulties in the execution of the task set will need to be borne in mind as we read the researcher's subsequent discussion of results.*

   ii.  *This latter observation also reflects my thoughts on the artificiality of what has been set up here as a test of listening comprehension. Aside from any constraints as a direct result*

*of the research design, our worries about the way time is used, together with the proce-
dures used to record comprehension, should alert us to the limitations on any generalisation of findings here.*

In the light of what you have read in this section, do you wish to amend, or add to, your
previous comments on group assignment, materials, and the potential threats to internal
validity of the data from attrition, history, or maturation?

*In previous sections, our attention had been drawn to the fact that information about
grouping was limited to the total numbers involved in each of the four groups who heard
one of the four versions. No further details are given here, but these had been drawn from
a total population of 208, and I still remain unaware of the criteria (if there had been any)
behind the original assignment of these two groups. The researcher may have felt that,
since all the participants were in the same section and studying the L2 at the same level,
group equality could be assumed, and there was no reason to provide any more information about this. Nevertheless, I remember that pre-test measures did reveal enough differences to eliminate over 13% (28 participants) from this original sample, which suggests that
the original population did, indeed, contain enough differences to warrant closer attention
and description. On the positive side, I do now know that versions were allocated randomly
to groups.*

*I had also enquired in the previous section about how the material was to be used and pro-
cedures scored, suggesting that "the dependent variable "listening comprehension" might be
measured as an interval or ordinal score" but noting that "number of recalls" might indicate frequency data. I learn here that the texts were previously divided into idea units, which means that
a fixed number of units would be available for scoring. This suggests continuous, closed scores,
which can be treated as interval data.*

6. Identify the basic type of design employed here and draw the design box. What immediate
   observations can you make about this design and its consequences for the study?
   *I read that four groups have been formed from intact classes. Each of three groups will hear one
   version of the text, and one group will hear an unmodified (control) version. In this between-
   group ex post facto design, there is no question of any experimental treatment being applied
   and tested here. Groups are to be compared on the basis of their reactions to hearing a particular
   version of the text. The effect of text version on comprehension/recall is to be studied without
   considering what went on before the experiment:*

Research questions: Is listening comprehension affected when
............ input includes more and longer pauses?
............ the speed of the input is diminished?
............ the syntax of the input is made simpler?
Is there any significantly greater influence of one of these modified input elements on comprehension than another?

Independent variable: Modified input (or Group)
Level 1: Pauses
Level 2: Speed
Level 3: Syntax
Level 4: No modification

Dependent variable: Listening comprehension/recalls

Design box:

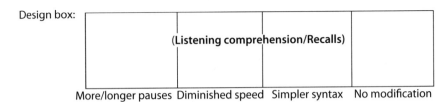

More/longer pauses  Diminished speed   Simpler syntax    No modification

*The tone of the research questions is seen as exploratory, rather than descriptive. We see how each level of the independent variable can be scored on the listening comprehension measure and compared with another level. These design boxes confirm the research questions in that the researcher will be able to compare scores at the interaction of listening comprehension/ recall scores and level of independent variable and will therefore also be in a position to decide which of the four (if any) has a greater influence on comprehension than others. It appears, from such a design, that the researcher will not be reporting on the supposed relative improvement **or** deterioration in listening comprehension previously understood from the research questions.*

*Since we are dealing with a comparison using an independent variable with four levels, it would appear that an analysis of variance might be appropriate to describe outcomes (rather than infer from) this context. Of course, what this design does not allow for – but which might prove an interesting piece of further research – would be a comparison of listening comprehension scores not only across the groups (or levels of the independent variable), but also by L2 proficiency level. In other words, groups could be selected from both beginner and intermediate classes and the comparisons drawn in two directions instead of the present one, using a factorial design. Even more interesting here would be to discover (using multiple regression) how well we can predict scores on the listening comprehension test from those of two or more independent variables. Using this procedure, we would even be able to suggest what combination of variables we need in order to predict performance on the listening comprehension test.*

7.   Attempt visually to classify the data-collection procedure, and comment on the perceived consequences of this for any eventual findings. Where necessary, suggest how this might have been improved, and why.
     *A pre-test is used here to establish "equal level in listening comprehension". Intact classes were used as the basic population, and there appears to have been no attempt randomly to assign group status, although the four versions of the text were subsequently randomly assigned to these groups. As it stands, the design is basically ex post facto. However, the researcher wants to see whether modifications of the text (the independent variable) can account for differences in listening comprehension success. Unlike the basic ex post facto design, the independent variable has been manipulated by the researcher into three ways of modifying the original input:*

Group 1 (O1)-X-O
Group 2 (O1)-X-O
Group 3 (O1)-X-O
Group 4 (Control) (O1)-X-O

*Such a design will indeed allow description of how the independent variable affects the dependent variable but will not permit generalisation beyond this context. The pre-test (O1) was used to establish group equivalence and provides some information about the sample, but it, too, has been the object of debate in our appraisal (hence it is placed within brackets in the above design). Amongst other things, I claimed it did not accurately describe the initial state of the selected students on the dependent variable as defined in the study itself (i.e., it tested listening comprehension rather than recall). If there is already doubt concerning what this pre-test told us about the groups' similarity on the dependent measure before hearing the manipulated text, it follows that it will be difficult accurately to infer any kind of effect on listening comprehension of text version here.*

For further practice in appraising this section of the research paper, turn to pages 256–261 in the Workbook.

# Chapter 7

# Method

## Data analysis

**Before you read this chapter, familiarise yourself again with the paper by reading the Procedures and research design 1 and Observations section of the worked sample appraisal paper on p. 94.**

## 7.1 Data analysis: Description of procedures

"What procedures are identified for data analysis, and do these deal adequately with the original objectives of the study? In the absence of information about procedures, suggest how this might be done."

In this section of the paper, the reader would be looking to see what was done to the data once they had been collected in the way described in the previous section. Some sources recommend that this section be embedded in the Results section (see, for example, the *APA Publication Manual*). However, I will separate them for appraisal here as there are a number of specific features of each which – for these purposes – are best considered apart.

Now that we know what the research question or hypothesis is, what variables are involved, how these are to be measured, how they are hypothesised to be linked, how these are to be operationalised in data, what groups and materials are involved, and how all these are to be used in the research design, we now have the tools to consider the appropriateness of the kind of data analysis proposed in the paper. Careful attention will now need to be paid to how, and why, the researcher opts for this or another analysis as well as to the sequence used in the process of analysis. Where descriptive or inferential statistical procedures are to be used, a major concern of the reader will be to consider, firstly, the appropriateness of such a procedure in the present research context and, secondly, whether the necessary rules or assumptions associated with each procedure have been adequately met both to permit such an analysis to be made, and also to obtain results in which we can have confidence. Once again, the specific publishing medium will often have determined the kind, and amount, of detail to be included about analyses. For example, the journal *TESOL Quarterly* concentrates on consumers of the research and recommends (in its "Guidelines for submission") authors include enough information "to allow readers to evaluate the claims made".

The *APA Publication Manual* reminds the author directly that analyses should be reported in enough detail to justify any conclusions made later.

If the statistical tests used are common ones (such as *t*-tests, CHI-SQUARE, analysis of variance, or correlation), the step-by-step details are often omitted in the text. Only the name of the procedure will be given and it will up to the reader to be in a position to consider the correct application in each case. Since our immediate objective is the appraisal of this section, and this requires our focussing on several of the steps involved in these tests and the principle assumptions behind them, the following summary is intended as a review of the key elements to which the reader should pay particular attention in their evaluation of the section. In this and subsequent sections of the book, it is assumed that the reader has some prior acquaintance with the basic concepts and language of descriptive or inferential statistical analysis. For a full description of how to perform these step-by-step statistical analyses, the reader is referred to the manuals in the "Further reading" list.

Try to determine what tests or procedures have been specifically identified by the researcher to analyse the data. The procedure(s) selected could then be immediately referred back to the hypothesis or research question to confirm how far the data bearing on all relationships or comparisons posed therein are likely to be subjected to these analyses. Since the data analysis and results sections are often combined for questions of space, it may well be that the reader will need to indulge in the useful exercise of predicting and discussing, rather than identifying and analysing, the most appropriate procedures, based on what he or she has read in the paper so far. These deliberations would then need to be confirmed in the subsequent Results section.

---

📖 **Now read this worked appraisal of the sample paper:**

1. What procedures are identified for data analysis, and do these deal adequately with the original objectives of the study? In the absence of information about procedures, suggest how this might be done.

   *The only information so far revealed (in the abstract) about data analysis has informed me that "t-test procedures" were used to reveal "more statistically significant reductions in the test groups' errors than in the control groups". Since t-tests are normally used to reveal differences between two levels or groups of one independent variable, this would seem initially to be reasonable here (but see below, questions 10 and 11). It remains to be seen whether the t-test used is parametric or non-parametric.*

   *A look back to the research hypothesis shows that two objectives were presented: the effect of feedback on students' (writing) skills (presumably addressed by the t-test analysis) and "detailed profiles to be made of the errors common to specific writing genres". This last would seem to be addressed by the program itself which, together with the parsing tool, is able to identify and track 45 special errors and provide "comprehensive descriptions" of these. What these "profiles" actually are, and how the program goes about creating them, is not clear, but the implication so far is that little more than counting will take place. I have made a note here to follow up on these profiles in the Results section.*

## 7.2    Data analysis: Appropriateness of procedures

**"Provide a step-by-step description of the elements involved in the data analysis so far, and decide on the appropriateness of any proposed analysis procedures in the light of this."**

As so often before in our reading, the key word in this section is "confidence". Statistical analysis is used to give the researcher and the reader confidence in the claims being made for the data. However, the reader's confidence in the outcomes reported will again need to rest on more than just a set of numbers in the Results section of the paper. Frankly, any statistical test on data can be made to turn out significant; the computers that calculate this for us do not know, and do not care, how the data got there in the first place! The interested reader appraising this section of the research paper would want to delve deeper into what has happened prior to the feeding in of data into the machine and use what he or she has read to establish or confirm the ideal descriptive or inferential statistical procedure to be used in the circumstances.

Descriptive statistics do just, and only, that. They describe data in a way that allows the researcher to inform us about how often something occurred in the data, what typical values or elements were found in the outcomes, or how such values were dispersed throughout the data obtained. Typical statistics which the reader should be looking out for in such cases are some measure of FREQUENCY, CENTRAL TENDENCY (such as the MEAN, MODE, or MEDIAN), and variability (typically the variance or standard deviation). All three measures can provide important insights into data and help us understand them better. In most of the research described in the previous section, however, the researcher will want to do more than just describe. Descriptive statistics will tell us finite information about our particular sample of participants; they do not, however, help us to think beyond this sample to the larger population. As in the research we have appraised so far, most researchers undertaking experimental or quasi-experimental studies will want to know whether the data described can be used to support hypotheses made or help to provide responses to research questions. According to the *APA Publication Manual*, the eventual data presentation (i.e., in the Results section) should be reader-friendly in the sense that sufficient information is provided therein to permit the reader to confirm the appropriateness of the analyses and any information about differences in scores or frequencies or other measurements. But both reader *and* researcher will probably want to know whether these differences are normal or large enough to make certain inferences about them and their causes. Statistical tests can be used both to describe and to infer. When a researcher uses them to describe, such tests help him or her to have confidence in the description made of the data. When he or she uses these tests to generalise (inferential statistics) the idea is to make inferences from our data to other participants and other learning contexts.

To begin to decide about the appropriateness of any proposed data analysis (or to predict what might be the most suitable analysis), it is useful to go through the same step-by-step assessment of the situation and objectives as the researcher should have done to arrive at the decision. There is a variety of choice open to the researcher for the analysis of data, but this will have been determined by the characteristics and measurement of the variables, the type of research problem, the research design, and the nature of the data obtained. We assume the researcher would have been seeking to analyse his or her data in a way which throws light on the research question or hypothesis. In the kind of research design that concerns us in this book, data will mostly be in original, or converted, numerical form, and the aim would be to submit this to some kind of descriptive or inferential statistical procedure.

The first step is to establish the number of independent and dependent variables and the number of levels of each variable. Secondly, confirm what kind of comparisons or relationships are sought: look back to the Method section and check on whether the researcher intends to compare the one group with another group on one task or different tasks (between-groups) or with themselves on one or more measures (repeated-measures). Thirdly, we will need to establish the way the variables are to be measured. In other words, look back and see if these are to be measured as frequencies (nominal), ordinal (ranked), or interval (score) data. At this point, we can consult the flow chart in the Appendix (p. 290) to establish the preliminary options available for analysis.[30] This chart describes some of the most common descriptive or inferential statistical procedures.[31]

For example, let us imagine we are reading a study in which one group of beginner-level L2 students were trying out a new reading-comprehension programme, and another group were acting as controls. Data to assess reading comprehension proficiency will be obtained on a specially-designed in-house test. While the researcher is aware that she cannot use inferential statistics to generalise any results – amongst other reasons, because intact classes are being used – she would like to see whether the new material has any significant effect on test scores within her classes. Thus, we determine

Variables:  Dependent = *Reading comprehension proficiency;*
　　　　　　Measurement = *Scores on in-house test (interval)*

　　　　　　Independent = *Groups (two levels);*
　　　　　　Measurement = *Nominal (experimental and control).*

Comparison or relationship to be tested = *Comparison between independent groups (between-groups).*

Turning to the flow chart, it is clear the researcher intends to "discover the effect of an independent variable on a dependent variable" here. She will "measure the dependent

---

30.　The flow chart is reprinted from Hatch, E., & Lazaraton, A. (1991). *The research manual.* New York: Newbury House Publishers.

31.　Readers are recommended to consult the tables in Brown, J.D. (1992) for considerations about more advanced statistical procedures. See "Further reading".

variable" from the in-house test (i.e., "scored" data). The chart now gives us three options, according to whether the design aims to use different, the same, or mixed groups. Here two different intact classes are involved so we choose "between" in the chart. At this point we must finally decide on the "levels" of variable involved. This study has two groups of one independent variable involved. The chart suggests "*t* test". Although the reader can use the chart on a reverse route (i.e., checking on the step-by-step logic behind a researcher's decision to opt for a stated procedure), more care is required here since a number of other assumptions (see below) may, and should, have gone into that researcher's decision.

Once we are aware of the basic test recommended, the logical first step would be to compare this outcome with the decision made by the researcher, assuming that has been given in the text so far. If our selections do not coincide, of course, the discrepancy will need to be immediately addressed, since it may indicate potential disagreement with the subsequent reporting of any results. If no decision has been forthcoming in the paper so far, the selection arrived at should be noted and re-appraised when the results are finally presented.

> 📖    **Now read this worked appraisal of the sample paper:**
>
> 2.    Provide a step-by-step description of the elements involved in the data analysis so far, and decide on the appropriateness of any proposed analysis procedures in the light of this.
>
> *Variables:*
>
> *Dependent = Scores on letters; Measurement = scores? (interval?)*
>
> *Independent = Groups (two levels); Measurement = nominal (experimental and control).*
>
> *Comparison or relationship to be tested: Comparison between independent groups (between-groups). The possibility also exists for comparison within the same groups (repeated-measures) on the five assignments.*
>
> *From the flow chart, I follow through the information provided: that the researcher wishes to "discover the effect of an independent variable on a dependent variable", that this variable is measured (apparently) as a test ("scored") measurement, that the main objective sees different groups being compared, and that two levels are involved in the independent variable. The t-test procedure is thereby confirmed as applicable here, and I have made a note to check in the next section on whether the researcher has opted for a parametric or non-parametric test. On the face of it, given the limitations of the design, it would seem that the researcher would be wiser to opt for a potentially less powerful (i.e., non-parametric) procedure.*
>
> *I do not know whether the researcher is interested in further comparison within (or across) the groups on the five assignments, but such comparison would suggest the option of using a 2 (group) by 5 (letter) ANOVA matrix.*

## 7.3    Data analysis: Statistical assumptions

"**Have the necessary assumptions associated with the stated or implied analysis procedure been met in a way that suggests the reader can have confidence in the results of the analysis?**"

Notice that I spoke above only of a preliminary decision being made as a result of any consultation with this chart. Each of the statistical procedures selected will carry with it a series of prerequisites or assumptions for its correct application.[32] Thus, the reader now needs to move on to the second of the two concerns mentioned at the beginning of this section: have the necessary assumptions associated with any proposed procedure been met to permit adequate analysis to be made (i.e., in which the reader can have confidence)? Assuming the specific analysis has been identified in the text up to this point, we should expect the researcher to be aware of, and have adequately addressed, the assumptions associated with their choice. Nevertheless, the reader will need to think about whether this is indeed the case for each assumption, since few editorial authorities require them to be specifically addressed in the paper itself. Furthermore, the realisation of some of these prerequisites can only be conjectured at this point in the proceedings and confirmed later when we are in possession of the results.

I have used the word "assumptions" deliberately here. They are not rules for using these analyses. Some of these assumptions are of more or less consequence depending on the nature of the procedure; others must be addressed if subsequent results are to be presented with confidence. Furthermore, failure to meet a particular assumption does not mean that the researcher cannot process the data with *any* statistical procedure. As we shall see below, and depending on the assumption potentially violated, an alternative or less powerful test will often be available. What the reader will have to assess in the face of assumptions not met, and/or less powerful tests adopted, is the extent to which his or her confidence in the outcomes is thereby weakened.

The table (see Appendix II) describes the assumptions associated with key statistical tests or procedures. Independence of groups or observations refers, in general, to the fact that a score given to one case must not bias the score of another case. In the case of group bias, this assumption would be broken if, for example, information was thought to have been easily passed between groups. Similarly, we would want to be assured that the researcher checked to see that no member of one group was able to appear in another. This is a particular problem, for example, when dealing with large groups in similar sections in a school. If participants are able to switch attendance between classes, a potential problem of this nature can arise. Clearly, any design that requires repeated measures to be taken from one group will not meet this requirement; happily, for many of the key descriptive or inferential statistical procedures we will see used, repeated-measures alternatives also exist. Similarly, independence of observation assumes that one individual score (or pair of scores in correlation) does not influence another. We can easily see how this assumption might be violated in research that calls for uninterrupted evaluation to be made of participant performance. Many readers might acknowledge how difficult it is to remain unbiased when scoring students' speaking performance one after another

---

32.  The reader is referred to Larson-Hall (2009) for detailed advice on the assumptions of typical statistical procedures used in L2 research. See "Further reading".

in an interview format: sometimes we might inadvertently judge the present student's performance by comparing him or her with the person we heard immediately before. In both these assumptions of independence, the reader will need to attend carefully to the information supplied by the researcher about data-collection in the Procedures section.

As can be seen from the table, normality is a key assumption in most of the commonly-used procedures for data analysis used in experimental and quasi-experimental research in our area. Initial information about this assumption will often need to be gleaned by the reader from the descriptions of the participants and their background/learning context and the selection procedures themselves. Other, more specific, information should be available in the Results section. There are two questions for the reader to think about here. Firstly, the more powerful, parametric tests of analysis (see below) assume that the data themselves form a NORMAL DISTRIBUTION: the mean and the standard deviation would be suitable statistics to describe the distribution. Secondly, we should be able to estimate a normal distribution in the population from which these participants have been drawn; in other words, they are representative of the same population outside the "laboratory". This latter tends to be more difficult to judge, of course, but the reader might initially rely on common-sense judgements in their appraisal. For example, if we read that a researcher is interested in studying the way second-year students in University X in Country D go about learning new L2 (German) vocabulary, the population to which the results are directed is limited. Thus, we might feel that two groups of 20 participants might well manage to be representative of the nature of the population the researcher has chosen for the study. Conversely, if we read that the researcher is interested in the behaviour of similar learners in the many other universities in Country D, two such groups (even if these were randomly selected, rather than in intact classes) are unlikely to be representative of the target population.

Our first, and less specific, appraisal of normality will come as a result of our reading about the numbers involved in the study. We might expect to see a normal population distribution formed when the number of participants is large enough. "Large enough" is relative, of course, but the larger the sample size, the greater the possibility of meeting this assumption. In many of the studies in our area, where participants are drawn from intact classes in educational institutions, sample sizes tend to be small. In such cases, normality in the data would be doubtful and the presentation of typical measures of central tendency and variability, such as the mean or standard deviation, might not be immediately meaningful. More specific information on normality of scores can be drawn from these very measures in the Results section. Try to imagine the typical BELL-SHAPED CURVE (see below) of the normal distribution; look for the mean and standard deviation (s.d.) figures in the descriptive statistics (hopefully) provided; finally, assume normality in the data if we roughly estimate that there is space in the curve for two or three of these standard deviation units on *either* side of the mean, and if there are apparently no extremely high or low scores obtained which might SKEW any potential curve. Clear evidence of lack of normality in a distribution should be treated with extreme caution by the reader; it will make the interpretation of results difficult and seriously affect the conclusions that can be drawn from them. Again, if this assumption is potentially violated, an alternative less-powerful, procedure would normally be available (see below).

As the table reveals, the assumption of equal variance is one that applies specifically to those tests or procedures in which differences between groups (rather than correlations) are sought. This assumption is also very much linked to the measures obtained above from the distribution. Since, mathematically, the variance is obtained by squaring the s.d. figure, the reader could obtain the variances of the groups involved and check that they are about equal. If they are seriously different, it would again suggest abnormality in the distribution, of course. Having said that, statisticians state that many of the more popular tests of group differences are strong enough to withstand violations of this assumption, as long as the group sizes are not highly dissimilar. Thus, the reader would do well to check up on the group sizes used in the study: problems are most likely to arise here when studies use small groups of highly uneven size. In obvious cases of inequality between groups, we would be looking to the researcher to have made the appropriate homogeneity of variance calculation and addressed the problem.

The assumption of LINEARITY is one which can only be judged from the data obtained in the subsequent Results section of the paper. The line we will need to be looking for there will ideally be found by drawing a straight line through points of data marked on a SCATTERPLOT. Basically, if a sufficiently straight line can be seen through these points, such linearity can be assumed. Once again, the scatterplot, or a description of it, may not be provided in the paper, so the reader will need to be particularly attentive to this potential problem when reading about studies in which linearity might be expected to fail. Imagine, for example, a study of the relationship between performance on a test of target-language phonetic transcription and time given up to study. At first, the transcription of what is heard into phonetic script is often difficult for many students. Little progress relative to time is demonstrated, and there will be a NEGATIVE CORRELATION (i.e., no positive relationship between the two axes of "time given up to study" and "phonetic test"). However, once they get the hang of it – and it can be an overnight change! – study time begins to pay off and relate more to successful outcomes on the test. The relationship between the two would then be expected to continue in a more linear fashion.

Related to this last prerequisite is that of (non)MULTICOLINEARITY, since this assumption requires that the variables not be highly inter-correlated. To check on this, the reader will once again need to see tables of correlations in the Results section of the paper to check if there are any correlations of .85 or above (or equally high negative correlation) among a number of the independent variables. When this happens, it will be very difficult for the researcher to interpret which is relating in more or less fashion to the dependent variable. Finally, HOMOSCEDASTICITY is threatened when the scatterplot reveals anomalies between sets of data. The reader needs to consider if the data points from the two variables around the straight line are at approximately similar distances apart all along the line. If not, this would tend to indicate that the amount of variability was not constant.

We should always keep in mind in our appraisal what claims the researcher wishes to make for their data, since the strict application of the specific assumption may change according to these needs. It is advisable to consult the specific manuals and reference books listed at the end of this book to understand what assumptions are considered fundamental to each statistical procedure and which are more flexible. We also need to be informed about the alternatives facing the researcher and what could or should have been done when one or more key assumptions were not met. Those relevant to the papers studied here will be described and discussed in the relevant workbook sections below.

For example, as can be seen from the table, the assumption of normality is one which is a *sine qua non* in the majority of the data analyses here. A researcher should be seen to have aimed for the most powerful test of their data. Power relates directly to an analysis that gives him or her more confidence in making any claims about eventual outcomes. Nevertheless, statisticians differ in their opinions about how comparatively powerful certain groups of tests really are. Normally-distributed data allow the researcher to choose from the ample range of powerful *parametric* analyses. These tests are more powerful because characteristics of the normal distribution are well-known and have been calculated for. The argument is that *non-parametric* tests, by putting scores into a ranked order, only measure the variability in scores indirectly and therefore do not take into account more information about the numerical differences between these and, consequently, the experimental conditions that produced them. Parametric tests are thought to be more sensitive procedures. This said, non-parametric tests *can* be used with interval or score data which the researcher – for some stated reason – did not feel confident about using in a more powerful procedure. Information about data would, however, be lost in opting for such an alternative. If we read that a researcher fails to meet certain key assumptions and opts for a non-parametric alternative, rather than criticise the statistical procedure as weaker, we need to consider the reasons for, and consequences of, such a decision, and the implications for the data collected. In our appraisal of papers in the workbook, the assumption will be that the researcher might initially aim for the most powerful data analysis.

Finally, we have noted throughout this book how our research contexts in the field of L2 learning inevitably restrict the kind of conclusions we can obtain from findings. When our participants are drawn from small intact classes, for example, and selection cannot be done randomly, it will be impossible to meet some of the assumptions required to use a statistical procedure for inferential purposes. In such cases, these statistical analyses can still be used to give us confidence in the descriptions of the data we are to be presented with, but *not* in the possibilities of extending these descriptions to a larger population. Whatever the eventual function intended, however, remember that the researcher should be aware of the need to have met the assumptions that lie behind the appropriate use of these procedures as far as possible. In circumstances of serious violation, the reader's confidence in the eventual findings is inevitably weakened. If one key assumption is ignored, and the researcher goes on to use the specific analysis normally, there will most likely be distortion of the significance levels reported. Since the end result could easily be meaningless data, the reader would then be looking to the researcher to qualify the results presented so that we can decide whether the end (i.e., the kind and quality of data obtained) justified the means (i.e., the use of a statistical procedure for which some important assumption was not met).

---

📖  **Now read this worked appraisal of the sample paper:**

3. Have the necessary assumptions associated with the stated or implied analysis procedure been met in a way that suggests the reader can have confidence in the results of the analysis?

   *The basic t-test has four assumptions assigned: independence of groups, independence of observations, normality, and equal variances. As regards independence of groups, no information was provided to suggest that the experimental and control classes in the Institute of Business Studies – from which six of the eight classes were chosen – could not have exchanged information about the study. Large groups of participants were deliberately used here, of course, to satisfy the objectives of the particular study; however, I wondered whether cross-attendance at classes was adequately controlled.*

   *There does, indeed, seem to have been independence of observations, since scores would appear to be based on the computer tally of errors (see p. 94) and not on the personal teacher assessment/ feedback. Certainly, the numbers involved are enough to suggest a normal distribution might be obtained. I might expect both the mean and s.d. to be appropriate measures for the upcoming t-test. However, the researcher seems to have implied that results from this study will be used to apply to large classes of "EFL…writers in Country X": I wonder how representative of such classes are 374 participants studying Business Studies in "two higher education establishments". Finally, a formal appraisal of equal-variance will need to wait for the s.d. measure in the Results section. I note at this point, however, that the n size of the experimental and control groups are most certainly not equal here (i.e., two control groups vs. six experimental groups) and that, therefore, this assumption might be violated.*

## Worked sample appraisal

**Re-read the Procedures and research design 2 section on p. 128.**

1.  What procedures are identified for data analysis, and do these deal adequately with the original objectives of the study? In the absence of information about procedures, suggest how this might be done.
    *The researcher has yet to reveal what analysis will be used to demonstrate the "significant improvement in oral comprehension" described in the abstract. Our design box and description of the variables suggests a possible "one-way" analysis of variance here, since we are presented with one dependent variable and four levels of one independent variable. Such a procedure would address all of the research questions presented for it allows for multiple comparisons between three or more groups. As with comparisons involving fewer groups, however, decisions will need to be made about whether a parametric or non-parametric procedure is suitable in the circumstances.*

2.  Provide a step-by-step description of the elements involved in the data analysis so far, and decide on the appropriateness of any proposed analysis procedures in the light of this.
    *The information provided so far suggests the following description of the situation:*

    Variables:
    Dependent = Listening comprehension
    Measurement = Scores, of idea units (interval data).
    Independent = Modified input/Group (4 levels);
    Measurement = Nominal (Levels = Pauses; Speed; Syntax; Control).
    Comparison or relationship to be tested = Comparison of four groups on the effect of modifying the L2 input on comprehension (between-groups).

    *We now turn to the flow chart and plug in the above information. The first decision made is that the researcher is trying to see the effect of an independent variable on a dependent variable. Next, the dependent variable will be measured as a score, and the comparison made between groups. Then, we know that the independent variable has "three or more levels", which brings us to the suggestion of the ANOVA (analysis of variance test). The question remains as to what kind of ANOVA this will be.*
    *Parametric tests assume that the mean (rather than the mode or the median) is the best measure of central tendency and that there is normality in the data and in the original population from which the sample is drawn. I have already noted that large sample sizes and random selection and assignment to groups are useful ways to promote such a normal distribution. This would give the researcher confidence in using the most powerful or the most sensitive procedure (i.e., a parametric test). Hopefully, I will later be able to check up on the normality of the data from any descriptive statistics offered. While parametric analyses such as ANOVA are considered to be robust to problems of normality, the use of intact groups here suggests that a non-parametric equivalent might be more advisable. This is not necessarily a second-best option: non-parametric tests are less powerful or sensitive in principle, but their strength does increase with the kind of large samples I read of in this study.*

3.   Have the necessary assumptions associated with the stated or implied analysis procedure been met in a way that suggests the reader can have confidence in the results of the analysis?

*Despite our observations in the previous question, we should begin by presupposing that the researcher will opt for the most powerful or sensitive test – unless we read otherwise. Our consultation of the relevant table shows that the between-groups ANOVA test requires four major assumptions to be met: independence of groups, independence of observations, normality, and equal variances. There is certainly no basic objection to the first two assumptions: scores here come from four different groups and each participant will contribute one score to only one group. I might note for any future discussion of results whether the physical proximity of classes (and participants) and the extended testing period might have encouraged information to be passed between the groups, but this can hardly be assumed seriously to have threatened data here. Similarly, I would have expected the researcher to have checked that there was no cross-attendance in classes. Consideration will also need to be given to whether the assumption of independence of observations was threatened by the kind of data-gathering and evaluation going on. The reader might want to consider whether data were threatened by the large numbers of participants who may have been taking the test in the same classroom and at the same time (you may remember that this was not made clear in the text). Could this have been conducive to participants copying from one another? Although the three evaluators seemed to have had a heavy work load in reviewing all the scripts from all the participants, this did not involve the kind of subjective judgements being made that might have led to bias, and disagreements about scoring were discussed. I have also already mentioned certain reservations about normality here. On the positive side, a large number of participants has been used in the study, and I might expect the mean would be the best measure of central tendency in the sample. On the other hand, I have expressed doubts about the established normality in the population from which these participants have been drawn, as a consequence of the intact nature of the classes. Finally, as always, confirmation of equal variances will need to await the detailed descriptive statistics in the next section, although we might remember that – in the previous section – we were told that group sizes are equal here.*

Observations

Look at each observation marked in this text and decide what kind of pertinent reaction could be made at each point. Help is given in the form of short prompts.

①   Can you suggest how these participants might have reacted to this information in these circumstances?

②   How might participants have reacted in their responses, given such a restriction?

③   What would you need to know about the way this was done, and why could it be important?

④   What problems could conceivably have occurred during scoring, given such a scheme.[33]

---

33.   The procedures, research design, and data analysis sections are treated together in the further guided and unguided appraisals in the Workbook (see pp. 256–261).

# Chapter 8

# Results

## The nature and presentation of findings

Before you read this chapter, familiarise yourself again with the paper by reading Research questions and variables 1 (p. 36), Participants and materials 1 (p. 62), and Procedures and research design 1 (p. 94). Then read the following section of the worked sample appraisal paper and the Observations associated with it.

**Results: The nature and presentation of findings 1**

As you are reading, in the **right-hand column**, write a few words which record your instinctive reactions to what you have just read as if you were talking to the researcher face-to-face. In this worked example, the column has been filled in to show you how you might go about doing this initial reading task.

| | |
|---|---|
| Table 1 shows the total percentage of errors made by all the groups across the five different letters. Only those errors that comprised 5% or more of the total are shown. | *So a lot of errors (of the other 38 categories) were under 5%, it seems?* |

**Table 1.** Total errors across classes and assignments

| Category type | % |
|---|---|
| Spelling | 27 |
| Typical | 18 |
| Noun Phrase | 10 |
| Punctuation | 9 |
| Sentence variety | 7 |
| Subject/Verb Agreement | 7 |
| Capitalisation | 5 |

*That seems a very large proportion of errors for "Spelling". I wonder why?*

*What does "Sentence variety" include as errors?*

| | |
|---|---|
| Those errors classified as "typical" formed a special category that was based on a data-base of over two hundred errors① that this researcher had collected during his marking of compositions over the previous two years in Country X. | *But did these come from the same kind of writers and writing as here?* |
| The next table presents the most frequently-encountered error types (> 5%) in the control group for each of the five letters and serves to show how error occurrence changed across this writing. | *Why should I only be interested in the most often-encountered errors in the control group?* |

**Table 2.** Most common error types across five letters for control group

| A | B | C | D | E |
|---|---|---|---|---|
| Spelling | Spelling | Spelling | Spelling | Spelling |
| Punctuation | Typical | Typical | Typical | Noun phrase |
| Sentence variety | Noun phrase | Capitalisation | Noun phrase | Sentence variety |
| Typical | Subject/Verb agreement | Noun phrase | Subject/Verb agreement | Subject/Verb agreement |
| Subject/Verb agreement | Sentence variety | Punctuation | Punctuation | Punctuation |
| Noun phrase | Capitalisation | Capitalisation | Sentence variety | Capitalisation |

A – Application; B – Inquiry; C – Response; D – Sales; E – Offer

*Are these in order – top most common to bottom least common?*

I noticed that the number of errors decreased at a significant rate for both groups the more letters written and the more time went on. In other words, the genre of letter required did not affect this decline. Having said this, the reduction in error rate computed for the experimental groups was greater (−1.14) than the control group. The following five tables show the mean error computations for the two groups across the five letters. Only those differences that turned out to be significant have been highlighted ($p < .10$).

*What do you mean by "at a significant rate"? And did the order in which the letters were completed correspond to any pre-determined criterion?*
*That seems like quite a low probability level. Is that the ALPHA level you chose?*

**Table 3.** Letter 1: Mean errors of control and experimental groups

| Error Type | Experimental Group Mean | Control Group Mean |
|---|---|---|
| Adverb② | .35* | .12 |
| Article | .38* | .41 |
| Spelling | 4.2* | 2.3 |
| Typical | 1.7* | 1.1 |
| Redundancy | .32* | .05 |
| Sentence variety | 1.3* | 1.7 |
| Poor adverbs | .02* | .3 |

*$p < .10$

*Graphs would have helped me to understand all this better.*

**Table 4.** Letter 2: Mean errors of control and experimental groups

| Error Type | Experimental Group Mean | Control Group Mean |
|---|---|---|
| Adverb | .13* | .33 |
| Infinitives/Gerunds | .11* | .19 |
| Noun phrase | .67* | 1.2 |
| Punctuation | .68* | .34 |
| Spelling | 1.5* | 2.6 |
| Typical | 1.2* | 1.8 |
| Verb object | .31* | .18 |
| Too-long sentences | 2.3* | 2.9 |
| Sentence variety | .5* | .31 |

*$p < .10$

**Table 5.** Letter 3: Mean errors of control and experimental groups

| Error Type | Experimental Group Mean | Control Group Mean |
|---|---|---|
| Adjective | .37* | .23 |
| Poor commas | .14* | .45 |
| Incomplete sentences | .35* | .46 |
| Verb object | .43* | .26 |
| Prepositions | .79* | 1.3 |
| Poor pronouns | .96* | 1.3 |
| Relative pronouns | .79* | 1.6 |
| Subject/Verb agr. | .77* | 1.3 |
| Spelling | 2.1* | 2.6 |
| Typical | 2.5* | 2.1 |
| Abbreviations | .44* | .29 |
| Question-formation | .68* | .42 |
| Split infinitives | .21* | .43 |

*$p < .10$

**Table 6.**  Letter 4: Mean errors of control and experimental groups

| Error Type | Experimental Group Mean | Control Group Mean |
| --- | --- | --- |
| Subordination | .41* | .67 |
| Adverbs | .57* | .98 |
| Verb forms | 1.1* | 1.7 |
| Tenses | .52* | .86 |
| Infinitives/Gerunds | .66* | .51 |
| Subject/Verb agr. | .62* | .84 |
| Spelling | 2.2* | 3.1 |
| Punctuation | .24* | .43 |
| Capitalisation | .22* | .49 |
| Slang | .19* | .43 |

*$p < .10$

**Table 7.**  Letter 5: Mean errors of control and experimental groups

| Error Type | Experimental Group Mean | Control Group Mean |
| --- | --- | --- |
| Article | .14* | .39 |
| Sentence connections | .36* | .85 |
| Poor pronouns | .43* | .96 |
| Spelling | .89* | 1.4 |
| Punctuation | .52* | .32 |
| Split infinitives | .31* | .11 |

*$p < .10$

It is hardly surprising that the first letter brought about such a relatively large amount of errors. Feedback had yet to be introduced to the group. More interesting outcomes can be studied by examining results of the subsequent letters (i.e., once feedback might be hypothesised to be having some effect). In order to see the amount of change that took place for the occurrence of each error type, the error mean committed by the experimental group was subtracted from that of the control group and the total result totalled for letters two, three, four, and five and for all the error types. Thus, for example, if the control group mean for "Punctuation" was totalled as 2.39 across the four letters and that of the experimental group 2.87,

*How did you judge when the feedback might begin to show some significant effect?*

the sum computed would have been −.48. Such a negative number would have been an example of an error type that occurred at a higher rate in the experimental group than in the control group. Conversely, positive results would indicate the opposite. These computations for the 45 error types showed that the experimental group's errors were less than the control group's for 32 types. Of these positive changes, the greatest improvements were found in "Spelling" (2.4), "Subject/Verb agreement" (.6), "Noun phrase" (.4), "Verb object2 (.3), "Verb form" (.2), and "Sentence connectors" (.1). Conversely, "Punctuation" (−.3), "Sentence variety" (−.2), "Possessives" (−.2), and "Typical" (−.1) types registered higher rates in the experimental group.

These results therefore show the kind of error that is susceptible to improvement using the software program③. By far, the "Spelling" type is seen to show the most sensitivity to improvement with the program. This was also where both groups committed most errors and was probably the easiest error to spot. The negative outcome for "Punctuation" is also interesting; the experimental group committed more errors than the control group. This might be because correct punctuation requires more profound knowledge of grammar than the computer can provide. The advantage for the teacher here is that spelling appears to respond well to such computer feedback and so the teacher would not need to spend so much time correcting poor spelling④. On the other hand, large amounts of punctuation error give the teacher the chance to dedicate more time in class to this kind of problem.

*How do you know what individual use each student made of the feedback given? Was this monitored?*
*So what is gained if the teacher ends up having to dedicate more teaching time to something?*

Observations

①   Comment on the kind of errors possibly contained in the "Typical" category.
    *The researcher asks the reader to accept the apparent significance of "Typical" errors in the over-*
    *all ranking and in Tables 3–5 with no information about their content or provenance other than*
    *that they were "a special category….based on a data-base of over two hundred errors" from the*
    *researcher's own previous marking of compositions. With so many errors apparently falling into*
    *this category, and with 44 other types to choose from, I wondered if there was no overlap with*
    *other types, and how any such doubtful cases were resolved in terms of grading.*

②   Think about any overlap between the categories mentioned here and elsewhere.
    *Once again, it would have been important to see – not least for replication purposes – a more*
    *detailed description of error types, for me to understand how apparently similar or inclusive types*
    *such as "Adverbs" and "Poor adverbs" or "Punctuation" and "Poor commas" were differentiated*
    *in practice.*

③    Comment on the implications of "therefore".

*This seems to imply there will be a positive direct effect found of using this program on the frequency of the errors mentioned in the previous sentences. This strikes me as a doubtful claim with so much information lacking about the research design and materials. There could be a more subtle indirect interaction going on between letter genre, feedback, and the type of student here (i.e., ESP-oriented).*

④    Comment on the implications of "…and so…".

*I am not sure that the relative amount of time spent by the teacher correcting spelling will decrease as a result of students using the feedback. Firstly, there is no information available about the comparative times spent correcting exercises, or giving feedback to the experimental and control groups. Secondly, the teacher would still have to correct other items that may take up just as much, if not more, time. The program might help clean up those items that were previously detected as incorrect, but it will not necessarily help prevent further deviance in other words.*

## 8.1    Adequacy of data provided

> **"Does your initial reading of this section suggest that enough data have been provided so as to have adequately responded to the research questions or hypotheses previously put forward?"**

Although in many papers the Results and Discussion sections will be compressed into one, they will require different approaches to appraisal and so will be separated for present purposes. This said, our reading of any results will inevitably be linked to our interpretation of these, and it will be useful for us to start considering what any data on the page are telling us – ideally before discovering the researcher's own interpretation of these. The immediate aim for the researcher now is twofold: he or she must report what happened in a readable and easily interpretable form and describe those findings in a succinct way, prior to more profound discussion of their perceived importance in the subsequent Discussion and conclusions sections. Most journals, for reasons of space, require brief summaries of results here. However, it is to be hoped that these include enough information about outcomes to be seen to have adequately responded to the research questions or hypotheses previously proposed. As readers, we will need to recall our appraisal of the research questions or hypotheses and check that – at least on a first reading – what was required by these has indeed been provided in terms of the data in this section. Obviously, the findings presented here will also need to be consistent with the method, procedures, and selected data analysis described earlier. Consequently, once again, our appraisal of the nature of outcomes needs principally to be based on our accumulated knowledge and evaluation of the study so far.

📖   **Now read this worked appraisal of the sample paper:**

1.   Does your initial reading of this section suggest that enough data have been provided so as to have adequately responded to the research questions or hypotheses previously put forward?
     *The original research hypothesis/question suggested that "objective measurements" and "feedback" from the software would positively affect "students' skills" (later qualified as "errors"), and that detailed information would become available about specific errors as a result of the data obtained. The tone suggested a directional hypothesis wherein some improvement would be seen in the relevant group. Furthermore, I thought the word "significantly"* **might** *indicate that results will satisfy a certain cut-off level of hypothesised probability (i.e., the alpha level) in the t-test.*

     *A first reading suggests that comparative data have been provided for the two groups involved and that these could show whether there was improvement as a result of the use of the program. A somewhat generous significance level (p < .10) has been provided, although no (alpha) cut-off point was suggested prior to these results. I also wondered how the feedback provided might give the "detailed profiles of…errors common to specific writing genres" promised in the second part of the research question/hypothesis. These "profiles" are presumably displayed in Tables 3–7 (see below).*

## 8.2   Graphical displays of results

> **"What tables or graphical displays of results are provided, and what do you understand from the data displayed? Are there any data that you feel might have usefully been added to the information provided here?"**

In the kinds of study that concern us in this book, the initial presentation of findings will often be by means of tables that help summarise the quantifiable findings in some easily-read form. Again, we will find variation in the amount of detail editors recommend to be included in such graphic presentations, but many agree with the *APA Publication Manual* that such graphics should supplement (rather than duplicate) information in the text.[34]

Generally, these presentations highlight the most significant information and results for the reader. As we shall see, however, the reader will again need to be attentive to both kinds of presentation of results (i.e., graphical and textual), since it is sometimes in this very data reduction that interesting tendencies go unobserved or weaknesses are concealed. Equally, we will need to be alert to any data which we feel might be missing or which might have provided further insight into what actually happened.

A useful initial awareness-raising procedure, therefore, is for the reader to locate these displays and try to interpret what he or she is being told therein *prior to* reading any reporting or interpretation of the same by the researcher in the main body of the text. This allows us to come to our own preliminary conclusions about the data, and it can also help clarify any previous doubts about the data analysis involved. As a result,

---

34.   See, in particular, Chapter 5 in the *Manual*.

we might be able to foresee points we would then like to see followed up or further explained in the text itself. Brown (1992) provides the basis for a useful check-list procedure that can be used as a first strategy in interpretation:[35]

Examine the table and, in the light of the statistical procedure used, confirm

a.  what results it purports to show and the relevance of these to the study and analysis procedures proposed.
b.  what the column and row labels and/or sub-labels stand for in the study. Check that these labels correspond to the groupings and/or variables envisaged in the Method section.
c.  what any statistical abbreviations refer to and their relevance to the analysis procedure.
d.  and decide on our initial reactions to any significant/non-significant outcomes described.

Similarly, the reader needs to be able to interpret any graphs and figures that have been used as a means of providing concise information about results. As we saw in the last section, for example, a number of assumptions associated with specific descriptive or inferential statistical procedures require information about the distribution and DIS-PERSION of data, the linearity, or homoscedasticity, much of which can be presented graphically through BAR GRAPHS, line graphs, HISTOGRAMS, and scatter plots. Although the way all this is presented varies from paper to paper, the reader needs once again to begin (or continue) his or her appreciation of results by responding to what these figures reveal, rather than be told about them initially from the (potentially subjective) viewpoint of the person who produced them. For example, bar graphs and POLYGONS (line drawings) are often useful initial insights into the descriptive statistics behind a particular study. The reader should look at the ways axes are labelled on these figures and begin to think about the implications behind the graphical display produced. In the case of polygons, for example, we might be being shown frequencies in relation to one another. Such displays may reveal results that seem not to belong in the data, or that seem to suggest that these were not as expected across the sample. In this case, the reader would want to start thinking about why this may have been so and the effect this observation might have on any further statistical analyses yet to be carried out. All this, of course, prior to confirming that the researcher has also noticed and addressed the question in the text.

Having read and come to our own initial conclusions about what is understood therein, we might now look to the researcher to direct our attention to those findings perceived as being most important. The *APA Publication Manual* suggests

---

35.    Adapted from Brown, J.D. (1992). See "Further reading".

particular focus should also be on any results that are inconsistent or do not accord with the hypothesis.

---

📖    **Now read this worked appraisal of the sample paper:**

2.  What tables or graphical displays of results are provided, and what do you understand from the data displayed? Are there any data that you feel might have usefully been added to the information provided here?

*I would have also been interested (Table 1) in seeing how many of the original 45 error types observed by the software were identified. It appears the remaining 38 types registered such low occurrence as to be of little interest to the researcher or the objectives of the study. If "detailed profiles" of errors are to be presented, it would probably be just as important to discuss both why certain error types occurred so often and why others were much less frequent.*

*The total percentage covered by these seven types is 83%, which means that the remaining 38 types accounted for only 17% of the remaining deviance. Perhaps some types even failed to register any error occurrences. This seems to present me with a very small number of error types accounting for a considerable amount of error across a large number of participants (N = 374). If, indeed, this data-base derives from "….the **most common errors** of EFL intermediate-level students in Country X when writing" (my emphasis), I wonder if these present writers are so typical of this population.*

*In Table 2, I am not told how results are ranked and/or what the interval score is that divided the ranks. The researcher claims that the information provided "serves to show how error occurrence changed across this writing". After the initial total group information about frequency of error types, does the ranked information about error types from only the control group add anything more to my knowledge of the success of the software feedback program? Similarly, I am not sure what is meant by "control group", since there were two classes involved. Is this ranking based on the mean data of the two?*

*I suggested the writing these students might have been doing as part of the normal business studies courses could have impinged on outcomes here. Thus, it would have been useful to see how far the frequency of error occurrence changed across both control groups, even though the overall ranking might have remained the same or very similar throughout the research period. My worries about any threats to attrition across the long (six-month) study period could have been allayed by providing details of the participant numbers involved at each assignment.*

*As the "detailed…Profiles" promised in the research hypothesis, the information in Tables 3–7 seems to be somewhat deficient. Only significant differences have been presented, but I would also have been interested in those error types that did not achieve significance or that narrowly missed the cut-off point – perhaps to see where the software feedback did not help so much. Groups were significantly different on only a relatively small number of the 45 types. Not all the significant differences revealed are favouring the experimental group. I note – in the third letter – that the latter group scored significantly more errors in "Adjective", "Verb object", "Typical", "Abbreviations", and "Question-formation" categories. Indeed, differences still exist after the final letter in "Punctuation" and "Split infinitives" categories. Might this, again, be evidence that the software program seems to help improvement in some, but not all, error types?*

*The probability level (p < .10) may be somewhat too low for me to have great confidence in the success of the software. However, as no alpha level was previously determined, I do not know if this probability was calculated as a post-hoc result after seeing the data or whether this represents, in fact, the (alpha) level of confidence the researcher had originally envisaged for the results. We might also note here that – in most journals in our field – it is assumed the p level is .05 or less, unless otherwise stated.*

## 8.3    Descriptive statistics

**"What information is provided by any descriptive statistics about the distribution of data?"**
**"Have the data been scored using the unit measurement predicted earlier and/or has any appropriate data conversion taken place?"**

In the kind of studies we have been concentrating on in this book, we could be look-ing for some information in graphical and/or textual form concerning the descrip-tive statistics for a given relationship or effect. Such results are to be considered as basic identification data, wherein the reader can obtain some initial idea about the distribution of data in the sample studied: how results were spread out across these participants, how often a certain observation occurred, or how typical these observa-tions were amongst these participants. Throughout most of the analyses that follow, we will need to be looking out for crucial indicators in these statistics, some of which have already been mentioned as providing us with essential information to decide on whether specific assumptions have been met appropriately.

Frequencies (f) are reported when some kind of counting of certain phenomena has taken place. These often begin as simple frequency counts where each participant is categorised (e.g., male/female, NS/NNS) or categorises themselves (e.g., yes/no answers given), and move to frequency-based *scores*, in which each participant might be awarded a percentage mark for performance based on the number of correct or accept-able answers. The former kind of results are often presented in graphic form through bar charts or graphs and descriptions offered, while scores might then be summarised and subjected to closer scrutiny and comparison through measures of central tendency and variability (see below). It is often impractical to provide such detail with large samples, but the reader should remember that individual FREQUENCY DISTRIBUTIONS (of certain scores on a test within a class, for example) can provide important insights into particu-lar tendencies *within* a group before any comparison is made with other groups. Such data are usually lost or unseen when only collective or mean data are offered.

Frequencies as raw data are of a nominal NON-CONTINUOUS nature, but researchers will often be seen to convert them into continuous, score data such as percentages or rates in order to be able to use these in more powerful parametric statistical procedures. As I have mentioned earlier, any data conversion needs to be fully explained or justified and the reader satisfied that the converted data meet any other assumptions applied in the statistical procedure in which they are then used. Conversion into percentages is a case in point: the researcher (and the reader) will need to think about other factors which go to make up a percentage total before coming to any conclusions about what appears to amount to just a simple score. Ideally, we would want to be informed of both the frequency *and* the converted per cent score since the raw frequencies might be small even if the per cent score looks impressive. For example, if a question was answered correctly by 5 participants in class A (n = 5) and this same question was answered correctly by 20 participants in class B (n = 40), the percentage scores would be recorded as 100% who got the correct answer in class A, and 50% in class B. As readers, we would want to look beyond the initially impressive 100% score-line to see how meaningful such a score really is in terms of the original raw frequency when placed in its initial context. Secondly, if the original groups contributing these converted frequency tallies were unequal to start with, it may well be that total percentage scores of correct answers from both groups conceal the fact that the larger (or more able) group contributed more to the final percentage (or had more opportunity to do so).

Continuous data may also be achieved by the conversion of raw frequencies to rates. This is often used in studies in which the frequency of some textual feature needs to be tallied. Thus, it would make more sense in such a study to report, say, the number of times a particular word occurred "per 100 words" than simply report a frequency tally. As with percentage scores, the conversion means that data can now be compared, rather than only described. While such conversion does not need to be explained in such circumstances, the reader might want to consider how logical, acceptable, or appropriate the final unit (i.e., "per $x$ quantity") appears to be in the context of the study. For example, research that used textual features as its "participants" and extracted data from a corpus might well report a standard unit of "per 1000 words", but such a rate would perhaps look rather excessive when data are drawn from 5-minute recordings of L2 beginners' descriptions of their daily lives. A unit claimed to be "per 100 sentences" for example, would require an operational definition of "sentence" in order to facilitate replication; in the same way, such a unit may seem inappropriate in a study where the object was to report the number of times participants corrected their pronunciation of a word.

Perhaps the most useful descriptive indicators of typical group behaviour that we should be looking out for are the measures of central tendency and variability. Once again, these measures of basic differences between the groups may often go unreported in studies where they are then to be used in specific formulae for inter-group comparison and the testing of significance. "Significant" differences and relationships between groups and variables will need to be appraised in the light of the amount of difference or relationship there was in the raw data. Not describing such crucial data is unfortunate since, in the majority of cases, the information is extremely useful to help the reader understand better the way individuals within each group performed on a data-gathering measure, the distribution obtained thereby, and, therefore, the appropriateness of the procedures eventually undertaken to compare the groups. Any decision made implicitly or explicitly here will have implications for both data analysis procedures and the descriptive/inferential use that can be made of any outcomes arising from such procedures. It will also indicate a certain predisposition on the part of the researcher towards the normality of the data he or she has obtained.

Of the three measures of central tendency, the *mean* is by far the most common in studies manipulating interval/continuous scored data. This is understandable in the sense that it is the measure most used in powerful parametric statistical procedures because of its stability and comprehensiveness. Notwithstanding such popularity, the consumer of the research will need carefully to consider the appropriateness of the choice made in the light of what we have been told. The mean is considered to be a comprehensive measure because it takes into account each and every score obtained in the group. No information is lost, and so any scores which somehow do not seem to fit in with the rest of the group's performance are also included in the calculation. This makes it a measure that is highly sensitive to extreme scores (also known as OUT- LIERS). Thus, a couple of very high- or very low-scoring participants in a relatively small group could displace this average measure to the left or the right of the mid- dle ground and seriously affect the distribution obtained. When the distribution is abnormal, it is unlikely that the mean would be a safe measure of group tendency. As we mentioned before, for reasons of space, individual performance indicators are often subsumed in collective data. Yet there are times when such figures can determine whether any subsequent analysis and findings are valid or not. When outliers are iden- tified, the researcher will need to decide whether to eliminate these data in order to use the mean (justifying their elimination and, perhaps, studying their uniqueness in another section of the research), or leave them in and use a less demanding measure of central tendency such as the median. Logic should tell the reader to be more wary of groups comprising small intact classes. In such contexts, (lack of random) selection procedures, together with the few participants involved, may well skew the normal distribution so often assumed in the most popular descriptive or inferential statistical procedures. Going on to use the all-embracing mean as a measure of central tendency in such circumstances would be unwise.

The other two measures of central tendency are the *mode* and the *median*. The former is the score most recorded within a data set. There are a number of prob- lems associated with its sensitivity and comprehensiveness. Most of these are logical consequences of using the most often obtained score. For example, if there happens to have been no one repeated score in a data set, there is no mode either! Also, one might imagine a disaster scenario wherein a particularly difficult test might pro- duce a high frequency of zero scores in a group. In this case, one might be faced with using a mode that will hardly be useful for any inferential statistical analysis that follows (although a series of 0 scores might be of interest in any subsequent descriptive statement). Having said all this, knowing the most frequently-obtained score in a group might reveal interesting tendencies if two very different scores were found to be often repeated in a data set. This bi-modal score distribution would be further evidence of abnormality in the group, since the suggestion would be that two different groups (i.e., with two distinct tendencies) seemed to have been formed within one group. The median is in the middle of a set of scores: fifty per cent of the scores fall above it and fifty per cent below. In this sense, it is less sensitive to extreme, outlying scores and would be the natural choice when there were problems perceived with using the mean. It too has its problems, since the calculation as to where exactly the half-way point between data lies is not always so clear-cut and for it to be meaningful there need to be many scores rather than only a few. Nevertheless, it remains a useful alternative to the mean when the numbers of participants involved are small and/or where the researcher has reason to believe that he or she will not obtain a normal distribution of scores from the group data. For this reason, the median is mostly found in non-parametric inferential statistical procedures, which do not make any strong assumptions about the normality of the data obtained and use rank-order as the basis for calculation.

Like the measures of central tendency, two of the three measures of variability available differ in their comprehensiveness. The most common measures are the range and standard deviation ($s$ or $s.d.$), both of which report how homogenous participants are in their reported behaviours. As far as appraisal is concerned, the reader will need to be attentive to the kind and amount of information reported in one or the other measure. The range is probably the crudest and most unstable of measures of variability, since it takes into account only the difference between the highest and the lowest score obtained. Thus, only two scores enter in the calculation. Any intermediate scores are disregarded for the purposes of the calculation, which means that no information will thereby be available on how the rest of the group performed relative to the measure of central tendency. Furthermore, it too is alarmingly sensitive to extreme scores: imagine how one lowest score of 0% or highest score of 100% in a group might alter the range completely! Of the two remaining measures, the standard deviation is probably the most useful and frequently-encountered measure of all (the variance equals the square of the standard deviation and is important in the calculation of various inferential statistics).

Both these measures have the advantage over the range of taking every score into account. As readers, we need to understand what the figure reported is telling us about the data and then use it to appraise what we are told (or not told) about the variability in the sample. The s.d. figure firstly informs us about how scores are spread out away from the mean ("0" in the diagram below) in both directions. Thus, a high s.d. would indicate that the data are widely dispersed around that figure and that participants did not perform very uniformly on the data-gathering measure. Secondly, once again there will be important implications for the normality of the data being used and, in consequence, for any analysis of these same data. As you see in the diagram below, standard deviation may be thought of like a ruler, dividing off equal sections from the central point of the distribution. Statisticians have calculated the percentage of scores that occur in each of these sections, if the distribution is normal:

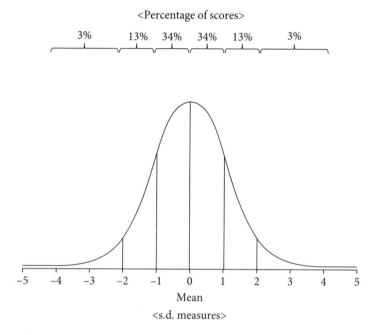

<Percentage of scores>

3%      13%  34%   34%   13%      3%

-5    -4    -3    -2    -1    0    1    2    3    4    5
Mean
<s.d. measures>

So, for example, by calculating if there is room for at least two reported s.d. measures on either side of the mean (given the total score possible for the test), the reader will be able roughly to estimate the normality of the distribution, without actually seeing a typical descriptive polygon like this of these results. Two reported s.d. measures on either side of the mean ("−2" to "2" in the diagram takes in around 94% of the scores (i.e., 13% + 34% + 34% + 13%)). Similarly, if there appears to be room for more than three of these s.d. values above the mean, it would indicate that 50% of the scores were above that point (34% + 13% + 3%). This, too, would suggest some abnormality in the distribution and a larger than normal amount of higher scores on the measure. To take a concrete example, if we read that the total score available on a test was 50, that the mean was 40, and the s.d. 10, we should note irregularity because there would only be room for one s.d. above the mean. As a result of any apparent abnormality, the reader would need to be particularly alert to the subsequent (and probably unjustifiable) use of any analysis procedure that required normality as one of its assumptions.

Thus, in any descriptive statistics of scored data, it is important for the reader to be on the lookout for the reporting of *both* measures of central tendency and variability. The reason for this is that both offer us complementary pieces of information about the data. For example, it is quite possible for a researcher to report the same means across two sets of data collected. Conversely, the researcher cannot then assume that the groups were the same. The only way of knowing if the groups really were identical would be to report a measure of variability that took into account every score and demonstrated if the distribution of scores around that same mean was equally comparable. Finally, even when normality can be assumed from what we have said so far, we would still be wise to check on the normality of the distribution curve itself. Such KURTO-SIS is rarely reported in these circumstances, although computer programs can easily calculate it, but it provides useful information on the shape of the peak in the normal distribution curve. If we think of the shape of a sharply-peaked "normal" curve, for example, we will understand that this describes a high frequency of results bunched closely around the mean line; the s.d. figure would most likely be small, confirming the minimal dispersion from the mean. Although the resulting curve is symmetrical, it may reveal a certain abnormality. With the normal distribution threatened again, we might expect problems in any subsequent statistical analysis.

> **Now read this worked appraisal of the sample paper:**
>
> 3. What information is provided by any descriptive statistics about the distribution of data?
> *The mean is used in the data as the measure of central tendency. However, there is no measure of variability reported. Consequently, there is no way the reader can know what the spread of scores away from these means actually looked like. Working backwards from the demands of the announced t-test, I have to assume that the s.d. was actually calculated to be used subsequently in the formula to obtain the t value. However, by not reporting the s.d., and by only reporting some of the means, it becomes impossible for me to consider the assumption of normal distribution of data here.*
>
> Have the data been scored using the unit measurement predicted earlier, and/or has any appropriate data conversion taken place?
> *Up to now in the paper there has been little clear information about the way error performance is to be scored. I was told only that "…the more errors that were revealed, the lower the final grade awarded". Presumably, some conversion of data must have gone on to convert the frequency of "the errors found by the program" to the kind of "grade" found in Tables 3–7. What the range of possible scores/grades is, or how this conversion was carried out, remains unknown.*

## 8.4 Statistical procedures

> "i. What, if any, specific statistical operations or calculations were carried out on these data, and do these seem to have been carried out appropriately?"
> "ii. In the light of what you have read in this section, do you wish to amend or add to your previous appraisal of the assumptions met for this procedure?"

In many papers, providing a description of the data through descriptive statistics may be the sole purpose of the research. However, these give us part of the picture, only telling the researcher and the reader about the tendencies in this particular sample and, where relevant, the differences between samples or the relationships between variables within a sample. The problem is that the data so described are based on samples selected and assigned to specific groups in the study. Group characteristics will inevitably vary greatly from one group to the next throughout the many L2 learning settings around the world. For this reason, we need to be cautious when reading conclusions based exclusively on calculating such descriptive statistics for one particular sample. The only way possible of checking on the reliability (and eventual generalisability) of such conclusions would be to replicate the study in many contexts and with a number of different samples. Such a method would prove a fairly reliable way of confirming conclusions in the long run, but is an extremely expensive and inefficient way of conducting science, since it relies only on the accumulation of knowledge rather than the considered interpretation of what we already know. For this reason, many researchers turn to inferential statistics when they wish to look more profoundly into the data obtained and, perhaps, say something about similar populations in similar settings.

Although the set of specific statistical operations we are about to discuss has this denomination of "inferential", it should be remembered that the same procedures can be used (and the significance level reported) to establish confidence only in the *description* of the outcomes. We would still be looking to check that the relevant assumptions behind each test or procedure had been met, of course, but there is no attempt or desire on the part of the researcher to go one step further and generalise beyond this description to other settings. In this case, the analysis is being used to give the researcher confidence that the calculated difference between groups or relationship between variables is existent for that one research context. As we have seen in many sections of the papers appraised so far, particular care is required on the part of the cautious reader here, for there can be a temptation to take the step towards generalisation without the minimum support of a research design which permits such a move (i.e., which meets the principal threats both to internal and external validity).

The common factor behind all of these procedures is the search for differences or relationships that show a significant enough level of statistical probability for the researcher to suppose that their occurrence is not due to chance factors alone. It is clearly beyond the scope of this book to describe each and every descriptive or inferential statistical procedure used in our field of study. In what follows, I describe the principle objectives behind a number of statistical procedures but – in line with the main thrust of this book – my main concern is to alert the reader to what needs to be considered when appraising outcomes from some of the most common statistical procedures used in the field of L2 learning.[36] I have assumed that readers are already familiar with the

---

36.    The choice of procedures also reflects Lazaraton's (2005) findings on those most prevalent in papers from four leading journals (see Lazaraton, A. Quantitative research methods. In E. Hinkel (Ed.). (2005). *Handbook of research in second language learning* (pp. 209–224). Mahwah, NJ: Lawrence Erlbaum Associates).

basic objectives, method, and function of each procedure; my focus here is on appraising the consequences for interpretation of using such a procedure to analyse the data. Space also dictates the specific variety of test (i.e., parametric/non-parametric) and design (i.e., between-groups/repeated measures) that can be discussed. Although our appraisal of results will be very similar in most cases, readers are encouraged to make use of the manuals listed at the end of this book for more detailed information about other versions of these tests. Furthermore, while the principal criterion for selection has been their widespread use in the field, these procedures (with the possible exception of regression and loglinear analyses) have also been selected because they are appropriate to the kind of research context in which many readers of this book will find themselves. Thus, I have also assumed that readers will need to be more familiar with procedures that admit relatively small numbers of participants or observations and can be carried out without the obligatory use of statistics software. While software can carry out these operations easily and efficiently enough, I include the basic calculations here so that readers can begin to appreciate how the results are arrived at and correctly appraise what might have been fed into the computer in the first place.[37] Readers are again referred to the references in the "Further reading" list for an explanation of more complex procedures.

### 8.4.1   Correlation

When the relationships between variables are being described, researchers commonly use correlation procedures to obtain the relevant correlation coefficient, which will normally be quoted as $r$, $r_{pbi}$ or $\rho$ (rho), depending on the specific procedure used. We can expect to see reported a coefficient that ranges from $-1.00$ (the strong relationship between variables moves in opposite directions) to $1.00$ (the relationship moves in the same direction). It should also be remembered that the sign + or – would only indicate the direction of the relationship. Thus, a correlation coefficient of $-.50$ would show us a stronger (more predictable) relationship in the negative direction than one of $+.30$.

In practice, it would be unusual to see many correlations of $0.00$. The problem for the critical reader is that even non-correlations such as these can turn out to be statistically significant! This is because some degree of correlation will almost certainly always be present through chance factors between two sets of score or numerical data. We will need to pay particular attention to the number of participants involved, since reported significance (and our appraisal of this) will always depend largely on sample size. So, for example, although a correlation of .65 may not be seen to be statistically significant with a small sample group of participants, it may well have turned out to be so had the researcher involved larger numbers in the study (see below, EFFECT SIZE). As so often

---

37.   Readers interested in using the statistical package SPSS with L2 research data are encouraged to consult Larson-Hall, J. (2009). See "Further reading".

in our appraisal of these studies, the focus will be on just how significant is "significant" given the relationship being tested and the context of that same relationship.

The tabular presentation of correlation results of a number of variables will often be through some form of correlation matrix:

| Variables | Reading | Writing | Speaking | Listening |
|---|---|---|---|---|
| Reading | 1.000 | .425* | .315 | .754* |
| Writing | .425* | 1.000 | .442* | .663* |
| Speaking | .315 | .442* | 1.000 | .851* |
| Listening | .754* | .663* | .851* | 1.000 |

*$p < .01$, $df = 62$

In this fictitious example of a PEARSON CORRELATION, we are shown how four independent variables (sub-tests of L2 proficiency) were seen to correlate. Since the relationships described are symmetrical, tables will normally be presented with only the top half filled in. Working down and across from each side of the matrix, we can see the origin and outcome of each correlation made. The researcher also presents the significance level ($p < .01$) of each correlation, ideally based on the preferred alpha ($\alpha$) level, which many editorial authorities require to be stated before any calculations are presented (see below).

Researchers will want to have used a statistical test to give them support for their findings, in order to be sure that any measured difference or relationship between groups was not due to chance alone. These $p$ figures refer to the probability level calculated. In this case, ($p < .01$), the researcher is stating that there is less than 1 per cent probability that an observed relationship this great would have been down to chance alone. It is also useful for the reader to pause and think a little about both the $p$ and alpha statistics offered. The alpha level of significance is the true cut-off point for judging what is likely or unlikely to be due just to the chances of sampling in a study. Ideally, we would be looking for the researcher to report this *before* any calculations are made. He or she might have had some stated or implied reason (perhaps based on previous findings or constraints on participant selection) to select a higher or lower (alpha) level of probability for any analysis. By previously opting for an acceptable level of probability, the researcher is seen to have avoided the temptation to have made the eventual probability reported sound as if it were what he or she was expecting anyway. On the other hand, we may often come across studies that only report the level obtained *after* calculations, as $p$. In such circumstances, the reader would need to assess the appropriateness of the level now reported in the context of what has been read. We would need to be particularly wary of any suggestions that a particularly low level of probability obtained (i.e., $p < .00001$) was somehow "better" or of "greater importance" than if the result had been significant at a higher level (i.e., $p < .05$) (see below, *t*-test).

The *df* figure (DEGREES OF FREEDOM) is an adjustment that the relevant formula takes account of in calculating observed statistics. Again, editors may or may not request this measure in data reporting, but it will help us to check on the probability level obtained and the significance of any results in statistical tables. These adjustments vary according to the procedure being used. In correlation, the *df* should have been computed as the number of pairs of results less two. In this case, for example, 64 participants took each sub-test; therefore, the *df* value is 64–2. In the table provided for the Pearson-product correlation procedure (p. 299) there is no line that specifies 62 as the *df*, so the researcher would normally have opted for the more conservative 60. The intersection of the *df* row and the p value shows the CRITICAL VALUE needed (equal or greater than this value in this case) to reject the null hypothesis. Nowadays – with the help of complex computer software – it is unlikely that researchers would have committed errors in the actual calculation of results; however, it may be useful practice to check in the tables provided at the end of this book – as far as possible – on the correctness of critical values and significance levels, given the *df* involved.

In our appraisal and interpretation of the correlation coefficient, critical attention should initially be drawn to two measures: the significance level reported and its importance in this context and the reported (or calculated by the reader) shared variance between the variables. As we shall see below, this will be the first of several occasions in our interpretation of statistical procedures when we will need to take care not to be dazzled by apparently impressive and highly-significant relationships. Statistical tables of correlations (or computer software) will give the researcher the information required about whether a certain relationship is to be reported as significant or not, but both the researcher and the reader will then need to interpret that outcome based on the context and content of the particular study and the results of any previous work on the same or similar sets of variables. Let us imagine a study where a researcher studies the relationship between L2 writing proficiency and L2 grammatical knowledge. We might expect the relationship to be a high one in many language learning contexts. Perhaps previous studies have reported this strength as significant at an *r* of 0.80 or more. If, after analysing their data, the relationship turned out to be "only" 0.60, we might still expect the researcher to address the reasons for the apparently weaker result, even though it turned out to be significant from the tables. Conversely, if a researcher is studying a relationship between two variables that would not normally be hypothesised to be highly related and/or for which little previous research exists, a weak (but also significant) relationship may be a noteworthy result and just as interesting to the field.

We should also bear in mind that a reported coefficient only tells us how well the two variables can be said to fit together. To understand the relationship better, it is more useful to see how far this relationship actually indicates that the two variables overlap or are providing similar information. An accompanying initial scatterplot reproduces graphically the direction of the relationship between two variables as plotted points on a graph around an imaginary straight line (i.e., representing what would have been a perfect correlation between the two variables). It is a useful additional aid to help the reader see what is going on and can often provide information that is hidden from view in the concluding *r* statistic. If such a scatterplot is presented in the text, the reader might wish to check on the apparent positive (bottom left to top right SLOPE) or negative (top left to bottom right slope) direction of the line through the plotted points and the general shape described. In particular, we would want to focus on any deviation away from the straight line and check to see if the graph looked linear or CURVILINEAR. The strength of any correlation will be graphically represented in the way the plotted points cluster near the imaginary straight line; the closer these are to that line, the stronger the relationship between the variables. Similarly, if no apparent line can be drawn through the points because these are so dispersed around the scatterplot, there is little or no real relationship between the variables and the causes would need to be addressed.

In the Pearson example, such shared variance or STRENGTH OF RELATIONSHIP is easily calculated simply by squaring *r*. Thus, a reported *r* of .52 significant at $p < .05$ would show a shared variance in our study of .27, suggesting that 27% of the variance in L2 writing proficiency is accounted for by L2 grammatical knowledge. While this appears to be a fairly strong correlation, just how meaningful that overlap really is again comes down to interpretation based on what we already know. Such a percentage may not seem to indicate the kind of overlap we might have expected in the circumstances. Much depends on the objectives of the researcher: if he or she had previously hypothesised that two measures should be testing the same thing, such an outcome would be surprising. Conversely, he or she might be content with even a small, but significant, shared variation if previous literature had suggested that there would be no significant relationship between variables, or that perhaps this relationship would exist in an opposite direction. Whatever the outcome, we might want to make a mental note to see this point addressed in any upcoming discussion.

This interpretation might also need to address what is classified as "error" in such an overlap (i.e., the remaining 73% of variance), and which is presumably largely due to variables other than those studied. Such error cannot just be ignored and the focus of scientific attention turned onto the calculated strength of relationship. This would be particularly important in cases where the researcher had hoped to show that the two variables basically measured the same thing. If the correlation is quite weak (and the more error is involved in the relationship), the less confidence the researcher will be able to have in any predictions of the outcomes from one variable based on the other. One formal way of addressing error, particularly if the researcher is interested in using a supposed correlation for the purposes of prediction, would be to obtain a measure of this error (known as the "standard error of estimate"), often quoted as SEE. This figure acts in a similar way to the s.d. measure, in that it shows the researcher the amount of dispersion around that straight line drawn through the scatterplot of the relationship (known as the REGRESSION LINE). This measure is useful on certain occasions for further interpretation of the overlap. It will tell us how much error may occur if we go on to use the correlation coefficient obtained to predict scores on one variable based on scores from the second variable. The larger this figure is, the greater the chance of error in predicting a score. As with the s.d. measure, there is no recognised cut-off point of acceptance. For the purposes of our appraisal, we simply need to recognise that the value gives us information about how wrong the researcher might be in predicting scores from the coefficient.

A cursory glance at our flow chart shows that the Pearson *r* is the only correlation procedure that works with interval data from both variables. Other correlation procedures require data that are ordinal or rank-ordered, while others can even be applied to nominal data. Of the non-parametric tests, one of the most popular is the SPEAR-MAN *rho* ($\rho$), used to compare two sets of ranks to estimate their level of equivalence. If the original data have been obtained in interval form, this can be converted (important information is, of course, lost thereby) to ranks and this test applied. A researcher might deem this useful in cases where the RAW SCORE data somehow seems to make more sense once it is ranked, for example when individual examiners are seen constantly to respond differently to the same marking scale. The computation of $\rho$ includes an operation of squaring differences, and so we cannot talk about strength of relationship in this case as $\rho^2$. Rather, the significance of $\rho$ will be confirmed in the tables, although, once again, the strength of the correlation gives us more information than the significance as such. We should also be aware that the Spearman *rho* does not respond well in situations where there are a fair number of equal ranks in the raw data. In such cases, the researcher would be advised to opt for Kendall's *tau* ($\tau$).

There are a number of other issues affecting correlation that need to be remembered as we digest the results (and discussion) of any analysis. By far the most important of these focuses our attention on the nature of the correlation itself. There is often a dangerous temptation to read much more into an observed co-relationship of variables; however, correlation itself cannot be used to suggest that the relationship between variables is causal, and to do so would indicate serious misunderstanding of the nature of such an analysis on the part of the researcher. Correlation data can be viewed in the light of cause-effect hypotheses in that they may show up areas that might usefully be subjected to hypothesis testing in further research. For example, if a high positive correlation is obtained, the arguments for a cause-effect hypothesis might be strengthened. But recording a significant correlation, low or high, does not demonstrate that one variable "causes" the other, or that one variable "affects" another. It only establishes a significant relationship – positive or negative – between them.

Secondly, there are a number of issues that relate to the distribution of the data obtained. As on previous occasions, when group data are simply plugged into formulae and run through the computer, this information may be lost from view to the reader (and the researcher), although descriptive statistics reporting the dispersion of data and measures of central tendency should provide valuable clues. Yet one or more of the following is sufficient seriously to distort any correlation analysis findings. Outlying data from one variable, (i.e., a result that does not seem to fit in with the rest of the data) may affect a coefficient. Likewise, we might also want to be sure that the data obtained do not bunch at extreme points along the continuum of scores, leaving large areas of the scale without any scores. This accumulation of high or low scores should also be evident from the descriptive statistics given. In both cases, data need to be distributed throughout the range of possible scores as far as possible; otherwise the assumption of normality cannot be met and no (parametric) correlation analysis appropriately carried out. This question of distribution of data also extends to the participants themselves. The researcher should have taken care that the sample from which data have been obtained has the necessary characteristics to guarantee a full range of scores in the first place. For example, if a researcher has decided to correlate L2 reading ability with age but uses only participants between the ages of 12 and 15, one of the variables will inevitably contain data from a very limited database. If initial restrictions on the range of data have been imposed by the participant sample itself, the correlation coefficient might turn out to be lower than it might have been if more wide-ranging data had been obtained.

Finally, the value of correlation – like any statistical procedure – ultimately depends on the quality of the data used to measure it. Ideally, therefore, the original data would have been tested for reliability. If either of the sets of data to be correlated has not been reliably measured, correlation can be affected in some way. Particular care should be taken in studies that claim to correlate a specific test with another L2 variable. We may find that the test – particularly if it is a commonly-used example – comes with its own reliability coefficient (which should have been quoted in the paper), but that the variable with which it is to be correlated has not been measured so carefully. If little or no formal information about reliability is provided, and the variable is then related to a test where reliability *has* been precisely calculated, the end result is unlikely to be one in which we could have great confidence. On the other hand, if the reliability was calculated and the researcher saw that this was clearly dissimilar in the two (or more) variables about to be correlated, an attenuation formula could be applied to the reported reliability, which would suitably adjust the correlation.

It should also go without saying that, in any appraisal of results, the reader should think back to their mental notes made in response to the assumptions apparently met (or not met) in the previous section of the paper. Now is the time to return to these thoughts and see whether the information provided in this section of the paper suggests we add to, or modify, those observations.

### 8.4.2   Regression

Regression allows us to go further than correlation and use the established linearity of the relationship (as shown in the straightness of the regression line) between the two variables to predict scores on the dependent variable from one or more independent variable(s). If the researcher claims to analyse the data using simple or LINEAR REGRESSION, the prediction is of only one variable based on the scores from the second. In the more wide-ranging MULTIPLE REGRESSION, the researcher has the opportunity to ponder a number of independent variables and report, not only on how each predicts performance on the dependent variable, but also which combination of these variables might better predict outcomes on the dependent variable.

It follows that our attention might first be drawn in such procedures to the correlation coefficient itself. If the reported $r$ is close to 1 (i.e., the perfect correlation), we can have confidence in any prediction of performance on the dependent variable. The opposite is the case if there is no correlation (i.e., the $r$ is around 0). If the error in prediction (often referred to as "residual" in reporting results) is likely to be great – in other words, if the correlation is weak – it will probably be best to turn to the mean score itself as the best (albeit informal) prediction of results on the dependent variable. Simple regression adds little to correlation, in fact, unless one wants to predict individual scores on one variable from another. If we see that the correlation was not strong to start off with, but that regression has still been used to predict results, we might expect to see the researcher report the formal SEE value (see above), so that the reader can also appreciate how wrong the researcher is likely to be in predicting scores for one test by using scores from another one. Analogous to the s.d. statistic, the SEE tells us about the dispersion of scores away from the regression line; thus, the greater this statistic, the more marked is the spread away from the line – and the more likely error will be made when predicting scores on one variable from those on another.

Any results from linear regression will have used descriptive statistics that we should see reported (even if they have been subsumed in the final calculation): the mean score on test A, the mean score on test B, and the calculation of slope of the regression line between the two variables (usually quoted as $b$).

Multiple regression is a more versatile procedure and provides a subtle description of the predictive effect of a number of independent variables on the dependent variable. It also has the advantage of showing the researcher which is having the strongest independent effect among several that may all separately have significant correlations with the dependent variable. As we read through the results of such regression, the reader needs to remember (not for the first time!) what is understood to be behind any figures reported. In other words, regression might be said to start where correlation leaves off, and so we are being asked to assume that any correlation values plugged in to the regression formula are accurate. Accuracy here includes attention to key assumptions for correlation procedures, particularly when regression is being used with an eye to generalising from any outcomes. As can be seen from the table, variables may interact with each other and may intercorrelate; thus, multicolinearity threatens multiple regression, and we will want to pay attention to the correlation coefficients to make sure these are not similarly high (note, for example, if correlation coefficients between variables are higher than .80). As with many other values plugged into formulae and perhaps thereby concealed from view, it would be as well to see the value of the coefficient and be assured that any combination of variables to be assessed for prediction were, individually, based on reliable measures from the outset (see above, "Correlation") and, if necessary, corrected for attenuation. Also, it follows logically from what was said earlier about sample size in correlation that – if more variables are going to be involved in predictive procedures – more participants are going to be needed. Most statisticians agree that multiple regression is not applicable to small samples and recommend at least 30 participants for each independent variable involved in the calculation.

As always, attention will need to be paid to any tabular presentation of results, particularly since a number of relative contributions to variable predictions will be displayed. Results tables will therefore normally inform about the comparative predictive weight of each independent variable either separately (entering the variable data all at once) or as each one is added (entering data in a stepwise fashion) on the dependent variable and the statistical significance level of the outcome, as in the following fictitious (and simplified) example of the predictive power of performance on an L2 spoken production test. In this example, data have been entered in a stepwise fashion:

| Variables | $r$ | $R^2$ | Change in $R^2$ |
|---|---|---|---|
| Error correction | .67 | .45* | .45 |
| Intonation | .54 | .46* | .01 |
| Vocabulary | .45 | .48* | .02 |
| Content | .36 | .48* | .00 |

*$p < .05$

In this example, imagine that the four variables have been found to provide a statistically significant contribution to the dependent variable. The table then has to show the reader the quantity of variance in the dependent variable scores (in this case, the test of L2 spoken production) that is explained by each independent variable ($R^2$). Immediately, we can see that "error correction" is a good PREDICTOR of performance on the test because it shares 45% of the variance. The "Intonation" independent variable has an $R^2$ of .46, showing that – once added to the "Error correction" variable – the combined variance is 46%. The final column (Change in $R^2$) describes the relative gain in predictive power obtained. Thus, "Intonation" only accounted for an additional 1% in prediction. If the next variable, "Vocabulary", is plugged in to the calculation, the three now make up 48% of the variance and 2% more predictive "value" is added. "Content", although it was significant in its contribution, does nothing to improve on this cumulative predictive value. As a group, these four independent variables explain nearly 50% of the variance in L2 spoken proficiency on this measure. Furthermore, the researcher has tested to see if the $R^2$ finding is due to factors other than pure chance at the level of .05 and reported that the addition of "Intonation", "Vocabulary", and "Content" adds significantly each time to the $R^2$. We also understand from the table that the four variables together account for more of the variance in the L2 spoken proficiency test scores than only one on its own.

Such a reading, however, also needs to be seen in the light of the original correlations. Here, we understand that – once error correction is included – the other variables add little. Thus, error correction comes out as having the dominant relationship. Nevertheless, if we look at the correlations of all the variables with each other, which is always advisable, that outcome might have come about because the other three variables have only relatively small correlations with the dependent variable (or because they have strong correlations with the dependent variable, but *also* strong correlations with error correction). For this reason, once error correction is included in a stepwise multiple regression (and untamed computer programs have a habit of inserting the strongest correlation with the dependent variable first), these three variables get discounted. Thus, we would be looking to the researcher to explain the procedures adopted since, by the nature of such stepwise calculations, the order in which data are entered into the equations will affect the amount of contribution assigned to each (and combined) variable(s). If the researcher chooses to enter the weakest (significant) correlation first (and we should expect this reversal of the norm to be explained), there will be no difference seen in the $R^2$ total result, in that the four variables here will account for 48% of the variance. However, the reversed order of entry may mean that the cumulative weights differ.

Logistic regression is the extension of simple linear regression. Many phenomena we may study in our field may present discrete or binary, rather than continuous or quantitative, data in their outcomes. Thus, something is observed or it is not observed: a student may opt to take on one course and not another, and they might then go on to finish the course or they might not, or a questionnaire may record Yes/No answers to a particular question. It is a procedure you might expect to see used in situations where the researcher is aiming to predict whether something takes place or does not or whether a characteristic is present or not. It combines the independent variables to estimate the probability that a particular event will occur, i.e. a participant will be a member of one of the groups defined by the binary dependent variable. Numerically, these results can be expressed in binary terms as "1" or "0". Linear regression is a statistical technique that is used to learn about the relationship between the dependent and independent variables. In linear regression, dependent and independent variables consist of continuous data values, such as test scores or student age. Binary logistic regression is often chosen if your dependent variable is binary in this way and the researcher wishes to explore the relative influence of continuous and/or categorical independent variables on this binary dependent variable, and to assess interaction effects between the independent variables. The usefulness of logistic regression for the researcher over other types of regression is that, firstly, it does not assume that the relationship between the dependent variable and independent variable(s) must be linear. In logistic regression, the independent variables do not need to show normal distribution nor equal variance in each group. The dependent variable also does not need to present normal distribution. However, logistic regression does assume the absence of outliers and we would need to make sure this has been adequately verified in the data before submitting it to this procedure. This is also a procedure where we would need to see much more data than in standard regression to achieve meaningful results. Statisticians recommend the researcher would need a minimum of 10 entries or data results for every independent variable used in order to obtain reliable and meaningful results. Thus, if you read of a paper using 5 independent variables, you would be looking for a minimum sample size of 50 consisting of at least 10 cases per variable, allowing for any outliers and/or missing data in cells. If this minimum sample size is not obtained, it should be clearly mentioned as a (serious) limitation to the study. Finally, as with multiple regression above, we would need to see that multicolinearity had been checked for. Given that I have restricted this section to procedures that admit relatively small numbers of participants or observations, I will not go into more detail here but, again, direct the reader to the relevant statistical method books such as those by Sheskin (2000), Cohen (2007), Johnson (2008), and Shaughnessy (2008) in the "Further reading" list.

### 8.4.3    *t*-tests

Perhaps one of the most used, and abused, of statistical procedures in our field, the *t*-test compares the means of two (only) groups and determines the confidence or significance level with which the researcher can describe the two samples as different due to some intervention or genuine difference in whatever variable created the groups – rather than pure chance. The first thing to remember here in our appraisal is to establish which of the several *t*-tests has been applied and whether this is appropriate. In theory, this decision will have been made obvious in the previous section and checked there by the reader as a result of using the flow chart. However, the specific test may not have been named there as such by the researcher, and it would be wise to check identification here. It is reasonable to expect the researcher to specify the *t*-test applied, both because of the variety available, and because there are subtle differences involved in each as regards the kind of data (and assumptions) that must be applied. Thus, as with all the procedures examined, the kind of *t*-test used should be viewed in the light of our appraisal of specific assumptions associated with these kinds of tests in the previous section. As in most of the descriptive or inferential statistical procedures reviewed here, an alternative non-parametric test will be available if a key assumption has not been met. However, the reader would again be advised to check carefully against the flow chart and table to establish the justification for any choice. If the researcher has chosen to ignore a particular assumption and go ahead with a specific test, the justification should be made clear. The appraisal is of vital importance: an incorrect choice of test can easily lead to a serious Type 1 or Type 2 error being committed. In the former, the researcher rejects the null hypothesis when he or she should not have done (e.g. he or she claims the experimental and control group were significantly different when they were not). A Type 2 error is committed when the null hypothesis is wrongly accepted as true (e.g. he or she says the groups were not different when they really were).

Results are typically presented as a statement or in tabular form: $t = 2.874$ $(34)$ (or $df = 34$), $p < .05$ or

| Group | n | Mean | s.d. | t obs | t crit | df | p |
|---|---|---|---|---|---|---|---|
| Experimental | 19 | 15.6 | 3.7 | 2.874* | 2.042 | 34 | $p < .05$ |
| Control | 17 | 11.4 | 5.3 | | | | |

In the above, "Group" denomination should correspond to those being compared according to the previous text (e.g. "Control" and "Experimental"). Check then to see that the numbers quoted correspond to what was mentioned in the previous Participants section. Any differences should have been explained in the text. The mean and s.d will need to be assessed immediately as descriptive statistics in the way mentioned earlier, particularly in the light of what they reveal about the normality of findings. The reader needs to be able to visualise the typical bell-curve design of the normal distribution and remember that – in such a distribution – there will ideally need to be room on either side of the mean for at least two s.d. measures (see p. 161). In these fictitious results from a placement test with a total possible score of 28 points, we can use the data immediately to visualise the curve. If 15.6 was the mean for the experimental group (and 28 points was the maximum they could have obtained) and 3.7 was the s.d., this would allow for about three s.d. measures on either side of the mean (i.e., $15.6 + 3.7 + 3.7 + 3.7 = 26.7$). We might notice from such estimates that there is actually room for four s.d. measures below the mean for the experimental group, which might alert us to the possible presence of outliers in the data. As regards the control group, we note a relatively larger measure of variability, and the fact that these results would also comfortably allow for three s.d. measures beyond the mean but only two below the mean. Reflected in the normal distribution (and assuming both groups did the same test!), this may indicate that more participants did rather better than expected in the control group despite not having received the treatment – this might have pulled the mean somewhat higher than it would otherwise have been. If it is felt this may have amounted to a serious threat for a *t*-test that assumes normality of results, we might hope to see the matter addressed by the researcher. Furthermore, this, (along with any other information drawn from such descriptive measures) would need to be considered carefully when appraising any results based on these data.

We then go on to read a "*t* obs" and "T CRIT" figure, and a measure for the degrees of freedom again. This latter adjustment to the sample should correspond (in the *t*-test) to the number of participants (in each group) −1, or 36−2 in this case. The *t* obs(erved) figure will be that observed after applying the data to the specific *t*-test formula used. It might be worth checking (if possible) the information given in the relevant statistical table (see p. 296). Once again, in the absence of a row for 34 *df*, the researcher might have applied the more conservative 30 *df* and obtained a *t* crit(ical) value for a probability of < 0.05 of 2.042. Since the *t* observed figure exceeds this value for the level of probability selected, the researcher is right to reject any null hypothesis that said there was no difference between the groups. As we have mentioned on several occasions already, calculating significance of results is a relatively simple matter nowadays with the use of computers; interpreting what surfaces from such calculations, however, requires much more critical insight. The reader will often be presented here with sets of tables and figures that may culminate in the kind of outcome illustrated above and in the other sections of this chapter.

Nevertheless, the hard work of interpreting these figures begins now. For the reader, their own critical expertise will also need to be to the fore at this point. Our reading of any Results section will have three objectives. Firstly, there has been the constant need to form our own initial impressions of what the data are telling us, before the researcher gives us their reading. Now, we need to read about what the researcher understands from the same data. Finally, we would want to compare these thoughts with our own reading of the results.

---

📖   **Now read this worked appraisal of the sample paper:**

4.   i.   What, if any, specific statistical operations or calculations were carried out on these data, and does this seem to have been carried out appropriately?

   ii.   In the light of what you have read in this section, do you wish to amend or add to your previous appraisal of the assumptions met for this procedure?

   i.   *The only specific naming of any statistical procedure to be used was in the abstract to this paper, where I read "t-test procedures revealed more statistically significant reductions in the test group's errors than in the control group". The particular version of the t-test used is not identified, and I cannot confirm its parametric or non-parametric nature. I cannot suggest what would have been the most appropriate test in the circumstances, since the necessary descriptive statistics are not complete enough to permit confirmation of the normal distribution of data here.*

> *The results of the t-test are not presented in any of the conventional ways: there is no evidence of the t values, the s.d. statistic, or the df. The researcher goes on to calculate any improvement as a result of receiving the experimental feedback by subtracting the experimental group means for each error type from those of the control group. This process of calculation, arriving at a negative or positive figure to establish improvement or otherwise, confirms that the success of the software feedback is to be measured as a consequence only of increasing or decreasing frequency counts, rather than of any variation in the quantity and type of error made. I have made a note here to see whether the researcher subsequently picks up on this limitation on outcomes.*
>
> ii. *In the previous appraisal, I made a note to check for more information in this section on the assumptions of normality and equal variances. It is impossible for me to imagine whether a normal distribution has been obtained here in the data, since insufficient information is provided about dispersion of scores. As no s.d. statistic is reported, it is equally impossible to confirm whether variances are equal. However, since group sizes are highly unequal, it does seem as though this latter assumption might not have been met in the study.*

## 8.5   Explanations of data

**"What is your appraisal of any other interpretations that the researcher makes of his or her data in this section?"**

As we read and react to what the researcher interprets from the results, it will be as well for us to bear in mind what these results can reasonably convey and what they cannot. Firstly, the application of a descriptive or inferential statistical procedure such as the *t*-test may tell us whether a significant difference exists or not between the two groups involved, but it does not – in itself – tell us why that difference came about. That is a question of interpretation and one in which we can only have confidence to the extent that the research has been well designed and the relevant threats met. For example, if we are reading a study in which the two groups involved were drawn from intact classes, and no pre-testing had gone on prior to any intervention to establish equality in the groups, we will understand that a statistically significant difference now does not mean that the groups were not already significantly different at the outset. Similarly, we need to understand the nature of the two groups who are now being seen to be at variance. Ask yourself how normal it is to find such a difference between these groups. A study that reports a significant difference between the success of a group of native speakers correcting their output and a group of foreign learners doing the same may not be reporting a difference that is very meaningful. Any difference reported as a result of the *t*-test may be due to the natives' overall better language ability rather than the specific "correcting-ability" variable. Once again, the focus of attention in our appraisal of both results and the researcher's interpretation of them is the real practical import or meaningfulness of any statistically significant outcomes in the context of the study (see below). Finally, it might be as well to confirm whether any significant results respond to the major question(s) being asked or some subsidiary one posed after seeing the results themselves.

Ironically, non-significant results might – in some cases – be just as interesting as significant ones. We would hope to see the researcher address any outcomes, of course, but we may often find less attention being paid to results that do not come out exactly the way the researcher might have hypothesised. This is a pity, because interesting trends might be evidenced by results that – although they do not quite make the cut-off point required by the proposed (alpha) level of probability – indicate that some effect or relationship of a variable is being observed. Imagine, for example, that a researcher wishes to see whether their revolutionary new method for teaching L2 vocabulary actually succeeds in making a difference to groups of learners. Although the design of the study – using intact classes and with no possibility of random selection or assignment to groups – will not allow for generalisation of any results, the researcher will use the $t$-test to support the description of any outcomes after applying the method in this context. The researcher opts for an alpha level of $< 0.05$ for any calculations, and the $t$-test shows that the differences between the groups on the post-test of vocabulary are not significant at this probability since the computer reports a significance level of $p < 0.058$. Although the result means that the null hypothesis (that the two groups are not different) cannot be rejected, it would be important not to throw the baby out with the data. The field needs to be informed about the trend here towards a significant effect of the new methodology, for it may mean that the researcher or the reader can suggest ways forward in a replication study or further research that counteract any possible weaknesses in the design and that could help to achieve "better" results.[38]

This said, we do need to be wary about any results (in this or any other statistical procedure) that are described by the researcher at various levels of probability. The $p$ measure essentially tells us about the probability of a particular result and, thereby, whether we can have confidence in rejecting the null hypothesis. Conversely, it tells us nothing about how much of the difference between the two groups is actually due to the effect of the independent variable (see below, "Effect size"). This also means that a result that turns out to be at a higher level of probability than the alpha level previously established for the calculation may not be more effective or important than a result that is "only" significant at the predetermined alpha level – and should not be claimed to be so. Similarly, the impression should not be given the reader that a particular result is "very" significant or "less" significant than another. Likewise,

---

**38.**    It is also worth remembering that there are occasions when a researcher would, indeed, choose to accept the null hypothesis (i.e, rather than not be in a position to reject it). Frick (1995) suggests that too many researchers see their inability to reject a null hypothesis as an indication of "failure". However, for example, there are experimental situations wherein it would be important to confirm that there is, indeed, no difference between two sets of data or groups (Frick, R. (1995). Accepting the null hypothesis. *Memory and Cognition, 23*, 132–138).

the probability level does not tell us about the probability of repeating this result in another context. The best way of determining the replicability of a result is by replication itself!

The bottom line in this kind of hypothesis testing is that the confidence obtained in results by the use of a particular statistical procedure will only give the researcher (and the reader) part of the story. Such unfinished stories are also, of course, what drives research forward, in the sense that they show us what other questions need to be followed up in order for us to get a clearer picture of what is going on. However, another aspect of the story behind a statistically significant result is that the outcome will always be influenced by other factors within the design itself. So far, we have looked mainly to validity factors as of fundamental importance to interpretation, but further information in this section of the paper will also help us to assess the true significance of what has been discovered.

> 📖   **Now read this worked appraisal of the sample paper:**
> 5.   What is your appraisal of any other interpretations that the researcher makes of his or her data in this section?
>
> *In general, the information provided by the tables is not expanded upon in the body of the text. The researcher comments after Table 2 that the number of errors "decreased at a significant rate for both groups the more..... time went on". However, there is no evidence for this presented in any table, and no data recorded for any between-letter comparisons. Indeed, this would have been an important statistic to calculate, for it would tell the researcher the extent to which both groups were improving (i.e., with or without the software feedback). I cannot see where the statistic of −1.14 comes from to show that the experimental group decrease is greater than that of the control group. There would appear to be implicit acknowledgement here that the control group was also committing fewer errors, and I wonder if the unspecified personal teacher feedback they received was helping and/or perhaps their normal L2 classes had an impact on results. "Spelling" is claimed to be the type most susceptible to improvement with the use of the program. I wondered if we can conclude that the link between software feedback and a reduction in errors is such a direct one. Presumably, a participant writing a totally different letter in a very different genre will be using different lexis to communicate content. Will error incidence and feedback on these in a previous letter necessarily act to lessen the number of spelling errors in the next letter? There might be direct help in the unlikely case that the participant chooses to use the same lexis as in the previous letter and remembers what the program told him or her. Otherwise, any decrease in spelling errors in the next letter might also be due to the writer's heightened awareness about spelling errors as a result of using the program.*
>
> *Finally, the researcher suggests the reason why there were more "Punctuation" errors registered in the experimental group was because the computer program was not able to supply the kind of knowledge required to see an improvement. I read into this that the help offered by his or her program may be limited to certain error types and not others. If, as it now seems, the program is only partially successful in helping decrease some errors in writing, and if the teacher will still need to input knowledge in other key areas of deviance, I wonder how useful the software program will eventually be in alleviating the kind of problems teachers of L2 writing face in Country X.*

## 8.6    Effect size

**"What information is made available or can be calculated about effect size of the outcomes?"**

Therefore, our critical focus now needs to move beyond the significance level obtained in any statistical procedure. Logic should tell us that the independent variable is unlikely to be the sole cause of any significant differences between the groups. As we have already seen in correlation procedures, there will always be some "error" involved in the variable relationship, often due to the inherent nature of sampling. Further research will be needed to determine if any other variable is at work but, for the moment, it would be interesting to see estimated the size of the effect of the independent variable or the STRENGTH OF ASSOCIATION between variables. Such a measure would again help us better to appreciate the real consequence of this variable in the relationship or effect studied. Indeed, many journals in our field now insist that statistical significance be accompanied by data on effect size. The understanding is that it would tell the reader how large the effect really is, something which the *p* value on its own does not.

A problem with the kinds of descriptive or inferential statistical procedures we often read about in papers is that outcomes are inevitably influenced by the sample size – making it difficult to assess the true effect or relationship achieved. For example, as can be appreciated from the statistics tables, it becomes easier to reject a null hypothesis when more participants are involved. Ideally, therefore, we would need a measure that gives us an idea of the real effect obtained, without regard to sample size or to the *p* value obtained. A first rough estimate can always be made by checking on the difference between the means of the groups. Ask yourself whether that difference seems to be a lot of scale points/marks in relation to the length of the scale: for example, a difference of 1.2 is quite big on a 5 point scale, but not on a percent score scale.

An effect size basically presents us with the quantifiable difference between two groups – the difference between two means of, say, the experimental group and the control divided by the s.d. of the two conditions. Precisely the division by the s.d. enables us to compare effect sizes across experiments. A number of more formal effect size measures exist that correspond to a particular statistical procedure, but these can be translated to the other comparable measure with little difficulty. It is a welcome sign that effect sizes are reported more and more nowadays and are even explicitly required by some journals (e.g., *Language Learning* and *Language Teaching*), but you may still see examples of results being taken only as far as the acceptance or rejection of a particular hypothesis. This is unfortunate, since the normal tests of statistical significance will only succeed in giving us part of the story – an indication of the existence or absence of relationship or effect from the independent variable. With information about effect size, for example, we would be able to summarise a series of experiments that used the same independent variable and then directly compare effects across these studies, regardless of the numbers of participants involved. Similarly, we might average these effect sizes across several studies to provide an estimate of the overall effect; such information would be particularly useful in an applied field like ours, where we so often need to understand the effectiveness of recent innovations and new methodologies and where L2 learning goes on in so many different contexts.

In the case of the *t*-test, effect size (Cohen's *d*) can be calculated by the reader with a simple formula and in a number of ways depending on the information which should have been provided by the researcher.[39] In this case we will use the *t* and *df* values provided by a researcher who quoted the outcome of her *t*-test on page 174.

$$d = 2t / \sqrt{(\mathrm{df})}$$

so, in this case, $d = \dfrac{2 \times 2.874}{\sqrt{34}} = 5.748/5.83 = 0.986$

The larger the effect size actually is, the easier it is to detect (i.e., fewer participants will be needed to detect it). Cohen (1992) describes a medium effect size for a two-group design as being .50, and small and large effects as .20 and .80 respectively.[40] However, Thompson (2001) has argued that researchers should not merely announce in rigid terms whether the effect is small, large or medium, but rather relate the numerical effect size announced to those of relevant previous studies.[41] Knowing the amount of effect a particular variable had will help the researcher (and the reader) in other contexts to decide on whether to apply this treatment in other less constrained situations. Information about effect size across similar studies is also extremely useful to the field when other researchers are trying to establish the most powerful statistical test to use for their study. The researcher will want to have selected a test that is powerful enough to give him or her the assurance that a Type 1 or Type 2 error will not be made in reporting results (see above).

---

39.   A useful set of calculations for obtaining Cohen's d for various procedures and with different data supplied by the researcher can be found in Thalheimer, W., & Cook, S. *How to calculate effect sizes from published research: A simplified methodology* (http://learningaudit.com/white_papers/effect_sizes/Effect_Sizes_pdf4.pdf) and more detailed discussion on effect sizes can be found in Rosenthal, R., & Rosnow, R. (2007). *Essentials of behavioural research: Methods and data analysis.* New York: McGraw Hill. A software program for calculating different effect sizes (The Effect Size Generator) can also be downloaded from a number of sites, including http://www.clintools.com/products/esg/effect_size_generator.html.

40.   Cohen, J. (1992). A power primer. *Psychological Bulletin, 112,* 155–159.

41.   Thompson, B. (2001). Significance, effect sizes, stepwise methods, and other issues: Strong arguments move the field. *Journal of Experimental Education, 70,* 80–93.

A second class of effect measure can be based on strength of association calculations (cf., strength of relationship in correlation procedures), which determine how much of the overall variability in the data can be accounted for by the independent variable. For the *t*-test, we can use ETA-SQUARED: $t^2/t^2 + df$. If we try this out with the results above, we obtain an *eta* of .19, which is not a very strong association. It tells us that 19% of the variability in this study is accounted for by the independent variable. At this point, the researcher and the reader would need to re-consider the objectives of the study. It may well be that the specific statistical test proposed aimed to discover the existence of a significant effect or relationship as a result of applying some or other theory to a set of data. In such cases, even a relatively weak effect would be worth our notice in that it shows us that the theory was confirmed in practice, and such a conclusion should be addressed in the text. At other times, such outcomes will not be those expected as a result of the previous work in the area. Once again, we would be looking to the researcher to address the apparent discrepancy. Such considerations of effect size might also helpfully point the field to other questions still to be answered. Here, for example, a significant effect has indeed been obtained at the alpha level of probability required, yet only 19% of the variability is accounted for by the independent variable. This leaves the question open (i.e., yet to be studied) as to what else could have been involved in the effect (i.e., to account for the 81% of error), or whether special characteristics of the sample, the context, or the task might have affected the outcome.

While we have already stated that parametric tests are essentially more powerful than non-parametric tests, the question is still none too clear, and other factors directly related to the sample size and effect size need to be taken into account. A common misconception is that power is increased by *any* increase in the size of the sample used (i.e., the bigger the sample, the more powerful one can claim the study has been). It is true that the more participants involved, the more likely that the statistical test used might detect a significant effect or relationship, since there will probably be a more representative sample. However, ideally, researchers would have performed a power analysis before collecting data, to estimate the ideal sample size requirements in their study. To do this, the researcher would need to have first estimated the effect size anticipated for the study. The larger the effect size, the greater the power in the study because less extraneous error will have entered the relationship between variables. Here again is where the importance of reporting effect size becomes evident, for an examination of the effect sizes obtained from previous studies of the independent variable can guide this estimate more clearly.

In meta-analyses, you will typically find an effect size being used as the common measurement to compare study outcomes. The effect size is a useful measure in such studies, particularly since the different effect size calculations can be converted into each other. The mean effect might then be calculated to discover the underlying commonalities and differences in the studies collected. When we do see the effect size reported in such studies, we would also want to make sure it is described together with a means of verification by the reader: the number of studies and the number of effects used to create the estimate and the CONFIDENCE INTERVALS to help us measure the consistency and reliability of the mean estimated effect size.[42]

While without doubt serving a very useful purpose in collating and statistically analysing results from potentially large numbers of research studies, we need to be very much aware in appraising the outcomes that – precisely by combining results from so many studies into one large study – we are likely to see blurred key distinguishing aspects of each study such as operational definitions of constructs or the more subtle differences in participant selection or procedures. In such circumstances, we must be wary when interpreting outcomes. Most of these are logical effects of the methodology used: the more similar the studies that are being added together, the more likely the meta-analysis will result in valid conclusions. We would want to learn of the criteria used to include or exclude a study. A less restrictive requirement of similarities between the studies allows more studies to enter the meta-analysis, which makes it easier to reach statistical significance. However, this can decrease the reliability of the conclusions of the meta-analysis. Since a meta-analysis is a summary of a number of separate studies, it is only as good as those studies combined within it. Thus, even if a very large study is poorly done and is part of a meta-analysis, the results of the meta-analysis can be adversely impacted by that study (statistical adjustment can compensate for this, however). In studies where different effects are being compared, we might want to assess how far the analysis highlights main effects to the detriment of any significant interaction effects. All this requires the researcher to have previously provided us with sufficient unbiased information with respect to study selection and criteria used for inclusion or exclusion. Similarly, in the very selection of studies that have been included in the analysis there is a built-in bias which, while inevitable, needs to be considered in any appraisal of the end result.[43]

Hopefully, the researcher has told us why the meta-analysis is being carried out. However, we might want to approach this reason with customary caution: it would be only human nature to be satisfied with a summation of studies that confirm a previously held opinion, particularly a published opinion, rather than set out to do a meta-analysis that refutes our own prior assumptions. Consequently, what we might

---

42.    A program for calculating confidence intervals can be downloaded from http://www.dimen-sionresearch.com/resources/calculators/conf_means.html

43.    Further information about some of the problems associated with meta-analyses can be found in Norris, J.M., & Ortega, L. (Eds.). (2006). See "Further reading".

call 'interpretive predisposition' is even more likely to occur when a meta-analysis is conducted by an author with a strong opinion in an area of controversy. Finally, our confidence in a meta-analysis might be increased by the presence of a "failsafe N" statistic of stability. One of the problems with meta-analysis is that it is easier to source published studies. Inevitably, there will be others – typically which did not find significant enough effects or differences to overcome publication bias towards significant outcomes. Had such studies been included, the effect sizes for those treatments would be smaller. The "failsafe N" is a handy calculation of the number of non-significant studies that would need to be added to the present meta-analysis to reduce the effect size to a non-significant value.[44]

> 📖  **Now read this worked appraisal of the sample paper:**
> 6.  What information is made available or can be calculated about effect size of the outcomes?
>     *In the light of the previous questions and appraisal, it is impossible formally to calculate effect size or power from the data made available. An informal judgement of this can be made from the actual sizes of differences between means, although data are still needed here to make such an estimate.*

## 8.7    Other statistical procedures

### 8.7.1    Analysis of variance

If a researcher conducts a number of *t*-tests on the same participants across a number of independent variables, the chance of making a Type 1 error increases as the number of group means being compared increases. The versatile ANOVA can also involve a comparison of group means but has no limitation on the number of group comparisons that can be made (always assuming, of course, that such comparisons are previously planned rather than the result of fishing around in the data available!). Researchers use ANOVA to examine the variability of scores within and between groups. Participants' scores within the same group will vary due to individual differences and random error. If there is a treatment effect found, there will be more variance between the groups than within them.

When a one-way ANOVA is to be used, we would be looking to see that the researcher has proceeded firstly to apply an omnibus *F* test, which will result in a RATIO of the two sources of variance – between-groups divided by WITHIN-GROUPS.

---

44.    See a full description of this calculation and a discussion of its use in Rothstein, H., Sutton, A., & Borenstein, M. (Eds.). (2005). *Publication bias in meta-analysis: Prevention, assessment and adjustments.* New York: Wiley.

The test will have determined whether any group mean is significantly different from any other group mean. The researcher would be looking for an $F$ of considerably more than 1 to show such a difference between the groups and to be able to proceed. If the final $F$ RATIO is not significant, there is no point in going any further, since the test has shown that all the group means are basically the same and the null hypothesis (i.e. no difference between the groups) cannot be rejected.

Results of the $F$ test will normally be presented as a statement or in tabular form: $F = 0.126$ (3, 92) $ns$ or $p = 0.945$ or:

| Source of variance | SS | $df$ | MS | $F$ | $p$ |
|---|---|---|---|---|---|
| Between groups | 6.688 | 3 | 2.229 | .126 | .945 |
| Within groups | 1620.006 | 92 | 17.608 | | |
| Total | 1626.694 | 95 | | | |

As always, we should first try to understand what the columns and rows are telling us, before assessing what is within the table itself. "Source of variance" informs us about the two sources of variance mentioned above. The total variance represents the sum of the variance between and within the groups. The "SS" and the "MS" columns are the "sum of squares" and the "mean square" respectively, and are steps in the calculation of the $F$ statistic. As always, it would be as well to check on figures as far as possible. The MS between groups should have been obtained by dividing the SS between groups by the $df$ between groups (i.e., 6.688/3). The MS within groups is obtained by dividing the SS within groups by the $df$ within groups (i.e., 1620.006/92). The $F$ ratio will have been obtained by dividing the MS between groups by the MS within groups (i.e., 2.229/17.608). There are a number of $df$ measures in the ANOVA procedure. The $df$ between groups is equal to the number of groups or independent variables minus one (i.e., 4 − 1). The $df$ for each group is n − 1. Since in this fictitious study there were 24 participants in each group, there are 23 $df$ within each of the four groups. Because all four groups are the same size, we can obtain the within-groups $df$ by multiplying the $df$ within each group (23) by the number of groups (4). The obtained $F$ value here is less than 1 and the outcome is not significant ($ns$). In this case, therefore, we cannot assume that there is any difference between the groups, and the null hypothesis cannot be rejected. Here the story might safely end, at least as far as the results of analyses are concerned (we would obviously be looking to see even non-significant outcomes addressed in more detail in subsequent sections).

If an $F$ ratio of more than 1 is obtained, the researcher must go on to decide if the null hypothesis can be rejected at the alpha level required. We, too, can check this using the F DISTRIBUTION (ANOVA) statistical tables and see what level of significance is obtained (see p. 294). In this table, slightly different from that seen so far, the *df* line is horizontal and vertical. The vertical *df* corresponds to the within-group measure and the horizontal line across the top to the between-group measure. When the calculation produces a statistically significant result, the researcher will be able to state with some confidence that manipulating the independent variable has produced a change in performance. This may again be where the story finishes as far as the researcher is concerned. The reader, of course, would now be interested in the interpretation of significance discussed above in the *t*-test. However, the *F* measure only allows the researcher to reject or fail to reject the null hypothesis; if the result was the rejection of the hypothesis, one of the key questions still remaining is *where* that significant difference is to be located. In other words, the reader would be looking to see further analysis made of any significant outcome here. The descriptive statistics (hopefully) provided – particularly mean and standard deviation – will be important here for they will provide a first suggestion as to where the differences might be found. However, more precise procedures should then have been used.

The general procedures and logic for designs that use repeated measures are similar to those described here. The main difference is that the F ratio is obtained in a different way to allow for the fact that we are not interested in how participants differ from each other, but rather in the way each participant performs differently across the different measures or at different times.

| Source of variance | SS | *df* | MS | F | |
|---|---|---|---|---|---|
| Participants | 32.87 | 5 | | 34.96* | *p < .01 |
| Presentation rate | 249.62 | 2 | 124.81 | | |
| Participants x Presentation rate | 35.74 | 10 | 3.57 | | |
| Total | 318.23 | 17 | | | |

These fictitious data show results from six participants all experiencing three experimental conditions: learning different lists of L2 words under slow, medium, and fast rates of presentation. There were 6 participants so the *df* is n − 1. There were three modes of presentation so the *df* is n − 1, and the "Participants x Presentation" simply multiplies the two numbers. The SS outcomes were obtained as a result of previous calculations; we might like to stop and think how the MS figures were obtained from the SS and *df* statistics. Note that the MS for participants is not required in such a design. We do not expect students to differ from one another or, at least, this is not the objective of the present exercise. Therefore, unlike the between-groups one-way

ANOVA, the MS within groups will not be used to determine the F ratio. Here the ratio is calculated by dividing MS between groups (i.e., the presentation rate) by the MS of the Participants x Presentation. The same distribution table is used to check on the significance of *F*, except that the two *df* to be consulted there are those for the Presentation rate (2) and the interaction (10).

Repeated measures procedures should have been subjected to the same assumptions for the between-groups ANOVA. Thus, in repeated measures designs, we would be looking to know a number of things, from the obvious but not always confirmed – that the data are from the same students and are normally distributed with equal variances – to the less obvious such as that that there is a minimum of 5 observations for each cell.

We should expect to find post-hoc comparisons made between the group/condition/treatment means. This is because a significant *F* means that at least one group mean is significantly different from another group mean. Two routes are open to the researcher: the first one depends on previous hypotheses being made about differences between groups and the second on the fact that the researcher began with a null hypothesis of no differences at all between any of the groups. In the first case, there would have been specific null hypotheses made about group differences. For example, perhaps the researcher hypothesised that the Group 1 mean would be significantly different from the Groups 2, 3, and 4 means, or that the means of Groups 1 and 2 would be different from those of Groups 3 and 4. The reader needs to be especially attentive here since the temptation to set out on another "fishing trip" looms at this point: this refers to the highly-unscientific habit of looking around in the data obtained for significant results. In the present case, we would want to see that any subsequent post-hoc tests were carried out based on the previous hypotheses of the study. Thus, the point would need to have been made earlier that, say, Groups 1 and 2 would obtain significantly higher results than the other two groups on a test of L2 speaking as a result of some intervention or treatment. If the researcher opts for the second route mentioned above, the understanding is that, after rejecting the null hypothesis, the researcher is merely interested in pinpointing the precise location of any differences and so comparisons are to be made. There should be no suggestion of tests being undertaken after receiving the information from the descriptive and inferential statistical procedures that there are, indeed, significant differences, which the researcher then proceeds to find. Hypotheses are – by definition – not made after we see the results, and/or claims then made that this was what was expected from the outset!

A number of these tests exist and each has its advantages and disadvantages for the researcher. The most popular tests are the SCHEFFÉ, the Tukey, and the Fisher exact tests. With each test, there is a risk run of making a Type 1 error, although this is less likely with the Scheffé test since this is the more conservative of the three in that it requires the most rigorous criteria for significance. We should expect to see the particular test named so that the specific consequences can be assessed for the data obtained. We would also expect to see results from these procedures presented in a way that group comparisons can easily be made, ideally in tabular form.

So far, we have been looking at the results from a One-way (BALANCED DESIGN) ANOVA: the researcher has used only one dependent variable and only one independent variable with three or more levels. However, analysis of variance is a particularly popular procedure in our field precisely because it enables the researcher also to study the effects on the dependent variable of a number of different independent variables at the same time. The advantage of such factorial designs is that the researcher will now be able to see both the effect of each of these variables separately, and also how different variables interact to produce a particular effect on the dependent variable (cf., the procedure of multiple regression, where we can see which one, or combination, of a number of independent variables best *predicts* results on the dependent variable). The simplest factorial design might see two independent variables each of which is manipulated at two levels: a so-called "2x2" design. Crucially, these designs give the researcher the possibility of identifying interactions between independent variables. An interaction will be seen to have occurred when the effect of an independent variable on the dependent variable is determined by the level of another independent variable. In any factorial design, therefore, it will have been possible for the researcher to have made and tested predictions about the overall effect of each independent variable while ignoring the effect of the other independent variable. This overall or main effect will then be interpreted by the researcher. The reader should bear in mind that such interpretation is critically dependent on whether a significant interaction has been revealed or not.

When a researcher adds a moderator variable (see p. 47), he or she would be testing whether or not the main effects (perhaps already studied in previous research) of the independent variable on the dependent variable are moderated by some other factor. In theory, he or she might hope cause and effect are clear-cut between the main variables and that nothing else *is* involved. When an interaction is found to be significant, any assessment of the relationship shifts to focus on that interaction, rather than on any significance of the main variables. In general, main effects need to have been interpreted with care whenever a significant interaction is evident. When no interaction has been observed, the main effects of each independent variable can be interpreted as separate relationships, as though they were part of two different studies.

As in all the statistical procedures we will see, the initial focus for appraisal would again be found in basic summary (descriptive) statistics such as the mean and standard deviation for the groups involved. These statistics are always extremely useful to help the reader come to initial conclusions about what happened:

|  |  | Learner status | |
|---|---|---|---|
|  |  | *Good learners* | *Poor learners* |
| **Method** | *Communicative approach* | n = 6<br>Mean = 27.3<br>*s.d.* = 1.58 | n = 6<br>Mean = 18.5<br>*s.d.* = 1.87 |
|  | *Audio-visual approach* | n = 6<br>Mean = 17.4<br>*s.d.* = 1.14 | n = 6<br>Mean = 31.2<br>*s.d.* = 1.30 |

Means for main effect of learner status:
  Good learners = 27.3 + 17.4/2 = 22.3
  Poor learners = 18.5 + 31.2/2 = 24.8

Means for main effect of method:
  Communicative approach = 27.3 + 18.5/2 = 22.9
  Audio-visual approach = 17.4 + 31.2/2 = 24.3

By eyeballing these results, we should be thinking that the means in each section of the matrix do indeed seem very different. For example, the poor learners' results with the Communicative approach are some twelve points below those they obtained with the Audio-visual approach. Having said that, our attention should also be drawn to the fact that there are only 6 participants in each group (statisticians recommend a minimum of 5 observations per section of the matrix). With such small numbers involved, the differences obtained in the means will indeed need to be large if they are subsequently to be found statistically significant. We should also notice that there would appear to be an interaction present: the highest of the two means for the "Good learners" was with the Communicative approach, and the highest for the "Poor learners" was with the Audio-visual approach. Finally, look to the *s.d.* statistics to provide useful information about the variation in each group. Looking across the four groups, we can see that the largest variation was in the *Poor learners/Communicative approach* group and the smallest was in the *Good learners/Audio-visual* section. The small difference between these two values would tell us there was little overall variation between the groups. Furthermore, the fact that the largest *s.d.* in any group was below 2 units on the post-test indicates there was not much variation within any of the groups.

Particularly helpful is a graph, similar to that below, in which we would see an illustrative representation of the means of the two groups of participants (Poor learners vs. Good learners) on post-tests after experiencing two different kinds of language teaching methodology (Communicative vs. Audio-visual approach):

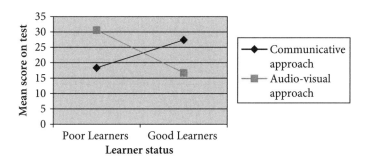

In this kind of graph, non-parallel lines would suggest an interaction and parallel lines suggest no interaction. In this example, the evidence is that, although good learners did considerably better if they were in the group studying with the Communicative approach, poor learners did better on the post-test if they were studying with the Audio-visual approach. However, the graph also confirms that there was an interaction (e.g., good learners did not perform so well when they were using the Audio-visual approach). Such an interaction means that the researcher cannot conclude that one teaching approach is more successful than another; things are not that clear cut as it might have seemed at the outset. In other words, the main effect of the variables now has to be seen in the light of this interaction. In a 2 x 2 design like this there can be only one interaction, but in a three-factor design each independent variable could interact with each of the other two variables, and they could all interact together. Therefore, the change to a three-factor design means that up to four kinds of interaction are possible. When the interaction is seen (or calculated) to be significant, the researcher should address the issue above that of the main effect. This is because the relationship of the main effects is no longer simple; in fact, the effects of one independent variable are different at various levels of the other independent variable. We should, however, be alert to any abuse of the factorial design's ability to study a number of different independent variables and levels. It is all too easy to design a FACTORIAL ANOVA with so many independent variables and possible multiple interactions that it becomes impossible to interpret outcomes with any degree of confidence.

The results from a factorial design are presented in a similar fashion to the *F* test above, as the same basic tool is used in one-way analyses and more complex designs. We would firstly expect to see that the omnibus *F* ratio test had been carried out (see above) and that a significant $F$ suggested that at least one relationship of mean scores was significantly different. The follow-up analyses are then needed to pinpoint these differences and interpret the initial omnibus test. In these 2 x 2 designs with two independent variables, however, there are three potential sources of variation. Each independent variable can produce a main effect, and the two independent variables can combine to produce an interaction effect. Such complexity is best presented clearly in tabular form in the source table rather than within the text itself:

| Source of variance | SS | df | MS | F |
|---|---|---|---|---|
| Method | 27.08 | 1 | 27.08 | 5.39* |
| Learner status | 15.14 | 1 | 15.14 | 3.01 |
| Method x Learner status | 103.75 | 1 | 103.75 | 20.67* |
| Residual Error (Within groups) | 82.01 | 20 | 5.02 | |
| Total | 227.98 | 23 | | |

*$p < .05$

The information in the ANOVA summary table is initially most usefully read in conjunction with the means reported in the descriptive statistics table. As we shall see below, the statistically significant $F$ for the interaction indicates that the pattern of results across the learners for the two methods is different. As we can read in the descriptive statistics table, the means reveal dissimilar results with each method and group. The means for the main effects of "Learner status" and "Method" below the table also reveal certain differences, although not as large. These relatively small differences are reflected in the significance of the $F$ tests carried out for main effects. The three $F$ tests were computed by dividing the MS value within groups into the MS for "Method", "Learner status", and the interaction. The specific probabilities were not reported as part of a computer program here, and so a table has been consulted (see below) to determine these at an alpha of $< .05$. Thus, the MS Residual Error is used as the denominator of all three $F$ tests. The MS for each main effect and for the interaction are used as the numerators for three independent $F$ ratios. These ratios then appear in the $F$ column. Although we can work downwards from the top of these ratios, it is best to fix our first evaluation on the interaction ratio (if there is one), since this will override any main effects (see above).

Since the $F$ ratios are all more than 1, the researcher can safely move on to the next step to see if this is large enough to allow the null hypothesis to be rejected at the cut-off point chosen. By looking at the table again and $df$ numbers (and it is always worth checking both according to the information presented us so far), a value can be obtained for these $df$s for each of three possible effects: method, learner status, and method x learner status. There were 24 participants in the study and the total $df$ is N – 1 or 23. These 24 were divided into four groups, and the *df* within groups is 24 – 4, or 20. There were two levels for "Method" and two levels for "Learner status". In both cases this amounts to 2 – 1, which gives us a *df* here of 1 for each. The *df* for the interaction between Method and Learner status is 1 – 1. The "Residual Error" is the variance associated with normal variability in performance (i.e., all the variance not accounted for by any main effects or interactions). It follows that such variance is not influenced by either independent variable or any combination of the two. In the statistical table (see p. 294), the position where the (between-groups) *df* meets the (within-groups) value (1, 20) gives us a critical measure of 4.35 to reject the null hypothesis at *p* < .05. Since the *F* ratio for "Method" is higher, there is a significant difference obtained at this level. On the other hand, the value obtained for "Learner status" is less than the critical value and not significant. The interesting point to note in this table, however, comes with the interaction value, which is also greater than *F* critical. This should immediately attract our attention, since it means there *is* a significant interaction between the two, as predicted by our initial eyeballing of the descriptive statistics. In other words, any effect generated by the variable "Method" will be moderated by the variable "Learner status", exactly as the graph also predicted it would.

In a complex design, as in the one-way version, some kind of follow-up analysis of this omnibus test is now required. The analysis (and our appraisal) would differ depending upon whether or not a statistically significant interaction has been obtained. If the interaction effect had *not* been significant here, the researcher would be able to go on to address more confidently the main effect of the independent variable. If the main effects of the variables are statistically significant, the source of that main effect can be specified more precisely by performing analytical post-hoc comparisons that compare two means at a time. If an interaction is not obtained in such a factorial design (and always assuming the researcher has conducted a sufficiently powerful and sensitive study to detect it), he or she would have the evidence to be able to support the generalisation of the effects of each independent variable across the levels of the other independent variable(s) within the experiment. Generalisation beyond this would depend on the usual kind of assumptions I have mentioned earlier in the book.

In the present case, we would want to see any significant interaction appropriately addressed and interpreted in this or the subsequent Discussion and conclusions section (see below). The basic reading of the results is that differences revealed in the two teaching approaches have to be consequent upon the fact that poor learners performed better if they were exposed to the Audio-visual approach and good learners did best if they were exposed to the Communicative approach. Such findings might suggest that (in this context) there is an argument to have two methods for these two streams; the practicality of that would need to be assessed in the paper. At this point, if the researcher wanted to identify where precisely any differences were in the groups, we might again be looking for post-hoc comparisons to be made between means, since there is at least one significant difference somewhere among the group means for "Method".

We would be looking to see the researcher address the nature of any relevant independent variable (i.e., one that has been seen to affect the dependent variable directly (in a main effect) or indirectly (in an interaction with another variable)). However, we may also read of the implicit dismissal of an independent variable as irrelevant simply because no effects were revealed. This would be another example of accepting an unfinished story. The advantage (or disadvantage!) of using complex factorial designs such as these, where a number of interactions might take place, is that the effects of a particular variable might well be hidden from view in other – as yet unstudied – interactions. It follows that we should think carefully before rejecting the effects of such a variable; a number of explanations for what happened still remain for further research to study, and it would be useful if the researcher points these out to the field. For example, it may be that a particular independent variable might well have had an effect if *other* levels of the independent variable had been tested. Furthermore, if an independent variable has no apparent effect in a 2x2 design, this is not to say that interaction will also be absent in a more complex set-up. Finally, there is the problem we have continually mentioned in these analyses: failure to reject the null hypothesis (or the absence of a statistically-significant result) does not necessarily imply the absence of any effect. It may well be that the researcher needs to check on the power used in the study and that a readjustment of this could bring about differences in outcomes in the future.

Once again, therefore, we would benefit from seeing effect size or strength of association calculated in some form or another in an ANOVA study. There are two basic choices for effect size, depending on whether the analysis is between-groups and/or has equal $n$ sizes, or is repeated-measures and/or has unequal $n$ sizes. The OMEGA$^2$ statistic is best calculated for the former and eta$^2$ for the latter case. I will again include their calculation here, for effect size is not often referred to in our studies, and it may again be up to the reader to measure this.[45] There are three possible calculations here for $\omega^2$: there were two main effect variables and one interaction present here. However, as a result of our calculations above, only the effects for "Method" and the interaction were significant; therefore, we do not need to calculate effect size for "Learner status".

$$\text{As } \omega^2 = \frac{SS_{\text{method or interaction}} - (df_{\text{method or interaction}})\,MSW}{SST + MSW}$$

For "Method" = 27.08 − (1) 5.02 / 227.98 + 5.02 ⇒ 22.06 / 233 = .09
For the interaction = 103.75 − (1) 5.02 / 227.98 + 5.02 ⇒ 98.73 / 233 = .42

---

45.   eta$^2$ for unbalanced designs and repeated-measures designs is easily calculated from information in the omnibus $F$ test = $SS_{\text{between-groups OR factor of interest}}/SS_{\text{total OR effect + interaction}}$. If the table is not presented, it can also be obtained from the $F$ ratio for the between-groups effect: $F\,(df_{\text{effect}})/F\,(df_{\text{effect}}) + df_{\text{error}}$. Either way, omega$^2$ tends to give a more conservative estimate of effect than eta$^2$.

It is now evident that the effect size for "Method" only accounted for about 9% of the overall variance, and this despite its significance in the ANOVA analysis. On the other hand, there was a much larger effect size for the interaction of about 42%. Therefore, the interaction appears to have been far more crucial than simply the method on its own. Having said all this, and noting that the effect size of "Learner status" would have been very small indeed, the fact also remains that nearly 50% of variance remains unaccounted for in the design. We would want to see this addressed somewhere in the text – perhaps with some suggestions from the researcher about how future research might follow up such an outcome.

We may also come across a number of more advanced uses of MULTIVARIATE ANALYSES, in which the design allows for the study of more than one dependent variable, which are thought to be related to one another. MANOVA is able to examine, say, two or more groups on one or two tests. As with *t*-tests, it is inadvisable to opt for a separate ANOVA on each dependent variable, as if these were unrelated. To do so would easily lead the researcher into committing a Type 1 error. Using MANOVA has the additional advantage of allowing the researcher to examine the relationships among the dependent variables and determine how the independent variable relates differentially to each dependent variable. Although space does not allow us to describe these more advanced techniques in detail, it is important that the reader understand the general similarities between all these kinds of multivariate tests. Once again, two steps should have been recorded. An initial omnibus test will have checked to see whether there are overall differences between groups on the combined dependent variables. If the answer is affirmative, and the difference is significant, the second step will be to see where the differences are, using follow-up tests. The reader is referred to the handbooks in the reference list for the procedures, advantages, and disadvantages of each follow-up test, the most common being univariate ANOVAS or discriminant analysis. Similarly, MANCOVA might be used to study the effect of an independent variable(s) on multiple dependent variables while controlling for other variables that are predicted to be related to the dependent variables. The principal aim of such analyses is to reduce the error by controlling for the relationship between the COVARIATE and dependent variable. As I mentioned in the section on pre- and post-testing, you might also see a procedure called ANCOVA being used. ANCOVA allows the researcher to remove biasing characteristics or error variance from a dependent variable that cannot be predicted from the independent variable. It can be used in other research designs, too, and you might commonly see it in a situation where the researcher believes a third variable may be responsible for the relationship observed between the independent and dependent variables. It treats this potentially confounding variable as one that can be neutralized rather than as a moderator variable (that is, one that needs to be measured). As with all the procedures we have seen, however, it too demands that certain assumptions are met (See Appendix 2) and – in the case of ANCOVA – it is always worth checking that of regression: in ANCOVA assumptions, the relationship between the independent and dependent variable must be linear.

### 8.7.2   Chi-square

CHI-SQUARE is one of the few statistical procedures that allows the researcher to address relationships between two nominally-measured variables. The analysis basically compares the frequencies obtained with other EXPECTED FREQUENCIES (i.e., if there had been no relationship between the variables) and sees how much variation from the predicted distribution is normal, and how different these should be for a conclusion to be reached that there *is* a relationship between the variables tested. As with all the analyses seen so far, the researcher should have met the critical assumptions associated with the specific procedure before analysis was undertaken. In this case, the two highlighted are independence of groups and of observations. However, the reader might also want to consider other elements of the test, which – while they are not strictly speaking assumptions – might affect the reading of findings here. Firstly, Chi-square will at best only reveal significant differences in frequency data and thereby test the relationship between the variables. There can be no suggestion made that Chi-square in itself reveals a cause-effect relationship, however. Also, although the implicit assumption that frequency/categorical data be used seems clear, it is worth checking to see how far these data are a fair measure from the whole sample. For example, we would want to be sure that frequencies were not artificially inflated because some participants were somehow able to contribute more to the results than others. In a study that looked at the relationship between introversion/extroversion and participation in class, for example, our experience might tell us extrovert participants would normally participate more often than introvert ones. Thus, any comparisons of the frequency of participation might well present a specious relationship. In such a situation there would be a major threat to the assumption of independence of observations, since participants would have been able to contribute more than others in each frequency cell. Chi-square is also a popular procedure to study survey data, which generally involves frequency data that are inappropriate for the other types of data analysis illustrated above. We would want to know how representative a frequency count of, say, the number of people answering "yes" or "no" to a certain question really was. If the question had been asked of 500 students in a telephone survey, for example, we would want to know what percentage actually responded to (rather than refused to answer) the question, in order to know whether the response frequency reflected fairly the number of people who were actually asked the question.

Secondly, it is worth checking to make sure that observations fall into mutually exclusive and/or logical categories (e.g., male/female, left-handed/right-handed, etc.,) rather than counting towards more than one frequency tabulation. We might also come across suspicious data-transformation, where categories have been set up based on data so specific to one context (such as converting scores on a reading comprehension test to "high", "low", and "intermediate" data) that they can no longer be generalised to other contexts. In other words, the extent to which the categorisation is logical or acceptable will need to be related to the research question or hypothesis itself. In turn, we will be looking to the researcher to justify this and also consider its consequences for any eventual generalisation of outcomes.

Finally, to have confidence in the results, we would want to be sure that at least 80 percent of the expected cell frequencies in the chi-square table presented us with more than 5 cases. If this is not so, and/or if the study carries a $df$ of 1, the researcher should be seen to have applied a correction factor (Yates') to compensate for the discrepancy that arises in these circumstances between the Chi-square distribution and the observed Chi-square value.[46]

In one-way chi-square analyses, the researcher is interested to see if frequencies from the dependent variable are significantly different with levels of another independent variable. My focus here will be on the two-way design as by far the more common procedure in our field.

Results from the Chi-square ($\chi^2$) test will normally be presented as a statement, possibly accompanied by a contingency table and summary statistics: $\chi^2 = 14.69$, $df = 4, p < .05$:

|  | L2 chosen | | | | | |
| --- | --- | --- | --- | --- | --- | --- |
|  | French | German | Russian | Hebrew | Italian | Totals |
| Female | 10.08 | 10.92 | 4.2 | 7.56 | 9.24 | 42 |
| Male | 13.92 | 15.08 | 5.8 | 10.44 | 12.76 | 58 |
| Totals | 24 | 26 | 10 | 18 | 22 | 100 |

$\chi^2 = 14.69, df = 4, p < .05$

In this example, the fictitious data come from a study where the objective was to relate choice made by L1 English first-year undergraduates of an optional L2 in University P to the sex of these participants. Although chi-square does not assume any directionality in the variables, we might want to think that there is one dependent variable here (Sex, two levels) measured as a frequency and one independent variable (L2 chosen, five levels) measured as a nominal (category) variable. The data refer to the expected values, rather than what was actually observed; in other words, how the frequencies

---

46.    See, for example, Sheskin (2000:502–503) for an explanation of this correction. See "Further reading".

would have turned out if there were no relationship between L2 choice and sex. We would have hoped to see the OBSERVED FREQUENCIES too, as we would then be able to see where differences were greatest and which cell(s) contributed most to any significant outcome. $\chi^2$ uses observed and expected frequencies to test a null hypothesis (here) that there is no relationship between sex and choice of L2 option. The *expected* frequencies of males and females choosing these options are those that would make these proportions the same and force us to accept the null hypothesis.[47] To the extent that the observed (i.e., real) frequencies differ from the expected frequencies, the results provide evidence for rejecting the null hypothesis. Once again, we should get into the habit of checking the data presented as far as possible (particularly since the original descriptive data are not provided). Firstly, the "Total" numbers around the table (known as the "marginals") refer not only to the row and/or column totals of expected frequencies here, but also to observed total numbers in the rows and columns in the original frequency table. The *df* here cannot just be calculated by subtracting 1 from the total number of groups. Here the researcher would also have had to subtract 1 from the participant options, of which there were 5. Hence the *df* for the groups is $2 - 1 = 1$ and that of L2 options was $5 - 1 = 4$. The multiplication of these two results gives us the total *df*, which is 4. The observed $\chi^2$ statistic (14.69) reflects the overall size of the differences computed between the observed and the expected frequencies. The greater this difference, the more likely this outcome is to be significant. We are now ready to check up the apparently significant difference in the $\chi^2$ statistical table (see p. 298). At the intersection of 4 *df* and the projected alpha of $< .05$, we see a figure of 9.49. $\chi^2_{observed}$ would need to be equal to or larger than this $\chi^2_{critical}$ (which it is) to be significant at this level of probability. An alternative, if a computer program were used, would have been for the researcher to tell us that statistical probability had been achieved, quoting the actual probability (here, by the way, .0054).

So far, so good. The reader will again need to be alert to how this outcome is interpreted in the light both of the limits of this kind of analysis and of the constraints placed on outcomes by the specific design itself. Our main concerns should be for any possible threats in terms of what was said above. We might note here that one of the expected cell frequencies was predicted to be below 5 (Female/Russian). The present example is border-line in this respect and it would probably be acceptable to include it in the analysis. We might be looking to the researcher to add a caveat about this low frequency and/or attempt to explain it. Then, we need to read carefully the researcher's immediate reactions to these outcomes. We would accept the researcher's claim that there *is* a relationship between sex and L2 option. However, we would not accept that being male or female actually causes the choice or vice versa! Other variables (i.e., yet

---

47.   In theory, we will never have to *accept* a null hypothesis. The outcomes of hypothesis-testing are that the researcher either "rejects" or "fails to reject" that hypothesis.

to be studied) might also be moderating the relationship. Finally, we would accept this outcome as confirming the description of these participants in this study, but we would not accept any generalisation to other contexts unless threats to external validity had been seen to be met earlier.

Perhaps most importantly, the researcher is now in a similar situation to that revealed after the omnibus $F$ ratio test in ANOVA. He or she knows that a significant difference exists between the frequencies expected and those actually obtained, but does not yet know for sure where that difference was actually located. It might have been in the frequency of any of the cells or a combination of these. Of course, the researcher might not want to go down this road and is content with describing a significant difference somewhere in the data or with highlighting which cells have the biggest expected-observed differences. There is nothing inherently wrong with this; however, he or she would have to understand that a concerned reader might well have reason to be interested in more precise location of differences. In this case, we might be looking out for post-hoc comparisons whereby each pair or cell is tested for its significance in individual $\chi^2$ analyses.[48] If this information is provided (usually presented in a similar table), and *if* the original (i.e., obtained) frequencies had also been given, the reader would be able to check to see that the outcome is roughly as expected after a perusal of the obtained data. Any apparent anomalies should be addressed by the researcher.

Despite the temptation to finish the story with a significant ending, it should remain of interest to both researcher and interested reader to discover just how significant "significant" really is in this context! We would once again, therefore, be looking for some calculation of effect size or strength of association to be made, and (either here or later in the Discussion section) reference to the practical significance or meaningfulness of what was found. The two – most common – options are PHI ($\varphi$), when 1 *df* is involved and Cramer's V when more than 1 *df* is computed. Naturally enough, it only makes sense to calculate effect when significance had already been obtained in the previous $\chi^2$ analysis.[49]

As before, the appraisal of the practical significance or meaningfulness of any statistically significant outcome here depends on common sense and recall of what we have been told about the research design and context so far. During our reading, it is as well to keep in the back of our minds that the original descriptive data may actually hold far more informative or revealing data for consideration. In the above example, the researcher might want to compare the $\chi^2$ statistic obtained at this probability level with those obtained in similar studies and go on to address any differences found both

---

48.    Post-hoc tests with chi square are not without complications, however, as multiple comparisons can inflate the probability of error considerably. Look out for the use of the so-called "Bonferroni correction", which divides the *p*-value by the number of comparisons being made.

49.    Phi and Cramer's V can be calculated online on a number of sites. See, for example, http://faculty.vassar.edu/lowry/tab2x2.html and http://faculty.vassar.edu/lowry/newcs.html.

in the end result and in the observed frequencies themselves. Similarly, we ourselves might want to see the observed frequencies so that, for example, we were in a position to judge whether any statistically significant difference between, say, the 10.44 males expected to opt for Hebrew as a L2, and the 15 who actually did, represents an interesting result over a sample of 100 students. If we read that the significant contribution to the overall Chi-square was found to come from the "Hebrew" cell, how might we then react to reading that only 1 female and 17 males chose Hebrew? Equally, of course, any comparisons that turned out *not* to be significant or that came close to the cut-off point might be interesting to ponder in the circumstances of the study.

A further, more complicated, technique you may come across is loglinear analysis. Behind the somewhat daunting name is an extension of the chi-square test in which the researcher has more than two nominal independent variables and wishes to test the relationship between them. Chi-square is insufficient when you have more than two such variables because it only tests the independence of the variables. When there are more than two, it cannot detect the varying associations and interactions between the variables and so cannot show which of the independent variables best predicts the present distribution and, as we know, it cannot test for causal relationships between variables. This is where loglinear procedures come in. Such a procedure allows the researcher to see what independent variables and interactions impact the dependent variable. When testing for any effects in loglinear analysis, we try to reduce the number of significant effects that it takes to explain the data. In this sense, the outcome ends once the results indicate non-significance for the level of effect you are testing. The final equation should contain only those effects which have been found to be significant (or necessary components of significant effects). Thus, loglinear analysis begins with a model where all possible direct and interaction effects are specified. A multivariate contingency table is constructed and the relationship between the variables is assessed. All the variables in the table are treated as independent variables, the dependent variables being the number of cases located in each cell of the table. Simpler models are then examined which remove some of these effects to see whether good fits to the data can be obtained with fewer effects. The linear model which results helps the researcher to predict cell frequencies. The more precise the model is, the closer the predicted frequency is to the observed frequency. Thus, the researcher may infer what variables are most important and what the pattern of effect actually is in the data.

It is a very flexible multivariate procedure, best adapted to analysing nominal measured variables. As an extension of chi-square, it has similar assumptions. One of the problems to be aware of as one reads the results of the above procedures is precisely that the inclusion and consideration of so many variables can make the interpretation of significant outcomes difficult. You should also again be aware of the independence of the data since only a between-subjects design can be used. The number of data entries is also important: loglinear analysis is for large numbers of cases and you would be looking to see at least five times the number of cases as cells in the data presented. So, for example, if presented with a 3 x 2 x 2 table you would need to have sixty cases. Finally, for all two-way associations, the expected cell frequencies should be more than one and no more than 20% should be less than 5. Failure to meet this requirement may mean that the power of the statistical procedure is reduced to a point where interpretation and analysis are meaningless.

## 8.8   Practical significance and meaningfulness

**"What initial conclusions do you come to about the practical significance and meaningfulness of these results? Do these coincide with the researcher's interpretation?"**

Throughout the text in this section, we will return to the need to appraise results of any descriptive or inferential statistical procedure in a way that separates their statistical significance from their practical significance or meaningfulness. It should already be clear that a so-called statistically significant relationship or difference could turn out to be of little import once placed within the wider context of what we now know about the study. Obtaining a significant result does not obviate the need for the researcher (or the reader) to assess that significance on a wider scale. In most cases, such assessment will be a matter of common sense. Remember that statistical significance can still be obtained with a minimum relationship between the variables or with a minimal difference between the means of two groups. Stand back and ask, for example, how we would assess the meaningfulness of a significant difference of a few points between the means of two groups when the test itself had a total score of 150 points? After considering factors such as the nature of the participants involved, the experience they had had with this kind of test, their level of knowledge, the kind of methodology followed in class, the content of the test and the procedures used to administer it, or even who did the marking and how, we may conclude that this difference does not really mean very much.

Imagine we are reading through the table of *t*-test results on p. 174. We have read previously that the significant differences in means in that table come from a study in which two groups of advanced-level Spanish-as-a-foreign-language students (N = 36) were tested on a multiple-choice type reading comprehension measure (total 28 points). The control group received normal tuition in class, which involved twice-weekly text analyses and multiple-choice questions to test comprehension. The experimental group received the same instruction plus one hour extra for ten weeks during which they wrote their own multiple-choice questions on these texts, received feedback on these from the teacher, and tested them out on each other. Do we feel that the eventual differences shown in the post-test are sufficient to be meaningful in this context? Would we have expected greater differences between them? Do we feel that the numbers involved in the study were not large enough to read much in to what happened? Do we even think that, at this level of L2 proficiency, reading comprehension is not meaningfully determined by multiple-choice questions only and, therefore, little of worth is revealed here about the abilities of the different groups to comprehend the L2? All such issues are perfectly legitimate reactions to the study from the reader's own reality. Clearly, the researcher will not be in a position to predict or address all of them. We would want to see, however, some attempt to place results in their true context, either in the present section or in the subsequent Discussion.

> 📖    **Now read this worked appraisal of the sample paper:**
>
> 8.    What initial conclusions do you come to about the practical significance and meaningfulness of these results? Do these coincide with the researcher's interpretation?
>
> *Firstly, if the program is only effective to a measurable extent with a restricted number of the 45 error types tested here, I wonder how useful it can really be claimed to be. Furthermore, I feel more confidence might have been placed in the software program (given the positive outcomes mentioned in the literature review from previous research with these kinds of programs) and a higher alpha level predicted. The chances of obtaining a statistically significant difference increases with sample size and statistical significance could have been obtained here at the cost of practical significance.*
>
> *I read that final computations of differences for the 45 error types showed that the experimental group had fewer errors for 32 types; however, I am not shown all these figures, so it becomes impossible to consider how meaningful these differences actually were. Although "Spelling" shows a large difference in favour of the experimental group, the other improvements seem to be very small in comparison, and those I do not see were probably even smaller.*
>
> *Finally, the eventual practical merits of a feedback program based on "the most common errors of EFL intermediate level students" would need to be tested in other, less specific, L2 learning situations and in response to other kinds of writing. While this does not weaken the results in this case, I have made a note to recall this as a perceived limitation on findings in the subsequent section.*

## Worked sample appraisal

### Results: The nature and presentation of findings 2

1.    Before working through this section of the paper, you should re-read the corresponding Research questions and variables 2 (p. 56), Participants and materials 2 (p. 85), and Procedures and research design 2 (p. 128).

2.    As you are reading, in the *right-hand column*, write a few words which record your instinctive reactions to what you have just read as if you were talking to the researcher face-to-face.

An alpha level was chosen of .01 for all the statistical tests undertaken①. The first test carried out was an independent group $t$-test on the outcomes from the control test②. No significant differences were revealed between the groups. Table 1 shows the descriptive statistics obtained for the groups on the recall test. Then the data from the 180 participants was fed into a one-way ANOVA procedure and the results obtained (see Table 2). A post-hoc Scheffé test on the ANOVA outcomes revealed a significant difference with regard to the control group.

**Table 1.** Descriptive statistics

| Group/Version | Mean | s.d. |
|---|---|---|
| Control | 46.3 | 13.8 |
| Diminished speed | 52.1 | 11.2 |
| Pauses inserted | 54.6 | 11.7 |
| Simpler syntax | 59.7 | 12.8 |

**Table 2.** One-way ANOVA

| Source | SS | df | MS | F |
|---|---|---|---|---|
| Between groups | 1788.911 | 3 | 596.303 | 13.731* |
| Within groups | 7643.023 | 176 | 43.426 | |
| Total | 9431.934 | 179 | | |

$*p < .01$

3.  **Read again the relevant section in the chapter, and then attempt to answer these questions. Finally, compare your responses to mine.**

    1.  Does your initial reading of this section suggest that enough data have been provided so as to have adequately responded to the research questions or hypotheses previously put forward?

        *The research questions asked how far modifying input using more and longer pauses, less speed, or simpler syntax would affect listening comprehension, and whether one of these modifications had more influence than another. I commented at the time that no direction was forecast in the research questions and that I would therefore be looking to see results that showed both any positive and negative outcomes on listening comprehension. The data I read here would appear to provide the basic information required to answer these questions, since the mean scores for each listening test with the separate modifications could be compared and suggestions made about whether listening comprehension is affected based on the control (i.e., unmodified) group score. Similarly, such data provide initial information about which, if any, modification is more efficacious.*

2. What tables or graphical displays of results are provided, and what do you understand from the data displayed? Are there any data that you feel might have usefully been added to the information provided here?

*The first table provided displays the central measures of tendency (mean) and the variability (s.d.) of each group and are pertinent to the study as they will show us how each modified input group performed relative to the control group. The mean scores should correspond to the number of idea units successfully recorded. Unfortunately, since we are unaware of the total number available in the text to start with, the information provided here will not help us easily understand the true meaning of the central tendencies and variability reported. Despite this, we should still begin to think about what the results seem to be showing us. First of all, it would seem that all groups receiving the modified input performed better than the control group. Just how significantly "better" a difference of nearly 6 points (in the "Diminished speed" group) or over 13 points (in the "Simpler syntax" group) really is will need to await further statistical analysis (see below). Secondly, the group receiving the modified text in the form of simpler syntax performed best. The second table shows the results of performing a one-way ANOVA on these means – this generally corresponds to expectations in the previous section. Our attention might immediately be drawn to the fact that a significant F ratio has been recorded and that, therefore, one group mean has been shown to be significantly different from another. This ratio is also significant at the alpha level established. A mathematical check on the figures shows these are correct. Although exact correspondences are not available in the tables for these df values, it is clear that an F ratio of this size is going to be significant when the data are run through a computer program. I would now expect the actual location of that significant difference to be found; the previous appraisal of Table 1 indicates this might well be in the group receiving "Simpler syntax" in their input, but a post-hoc analysis is the only way of knowing for sure. Unfortunately, although the text indicates this was carried out and a result obtained, the specific details are not provided in tabular form (see below, question 5). Likewise, mention is made in the text of the prior control test to check on the equality of listening comprehension level across all the groups involved, but details are not provided. I have to take the researcher's word that the end result showed no significant differences between the groups, but the reporting of such information here might also have helped the reader better understand the nature of the groups and, in particular, why some participants were eliminated from the study as a result of this test.*

3. What information is provided by any descriptive statistics about the distribution of data?

*As I mentioned above, it is impossible to make a rough estimate of the distribution of data, since I am not told of the scale used in scoring idea units. I note that the mean has been chosen as the measure of central tendency. This measure is highly sensitive to outlying scores, of course, but the assumption is that previous high- or low-scoring participants would have been removed beforehand as a result of the control test (but see the comments on the content of both tests, p. 89). The hope, therefore, is that remaining participants are now more uniform or "normal" in their responses. Certainly, the s.d. data seem to indicate similar spreads of scores across the four groups.*

4.  Have the data been scored using the unit measurement predicted earlier, and/or has any appropriate data conversion taken place?

    *In the previous section it was made clear that listening comprehension would be scored by "the number of recalls". Although I conjectured this might refer to open data such as frequencies, I read that the text had been scanned for a fixed number of idea units and that participants would be "given a score based on the amount of correct units of ideas found therein". This, presumably, corresponds to the closed score data presented here. A number of doubts were raised and remain at this point about how scoring was carried out, and I would be looking to see if these are addressed in the final section of the paper.*

5.  i.   What, if any, specific statistical operations or calculations were carried out on these data, and does this seem to have been carried out appropriately?

    ii.  In the light of what you have read in this section, do you wish to amend or add to your previous appraisal of the assumptions met for this procedure?

        i.   *The researcher has carried out a one-way ANOVA test on the listening comprehension data. If, as it seems, he or she has opted for a parametric test, we should bear in mind as we read the results that random assignment has not been a feature of the design and that normality cannot be assumed merely by virtue of the large numbers involved. As far as I can tell, the procedure has been executed correctly, and a significant F ratio has indicated that there are significant differences among the four groups. The post-hoc test reported on has been identified as the more rigorous Scheffé test; however, the outcome reported – "a significant difference…[was revealed]…with regard to the control group" – will not suffice. Of the two routes mentioned in the preamble to this section, it would seem that no specific differences were previously hypothesised by the researcher in previous sections – indeed the review of the literature also seemed to point towards this, as previous studies had provided somewhat inconclusive evidence. Therefore, the post-hoc test embarked upon here is used merely to pinpoint the exact location of the significant differences observed, rather than confirm a priori differences between, say, the "simpler syntax" group and the "diminished speed" group. The problem here is that I am still no wiser as to which groups differ from each other. Eyeballing of the descriptive statistics did reveal some information, but only the full results of the test can confirm this.*

        ii.  *Based on the assumption that a parametric test was opted for (a non-parametric equivalent here would have been the Kruskal-Wallis test), there were four major assumptions identified in the previous section. Of these, I thought that "independence of groups" and "independence of observations" were – most probably – met. My doubts about normality, however, remain, as insufficient information is provided in the descriptive statistics reported. Large numbers of participants were used, but these came from intact classes and were not randomly assigned to groups; moreover, the "best" and "worst" performers have already been taken out of the sample. Therefore, I cannot be sure that these are now representative of the population outside the current experimental context. As regards the assumption of equal variance, I am given the s.d. values here, and by squaring these I can see whether the variances are near enough the same. Here the variances range from 190.4 to 125.4. However, since the group sizes are balanced in this design (i.e., 45 participants in each group), any dissimilarity is unlikely to have had a serious effect on outcomes.*

6.  What is your appraisal of any other interpretations that the researcher makes of his or her data in this section?
    *The researcher has limited this section only to the reporting, rather than the interpreting, of results. Presumably, interpretation will be made in the Discussion section.*

7.  What information is made available or can be calculated about effect size of the outcomes?
    *Effect size through strength of association has not been calculated here, but the data made available mean it is only a short calculation away. The advantage of making such a calculation is that I will then know the proportion of the variability in the listening comprehension data that can be accounted for by modified input. You might notice from the F distribution tables provided at the back of the book that, as the number of participants involved in the study increases, it becomes easier to reject the null hypothesis of no-difference between groups. By calculating the effect size, I will be able to judge just how strong such an outcome really is, regardless of the number of participants involved.*
    *Since we have a between-groups and balanced design we can opt for the ω2 formula:*

    *As $\omega^2$ in one-way ANOVA =*

    $$\frac{\text{SS Between groups} - (df \text{ Between groups}) \times \text{MS Within groups}}{\text{SS Total} + \text{MS Within groups}}$$

    *We can plug in the data from the table provided as 1788.911 − 3 x 43.426 (=1658.633)/ 9431.934 + 43.426 (=9475.36) = 0.17. We now know that the effect size, as measured by the strength of association formula, is not strong – we can account for only 17% of the variability in the listening comprehension score by knowing the modified input group data. Despite the apparent weakness here, our interpretation of this outcome depends on the objectives of the researcher and, amongst other considerations, whether he or she had hypothesised or hoped for a better effect than this. In the present case, the previous research cited had been inconclusive: modifying the input seems to help on some occasions and with some students. The findings here do not seem to be any more convincing. Nevertheless, this researcher has chosen to explore the modification of input using different criteria and with beginner-level participants. An argument could have been made here (or in the subsequent discussion) that such an effect size did indeed show an interesting trend, given what is known about the effect of this variable in other circumstances and with other kinds of participant (see below, question 8).*
    *The 83% remaining error in the variability also needs to be addressed here or in the subsequent discussion, although the reader might again usefully form his or her own reactions before reading the researcher's interpretations. After reading the review of the literature, I suggested that the inconclusive findings might also have been due to a number of other intervening factors or "error", such as the material used for listening comprehension, the amount of time studying the language, or the way these participants are normally taught*

*this skill. Although the researcher did not actually calculate the effect size, I might make a note here to see whether he or she suggests these or other further areas for study in the subsequent pages, and based on what evidence.*

8. What initial conclusions do you come to about the practical significance and meaningfulness of these results? Do these coincide with the researcher's interpretation?

*We can begin to think about the practical significance of these findings in terms of what they might mean for the teaching of listening comprehension in this context. The researcher has not informed me of what usually happens in this regard in the participants' normal classes, but – faced with the kind of effect size here – I might imagine he or she would need to experiment with other factors before incorporating the results into any formal teaching programme. Furthermore, there is still the knotty question of whether the kind of listening comprehension tested here (i.e., recall of idea units) is an operational definition that will be useful or acceptable to other teachers and methodologists. Perhaps the author will take this up in more detail in the subsequent section. However, the results do contribute to what I already know about the topic, presenting evidence for the influence of modified input on L2 comprehension.*

*I also need to think about whether the differences revealed here are meaningful in the context of what I have been told so far. In the present case, I suggested that successful listening comprehension may depend much more on the nature of the interaction itself (see above) than on that of the input. If this is so, how far can group data of this kind, based on the results of one text, provide meaningful evidence about the influence of modified input on listening comprehension? Indeed, how far do these data conceal from view certain individual strategies that might be used to help improve comprehension in specific situations? The preamble also suggested that the appraisal of meaningfulness should look to questions such as the procedures used in the measurement of a particular variable. I argued earlier that any such accurate measurement of the effect of a variable on listening comprehension would probably need to obtain data from **all** the participants interacting with **all** three kinds of modified input and across an ample time-span. This is particularly important when the researcher, as here, is interested in discovering which, if any, of the three modified input situations has more influence on listening comprehension outcomes.*

## Observations

Look at each observation marked in this text and decide what kind of pertinent reaction could be made at each point. Help is given in the form of short prompts.

① Why do you think this somewhat higher alpha level was chosen, and might it be based on any previous discussion of the literature?
② Since the *t*-test is used to compare two groups at a time, what is your reaction to this information?

For further practice in appraising this section of the research paper, turn to pages 261–266

# Chapter 9

# Discussion and conclusions

**Before you read this chapter you should familiarize yourself with the previously appraised sections of the paper. Then read this section and the accompanying Observations:**

**Discussion and conclusions 1**

**When you have read a paragraph, stop and write in the *left-hand column* a few words which summarise the gist of that paragraph, to help you understand and focus on what the researcher is saying. Then, in the *right-hand column* write a few words which record your instinctive reactions to what you have just read as if you were talking to the researcher face-to-face. In this worked example, the columns have been filled in to show you how you might go about doing this initial reading task.**

| | | |
|---|---|---|
| *Results support previous findings; software use leads to reduction in errors and better understanding of L2 writing process in specific genres.* | The findings here support results from our previous studies①, wherein we also saw that feedback from the computer brought about a reduction in the number of errors revealed. Since results here showed significant reductions in the test group's errors compared to the control group, it is clear that using such software and its subsequent feedback can serve as the starting point for a better understanding of how students go about writing and the way they do this in specific writing genres. | *Sorry, I don't see the connection – how does the use of the software, as explained here, help us "understand" more about the L2 writing process?* |
| *Separate error profiles showed few differences between groups, but cumulatively test group were better by the end.* | A different profile of participants' errors was presented after each of the five letters written. There were few differences noted in these profiles between the experimental and control groups, although the test group had significantly fewer error types by the end of the study period②. Some of the 45 types monitored by the program showed excellent responses in terms of their reduction. | *How much information was shown us in these "profiles"? Is there any reason why some showed better responses than others?* |

Pedagogical implications

*Advantages for the teacher of writing in large classes: information provided which helps predict student errors means less correction for teacher. Objective is to create more error profiles to help teachers in class preparation.*

As regards teaching practice, there can only be advantages for any teacher of writing in large-class situations like those in Country X ③. It has become clear that, by analysing the kind of information provided by this software, a teacher can obtain valuable information about where his or her students are most likely to commit errors in their writing in these five kinds of genre; consequently, these teachers will feel less weighed down by the amount of correction they normally would have to do. Ideally, what now needs to happen is for research to go on getting more results from more students in more teaching contexts in this country until we have obtained many thousands of profiles, rather than "only" the 374 obtained here. After many years of working with, and obtaining information from, this program, a teacher could then use these profiles to guide him or her in the preparation of classes. It is clear that certain error types are helped by the use of the program, and the teacher can use specially-designed classes to handle the more resistant errors such as those of punctuation and sentence variety in a more traditional way in the class.

*…but this will not help "any teacher of writing" – as you say later, it depends on the kind of writing/genre being produced.*

*How long is "many years"? Are you saying that the eventual benefits of the software are such a long way off?*

Observations

① What more information could have been useful here about these studies?
*It is not immediately clear which study is being referred to. In the literature review, I read about work (References 12 and 13) using computer programs, although I did not read that this involved the kind of feedback mentioned here. Indeed, since these are the only references to previous work using computers in L2 writing in Country X, it would have been interesting to read how the present results compared with these studies.*

② Comment on the use of "significantly" in the context of this study.
*This may be read as indicating that some statistical procedure revealed such differences. However, the Results section only talked of "..errors that were less than the control group's for 32 types" (p. 152). I do recognise, however, that this was a majority of types (out of the 45 monitored by the program). Unfortunately, as the "some" in the next sentence reveals, the feedback can also be said to produce different degrees of response depending on the error.*

③   Has enough information about operational definitions been provided in the paper to sup-
    port this?
    *At the beginning of my appraisal of this paper, I noted that very little was revealed about*
    *what actually constitutes "large-class situations like those in Country X". Clearly, massifi-*
    *cation in classes is highlighted throughout, and the background to the problem and the*
    *problem statement talked of the pressures of getting students to examination levels in L2*
    *proficiency. However, how this translates into actual class numbers and the specific teach-*
    *ing and correcting responsibilities of the instructor is unknown. Consequently, at this*
    *point, it is impossible for an interested reader to compare his or her own research context*
    *with that of the study and decide whether the outcomes reported are, indeed, likely to be*
    *as advantageous.*

## 9.1   Outcomes in terms of the original research questions/hypotheses

This part of the paper highlights the cyclical nature of any research study: what
follows now should be an attempt on the part of the researcher to take the reader
back to the introductory sections of the report and, in a descriptive and interpretative summary, show the extent to which findings have answered the questions or
hypotheses proposed at that juncture. To that end, the reader him or herself will
also need to recall what was said (and appraised) at that point and decide whether
what was argued then has now found an adequate and appropriate response in the
findings and the subsequent discussion and conclusion. We would also be hoping to
see the researcher move beyond the confines of the present research study and show
us how the outcomes fit in to a wider context and contribute to the advancement
of knowledge in the field. With this in mind, we would be interested to read how
the researcher sees their results relating to current knowledge, how this knowledge
might have been improved or modified by what has been learnt, whether these results
might have practical implications for L2 learning, and whether further research is
suggested or recommended as a consequence of what has been revealed. Moreover,
by laying out the implications of the study for current theory and further investigation, the researcher is simultaneously providing the reader with the kind of information that helps him or her advance in their own study of the topic. Bear in mind that
one of our initial objectives in reading the paper in question may well have been to
acquire more background data about a specific aspect of the field, prior to mount-
ing our own study and venturing empirically-based interpretations of a particular,
related language-learning event.

It should already be clear from this introduction that the Discussion and conclusions
section of the paper is a particularly appropriate juncture for both researcher and reader
to be engaged in a tacit exchange of opinion about what has happened, what conclusions

can be drawn from this, and what remains to be done. Therefore, we will want continually to be alert to the theoretical and empirical support for any opinions offered here, as well as to the logic of the manner in which they are expressed. Our own thoughts about the research as a whole will need constantly to be compared with those of the researcher. Such reaction on our part is again best realised through frequent questioning of the text: do we agree with the researcher on the general conclusions to be drawn here? Does a particular claim follow logically from the evidence or support provided? Do we think some results support what has been hypothesised earlier, but others do not? Do we feel that current knowledge in the field – as described in the introductory sections – has been appreciably enhanced by what has been discovered? Do we agree with the researcher about what remains to be done and/or how this should be done? Most of these reactions will implicitly reflect the confidence we have gained in the researcher's work as a result of reading the paper. Apart from the research design and execution itself, this confidence will also be based on the logic and strength of argument with which the researcher seeks to defend the outcomes obtained and the conclusions drawn from them.

### "What conclusions were drawn from the study, and how do these reflect on the original questions and/or hypotheses?"

Because this section is basically interpretative in nature, there is no established sequence as such in the narrative. However, ideally we would be looking to read and appraise a number of different perspectives on the findings. The first of these would be a concluding summary of findings: the reader would want to be clearly informed of what the researcher has learned from the study. This statement would ideally include the responses to the research questions, or the support or non-support of the hypotheses as formed in the introductory section, perhaps in the form of a broad statement rather than a mere repetition of the specific results. As we read this statement, we should also be concerned to see that it is consistent with what we have just read in the Results section. A researcher may include "new" findings in this conclusion and/ or then proceed to over-interpret what the global outcomes mean. Likewise, at some point here, we should expect the researcher appropriately to address any results that have not come out in the way hypothesised or expected. Some kind of explanation might be ventured for these apparent discrepancies, although we should consider such post-hoc explanations only tentative, since they would not have been submitted to the empirical testing involved in the main part of the study. Nevertheless, such suggestions are useful for they could form part of any future research in the area that might seek to clarify the situation more (see below). Finally, once this section of the paper has been digested, we ourselves might want to think back to the reasons for the study as set out in the background to the problem and the problem statement and consider the extent to which findings are now seen to respond to the problems expressed there.

📖   **Now read this worked appraisal of the sample paper:**

1.  What conclusions were drawn from the study, and how do these reflect on the original questions and/or hypotheses?

    *As "...feedback from the computer brought about a reduction in the number of errors revealed", the directional intention towards improvement implicit in the original hypothesis is now said to have been confirmed. While this summary does respond in part to the original statement of intent, I think it might also over-simplify the kind of results obtained. I remember that improvement was noted in both control and experimental groups here, albeit the latter at a faster rate. This some- what unexpected outcome for both groups has not been addressed here or previously in the paper, despite the fact that it apparently detracts somewhat from the perceived effect of the software program (see below, question 2). Observations will also need to be made concerning the extent to which these results shed light on the problems envisaged in the original problem statement (see below).*

## 9.2   Inferences drawn from outcomes

> **"What is your appraisal of the general inferences which the researcher draws from the findings? How do these compare with your own reactions to what you have been told throughout the paper?"**

A central focus in this section will be on what the researcher infers from their find-ings. Indeed, the *APA Publication Manual* encourages researchers at this point to feel free "to examine, interpret, and qualify the results, as well as draw inferences from them." (p. 18). By definition, interpretation will obviously need to go beyond the mere description provided in the previous section. While any interpretations ventured there may have been at a level quite close to the data, now the inferences may involve con-siderably more abstraction, perhaps to the level of a larger theory (see below). We will now want carefully to compare our own cumulative appraisal of what has come out of the research with that of the author's, in particular regarding what happened within the set-up and conduct of the study to account for the findings. It is crucial for the reader appraising such interpretations to learn how to pause in their reading to consider the reasonableness and acceptability of these interpretations given our own reading of the study. In other words, we will need constantly to ask ourselves whether the explanation or interpretation being offered is reasonable in the circumstances of the study and, if necessary, once in the wider perspective. For example, our earlier appraisal of the sta-tistical procedures used in a paper may implicitly have endorsed the results obtained as a consequence of using that procedure. Nevertheless, the way the researcher then goes about *using* these outcomes in their own interpretations of data will still need to be examined. While we may agree with the results themselves, it is perfectly legitimate to disagree about what they mean. No findings speak for themselves; the researcher will need to interpret these for us and, almost inevitably, will do so from their own particular perspective. The angle from which he or she reads into these data will, by definition, not be the only one available.

A researcher may give us to understand that his or her results are unlikely to have been affected by any intervening variable or other more observable feature, but we ourselves might have identified certain threats on this score in an earlier appraisal. We might then wish to challenge that interpretation of outcomes on the grounds of its acceptability. Similarly, reasoned speculation is to be expected at this point but, as a result of our reading, we might find it *un*reasonable to see it suggested that results from a small group of intact classes in one school can be appropriately generalised to other schools in that country, let alone further afield. Our interaction with the researcher and his or her interpretation of the evidence should also mean that we are actively engaged in looking for alternative explanations: we might read of the improvement noted between pre- and post-test measures of L2 proficiency but feel that this may be just as easily explained by parallel language-learning experiences as by any special treatment the participants had been receiving.

---

📖 **Now read this worked appraisal of the sample paper:**

2. What is your appraisal of the general inferences which the researcher draws from the findings? How do these compare with your own reactions to what you have been told throughout the paper?

*I wondered how justified is the inference that computer feedback "…brought about a reduction…", since it could be understood from this that the software has actually caused the outcomes. Indeed, previous references to this software in the literature review also speak of a program that "produced" (p. 21) overall improvement. However, the research design employed simply does not allow us to say for certain what led to any improvement. Any of the following factors, or some subtle combination of them, could have intervened in the experimental group performance: attitudes towards using the computer, the method of using the software feedback, the amount of time each student interacted with the feedback, the personal teacher feedback obtained, and even the nature of normal class teaching. Also, the understanding I gained in the Results section was that improvement has come about basically through the amount of contact with the feedback, rather than the quality of that contact. Finally, I wonder how far the overall success of the program may be being judged as a result of the effect on relatively few error types, rather than across all 45 original categories.*

*The researcher also goes on to widen the perspective of his or her interpretation by suggesting that "since" there were significant reductions in error frequency, the software and its accompanying feedback can help us to understand "how students go about writing and the way they do this in specific writing genres". I do not see a logical link between the reason (i.e., "significant reductions in error" as a result of using the feedback) and the claim that we are thereby able to have more insight into the individual writing process. These error frequency counts tell me something about the product of the group writing process; I do not see what has been learnt here about the way individual writers actually process errors or go about correcting, for example.*

## 9.3   Outcomes related to literature review

**"In what ways are the findings related to current theoretical and empirical knowledge on the topic?"**

Finally, the interpretation of any findings could now move away from the confines of the immediate research context to relate the results and interpretation of these to the existing theoretical and empirical literature, much of which will already have been referred to in the previous review. The distinctive cyclical development of a research study and the cumulative nature of research itself can signal a need now to re-assess this literature taking into consideration the present findings, particularly literature cited as part of the background justification for the study in question. For example, if we were told then that gaps existed in current knowledge, we should be interested to know how far these have now been filled by these data. Has consistent or conflicting information been added? Any apparent conflicts or inconsistencies noted with this research should not be left without explanation, of course, and we will again want to consider the adequacy of these clarifications. Indeed, if the researcher does not re-address this work, we might usefully consider what was described in the review of the literature and attempt ourselves to assess the contribution of the present findings. Any pertinent knowledge we might possess of the current state of the field might also alert us to any intrinsic bias here. There may be a temptation for the researcher to seek to defend a particular position suggested by their findings by only citing the literature that supports such a view. If, on the other hand, we have been told of, or are aware of, opposing viewpoints or conflicting evidence, such information could be exploited to enable us better to place results in their true perspective.

In many cases, such considerations of past and present findings might also help the researcher and reader to broaden the interpretation of the immediate findings to place them in the context of any larger theoretical problems addressed by the project. In this way, we will be better able to assess the contribution of the work to current thinking on the subject and/or link the results to other areas that are theoretically or empirically related to the study. Such attempts to extract meaning and principles from findings are especially useful to the field in studies that have found their starting point or rationale in a particular theory and/or have set out to provide contributory data to confirm or refute this. We may remember that one aspect of our earlier appraisal of the background to the problem and the problem statement was precisely the likely contribution of the study to current theory. At that point we emphasised – amongst other things – the need for findings to have the potential to help us "better evaluate a number of previous explanations or models" (p. 15). Then, we were looking for references to prior thought or previous theories that directed us to where the present research would fit in with what is already known and, potentially, contribute with further evidence. Now, it might be useful to see this contribution made evident by the researcher, integrating findings into an already-existing theory or model or using them to formulate an original theory or model. Indeed, one of the advantages for the interested reader of a researcher integrating their findings into existing theoretical knowledge is that theories tend to be heuristic: they serve to generate ideas and, by integrating outcomes within existing models or using expected or unexpected outcomes to form new suppositions and hypotheses, theory can stimulate the future research needed to test them.

---

📖 **Now read this worked appraisal of the sample paper:**

3. In what ways are the findings related to current theoretical and empirical knowledge on the topic?

*There is no direct re-assessment of the literature in the light of these findings, beyond a claim that the authors' previous findings in Country X have thereby been supported (see below, Observation 1). I was told that computer-generated feedback had received "positive results" with L1 speakers, and clearly these outcomes will now provide more support from an L2 context. The author also mentioned the need for data from "EFL/ESL students over longer periods of study", but the relevance of this longitudinal study is not subsequently elaborated upon here.*

*The researcher does not take up his or her own suggestion that these data might contribute to what is already known about computer-assisted language learning (CALL) and L2 writing. Perhaps these findings could have been related to current theory about the process nature of L2 writing. For example, in a process model, error correction can take place at any stage in the process of composition, rather than only once writing has been completed. It might have been interesting to know whether the software and subsequent feedback provided "as they are working" (see p. 63) encouraged the experimental group to proofread for errors only before handing in their finished work or to undertake more subtle revisions while they were actually writing.*

---

## 9.4 Limitations and future research

> **"What limitations or weaknesses have you or the researcher identified, and how might any future research seek to contribute further to what has been revealed in the study?"**

As we mentioned above, as readers, we will also implicitly have been noting any shortcomings and weaknesses in the study during our reading and appraisal. Now is the time to recall any of the outstanding concerns (particularly those pertaining to reliability and internal/external validity threats) and compare them with the researcher's own views of any limitations on the results obtained or deficiencies in design. The *APA Publication Manual* recommends researchers include in this section "[remarks]…on certain shortcomings of the study, but not [to] dwell…on every flaw. Negative results should be accepted as such without an undue attempt to explain them away." (p. 19). Such statements by the researcher are not to be seen as a signal that the study is flawed, nor their absence interpreted as an indication that the researcher thinks it is perfect! Quite the reverse, in fact, for they demonstrate a researcher who is able to stand back from the work and, with hindsight, recognise where things could have been improved.

It can be safely assumed that no empirical research is perfect. As interested readers and/or prospective researchers, we have much to learn by seeing these shortcomings fully discussed and explained (rather than "explained away", as the *Manual* puts it!) and then followed by descriptive proposals (to which we will need to respond) for additional research which perhaps seeks to correct these deficiencies, clarify any ambiguous results, or test any new hypotheses that are suggested by these findings.

Aside from this perceived need for further research consequent upon inherent shortcomings in the study, we would also be interested to read suggestions that point the way ahead for any further study and research in the particular field. By considering what could have improved the design of the research, by looking for alternative explanations to outcomes, and by comparing evidence from previous studies or existing theories, the researcher may now be in a better position to tell us where to go from here. This is, potentially, one of the most productive sections of the paper for the reader: he or she can use these suggestions (together with their own ideas) as a guide towards acquiring further knowledge about the topic and, perhaps, as a stimulus for their own research project. Clearly, however, any recommendations we read or suggest should be seen to have developed logically from the findings obtained in the present study. The discussion itself would hopefully have motivated the reader and the researcher to consider questions that remain unanswered along with the kinds of research that would help provide responses to them. When appraising the author's own suggestions, we might hope for something more precise than a sweeping statement suggesting future research should, say, try this out with more mature non-native students and over a longer period of time. The reader and the field are much better served if we are given some guidance by the person making the recommendation about *how* he or she hypothesises any future outcomes might vary with these kinds of participants and *why* more engagement with this population should prove fruitful.

Often, as a result of our reading, the data and the subsequent discussion fail to convince us that there is adequate support for the researcher's position at the end of the paper. In the absence of specific recommendations from the researcher, we might ourselves – as part of our appraisal – then consider replication of the study, perhaps with different participants, a modified data collection procedure, or design – all with the aim of obtaining more evidence for or against the researcher's conclusions. Conversely, the way ahead may be illuminated by further study of certain aspects of a particular L2 learning phenomenon brought to light as a result of our reading of the present research. For example, as a result of statistical analyses of data, a researcher might have shown that participants who have been taught L2 pronunciation in language-laboratory classes acquire better pronunciation skills than those taught with conventional classroom methods. However, as we ourselves read these outcomes, we might have made a mental note about the need for more study of the way participants actually acquire pronunciation in the language laboratory. In other words, we are not questioning the outcomes here and/or suggesting replication; our appraisal of what happened has sent us thinking about discovering how these participants might have been processing what they heard to account for their subsequent improvement.

> 📖  **Now read this worked appraisal of the sample paper:**
>
> 4.  What limitations or weaknesses have you or the researcher identified, and how might any future research seek to contribute further to what has been revealed in the study?
>
>    *There is no statement here about possible limitations of the results or weaknesses in the study. My reading of the text indicates a continuing desire to generalise outcomes: for example, "it is **clear**.... can serve as the starting point for a better understanding of how **students**...." or that there are "... advantages for **any** teacher of writing in **large class situations like those** in Country X." (my emphasis). However, external validity threats were apparently not met in this design (see p. 76), specifically with regard to participant selection and assignment to groups. In such circumstances, the findings could, at most, only be applied to groups of a similar nature and provenance and in a similar context in Country X.*
>
>    *A number of problems were envisaged with regard to history factors affecting the sample. In particular, it remains unclear to me if (and how) the researcher had been able to ensure that the only L2 writing performed, and the only feedback available on participants' writing, during the whole six-month period of the study actually came from the specific procedures in the experiment.*
>
>    *Little information has become available about the functioning of the software. I have argued that any hypothesised benefit from using the software might, therefore, be very much dependent on individual interaction with it. There is also little address of the results that showed the control group improving over the experimental group. It may be of concern, for example, that three of the most-encountered errors across classes and assignments reported in the descriptive statistics (Table 1: "Punctuation", "Sentence variety", and "Typical") ended up registering higher incidence rates in the experimental group than the control group.*
>
>    *The researcher sees the way ahead for further research as "getting more results from more students in more teaching contexts in this country until we have obtained many thousands of profiles...". I would like to have seen some specification of what teaching contexts should ideally be studied, and why. For example, does this mean the researcher sees teaching context as potentially intervening in the perceived link between software use and improvement? I also think this software offers the opportunity for researchers to obtain more specific information on individual writing performance and error correction by concentrating on the individual processing of the feedback, rather than solely on the end product in terms of error frequency.*

## 9.5   Practical implications

> **"What is your appraisal of any practical inferences which the researcher draws from the study in terms of pedagogical implications or recommendations?"**

L2 learning is essentially an applied field of research and, as such, studies conducted in this area could helpfully generate some recommendations for modification in educational practice. It should go without saying, of course, that any such proposals for the application of findings must be seen to proceed logically from the actual results obtained or from the general theory or model to which these results have now been applied. Once again, there may be the temptation to seek to recommend the application of findings to other participants or other language-learning settings without having minimally pre-pared for such generalisation in the research design itself. Therefore, we would want to think about any such pedagogical implications carefully. This is particularly the case when a novel methodology, test, textbook, or other learning approach has been the subject of experimental study in the research. In the light of what seem to be significant results from some innovative intervention in the language learning process it is, indeed, appealing to wish to tell everybody the good news and recommend we all take up the new approach as soon as possible.

Nevertheless, much of the research we read will have been carried out in rela-tively small-scale language-learning operations with few, if any, guarantees of adequate external validity. In such cases, enthusiastic pedagogical recommendations will need to be tempered with the knowledge that there are many, very diverse, L2 learning con-texts throughout the world. It would be presumptuous on the part of the researcher to think that his or her intervention will bring about the same success in any situation, let alone to make recommendations about how each such context might best be modified by taking these findings into account. Indeed, many such specific pedagogical implica-tions are often best levelled nearer home, the researcher directing the more extensive recommendations of the research towards what still remains to be discovered about a particular phenomenon in the present context before any firm proposals for general practice are made. That the reader is not cognisant of the specific language-learning context to which the results are to be applied should not be an obstacle to our apprais-ing (or making) these recommendations on the basis of their common sense, per-ceived usefulness, or workability.

For example, we might consider carefully a proposal for introducing to beginner-level students a previously successful training course that taught dictionary-use strategies to L2 intermediate-level participants. Depending on a variety of other factors, we may feel the way an L2 beginner needs to go about using the dictionary (and the type of dictionary itself) may be rather different from that of an intermediate student, and the training might need to be suitably modified before wider application in the context. Likewise, the fact that a study has revealed significant evidence that shows participants with home access to the Internet enjoying more success as L2 learners may not, in itself, be sufficient even to recommend the immediate massive acquisition and incorporation of on-line computers in language learning classes at a particular school. It may well be that some of the projected recipients of the scheme will need non-specific computer training prior to their using the machines for any explicit language-learning use. Any hypothesised improvements in L2 learning as a result of using the computers may be dependent on how successful this initial training turns out to be. Finally, the researcher should be seen to limit his or her proposals to those that follow appropriately from the present research context. We might want to question, for example, an unqualified sug-gestion that a particularly successful children's beginners L2 learning programme might be equally successful with young adult beginners.

Earlier, I emphasized the fact that the tacit exchange of opinion between the researcher and the reader – which has, in fact, been the mainstay of our appraisal method throughout the paper – should be even further stimulated by this discussion of results. However, our understanding and appreciation of the appropriateness and logic behind the researcher's conclusions inevitably depends on the way those opinions are expressed. Our appraisal of a paper has assumed throughout the need to address the precision with which arguments, facts, and findings are communicated; however, arguably, here more than anywhere else in the paper, we must pay particular attention to the language used to present a case or conclusion. It is the reader's responsibility to think about the argument being presented and then evaluate it. This whole process is less straightforward than it may sound, since it requires us to look rather more closely than we might normally do at the words and expressions used to make claims, present evidence for those claims, and draw conclusions. We will need to be able to identify the strengths and weaknesses of an argument in order to appraise its significance. We will need to establish which elements of the argument proposed are useful and which might need to be discarded or re-phrased. By so doing, we are performing a useful service both to the author and the field and will perhaps be able to re-formulate what has been proposed to produce a new slant on the topic and, thereby, point the direction to new research in the area. Nevertheless, our concern should always be to focus on the kernel of what is being proposed rather than the person making it; the convention in appraisal of another person's work and opinion is that this is treated with due respect at all times.

However, it is worth making the effort here because we will then find it easier to appraise insight, strength, inadequacy, lack of plausibility, or even fallacy in the arguments or conclusions being presented. If we do decide that something has been found wanting in an argument, this should then be explained in a way which makes it clear *what* we have found wrong. There follow a number of typical textual elements of this academic style of writing which may help in an appraisal:

–   There is a natural tendency to hedge one's bets when presenting conclusions or implications based on empirical data. We might read that something will "probably" happen, that "some" language learners will benefit from a particular methodology, or that "generally" L2 learners will demonstrate this or another problem. These are arguments presented with qualifiers, words that serve to limit the scope of a claim in order to make it more immediately acceptable and delimit its application. There is nothing inherently wrong with this, and the research design used may actually recommend such a stance, but it does mean that we will have to assess the implications of such constraints for the strength of the conclusions being drawn.

–   Look out in the text for words that are used to structure an argument and adopt a posture. It is essential to have the structure of an argument clear in our minds before it is appraised. Basically, we should be looking to ponder both the conclusion drawn and the premises behind it: what needs to believed, or what evidence would we need to have to justify our accepting the conclusion? To be able to do this, we need to decide what can reasonably be admitted as evidence. These standards are not universal, but rather subject specific in the present case. Our appraisal of what we have read so far in the paper will be our principle guide in deciding upon the strength of argument here.

– Words such as "thus", "therefore", "hence", or "consequently" can be used to link evidence with claims and suggest inference, reason, and conclusions. Isolate the sentences in which these occur and consider how far the conclusion actually follows from the premise. Taking the conclusion expressed by these words, stop and ask what reasons are presented in the text for believing this conclusion, or why we are being asked to accept the conclusion. Typically, look out for words like "because", "since…", "it follows…", and so on as introductions to reasons. By being suitably sceptical at this point, we will be in a better position to reveal mistaken assumptions, faults in reasoning, and misleading notions in arguments, all of which will help us to build up an appropriate response to what we are reading.

– Look at the claim being made and try to appraise it from a number of angles. For example, call attention to any vagueness in what is being claimed, often observed as a result of referring to something without clearly defining it, or defining something in one way early in the paper and in another way now. Similarly, consider the response to any apparent attempts to convince the reader of the reasonableness of an argument by exaggeration or over-statement. For example, we might follow a particular claim throughout the paper and see whether or not it differs each time it is presented, particularly when the same evidence is being used to support it.

– We should consider the consequences for any conclusions drawn of other typical inaccuracies when constructing arguments. Sometimes, authors over-generalise in their use of language: they may use "all" language learners when they mean "some", or "most" L2 students, when they would rather mean "those participants I have studied". This kind of careless over-generalisation has the effect of implicitly discarding or underestimating any contradictory examples – which the reader may then identify. Conversely, we might often need to highlight arguments based on restricted instances of a particular phenomenon. In this case, the researcher may be building up a shaky proposal, as it is founded on unusual or unrepresentative examples. Care also needs to be taken when appraising conclusions presented with the appeal to a respected authority. An author should indeed tell us if their results mirrored those reported by a well-known specialist (or any other researcher, for that matter). It is quite another thing to suggest that the conclusion or proposal gains in strength *because* some respected author has reached the same conclusion or suggested a similar stance. An argument should be able to stand up on its own because of the evidence produced, rather than because any number of colleagues have implicitly backed this up. Finally, we might also want to decide on the appropriateness of adopting radical positions on the outcomes. An author may mistakenly think a conclusion becomes more acceptable because he or she ignores the centre-ground standpoint on the data and, instead, focuses only on the extreme perspectives.

---

📖    **Now read this worked appraisal of the sample paper:**
5.    What is your appraisal of any practical inferences which the researcher draws from the study in terms of pedagogical implications or recommendations?
*The practical conclusion drawn is that the software helps the teacher because the analysis of its outcomes provides him or her with "..valuable information about where...students are most likely to commit errors...in these five kinds of genre". The implication is that the usefulness resides in its capacity to predict error occurrence. However, what I have read here are descriptions of these particular students' errors using the software; no evidence has been presented that suggests the software can accurately predict errors. Moreover, although large numbers of participants have been used here, they are all studying in one specific area, so their results can hardly be said to help other teachers in other situations to predict the errors of their own students.*

*Interestingly, the researcher goes on to conclude ("...consequently....") that this feature of the software is where teachers themselves will most benefit. As early as the abstract, the researcher talked of an aim to "alleviate teacher obligation in the correction of written work" in large classes. My suggestion was that the instrument might be relatively effective in alleviating part of the problem, but not solving it. What follows here may arguably signal more work for the teacher: apparently "more resistant" errors – upon which the program seemed to have less effect – are recommended to be the subject of more detailed "traditional" attention in class, anyway.*

---

## 9.6    Assessment of overall confidence

Throughout this book I have emphasized the need for the researcher to help us build up confidence in the study being described. This has been highlighted in a number of ways in each section, and our reactions to what we have read now need to be collated for us to establish what I described in the *Introduction* as "the amount of confidence we might reasonably have both in the findings and the interpretations made from these" – in other words, an overall confidence level in the work.

**"Assess your overall confidence in the paper you have read."**

The above questions on the theoretical and practical inferences of the study should have already encouraged you both to think about the researcher's own interpretation of events and compare them with our own and also to assess the strength of argument with which the researcher defends the outcomes obtained and the conclusions drawn from them. However, our assessment of overall confidence should be the result of a cumulative process engaged in throughout our reading and, now, we might usefully recall, and reflect on, some of the most important confidence indicators encountered up to this point in the text and which help us arrive at an overall judgement:

- Has the problem statement and/or have the research questions turned out to be a comprehensive statement of what you have now read? In other words, has the original objective and/or commitment we read here been fulfilled? You might ask yourself whether it has since become clear that other areas of study are involved to a large extent or, perhaps, that other dependent variables than those mentioned have played a key role in the paper (see pp. 11–16).
- Has an acceptable case for the present study been made in the review of the literature by means of sufficiently critical and analytical engagement with the previous litera-ture on the subject? Of particular interest here was the way in which any apparent conflicting evidence from studies was handled by the author (see pp. 22–28).
- Have any independent, dependent and intervening variables and levels of these been satisfactorily identified and described? We need to have been able to follow which variables play which role in the study so that we can better understand the significance of any observed influence or relationship (see pp. 45–51).
- Have the constructs used been satisfactorily defined and in a way which allows them to be studied, examined and measured here, and replicated in future work? Operational definitions of key constructs or concepts to be studied are understood to be the way the researcher has chosen to delineate these aspects. Thus, now that we have read the whole paper, are we able to agree that such definitions have been maintained in the subsequent sections? (see pp. 52–55).
- Has the internal or external validity of the study been established and have any poten-tial threats to either been satisfactorily addressed? We asked ourselves during our reading whether key components such as the participant selection, research design, materials or procedure used could now be seen as valid since, if they are not, we can have little confidence in the findings obtained from the use of these components. Has the researcher addressed questions of reliability in data measurement and any poten-tial or actual threats to validity in a satisfactory way? (see pp. 72–76 and 78–83).
- Are you satisfied that correct ethical principles have been followed throughout? Here you should consider not only the recommendations in official policy docu-ments such as those mentioned on p. 99, but also what we might see as the basic principles of participation, anonymity, prior information given and confidential-ity of data obtained (see pp. 99–102).
- Does the kind and amount of detail included in the results/data analysis allow you to have confidence in the claims made? In looking for more confidence in any statistical evidence provided I suggested we might well look beyond the detailed tables and appraise "what has happened prior to the feeding in of data into the machine" as the basis for our confidence-building. I suggested, for example,

looking closely at any descriptive statistics provided to confirm the appropriateness of the analysis undertaken. As part of our confidence report, we would also want to assess the extent to which any assumptions associated with this procedure were apparently taken into account (see pp. 138–145 and pp. 153–162).

–  In any relevant statistical procedures, has the interpretation of outcomes been executed satisfactorily, and has a suitable statistic of effect and/or reliability been cited? Our overall confidence in a paper will clearly be boosted if we see that the statistical outcomes presented have been interpreted in a sound and logical manner. A number of aspects were mentioned in the text, but we would be interested in seeing how eventual significance levels have been addressed and explained (see pp. 162–178). Secondly, we emphasised the importance of being provided with some sort of statistic to take us beyond the main significance level, enabling us to estimate, for example, the size of the effect of the independent variable or the strength of association between variables (see pp. 179–183).

–  Given your reactions above, where do you feel the study had its principal weaknesses and strengths? Do you agree with the limitations of the study as expressed by the researcher and the way forward in terms of the theoretical and practical recommendations made?

---

📖  **Now read this worked appraisal of the sample paper:**

6.  Assess your overall confidence in the paper you have read.

*The problem statement was not clear in the opening section but the intention to demonstrate improvement has been achieved – albeit with some degree of doubt on my part since improvement was across both groups. Similarly, the hypothesis was imprecise, and I was left in doubt whether this would be a descriptive or a comparative study. The text confirms it was a comparative study but several doubts remain about the execution and analysis (see below). In the literature review, I remarked that there was no critical address of the literature and it was unclear how the present study was to help the field move on from its present state of knowledge. There were hints that previous studies lacked better "reliability and validity" but the problems were not specified. Variable measurement was not made explicit enough but subsequent procedures make it fairly clear what independent/dependent variables were used although intervening variables are not considered. Operational definitions were unclear throughout the study, which also makes replication difficult. Issues concerning validity remained throughout my reading, most noticeably in questions of internal validity such as initial equality of participants and the fact that generalization to other students studying other subjects was thought to be inadvisable. The freedom to participate and the guarantee of anonymity were not made clear in the text. Results were presented in quite a detailed way, but a number of questions I had formed in my previous reading remained unanswered in this section. I also felt the probability level accepted in this analysis did not give me confidence in the success of the software. Similarly, I was not happy that some descriptive measures were not reported and doubts remain about the normality of the sample and equal variances. Results from the t-test were not clear to see and the specific t-test used was not identified and so there is no way of knowing if the most powerful procedure was used here. In general, too much work of interpreting the data had to be done by me rather than reading detailed explanations from the researcher.*

> *No effect size or power statistic was calculated. No limitations or weaknesses in the study are suggested by the author but, overall, and although large numbers of participants have been involved, I feel the study presents many weaknesses in key areas of confidence building and, crucially as regards the aims of the research, the design of materials and the way these were used by the groups does not allow the researcher to pinpoint with any certainty what led to any improvement (see below).*

7.  Are there any additional points raised during your appraisal of the paper that you would like to have seen discussed in this section?
    *I did wonder whether the program devised by the author was itself bringing about an effect on error frequency or whether this effect was in some way due to the addition of the parsing program Grammatik©. The way the two programs differed and were subsequently integrated has never been clarified for the reader. Since very little information is given about the specially-designed software itself, it remains unclear what the combined effect of these two programs actually was. I also questioned earlier what feedback a computer might usefully give, beyond indicating the error and, perhaps, providing the correct version. I wondered whether future research with this instrument might usefully consider studying how far a combination of machine response and directed individual "traditional" teacher feedback could bring about improvement.*

## Worked sample appraisal

### Discussion and conclusions 2

1.  Before working through this part of the paper, you should re-read the previously-appraised sections of this study.
2.  When you have read a paragraph, stop and write in the *left-hand column* a few words which summarise the gist of that paragraph, to help you understand and focus on what the researcher is saying. Then, in the *right-hand column* write a few words which record your instinctive reactions to what you have just read as if you were talking to the researcher face-to-face.

| | | |
|---|---|---|
| | These findings do not reflect previous research in the area. Researcher 7 (1990) and Researcher 5 (1980) both suggested that the most important tool in aiding listening comprehension was to be found in the pauses. Researcher 9 (1988) and Researcher 2 (1985) both came to the conclusion that speed was the most telling feature. The present findings indicate modifying the input helps beginners' listening comprehension, and that modifying syntax has a significant effect on listening comprehension at | |

the beginner level. Speed and pauses, on the other hand, did not reveal any significant differences.

However, I identify one specific limitation on these data as a consequence of the research design. The version with modified syntax might have been made easier to comprehend than the control version because of the redundancy incorporated. More research clearly needs to be undertaken so that the field is informed about the following questions:

– Which specific features of syntax actually contribute to improving beginners' listening comprehension?
– Do adjustments in lexis and semantics aid listening comprehension for such students?
– Are the present findings replicated for higher level students? ①

There is important information here to contribute to the current debates about L2 acquisition and L2 teaching. It has been shown that modifications of syntax are easy to implement ② and potentially significantly assist non-native speakers ③ in receiving the input in a way that helps them acquire the L2 more successfully. Moreover, these outcomes provide further examples to add to the growing body of knowledge about what comprehensible input consists of. ④

3. **Read again the relevant section in the chapter, and then attempt to answer these questions. Finally, compare your responses to mine.**

1. What conclusions were drawn from the study, and how do these reflect on the original questions and/or hypotheses?
   *The summary statement of findings is embedded here in the first paragraph and states that "…modifying syntax has a significant effect on listening comprehension at the beginner*

*level. Speed and pauses…did not reveal any significant differences". Although eyeballing of the descriptive results tended to confirm this, the use of the ANOVA and post-hoc test still left us in some doubt about the exact location and significance of any differences (see p. 203). In general, these conclusions correspond to the original research questions put. The background to the problem addressed the need for more information about how "conscious language alterations" might affect comprehension at this level, and these findings will contribute interesting data to the debate. How far these data will help us understand the way L2 acquisition itself is affected – as was also suggested at that point in the paper – is more open to debate (see below).*

2.   What is your appraisal of the general inferences which the researcher draws from the findings? How do these compare with your own reactions to what you have been told throughout the paper?

*No initial interpretation of results was made in the previous section, and little more is ventured at this point. I read that "the present findings indicate modifying the input helps beginners' listening comprehension". Certainly, descriptive statistics indicated that all three modes of presentation resulted in higher scores than those of the unmodified control group. However, again, the statistical significance of these differences has not been accurately reported, so I cannot be sure of the real extent of the help provided by such modified input. Secondly, the overt generalising tone of this interpretation is not warranted in such a design. I had previously noted that the assumption of normality was apparently not met here and that the parametric test used for analysis was, therefore, inappropriate. There were, moreover, other elements of the research design that did not support such generalisation (see Procedures and research design 3, Questions 5–8). The researcher wisely uses the word "indicate" (i.e., rather than "prove" or "show") to describe the possible benefits offered here by modified input. Our own calculation of the effect size of this variable (p. 204) showed that only 17% of the variability in the listening comprehension scores could be accounted for by knowing the modified input group. It might also be worth reminding ourselves at this point of our previous reservations about the definition of "listening comprehension" in this study (p. 60). You might remember that what was measured and, therefore, "helped" by modifying the input in this case was the amount of "idea units" recalled. This was, I suggested, only one element of L2 listening comprehension (see below, question 4).*

*It is also appropriate to remind ourselves that the link between modified input and effects on listening comprehension may not be a clear-cut one here. The researcher does not point to any possible contributory factors, but I had suggested that features inherent to the materials – such as the medium used for communication, the vocabulary range of the input, or the instructions given the participants prior to recall – might all have played their part in how much was remembered. I also ventured an alternative explanation of results in that the modifications present in the texts (pp. 90–92) would have led to all three versions being produced at a slower speed. My suggestion was that it might have been such overall speed reductions that brought about any differences, rather than the specific modifications themselves.*

3.   In what ways are the findings related to current theoretical and empirical knowledge
     on the topic?

*The researcher begins the section referring the present findings back to some of those cited
in the literature review, concluding that – unlike previous studies – speed and pauses did
not have any "significant effect" on comprehension. At this point, I would be looking for
some attempt to explain this apparent conflict, but this is not addressed. If we look back to
our appraisal of this section, our overall reaction to the literature was that few clear trends
had been identified. In that sense, these results might be thought only to add to the existing conflict! On the other hand, it would appear from the literature review that little, if any,
prior work had been done with beginner-level L2 students. Although this description of
level has been the subject of some doubt in our appraisal (pp. 87–88), the findings might
have been usefully compared to Researcher 6's work, wherein the present researcher had
previously criticised the weaknesses resulting from the heterogeneous participant selection
(p. 31). Furthermore, the researcher can specifically challenge Researcher 4's hypothesis that
pauses are important as "listeners need time to process what they hear" on the grounds
that syntax was shown to be the telling feature with these beginners, and not pauses. Similarly, these findings from a different proficiency level and L2, and following Researcher's
9's suggestions as regards the simplification of syntax, do provide more insight into what
specific elements of syntax may be most susceptible to easier comprehension at this level
of L2 Spanish learning.*

*The researcher made the point earlier that current theory behind communicative meth-
odology underlines the importance of the negotiation of meaning between interlocutors
through comprehensible input. I suggested (p. 18) that this study's findings might potentially provide more insight into how input becomes more comprehensible. However, I then
read that input was artificially manipulated beforehand; the researcher did not study live
interactions in a way in which he or she could state with confidence how input was being
negotiated. I would question, therefore, the extent to which the data add to "the growing
body of knowledge about what comprehensible input consists of". Moreover, what the
listeners themselves did to make input more comprehensible has not been the subject of
study (see below, question 6).*

*The researcher then returns to his or her original idea (p. 17) that such modifica-
tions may actually aid L2 acquisition, since what the listener comprehends encourages
this. As I mentioned earlier in the appraisal, it was always going to be difficult to provide data from a cross-sectional sample that supported such an idea. I certainly cannot
hypothesise from these data on the way "non-native speakers receive the input" and,
therefore, whether this "helps them acquire the L2 more successfully". I simply do not
know what these participants did with the input to recall what they did, and I remain
unaware of whether the end result will be more successful acquisition. On the other
hand, there might have been a case here for the researcher to call for further research
over longer periods of study with a different form of data collection, which investigates
what these participants actually do acquire as a result of longer periods of exposure to
such modified input.*

4. What limitations or weaknesses have you or the researcher identified, and how might any further research seek to improve upon what has been revealed in the study?

*Only one limitation is recognised by the author: better results from the modified syntax version might have come about because of the redundancy introduced as a consequence of the modifications. I had also made the observation that all the modified versions might have become easier – irrespective of the specific modification incorporated – as a result of slowing down the delivery (see above, question 2). On the face of it, however, it would seem difficult to control for this variable in any future studies or replications. The open-endedness of the modified-input variable itself (we could, after all, be studying the effect on L2 listening comprehension of an infinite number of speed and/or syntax variations) suggests that further research might more usefully study how far the effect of such modifications is dependent on person- and context-related variables (see below, question 6).*

*A major concern in our appraisal has been with the possible weaknesses in the procedures used, and with the validity of the test instrument itself. In other words, did this succeed in accurately describing what it was designed to describe. Firstly, concern was expressed about the fact that the pre-test used to establish equality of performance in listening comprehension did not test the same kind of understanding as in the experiment itself. Consequently, there may also have been abnormalities in the eventual population selected (pp. 87–88). Secondly, the instructions given participants may have limited the validity of eventual outcomes. I was not told the amount of time participants had to write down their recalls, nor whether they were informed of any specific time limit. I hypothesised, however, that this may have affected how much was actually presented on paper for scoring (p. 130). Similarly, the choice of what was written down as a recall was suggested to have then depended on the ease with which the participants could translate the element from Spanish to English in this hypothetical time period (p. 131). I also debated whether asking participants to recall "any single thing they could remember from the tape" (p. 131) made the exercise a valid test of whether a participant had actually comprehended what had been heard.*

*As regards reliability, there have to remain doubts about the test instrument itself, since I am not told of any piloting or formal reliability testing – neither of the instrument nor the scorers (p. 132). I also expressed my worries about whether such a procedure is likely to obtain similar results across different populations when the comprehension process itself may be so person- and context-dependent.*

*The researcher sets an agenda for future research that – as often happens – tends to assume that the present study has enough internal validity to recommend moving on forthwith from these outcomes to other studies with other populations, or to the study of specific features of the modifications themselves. The question the reader needs to ask him- or herself is whether they are sufficiently convinced by what has led up to these results to accept such an advance. However promising such studies could be, the reader might feel that the present research needs first to be replicated in other situations and/ or with corrections to the design so that the conclusions may be further verified. How useful is the mere accumulation of more knowledge about what makes input comprehensible when there remain doubts about what we already know? In the present case, there have been interesting findings made that add to what has already been discovered. However, the conclusions drawn are based – for the most part – on a low effect size (see below) and also need to be tempered with the knowledge that lack of details about the method and procedures used has itself placed limits on what the reader can understand from these interpretations. For example, more information was called for about the age range of participants or other FL knowledge (pp. 87–88), a fuller description of the way modifications were carried out, and further information about how typical this kind of exercise was for these students (p. 88).*

*Since our calculation of effect size revealed 83% of the variability unaccounted for by the modification variable (p. 204), there still needs to be study of what else might be bringing about any differences between the groups. I suggested that future replications might consider factors such as the material used for comprehension or the individual strategies used to recall or comprehend the text (see below). Our appraisal also helped us suggest adjustments to the design that might throw more light on the findings. There is an argument, for example, that more prolonged observation of participants might lead to more reliable evidence of the long-term benefits of modified input on comprehension. Post-test interviews were suggested as a means of finding out more about what participants really comprehended of the text, and the strategies they used. A more complex ANOVA design was proposed by which comprehension could be compared across versions and proficiency levels or suggestions made about which combinations of variables best predict performance (using regression formulae).*

*Finally, the preamble to this section mentioned how our reading of the discussion or conclusion might call to mind other aspects of the L2 learning experience under study that could prove of interest to follow up. Thus, as I read the results of applying these modifications, I found myself thinking about the critical role memory must play in any recall of the text and, specifically, about studying the kind of L2 linguistic features these participants may be consciously or unconsciously focussing on to complete the task successfully.*

5.  What is your appraisal of any practical inferences which the researcher draws from the study in terms of pedagogical implications or recommendations?
    *No specific recommendations for educational practice are made; indeed, there has been little, if any, information about how Spanish listening comprehension is currently taught here. Consequently, there is little basis upon which the reader might assess any such proposals. The assumption behind the original contribution to practice was that, by finding out about how input is made more comprehensible, we could help teachers and materials writers in their presentation of language in the classroom. Having said this, the effect size obtained in this study for the modification variable would mean considerable research still needs to be done before any firm recommendations for classroom practice can be ventured. As I have indicated throughout, recall of key elements of the text is by no means the whole process of comprehension, but it is an essential first step to understanding what has been received. Perhaps these results could be used to formulate a tentative recommendation for designing input that helps beginners store this initial trace of the content. The rest of the process towards successful comprehension remains to be studied, of course: how do*

*participants use what has now been recalled on the way towards better understanding of what they hear? Can this process be taught as such, or is it part of an inherently idiosyncratic process (see below)?*

6. Assess your overall confidence in the paper you have read.

*I noted above that the conclusions correspond to the original problem statement and research questions. I commented also that the promise that findings would somehow contribute to the wider area of L2 acquisition has not been fulfilled in the data itself. The literature review was a satisfying and critical review of the problem background and paved the way for more information to be provided from this study. I also confirmed that the principal variables were readily identifiable although I suggested there were some possible intervening variables which remain unaddressed in the remaining text. I expressed concern at the time that "Listening comprehension" was rather loosely defined and my observations as regards scoring confirm that listening comprehension has only been defined in terms of the number of previously-determined ideas noted. Many would argue with such a narrow interpretation if generalization is to be involved. My main worries in this paper have centered on internal and external validity: while it was good to see that large numbers of participants were involved, the pre-test measure was not the same as that used in the experiment itself, the control measures revealed considerable differences in the pool and diminished the original participant pool by 28 , and I do not learn which class was most affected. Likewise, my concerns about the test instrument validity have not been allayed. A reliability measure for this test was also not forthcoming, nor was information about prior piloting. Concern was also expressed about some aspects of research ethics displayed here: there was an unexplained decision made not to tell participants the real reasons for the research, and they might have been made unnecessarily anxious by being told the local authorities were in some way involved in the research. In data analysis, my concerns about the normality of the original and final sample meant that the outcomes and interpretation of the statistical procedures need to be treated with caution, and this drawback is not mentioned by the researcher as a limitation. Having said this, the presentation of data and statistical outcomes is generally acceptable although a missing effect size calculation revealed interesting outcomes not addressed by the researcher. In general, therefore, I find the strengths of the paper in the earlier sections; procedures and interpretation of the outcomes have been less convincing, however, and there should at least have been a call for further study of recall through modified input with replication of the present study with similar groups of participants.*

7. Are there any additional points raised during your appraisal of the paper that you would like to have seen discussed in this section?

*Normal interaction between speaker and listener is probably a highly unpredictable process and, consequently, the negotiation of input a rather more complex matter than that envisaged here. The "conscious language alterations" mentioned earlier in the paper clearly could not be accurately reproduced with the text and media used in this experiment. My question was that, given the unpredictability of these interactions, how far is comprehensible input negotiated on-the-spot on most occasions and contingent on the perceived needs of the protagonists? In such circumstances, comprehension becomes highly context-specific and, as a result, a complex skill to teach. It also follows that findings from studies such as this might have limited application beyond the immediate experimental simulation. Perhaps future research might usefully focus on the receiver of the message rather than the producer and investigate, for example, whether these learners call on similar strategies with the L2 as they use with their L1 to make input more comprehensible.*

## Observations

Look at each observation marked in this text and decide what kind of pertinent reaction could be made at each point. Help is given in the form of short prompts.

① Based on what results in the study might the researcher have seen the need for this further research?
② Do you think this has been shown in the text?
③ What more needs to be specified here about the "assistance" observed in this study?
④ What kind of "comprehensible input" have we read about in the results of the study?

For further practice in appraising this section of the research paper, turn to pages 267–272 in the Workbook.

# Workbook

# Workbook
## (guided and unguided appraisals)

### Abstract 3 (Guided appraisal)

1.  Read this abstract. When you have read a paragraph, stop and write in the *left-hand column* a few words which summarise the gist of that paragraph, to help you understand and focus on what the researcher is saying. Then, in the *right-hand column* write a few words which record your instinctive reactions to what you have just read as if you were addressing the researcher face-to-face. Advice on how to go about reacting spontaneously to the text was provided on p. 4.
2.  Read the textbook introduction to this section again and then respond to these questions, using some of my prompts if you wish.

|  |  |  |
|---|---|---|
|  | A case-study① was set up to investigate how far overt teaching of revision② affects a group's written production and also the way they perceive the writing process. First, participants, taken from two classes of High School Streams③ in Country B, were taught to revise④. This teaching took place once they had written a first draft of the composition. Also all the participants answered a specific set of questions before and after the study. A number of students were interviewed⑤. An holistic measurement of performance⑥ in writing tasks was made once at the beginning and once at the end of the research period ⑦and the results compared with those participants who were not taught revision strategies⑧. |  |
|  | A description is given of the nature of this instruction and results are reported on the effects of the overt teaching. It appears that this teaching did have a significant influence on production. After analysing the data, it was seen that participants varied as regards the |  |

way they thought about writing and revision⑨. I suggest that writing teachers might think about using the system of different drafts of a piece of writing instead of completing a piece of work in class, since results from this study indicate that overt teaching of revision can help students become more conscious of how foreign-language writing can be influenced by certain elements of the discourse itself.

2. **Read the textbook introduction to this section again and then respond to these questions, using some of my prompts if you wish.**

   a.   Can you see a clear statement of the topic and aim of the paper?
   b.   Is there a concise description of the sample and materials used?
        *Are there any possible implications of "participants, taken from two classes.."? What information would you be looking for about participant selection?*
   c.   What details are provided about the procedures used and the way data were later analysed?
        *Is there a noticeable difference between participants being "taught to revise" and also "taught revision strategies"? Where would you look in the paper for more information?*
   d.   Is there a brief summary of results, or the general trend of these, and are you told what conclusions are drawn from these?
        *What do you understand here by "a significant influence on production" as a result of the teaching?*

Observations

①   Think about what could be meant by "case-study"?
②   What do you understand by "overt teaching", and where would you expect to see this explained?
③   What more would you want to know about these "High School Streams", and where would you look for this information?
④   What information would you need about this teaching and the students' experience?
⑤   What would you need to know about this interview and those selected for it?
⑥   What differences might there be between "holistic" and any other kind of evaluation, and how might outcomes be affected here?
⑦   Think about the potential importance of the time-scale in this research and how this might affect the reliability of the measurement. Where would you look for more information, and what would you want to know?
⑧   What would you want to know about the two groups, and where would you expect to find this information?
⑨   What do you think this variation might likely consist of, and where would you find these details?

## Abstract 4 (Unguided appraisal)

1.  Read this abstract. When you have read a paragraph, stop and write in the *left-hand column* a few words which summarise the gist of that paragraph, to help you understand and focus on what the researcher is saying. Then, in the *right-hand column* write a few words which record your instinctive reactions to what you have just read as if you were addressing the researcher face-to-face.

| | | |
|---|---|---|
| | I suggest here that individual language performance① changes in significant and clear ways② regarding the kind of language chosen and the accuracy employed in different situations. While we know much about such variability in L1 production, there have been few studies of L2 production and most of these have focussed on the speaking skill. The aim here is to fill that gap, by studying the ways in which the reader's perceived age affects written composition. Participants were a group of 22 secondary-school teachers③ in Country M, who were all asked to write short letters to three imagined people④ whom they had met while travelling abroad recently. These imagined readers were: (a) a person older than themselves, (b) another who was of a similar age to themselves, and (c) a much younger person. This writing was subsequently given a score and also analysed⑤. It is shown that these participants were methodical⑥ in the way their language varied in letter-writing. Statistical analysis of the scores⑦ produced significant effects for perceived audience age, and it is concluded that this variable systematically ⑧ affects L2 variability in such scenarios. | |

2.  Read the textbook introduction to this section again and then answer these questions.

    a.  Can you see a clear statement of the topic and aim of the paper?
    b.  Is there a concise description of the sample and materials used?

    c.    What details are provided about the procedures used and the way data were later analysed?

    d.    Is there a brief summary of results, or the general trend of these, and are you told what conclusions are drawn from these?

Observations

Look at each observation marked in the abstract and decide what kind of pertinent reaction could be made at each point.

① 

② 

③ 

④ 

⑤ 

⑥ 

⑦ 

⑧ 

## The background to the problem and the problem statement 3 (Guided appraisal)

1.    Read Abstract 3 again (p. 233).

2.    When you have read a paragraph, stop and write in the *left-hand column* a few words which summarise the gist of that paragraph, to help you understand and focus on what the researcher is saying. Then, in the *right-hand column* write a few words which record your instinctive reactions to what you have just read as if you were talking to the researcher face-to-face. Advice on how to go about reacting spontaneously to the text was provided on p. 4.

| | | |
|---|---|---|
| | For many researchers and teachers, student writers need to be able to learn more effective revision procedures①; on the other hand, there is no firm agreement on the question of whether any significant progress can be made by direct teaching of task-based revision techniques. My basic assumption here in this study was that direct teaching of revision is feasible. An investigation was set up to determine the extent to which direct teaching of revision strategies affects both participants' writing abilities | |

and the way they see their writing②. The basic objective set out was to study what effects such instruction had in the teaching context of Country B's secondary schools③. I decided to experiment in this study with the use of direct teaching of revision subsequent to initial drafts and prior to the writing of final versions of compositions.

Currently, little or no use is made of such multiple drafts in secondary schools in Country B. It may at first surprise that the practice of using single drafts lingers on in Country B, especially considering the swing in writing methodology over the past years from concentration on the one-version product to focus on process. At the moment, the normal requirement of an L2 student here is to write only a final version of up to ten or twelve compositions per year. Once compositions are corrected by faculty, these are returned so that the student may correct any grammatical errors. Any positive effects of the treatment here might signal the need to consider the introduction of a system of multiple drafts into schools' L2 writing curricula.

3. **Read the textbook introduction to this section again and then respond to these questions, using some of my prompts if you wish.**

   1. Is the background to the problem described? If so, what is it?
   2. Is there a problem statement? If so, what is it in your own words?
   3. From the problem statement, do you understand: (a) the variables to be measured? and (b) the functions of these variables? If not, what values would you assign from what you have been told so far?
   *How many dependent variables appear to be involved? On what are the groups being compared here?*
   *Can you think of any control variables that might have been used in this design? If so, to what end?*
   4. Is there a contribution claimed to theory and to practice?

Observations

① How do you react to the expression "For many researchers and teachers.."?
② Think about the possible definitions of "writing abilities".
③ How immediately realistic do you find this objective? What implications does it have for the research design?

## The background to the problem and the problem statement 4 (Unguided appraisal)

1. Read Abstract 4 again (p. 235).
2. When you have read a paragraph, stop and write in the *left-hand column* a few words which summarise the gist of that paragraph, to help you understand and focus on what the researcher is saying. Then, in the *right-hand column* write a few words which record your instinctive reactions to what you have just read as if you were talking to the researcher face-to-face.

| | | |
|---|---|---|
| | Individual language performance ① changes according to context and circumstance. An individual's language production can be thought to change in observable ways along with the kind of language chosen to communicate something, as well as with the kind of formal accuracy employed in that language②. Such change may be hypothesised to be produced as a result of certain linguistic, sociolinguistic and/or psycholinguistic variables③ and may, in turn, respond to certain rules. | |
| | Research in the field has, over many years, confirmed these intuitions to a large extent and findings are now being applied to methodologies of communicative language teaching. However, the majority of this research has been concerned with L1 changes; L2 studies are few and far between, the most recent work focussing on change within L2 participants' spoken interlanguage (Researcher 1, 1994); other work has also revealed interesting anecdotal findings about such change within interlanguage | |

(Researcher 2, and 3, 1995, 1996). There should be great interest in discovering more about the way L2 learners change their language output and whether this is done systematically, both for the theoretical and practical implications of such findings and for their hypothesised effect on the teaching and assessment of proficiency in a foreign language④. On one hand, it would be interesting to know how far context is an important factor: do L2 learners, for example, consciously decide whether, and how, to modify their production to reach certain objectives in specific situations? Furthermore, does this variation also depend on the perceived nature or status of the person they are communicating with?⑤

In addition, if production is indeed seen to be subject to modification in terms of accuracy in accordance with certain elements in the socio- and psycholinguistic context, it would be of interest to discover what those elements were precisely – and any constraints upon them – to enable teachers better to guide L2 learners in managing their output in these contexts. This empirical study aims to show how far written language output is seen to be affected by knowledge of the nature and status of the audience. In this case, the intended audience is imaginary and, as such, is not intended to have any particular expectations from the writer concerned. The main objective here is to use these findings to establish (i) whether knowledge of the audience is an observable and important element in written interlanguage, (ii) the nature of any effects of this element and (iii) to study the extent to which such effects may be due to certain cultural constraints.

3.    **Read the textbook introduction to this section again and then answer these questions.**

Is the background to the problem described? If so, what is it?
Is there a problem statement? If so, what is it in your own words?
From the problem statement. do you understand: (a) the variables to be measured? and (b) the functions of these variables? If not, what values would you assign from what you have been told so far?
Is there a contribution claimed to theory and to practice?

Observations

Look at each observation marked in the text and decide what kind of pertinent reaction could be made at each point. Help is given in the form of short prompts.
①    What do you understand by this term?
②    What changes do you anticipate these might be?
③    Can you suggest any examples of these variables and why they would bring about changes?
④    How do you expect any such findings might have an effect on the way a foreign language is taught?
⑤    In what way(s) do you think perceived nature and/or status of the person we are talking to might affect this variation?

## The review of the literature 3 (Guided appraisal)

1.    Before you read this review of the literature, familiarise yourself again with the paper by reading Abstract 3 and The background to the problem and the problem statement 3 on pages 233 and 236.
2.    Read this section below, written in 1998. When you have read a paragraph, stop and write in the *left-hand column* a few words which summarise the gist of that paragraph, to help you understand and focus on what the researcher is saying. Then, in the *right-hand column* write a few words which record your instinctive reactions to what you have just read as if you were talking to the researcher face-to-face. Advice on how to go about reacting spontaneously to the text was provided on p. 4.

|  | A common idea throughout the recent literature is that revision strategies may not have received sufficient attention from teachers in the classroom. There is an observation by Researcher 1 (1995), for example, who feels that teachers tend to spend more time reading about such strategies than actually teaching them. Moreover, there has also |  |

been debate as to whether the explicit teaching of revision is pedagogically useful or advisable. One of the reasons for this is that revising may easily be understood by students to be a quick-fix solution when writing compositions. Results from many studies have shown students revising at surface text level①, and more often than not failing to address revision of meaning at all. In the face of so much evidence that these writers prefer to avoid revision beyond the surface level, it has been suggested that such concerns might be better addressed, and with more effectiveness, before pen is set to paper (Researcher 2, 1993). Textual revision may also take in other areas, such as discourse-related awareness of reader, along with the aim of the writing and its internal coherence and flow.

The teaching of revision has been approached in many American college classrooms as a peer work activity with a collaborative approach, precisely to avoid seeing revision as part of a prescriptive process. Here, such peer work and group conferences are the usual way revision is taught. It is also possible to use activities which involve the whole class, and a number of tasks might be employed which actively exploit the use of the teacher at the front of a whole class, such as a combined critique of a particular text (Researchers 3 and 4, 1996). Researchers 5 and 6 (1990) and Researcher 7 (1986) have also described other activities which help students of a foreign language revise more efficiently②.

On the other hand, we do not read of conclusive findings with regard to the success of instruction in revision in L1. Researcher 8 (1982), for example, showed that explicit teaching can result in improved performance ③ of school students, but

Researcher 9 (1978) reported no significant changes in the writing performance of thirteen college writers after direct teaching of revision strategies. Conversely, other researchers have found that less than ten minutes of direct teaching can produce significant progress in the second draft of compositions compared to a control group who had not received any instruction at all (Researchers 10 and 11, 1991).

Those who have compared L1 and L2 revision have discovered that the two processes are analogous (Researcher 12, 1990; Researcher 13, 1986); it follows that we have sufficient information to enable us to study how far direct teaching of revision strategies affects L2 writing proficiency④. The little research that has been conducted up to now suggests that L2 revision does not always produce improvement in writing. Researcher 13 (1995), for example, discovered that revision actually led to more errors being made in writing and also had a negative effect on writing anxiety. Researcher 14 (1996) reported on a study with unsuccessful EFL student writers and showed that they were unable to revise for meaning. He further suggested that these learners needed formal instruction in revision. The teaching profession itself has also joined the call for more studies into revision strategies (Researcher 15, 1995; Researchers 15 and 16, 1994). The problematical connection between exercising revision in an L2 text and seeing improvement was also reported by this author in 1998⑤.

Finally, studies have revealed that encouraging students to write over a number of drafts is not often used in schools in Country B and that the normal practice is for schools to apply prescriptive rules for the way L2 writing is to be produced (Researcher 17, 1991; Researchers 18 and 19, 1995). Typical

| practice is that writing staff are told to ask for a minimum number of class compositions and, as an integral part of staff inspection, these compositions are regularly checked by the Head of Department⑥. | |
|---|---|

3.  Read the textbook introduction to this section again and then respond to these questions, using some of my prompts if you wish.

Are you satisfied that the review (a) describes the most relevant work done and indicates its relative importance, (b) has sufficient critical address of the literature, (c) communicates the main points related both to the background to the problem and the problem statement/independent and dependent variables, (d) covers an adequate time-span, (e) has adequate reference, where necessary, to empirical work? In general, does it convince you of the need for the study?

a.  How relevant to this paper are studies about revising without specific instruction, and those referring to one specific country?
How relatively important are studies carried out in the same country as this present study?

b.  Do you read of any apparently conflicting or controversial results here that seem to require more critical address?

c.

d.

e.

Observations

①  What more might you want to learn about these studies?
②  What else might you be interested to learn here?
③  Consider what could be meant by "performance" in this context.
④  Comment on the logic in this sentence.
⑤  What is your reaction to this comment on the author's previous finding?
⑥  Consider the possible local consequences of such procedures for the application of any successful outcomes from the present study.

## The review of the literature 4 (Unguided appraisal)

1.  Before you read this review of the literature, familiarise yourself again with the paper by reading Abstract 4 and The background to the problem and the problem statement 4 on pages 235 and 238.

2.  Read this section below, written in 1998. When you have read a paragraph, stop and write in the *left-hand column* a few words which summarise the gist of that paragraph, to help you understand and focus on what the researcher is saying. Then, in the *right-hand column* write a few words which record your instinctive reactions to what you have just read as if you were talking to the researcher face-to-face.

Most research which has studied the way interlanguage varies has been directed towards spoken output (Researcher 1, 1971; Researcher 2, 1971; Researchers 3 and 4, 1974; Researcher 5, 1974; Researcher, 6, 1975; Researcher 7, 1976; Researcher 8, 1979, 1983, 1985; Researcher 9, 1979; Researcher 10, 1981; Researcher 11, 1982; Researcher 12, 1983; Researchers 13 and 14, 1985; Researchers 15 and 16, 1985; Researcher 17, 1986; Researcher 18, 1989; Researcher 19, 1989; Researcher 20, 1990)①. There is very little research specifically concerned with studying any significant variables which affect L2 writing. A number of possible variables have been proposed, including topic (Researcher 21, 1983; Researcher 22, 1990); genre and rhetorical structure (Researcher 23, 1991); purpose (e.g., Researcher 24, 1990), and audience (e.g., Researcher 25, 1993). However, more "individual" type variables that might be hypothesised as impinging on writing performance, such as the nature of the reader to whom the writing is addressed, are rarely treated②.

Where work has been done on this variable this has tended to be within the area of English for Academic Purposes; here the potential reader is thought to exercise certain power over the writer and have certain expectations of him or her.

Other intuitive data from Country M has been offered which suggests that age is a culturally significant variable here (Researcher 26 1953; Researcher 27, 1974; Researcher 28, 1977; Researcher 29, 1979). This is not an exclusive characteristic of society in Country M; indeed, it might be suggested that age is a significant variable in all societies③. Nevertheless, this does seem to be a particular strong characteristic in society in Country M (Researcher 28, 1977).

> As such, it may impact on social interaction in distinct ways and to differing extents. If we accept such an hypothesis, it is possible that the L2 interlanguage output of learners in Country M might be seen to respond in a similar way to the relative or definite age of the audience as does their output in the native language (cf., Researcher 29, 1975).

3.   **Read the textbook introduction to this section again and then answer these questions.**

Are you satisfied that the review (a) describes the most relevant work done and indicates its relative importance, (b) has sufficient critical address of the literature, (c) communicates the main points related both to the background to the problem and the problem statement/independent and dependent variables, (d) covers an adequate time-span, (e) has adequate reference, where necessary, to empirical work? In general, does it convince you of the need for the study?

a.

b.

c.

d.

e.

Observations

Look at each observation marked in this review and decide what kind of pertinent reaction could be made at each point.

①

②

③

## Research questions and variables 3 (Guided appraisal)

1.   Before you read this section of the paper, familiarise yourself again with the paper by reading Abstract 3, The background to the problem and the problem statement 3, and The review of the literature 3 on pages 233, 236, and 240 respectively.

2.   When you have read a paragraph, stop and write in the *left-hand column* a few words which summarise the gist of that paragraph, to help you understand and focus on what the researcher is saying. Then, in the *right-hand column* write a few words which record your instinctive reactions to what you have just read as if you were talking to the researcher face-to-face. Advice on how to go about reacting spontaneously to the text was provided on p. 4.

Two research questions were investigated:

1.   Does overt teaching of revision strategies bring about greater improvement in written production than the traditional way of teaching revision?
2.   Does this teaching of revision strategies have any effect on the way students perceive the writing and revision process, and if so, how?

[From Method section .. I decided on the method and content of the revision strategy teaching together with the teacher involved. We agreed detailed revision teaching plans which would aim to stimulate audience needs/reader awareness in the writers and would focus on three main areas: Evaluating, detecting, and repairing problems. We further agreed on a focus of teaching which encouraged students to read each others' work and through which the students might appreciate how their writing could be made easier to read by concentrating on a text's appropriateness of style and good organisation of information.

The control group, who received the traditional teaching, had input for their compositions before starting to write①. They were told to complete their compositions in class② and were given a little help in the form of teacher correction of their surface mistakes.

Improvement in writing was measured as the difference between the pre- and post-test marks assigned to the student. To discover students' views on writing and revision, students in the two revision groups were asked to complete questionnaires in class before and after the study. Participants in the control group completed a similar version with fewer questions. I also carried out a number of semi-structured interviews with some of the participants from one of the experimental groups③, which helped  provide further insights into the influence of this teaching on students' views of the writing and revision process.]

3.  **Read the textbook introduction to this section again and then respond to these ques-
    tions, using some of my prompts if you wish.**

    1.  (a) Are research questions or research hypotheses formulated? If so, what are they? (b)
        Are the research questions exploratory, descriptive, or explanatory? (c) Are the hypotheses
        offered directional, and do they predict differences or relationships between variables?
        (d) Are the research questions/hypotheses unambiguous, consistent with the problem
        statement, feasible, and supported by the review of the literature?
        a.
        b.  *Do you feel the researcher is aiming to build or to test an hypothesis here?*
        c.
        d.  *Has the previous literature review adequately supported these questions as regards the
            local teaching situation?*
    2.  Can you identify the principal variables of the study, and are these to be measured
        as nominal, ordinal, or interval scales? Comment on the perceived appropriateness of
        these scales. Are moderator or control variables evident?
    3.  Can you predict any intervening variables or contributory factors – if not stated here –
        that might affect findings?
        *What other local factors might affect students' perceptions about the revision and writing
        process?*
    4.  What were the constructs used and have these been adequately delineated to permit
        operational definition? How have these constructs then been defined operationally,
        where necessary, and is this description acceptable in its present form?

Observations

①  What more would you want to know about this input, and where would you look for this
    information?
②  Can you think of any possible conditions, and consequences, of writing "in class" which
    might affect outcomes here?
③  Consider the possible reasons for, and consequences of, this selection of participants.

## Research questions and variables 4 (Unguided appraisal)

1.  **Before you read this section of the paper, familiarise yourself again with the paper by
    reading Abstract 4, The background to the problem and the problem statement 4, and
    The review of the literature 4 on pages 235, 238, and 243 respectively.**
2.  **When you have read a paragraph, stop and write in the *left-hand column* a few words
    which summarise the gist of that paragraph, to help you understand and focus on
    what the researcher is saying. Then, in the *right-hand column* write a few words which
    record your instinctive reactions to what you have just read as if you were talking to the
    researcher face-to-face.**

It is unlikely that an L2 learner's varying sensitivity to age in his or her output – even if constrained by certain cultural factors – will be limited only to his or her spoken output. Written production may also be affected. Such variability responding to age factors in written production might also be reflected in composition quality, as measured by any of the widely-accepted marking scales currently in use today①. This study used the popular Composition Profile designed by Researchers 1 and 2 (1984) (sample mark sheets in the appendix)②. Our first hypothesis was:

1. Marks awarded to compositions will vary in a systematic③ and significant way (p < .05④) as a result of⑤ the age of the supposed reader relative to the age of the writer.

Assuming this hypothesis is proved correct, we will still not be able to say if better performance in writing is always found when writers address older readers, and worse performance always when they address younger readers. Assuming participants are taught to give greater respect in their writing to older readers, this could also mean that they decide to be more careful in their writing. Thus, they could attend more to accuracy in their syntax and vocabulary, as well as concentrating more on organising the text better and getting better cohesion, and so on. As a result, they may get better marks. On the other hand, we could suggest that the writer feeling more comfortable addressing younger readers might also feel more confidence and have this confidence realised in greater fluency in his or her writing, with a wider range and more elaborate use of vocabulary and syntax; they may even become more accurate in their writing. Conversely, addressing an older reader could result in the writer feeling more anxiety while writing, resulting in an obsessive attitude to accuracy and, therefore, lower marks⑥. In both situations we might naturally expect writing to be easier when addressed to a same-aged reader, and assessment to reflect this.

The first of these situations is more typical of the writing context in Country M, so⑦ we decided to test the following hypothesis:

2. Compositions written to a reader considered to be the same age as the writer will receive the highest marks and those written to a supposedly older readership would receive higher marks than those directed to younger readers.

3. **Read the textbook introduction to this section again and then answer these questions.**

   1. (a) Are research questions or research hypotheses formulated? If so, what are they? (b) Are the research questions exploratory, descriptive, or explanatory? (c) Are the hypotheses offered directional, and do they predict differences or relationships between variables? (d) Are the research questions/hypotheses unambiguous, consistent with the problem statement, feasible, and supported by the review of the literature?
   2. Can you identify the principal variables of the study, and are these to be measured as nominal, ordinal, or interval scales? Comment on the perceived appropriateness of these scales. Are moderator or control variables evident?
   3. Can you predict any intervening variables or contributory factors – if not stated here – that might affect findings?
   4. What were the constructs used and have these been adequately delineated to permit operational definition? How have these constructs then been defined operationally, where necessary, and is this description acceptable in its present form?

Observations

Look at each observation marked in this text and decide what kind of pertinent reaction could be made at each point.

① 
② 
③

④
⑤
⑥
⑦

## Participants and materials 3 (Guided appraisal)

1.  Before you read this section of the paper, familiarise yourself again with the paper by reading Abstract 3, The background to the problem and problem statement 3, The review of the literature 3, and Research questions and variables 3 on pages 233, 236, 240 and 245 respectively.
2.  As you are reading, in the *right-hand column*, write a few words which record your instinctive reactions to what you have just read as if you were talking to the researcher face-to-face. Advice on how to go about reacting spontaneously to the text was provided on p. 4.

---

One high school was selected for the study and four fourth-year (of five) classes chosen. Since local education authorities would not agree to random selection of either school or classes, these four classes were decided on by the principal of the centre, a school which in turn had been allocated by the head of the local education authority. All the class members were female and between fifteen and sixteen years old. The family backgrounds of these children were varied, with an overall rich mixture of middle- and working-class families①.

From these four original classes, the principal and two of the school's English teachers proceeded to select two which would receive the revision strategy treatment. The participants in these two treatment groups were then informed by their teachers what different kind of teaching they would be given②. The third class was only to be used to demonstrate the improvement in writing performance. The fourth class was not involved for comparison purposes since students there were mainly studying History of the English Language as a subject and so merely received some extra hours of English per week.

Teaching staff were the following: during the first six months of the study one of the groups who received revision strategy instruction was taught by a local (non-native) teacher, who also gave classes to the third (control) class. A native English teacher taught the other revision group. However, late into the study, this latter teacher left the school and – in the last three months – his teaching was taken on by two new teachers. Such changes were not thought to have been a serious threat to the findings since these teachers continued with the same revision teaching procedures.

Classes in the school are typically large, with over forty pupils in each. Although pupils talk to each other in their native language, the majority of core subjects in the school are taught in English. The normal teaching procedures used in the school with regard to EFL writing were the following: very little direct teaching of such writing goes on at this level and class time is usually taken up with timed compositions in class and/or doing the corrections to the same. School policy requires teachers to give back compositions with any errors clearly marked, and students then have to correct the grammatical mistakes underlined. Students are normally expected to present for the Cambridge First Certificate examination near the end of their studies, where the composition plays a major role; therefore, much of the EFL writing centres on learning how to present acceptable writing of this kind with few grammatical mistakes, but content is not considered such an important feature.

As regards the materials used, all participants were given the following written instructions for their writing task before the study began and then again a year afterwards, after the end of the research period: Write a composition on the following, giving reasons for your arguments: "Smoking should be banned in all public places" Do you agree? [3].

These pre- and post-test compositions were given to two examiners who were not taking part directly in the study. They handled all the compositions from both experimental and control groups between them. These examiners used the same guidelines and composition marking scale as that used by Cambridge First Certificate examiners. No pre-marking coordination meeting was held between them as they were both experienced examiners [4]. The writers' names were whitened out of the papers before these were marked, and examiners were not told which compositions came from which group nor which sitting (i.e., before or after the study). An inter-rater reliability coefficient was calculated after the marking was completed and considered satisfactory at .89 for the compositions written before the study began and .78 for post-study writing.

Interview data were collected as the study was nearing its end [5]. Eleven students from one of the revision classes had an interview, the aim of which was to obtain more personal accounts of what these participants thought about revision and the teaching they had received. A pool of participants was made (n = 18), based on those that appeared to have made the best and the least improvement during the year, and each participant approached. Eleven volunteered to be interviewed by the researcher. Semi-structured interviews were recorded and aimed to collect data about what participants saw revision to be about, if they thought it was important, and the importance they attached to the reader⑥. All interviews were tape-recorded and participants' replies analysed and collated. Student opinion about the teaching received was also collected from questionnaires (see sample, below) which were given out before and after the research to those participants in the two groups receiving the revision strategy instruction (see below). As participants were obliged to complete these questionnaires in class, there was a 100 per cent return rate on these. The aim was to see the effect of the revision teaching received on the way these participants saw the writing process. Questions were divided into sections, which concentrated on: what they thought would constitute a good piece of writing, what they liked and disliked in the special teaching they had received, and what they thought revision is all about. The control group had to fill in a similar version of the questionnaire but which had fewer questions under each sub-section⑦.

## Extract from questionnaire for experimental class
Name:

**I want to know what you think about the writing and revision classes you have had.**
1.    Now that you know how to revise, are you happier writing your compositions?
      Yes/No
2.    Now that you know how to revise, do you think you write more effectively?
      Yes/No

**See how far you agree or disagree about the following statements:**
3.    i.    Learning how to revise has been a great help for me. Yes/No
      ii.   Revising is not very interesting for me. Yes/No
      iii.  Learning how to think about the reader of my writing was a great help for me. Yes/No
      iv.   Learning different ways to make a plan of my composition was a great help for me. Yes/No
      v.    Learning how to evaluate someone else's composition was very helpful. Yes/No
      vi.   These classes will help me when I take the Cambridge First Certificate. Yes/No
      vii.  I liked the idea of my friend checking my own composition. Yes/No
      viii. I will be able to use the strategies I have learnt on my own from now on. Yes/No

4.    **Circle ONE of the following options as the most important according to your point of view.**
      i.    "For a good composition, you need to have…."
            interesting content
            good paragraph structure
            few grammar mistakes
      ii.   "For a composition to be organised correctly, it should have…."
            a topic sentence
            five paragraphs
            spaces between paragraphs
            an introduction and conclusion

iii.    "Revising a composition correctly means……"
        correcting any grammar mistakes
        reading through the composition and changing any confusing content
        reading through the composition, thinking of the reader, and changing things as a result
        checking for, and changing, any spelling mistakes

**3.    Read the textbook introduction to this section again and then respond to these questions, using some of my prompts if you wish.**

1.    What basic identification data are provided about the participants, and are these data sufficient to permit replication?
      *How similar do you think the groups might have been? Is it important?*
      *What specific information would you want to have about L2 teaching of writing in the school? Is enough given here?*
2.    a.   What are your initial reactions to any groupings envisaged?
      b.   Do these groups reflect the original pre-group sample in terms of their basic characteristics, and is any justification provided for the eventual group size?
           a.   *What information would it be useful to have regarding these four intact classes?*
           b.   *How might the discarding of the fourth group affect the final data obtained?*
3.    Can you see any potential threats to internal validity of the data from attrition, history, or maturation factors?
      *How might the parallel teaching of other participants affect results here? What observations might be made concerning the teachers involved in the study?*
4.    What information is presented concerning the way participants were selected and/or group membership assigned? What do you see as the consequences of this as regards eventual generalisation of findings?
      *What observations could you make about the selection for the interview?*
5.    Has any material or instrument of testing/measurement been satisfactorily described and/or samples provided? Where appropriate, has its development/design and scoring been adequately discussed?
      *Comment on any other material (i.e., apart from the questionnaire and interview schedule) that appears to have been used.*
6.    For any instrument of testing or measurement used (including observation), what evidence of reliability was given, and how acceptable is this evidence?
      *Comment on the perceived precision of the questions in the questionnaire and the fact that they are presented in the L2.*
      *What do you think might be gained or lost by eliciting responses using closed (yes/no) questions and multiple choice items?*
      *How do you react to the fact that questionnaire sheets asked for participants' names?*
      *What informal elements of the marking may increase our confidence in the reliability here?*
7.    For any instrument of testing or measurement used, what evidence of validity was given, and how acceptable is this evidence? If none is given, what do you consider to be possible threats to validity here?

*Judging from this extract, how far do you think this questionnaire might succeed in gathering accurate/valid data about "the effect of the revision teaching....on the way these participants saw the writing process"? And what about the data from the interview? What more might you want to know about the "guidelines and composition marking scale" used, given the first research question (see p. 246)?*

8.    How have the main independent and dependent variables been realised within the method itself, and how satisfactory do you find this?

Observations

① How might socio-economic background have affected results?
② Consider the possible consequences of this information given the participants.
③ What other information about the conditions for writing might be relevant here?
④ Examiners of....?
⑤ Compare, and comment on, the period of data collection from the interview and the questionnaire.
⑥ How might the demands of these participants' current learning context also have affected these opinions?
⑦ Given the research questions, why do you think such data were gathered from the control group?

## Participants and materials 4 (Unguided appraisal)

1.    Before you read this section of the paper, familiarise yourself again with the paper by reading Abstract 4, The background to the problem and the problem statement 4, The review of the literature 4, and Research questions and variables 4 on pages 235, 238, 243 and 247 respectively.
2.    As you are reading, in the *right-hand column*, write a few words which record your instinctive reactions to what you have just read as if you were talking to the researcher face-to-face.

---

The initial population in this study were the secondary-school teachers in the capital city of Country M who were studying English as a foreign language① and who – in a government-aided scheme as part of their studies – had been to England within the last two years② for a three-month stay. Before the school year began, the 16 participating③ secondary-schools were allocated a number. Three institutions were then drawn at random to participate in the study. The teachers in these schools who had been abroad on the scheme totalled 36. These were also numbered and then 22 chosen at random as participants for the study. All these teachers were female④ with an age range of between 20 and 29⑤.

All the participants were asked to write letters addressed to three different people. Given that all the participants had been abroad within the last two years, a realistic letter-writing activity was thought to be one directed towards someone they had got to know during that stay. Three letters were required of each participant and each letter was to be no longer than one side of A4 paper⑥. Each letter was to include reference to a theme supplied by the researcher, one thought to be very familiar to the students and which they would be ready to comment upon: the current wave of people emigrating from Country M to neighbouring countries in search of a better job. The three addressees were: A. to a person of a similar age to themselves, B. to a person older than themselves, and C. to a person considerably younger than themselves.

The writing was given a grade based on the University Composition Evaluation Scale (UCES), widely used in Country M⑦. On this scale, evaluation is based on five criteria, with a possible range for each criterion of four marks (i.e., four through to one in decreasing order of perceived merit). A trial pilot test evaluation of ten letters⑧ led to considerable discrepancy amongst several examiners, all of whom felt that the suggested relationship described in the University scale between mark awarded and performance was not clear enough to ensure reliable evaluation. Consequently, and after discussion with the researcher, all examiners agreed to award grades on a letter basis with the addition of a plus or a minus sign as a further indication of performance level (i.e., A–, B+, etc.). This researcher then converted all such grades into their numerical equivalents (as a percentage) for the purposes of the analysis.

3. **Read the textbook introduction to this section again and then attempt to answer these questions.**

   1. What basic identification data are provided about the participants, and are these data sufficient to permit replication?
   2. a. What are your initial reactions to the numbers involved or any grouping envisaged?
      b. Do these groups reflect the original pre-group sample in terms of their basic characteristics, and is any justification provided for the eventual group size?
   3. Can you see any potential threats to internal validity of the data from attrition, history, or maturation factors?
   4. What information is presented concerning the way participants were selected and/or group membership assigned? What do you see as the consequences of this as regards eventual generalisation of findings?

5.   Has any material or instrument of testing/measurement been satisfactorily described and/or samples provided? Where appropriate, has its development/design and scoring been adequately discussed?

6.   For any instrument of testing or measurement used (including observation), what evidence of reliability was given, and how acceptable is this evidence?

7.   For any instrument of testing or measurement used, what evidence of validity was given, and how acceptable is this evidence? If none is given, what do you consider to be possible threats to validity here?

8.   How have the main independent and dependent variables been realised within the method itself, and how satisfactory do you find this?

Observations

Look at each observation marked in this text and decide what kind of pertinent reaction could be made at each point.

①
②
③
④
⑤
⑥
⑦
⑧

# Procedures and research design 3 (Guided appraisal)

1.   Before working through this section of the paper, you should re-read the Participants and materials 3 text and appraisal on p. 250.

2.   As you are reading, in the *right-hand column*, write a few words which record your instinctive reactions to what you have just read as if you were talking to the researcher face-to-face. Advice on how to go about reacting spontaneously to the text was provided on p. 4.

| | |
|---|---|
| Before and after the study, all the participating groups provided a sample of their writing in order to get data on writing proficiency. Improvement in writing was measured as the difference between these pre- and post-test marks assigned to the student. They also completed a questionnaire. For the six compositions written by the experimental group and the twelve written by the control group① the procedures adopted in the experimental and control classes were the same. | |

Each class lasted 75 minutes. In the first lesson the experimental (revision strategy) group were given certain pre-composition input. They then started the composition in class and returned a first draft of the same some time later②. The control group would follow the traditional mode whereby they also received the input but started and finished the composition in class. In the second class, the experimental group were handed back their first drafts with teacher feedback for perusal and were given initial revision strategy information and practice; the control group received their marked compositions back and were given a short time to correct these. They then also received the input, and then started and finished the next composition in class. In the third class, the experimental group received more detailed input and practice on revision and applied this to their own and a partner's composition. They then started another draft of the same composition, which was given in the following week. The control group were given their marked writing back and were again given time to correct the mistakes③. In the fourth class, the experimental class received comments on their final versions and pre-composition input on the next composition. Again they started the next composition in class and returned a first draft of the same some time later. The control group also received the input but started and finished the composition in class.

Subjects and titles of the compositions had to be agreed with the class teachers responsible and the principal of the centre, and there was constant interaction between these throughout the study. We agreed detailed revision teaching plans④ which would aim to stimulate audience needs/reader awareness in the writers and would focus on three main areas: Evaluating, detecting, and repairing problems. We further agreed on a focus of teaching through which the students might appreciate how their writing could be made easier to read by concentrating on a text's appropriateness of style and good organisation of information.

3.    **Read the textbook introduction to this section again and then respond to these questions, using some of my prompts if you wish.**

1.    What is your appraisal of the timing of events, and is this information sufficient to permit replication?
*What further information about timing of events for each group both within and across classes might have been useful for the reader?*

*How might the timing of the interview/questionnaire data collection possibly affect the data obtained?*

2. Are there any potential threats to internal validity as a result of test or practice effect?

3. What is your assessment of any prior information about the study given the participants and the instructions they received?

   *Discuss to what extent participation seems to have been voluntary or obligatory. Could the disruption of classes have been significant? Was anonymity assured? Comment also on the instructions given participants for filling in the questionnaire.*

4. What potential threats of reactivity do you see with respect to i. observer/scorer effects and participant expectancies, and ii) observer/scorer bias?

   ii. *Comment also on how potential bias was or was not controlled for the evaluation of the interview/questionnaire data.*

5. i. What details are provided about the environmental conditions of the study and could these have affected outcomes?

   ii. What observations about external validity can be made in the light of these details?

6. In the light of what you have read in this section, do you wish to amend, or add to, your previous comments on group assignment, materials, and the potential threats to internal validity of the data from attrition, history, or maturation?

7. Identify the basic type of design employed here and draw the design box. What immediate observations can you make about this design and its consequences for the study?

8. Attempt visually to classify the data-collection procedure, and comment on the perceived consequences of this for any eventual findings. Where necessary, suggest how this might have been improved, and why.

   *What purpose(s) does the pre-test appear to serve here?*

   *How might matched participants provide an alternative approach to this design?*

   *How might the following design also provide a further source of interesting data?*

$$X(1)-O(1)-X(0)-O(2)-X(1)-O(3)-X(0)-O(4)$$
$$\longrightarrow \text{etc.}$$

*where X(1) is the experimental treatment and X(0) is some other kind of treatment?*

9. What procedures are identified for data analysis, and do these deal adequately with the original objectives of the study? In the absence of information about procedures, suggest how this might be done.

   *The second research question suggests the possibility that the teaching of strategies has somehow affected opinions of writing and revision: how far do these procedures promise adequate comparative pre-/post data?*

10. Provide a step-by-step description of the elements involved in the data analysis so far, and decide on the appropriateness of any proposed analysis procedures in the light of this.

11. Have the necessary assumptions associated with the stated or implied analysis procedure been met in a way that suggests the reader can have confidence in the results of the analysis?

Observations

① Comment on the possible consequences of the different amounts of writing completed by both groups.
② Comment on the possible consequences for outcomes of the different conditions for writing and revision experienced by the experimental group.
③ Comment on the differences in the distinct class procedures for the control group.
④ Do you think these obliged consultations and "constant interaction" might affect outcomes? If so, how?

## Procedures and research design 4 (Unguided appraisal)

1. Before working through this section of the paper, you should re-read the corresponding Participants and materials 4 text and appraisal.
2. As you are reading, in the *right-hand column*, write a few words which record your instinctive reactions to what you have just read as if you were talking to the researcher face-to-face.

---

To make sure that any differences in writing outcomes were not the result of the order in which they were written, participants from the three institutions were assigned to each of the following sequences in equal numbers:

Order I= Letters B, then A, then C.
Order II= Letters C, then B, then A.
Order III= Letters A, then C, then B.

The letter-writing activity was presented by the class teacher in normal class periods①. After questions were answered, each participant received a sealed envelope containing all the instructions and paper necessary to complete the task. Together with this information, participants were asked to fill in a questionnaire② which collected information about their visit abroad. The teacher told the participants that all the writing could be completed at home③ and should be returned to that teacher within one week.

Once the letters had been completed, the data consisted of 66 scripts (i.e., 22 participants writing three letters each), which were then photocopied. Each examiner was then sent a packet containing a set of 22 letters, each set being made up (as far as possible) with one type A, B, and C letter from every participant④.

In order to obtain reliable data from the examining, 30 examiners (20 women and 10 men)⑤ were involved and each one rated one set of 22 letters. Therefore, each letter was marked ten times (30x22/66 scripts) All the examiners were experienced teachers⑥ and received pre-study training⑦ in using the scale until a fair rate of consistency was achieved⑧. Inter-rater reliability was not calculated since so many examiners were used in the study as to suggest this would be high in any case.

The score for each letter to be used in calculations was obtained by taking an average of the ten individual scores given by the examiners. Since the rest of the study met the assumptions of a repeated-measures one-way analysis of variance, we decided to use this procedure to obtain the significance of the resulting grades. We also used correlation formulae on the grades given each letter to see what differences there were between performances on each letter-writing task.

3. **Read the textbook introduction to this section again and then attempt to answer these questions.**

   1. What is your appraisal of the timing of events, and is this information sufficient to permit replication?
   2. Are there any potential threats to internal validity as a result of test or practice effect?
   3. What is your assessment of any prior information about the study given the participants and the instructions they received?
   4. What potential threats of reactivity do you see with respect to (i) observer/scorer effects and participant expectancies, and (ii) observer/scorer bias?
   5. i. What details are provided about the environmental conditions of the study and could these have affected outcomes?
      ii. What observations about external validity can be made in the light of these details?
   6. In the light of what you have read in this section, do you wish to amend, or add to, your previous comments on group assignment, materials, and the potential threats to internal validity of the data from attrition, history, or maturation?
   7. Identify the basic type of design employed here and draw the design box. What immediate observations can you make about this design and its consequences for the study?
   8. Attempt visually to classify the data-collection procedure, and comment on the perceived consequences of this for any eventual findings. Where necessary, suggest how this might have been improved, and why.
   9. What procedures are identified for data analysis, and do these deal adequately with the original objectives of the study? In the absence of information about procedures, suggest how this might be done.

10. Provide a step-by-step description of the elements involved in the data analysis so far, and decide on the appropriateness of any proposed analysis procedures in the light of this.

11. Have the necessary assumptions associated with the stated or implied analysis procedure been met in a way that suggests the reader can have confidence in the results of the analysis?

Observations

Look at each observation marked in this text and decide what kind of pertinent reaction could be made at each point.

① 
② 
③ 
④ 
⑤ 
⑥ 
⑦ 
⑧ 

# Results: The nature and presentation of findings 3 (Guided appraisal)

1. Before working through this section of the paper, you should re-read the corresponding Research questions and variables 3, Participants and materials 3, and Procedures and research design 3 texts and appraisal on pp. 245, 250 and 256 respectively.

2. As you are reading, in the *right-hand column*, write a few words which record your instinctive reactions to what you have just read as if you were talking to the researcher face-to-face. Advice on how to go about reacting spontaneously to the text was provided on p. 4.

First of all, I compared the two scores obtained on the pre-test measure and the post-test measure for the 84 participants in the experimental group (classes 1 and 2) and 34 in the control group (class 3). The figures in Table 1 below show these scores, together with the increases or decreases in the means for each group. The maximum score available in the holistic scale was 17. Pre-test results show that the control group had the highest mean (11.14), together with a relatively small variability (s.d. = 1.32) when compared with both experimental groups.

The post-test results, however, present a very different picture: now the mean for one of the experimental groups (class 2) is the highest of the three (12.79). By the end of the study period, the improvement for the control group is only .74, but in both experimental groups this improvement is registered at least at over four times this figure.

**Table 1.** Pre/Post-test scores and gains for experimental and control groups

| Group (Class) | Pre-test Mean | s.d. | Post-test Mean | s.d. | Points gained | s.d. |
|---|---|---|---|---|---|---|
| Experimental (1) | 8.01 | 1.29 | 11.26 | 1.44 | 3.25 | 1.31 |
| Experimental (2) | 8.79 | 2.31 | 12.79 | 2.40 | 4 | 2.98 |
| Control (3) | 11.14 | 1.32 | 11.88 | 2.29 | 0.74 | 2.86 |

Data from the two experimental groups show that Class 2 improve considerably more than the other groups. Indeed, they already were higher than the other experimental group in the pre-test. Having said this, this group also showed the greatest variability of scores. Indeed, Class 2 was seen to be a very diverse group before the experiment started. Class 1, on the other hand, would have been less interested in English as they were not going on to further study in this subject. Table 2 shows graphically the improvement/deterioration in each of the experimental groups.

**Table 2.** Pre/Post-test improvement/deterioration for experimental groups

| Pre-test to Post-test | Class 1 | Class 2 |
|---|---|---|
| −3 | 4 | 1 |
| −2 | 2 | 0 |
| −1 | 2 | 3 |
| 0 | 7 | 2 |
| 2 | 3 | 5 |
| 3 | 6 | 8 |
| 4 | 6 | 3 |
| 5 | 4 | 3 |
| 6 | 2 | 7 |
| 7 | 2 | 2 |
| 8 | 0 | 2 |
| 9 | 0 | 2 |
| | n = 41 | n = 43 |

It is clear from this table that 13 students in Class 2 made an improvement over the two tests of six or more points, compared to only 4 in Class 1.

Questionnaire data back up the gains made by Class 2 in that many participants in that group made a point of saying that the instruction was enjoyable and motivated them to revise more. Those interviewed who had made the greatest improvement said they felt that using these strategies helped them directly to improve their writing. Having said this, overall questionnaire returns from both experimental groups showed a majority preferring a return to the traditional system while recognising that the revision instruction might be useful in the Cambridge examination. Finally, there was a clear trend in these responses towards understanding writing more in terms of both content *and* accuracy after the instruction was completed.

The few interviews carried out threw more light on some of these questionnaire responses. Most participants interviewed suggested that the instruction had helped them to account for audience in their writing. They thought it had become easier to see what the teacher wanted in their work since the instruction was felt to have revealed the reasons behind the evaluation that went on①. Interestingly, several participants remarked that they saw the new instruction as contrasting with the normal way of focussing on accuracy in evaluation, and three expressed their worries about whether employing the method in the future would act against them once out of the experimental period②.

3. **Read the textbook introduction to this section again and then respond to these questions, using some of my prompts if you wish.**

1. Does your initial reading of this section suggest that enough data have been provided so as to have adequately responded to the research questions or hypotheses previously put forward?
2. What tables or graphical displays of results are provided, and what do you understand from the data displayed? Are there any data that you feel might have usefully been added to the information provided here?
   *What do you think might have brought about the initial inequality in the groups?*
   *Consider alternative explanations for the improvement/non-improvement shown.*
3. What information is provided by any descriptive statistics about the distribution of data?
4. Have the data been scored using the unit measurement predicted earlier, and/or has any appropriate data conversion taken place?

5.  i.   What, if any, specific statistical operations or calculations were carried out on these data, and does this seem to have been carried out appropriately?
    ii.  In the light of what you have read in this section, do you wish to amend or add to your previous appraisal of the assumptions met for this procedure?
6.  What is your appraisal of any other interpretations that the researcher makes of his or her data in this section?
    *How justified is the concentration on Class 2 for initial interpretations of data?*
    *How do you react to the majority comment from both experimental groups that they would prefer to return to the traditional teaching method?*
7.  What information is made available or can be calculated about effect size of the outcomes?
8.  What initial conclusions do you come to about the practical significance and meaningfulness of these results? Do these coincide with the researcher's interpretation?

Observations

①   Comment on the apparent validity of these data in terms of who made the comments, how they were analysed, and when they were obtained.
②   In what ways do you think the demands of the present writing context might affect the wider introduction of the experimental treatment?


## Results: The nature and presentation of findings 4 (Unguided appraisal)

1.  **Before working through this section of the paper, you should re-read the corresponding Research questions and variables 4, Participants and materials 4, and Procedures and research design 4 texts and appraisal.**
2.  **As you are reading, in the *right-hand column*, write a few words which record your instinctive reactions to what you have just read as if you were talking to the researcher face-to-face.**

Table 1 presents the descriptive statistics for each sample, where the distributions obtained clearly suggest the suitability① of a repeated-measures ANOVA for the analysis of data. These data also show that mean differences between scores and statistics for variability are not great, which is consistent with results obtained from the same participants on different measures.

**Table 1.** Descriptive statistics

|                                    | n  | Mean (%) | s.d. | Range |
|------------------------------------|----|----------|------|-------|
| Addressed to older reader          | 22 | 68.77    | 6.11 | 23.31 |
| Addressed to similar age reader    | 22 | 64.52    | 6.74 | 31.49 |
| Addressed to younger reader        | 22 | 63.41    | 5.93 | 24.83 |

I then proceeded to carry out a suitable② ANOVA test on these scores, the results of which are presented in Table 2.

**Table 2.**  Repeated-measures one-way ANOVA

| Source of variance | SS | df | MS | F |
| --- | --- | --- | --- | --- |
| Participants | 2484.93 | 21 | 118.33 | |
| Type | 326.65 | 2 | 163.32 | 18.66* |
| Letter x Type | 367.53 | 42 | 8.75 | |
| Total | 3179.11 | 65 | | |

*p < .01

These results clearly support the hypothesis that knowing about the nature of the audience for the writing has a significant effect on the scores obtained in the task.
A post-hoc test was then used to locate any differences more precisely:

**Table 3.**  Post-hoc Scheffé test

| Means | Addressed to older reader | Addressed to similar age reader | Addressed to younger reader |
| --- | --- | --- | --- |
| Addressed to older reader | | 8.45* | 19.32* |
| Addressed to similar age reader | | | 1.98 |
| Addressed to younger reader | | | |

*p < .05

These data reveal that there are significant differences between scores given to letters directed to older people and those of a similar age to the reader, with the greatest difference in the "Addressed to older reader"-"Addressed to younger reader" comparison.

Finally, Spearman correlation tests were carried out to compare test measurements and confirm how systematic was the effect of the variable of perceived age on the scores. The significant correlations show that the rankings between scores on the separate tests are related.

**Table 4.** Correlations (Spearman *rho*)

| Correlation | Rho | p |
|---|---|---|
| Older-Similar reader | .831 | <.001 |
| Older-Younger reader | .696 | <.003 |
| Similar-Younger reader | .762 | <.001 |

It was also shown that participants made changes in a consistent way in order to address the perceived audiences. Thus, they altered their handwriting to make the text easier to read; letters addressed to a younger reader would often be written on every other line and have additional line drawings; more detail was used when writing to an older reader; and most participants would try to write simpler syntax when writing to a younger reader.

3. **Read the textbook introduction to this section again and then answer these questions.**

   1. Does your initial reading of this section suggest that enough data have been provided so as to have adequately responded to the research questions or hypotheses previously put forward?
   2. What tables or graphical displays of results are provided, and what do you understand from the data displayed? Are there any data that you feel might have usefully been added to the information provided here?
   3. What information is provided by any descriptive statistics about the distribution of data?
   4. Have the data been scored using the unit measurement predicted earlier, and/or has any appropriate data conversion taken place?
   5. i.  What, if any, specific statistical operations or calculations were carried out on these data, and does this seem to have been carried out appropriately?
      ii. In the light of what you have read in this section, do you wish to amend or add to your previous appraisal of the assumptions met for this procedure?
   6. What is your appraisal of any other interpretations that the researcher makes of his or her data in this section?
   7. What information is made available or can be calculated about effect size of the outcomes?
   8. What initial conclusions do you come to about the practical significance and meaningfulness of these results? Do these coincide with the researcher's interpretation?

Observations

Look at each observation marked in the text and decide what kind of pertinent reaction could be made at each point.

① 

②

## Discussion and conclusions 3 (Guided appraisal)

1.  Before working through this part of the paper, you should re-read the previously-appraised sections of this study.
2.  When you have read a paragraph, stop and write in the *left-hand column* a few words which summarise the gist of that paragraph, to help you understand and focus on what the researcher is saying. Then, in the *right-hand column* write a few words which record your instinctive reactions to what you have just read as if you were talking to the researcher face-to-face. Advice on how to go about reacting spontaneously to the text was provided on p. 4.

|  | The results of the study were as expected: the experimental groups improved to a greater extent in the post-test measurement, even though the control group scored highly on the pre-test. Results from the questionnaire data showed that participants were being attentive to a wider range of factors① in their writing as a result of the revision strategy teaching. Having said this, data from the interviews tended to contradict this; some participants expressed a narrower view of revision, which reflected the kind of instruction they received in their normal L2 writing classes. |  |
|  | What was clear, however, from both questionnaire and interview data was that participants had begun to form an awareness of the reader. Admittedly, they may still have seen this reader in terms of their immediate writing context, in other words, their teacher. As Researcher 13 (1995) had found, participants showed a certain anxiety about writing grammatically correct forms; the interview data reveals participants who expressed this anxiety in terms of the possible repercussions on any eventual exam grade. The impression gained was that they were still unsure about whether this kind of revision would fit in with the way their compositions were normally evaluated. |  |

Pedagogical implications

These findings support the view that the teaching of L2 writing needs to take into account a number of factors, and not just surface accuracy. The common practice (Researcher 20, 1981; Researcher 21, 1983)② of encouraging initial L2 writing training by concentrating on surface correctness needs to be amended to include more instruction about discourse-related skills and/or how to focus on content in revision. Improvement in the control group was not as much as the experimental group; therefore, it seems that writing more, and on more subjects, and correcting surface errors only does not actually help to improve writing.

Limitations

Although findings do indeed suggest that the experimental groups profited from the instruction in terms of their points gain, it must also be admitted that no control was made in the study for what happened in each separate lesson or for the gains which might naturally accrue as a result of their normal English learning during the period③. Also, it should be recalled that only a few students were interviewed and that these were volunteers. Thus, these cannot be said to represent the views of the whole sample. Since this study only sought to describe what happened in one experimental situation, more research is needed to establish firm tendencies.

Encouraging more reader-based views about revision means encouraging the kind of peer reading and writing integration built in to the experimental teaching given here. Thus, as the experimental groups were reading each other's texts, they were also being taught revision strategies. The control group did not receive such benefits, and this could explain the comparatively small gains made overall pre- to post-test.

It follows from this evidence that revision instruction certainly seems to be a recommendable practice. These groups of participants were able to stand back from their work and assess the need for more global revision as a result of this instruction. The question for curriculum writers in Country B is whether an alternative should now be sought to the current practice of only encouraging the kind of frequent L2 writing in class practised here by the control group.

3. **Read the textbook introduction to this section again and then respond to these questions, using some of my prompts if you wish.**

1. What conclusions were drawn from the study, and how do these reflect on the original questions and/or hypotheses?
2. What is your appraisal of the general inferences which the researcher draws from the findings? How do these compare with your own reactions to what you have been told throughout the paper?
   *Consider again the implied link between instruction and improvement here?*
   *What other factors might have contributed to participants' perceptions about the writing and revision process?*
   *What other factors might have contributed to improvement in the main study?*
   *Are you satisfied with the conclusions drawn about the control group's performance?*
3. In what ways are the findings related to current theoretical and empirical knowledge on the topic?
4. What limitations or weaknesses have you or the researcher identified, and how might any future research seek to contribute further to what has been revealed in the study?
   *How might the structure of the final group of interviewees have affected responses obtained?*
   *Consider any limitations imposed on the study by the school authorities.*
5. What is your appraisal of any practical inferences which the researcher draws from the study in terms of pedagogical implications or recommendations?
   *How appropriate are the recommendations made in the light of current constraints on writing in Country B?*
6. Assess your overall confidence in the paper you have read.

7.  Are there any additional points raised during your appraisal of the paper that you would like to have seen discussed in this section?
    *What more details would have been useful about the revision strategies taught?*

Observations

①  What information has been provided about these "factors" in the paper?
②  What might be deduced from the dates of the research cited here compared to when the paper was written (1998)?
③  To which groups does this limitation refer?

## Discussion and conclusions 4 (Unguided appraisal)

1.  Before working through this part of the paper, you should re-read the previously-appraised sections of this study.
2.  When you have read a paragraph, stop and write in the *left-hand column* a few words which summarise the gist of that paragraph, to help you understand and focus on what the researcher is saying. Then, in the *right-hand column* write a few words which record your instinctive reactions to what you have just read as if you were talking to the researcher face-to-face.

| | | |
|---|---|---|
| | It is obvious from the evidence presented here that there is a fair amount① of support for our first hypothesis, which stated that grades given would vary in a systematic and significant way② according to the age of the reader as seen by the writer. Highest scores were given to letters written to audiences seen to be older than the writer; lowest grades went to those perceived to be younger. This was observed not only in the overall score, but also on 4 of the 5 elements③ of the scale, the exception being "Sentence style". This was not considered surprising since many of the examiners had expressed doubts about its definition during marking. | |
| | The second hypothesis, however, is not supported. I had thought that this piece of writing would be easier for the participants and turn out to be a more fluent piece of writing④. But this did not happen. The | |

participants would typically put in more personal information in letters addressed to readers seen to be of a similar age but would use more complex language when writing to older readers.

The significant correlations obtained with the Spearman analysis also give further support to the idea that the writing tasks set systematically affected performance.

The cursory qualitative examination of the writing showed that the letters also included elements directed towards specific audiences⑤: handwriting was changed to make it easier for "young readers" to read the text, drawings were also added for this aim, and syntax was visibly simplified.

My reading of these outcomes is that, for writers in this country, EFL writing varies significantly along with the perceived reader, and, in particular, the age of that reader as seen by the writer. Thus, audience awareness is clearly an important variable in EFL writing in this country. Beyond the confines of this specific context, there is now evidence to support the idea in the literature that learners will consciously modify their language when writing to specific readers and this contributes to current knowledge of the importance of such variables. However, there remain many more questions to be answered, not least of which is how these findings might be applied in the classroom itself.

3.   **Read the textbook introduction to this section again and then answer these questions.**

1.   What conclusions were drawn from the study, and how do these reflect on the original questions and/or hypotheses?
2.   What is your appraisal of the general inferences which the researcher draws from the findings? How do these compare with your own reactions to what you have been told throughout the paper?

3.  In what ways are the findings related to current theoretical and empirical knowledge on the topic?
4.  What limitations or weaknesses have you or the researcher identified, and how might any further research seek to improve upon what has been revealed in the study?
5.  What is your appraisal of any practical inferences which the researcher draws from the study in terms of pedagogical implications or recommendations?
6.  Assess your overall confidence in the paper you have read.
7.  Are there any additional points raised during your appraisal of the paper that you would like to have seen discussed in this section?

Observations

Look at each observation marked in this text and decide what kind of pertinent reaction could be made at each point.

①
②
③
④
⑤

# Glossary of key terms in quantitative research

**Alpha (decision) level (α)**  (see Statistical significance level)

**ANCOVA**  (see ANOVA)

**ANOVA**  Analysis of variance (ANOVA) is used to test hypotheses about the differences between two or more means. The *t*-test can only be used to test differences between two means. When there are more than two, it is possible to compare each mean with each other mean using *t*-tests. However, conducting multiple *t*-tests can easily increase the possibility of making a Type I error (see below). Analysis of variance can be used to test differences among several means for significance without increasing the chances of committing a Type I error.

Among the statistical procedures used in the analysis of data are the analysis of variance (ANOVA), analysis of covariance (ANCOVA), multivariate analysis of variance (MANOVA), and multivariate analysis of covariance (MANCOVA). These procedures aim to divide the total variance into its components by the analysis of sums of squared terms taken from the data.

**Assumptions**  Statistical methods such as those we have studied in this book require the data to satisfy various conditions. For example, the data should follow a normal distribution and be independent. When using such a method, we assume that these conditions hold: these are the assumptions required for the method to be valid. It is good statistical practice to check the assumptions as far as possible.

**Balanced design**  Another important aspect of the two-way ANOVA test is related to the number of participants in each cell of the design. If the between-groups independent variable has equal numbers of participants in each of its levels, then you have a balanced design. With a balanced design, each of the two independent variables and the interaction are independent of each other. Each independent variable can be significant or non-significant, and the interaction can be significant or non-significant without any influence from one or the other effects.

**Bar graph (chart)**  A bar graph is similar to a histogram, except that there is a small space drawn between the columns. It is often used in summarising a set of categorical data. A number of rectangles are used, all of the same width, each of which represents a particular category. The length (and hence area) of each rectangle is proportional to the number of cases in the category it represents.

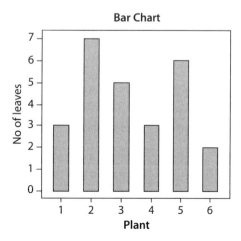

Bar Chart

**Bell-shaped curve**   (see Normal distribution)

**Between-groups designs**   Between-group variables are independent variables or factors in which a different group of participants is used for each level of the variable. If an experiment is carried out comparing four teaching methods and if a different group of participants is used for each, then teaching method is a between-groups variable. If every variable in an experimental design is a between-groups variable, then the design is called a between-groups design. Some experimental designs have both between- and within-group variables (cf., Mixed designs; Within-group designs).

**Category (variable)**   A set of data is said to be categorical if the values or observations belonging to it can be sorted according to category. Every value should belong to one and only one category, and there should be no doubt as to which one. For example, people have the characteristic of `gender' with categories `male' and `female' (see also Nominal data measurement).

**Causal relationships**   If there has been an identified probability of one event influencing another event, it is suggested that a causal relationship exists between the two events. In order to attribute a causal relationship between two events, A and B, three conditions are typical: (a) B must not precede A in time, (b) A and B must covary together to a recognisable degree, and (c) no alternative explanation accounts as well as or better for the covariation between A and B.

**Central tendency**   Measures of central tendency locate the middle or the centre of a distribution of data. There is deliberate vagueness about the way "middle" or "centre"

are defined. Thus, the term "central tendency" can refer to a wide variety of measures. The mean is the most commonly used measure of central tendency. Others are the "median" and the "mode". For normal distributions, these measures are all the same. For skewed distributions, they can differ considerably (see also Mean; Median; Mode).

**Chi-square test**   The chi-square test of independence is a test of whether there is a relationship, for example, between participants' characteristics on one variable and those on another. The test is based on the chi-square distribution, the most common use of which is to test differences between proportions. Although this test is not the only one based on the chi-square distribution, it has come to be known as the chi-square test. The test compares the observed frequencies in each of the cells of a contingency table with the expected frequencies for each cell if these differences were only due to chance. The greater the difference between observed and expected frequencies, the more likely the result is to be significant.

**Confidence intervals**   These are limits or ranges of values within which we can be certain (in terms of probability) that, say, the mean value of the population from which the sample is drawn can be found. Typically, these are *per cent* limits and 95% ones are commonly used (i.e. limits within which we can be 95% sure). (cf., Probability level).

**Confounded research design**   Two variables are confounded if they vary together in such a way that it is impossible to work out which one is responsible for an observed effect. For example, imagine a study wherein two L2 teaching methodologies were compared. The first was given to a group of teenage students and the second to a group of adults. If a difference between treatments were revealed, it would be impossible to tell if one treatment were more effective than the other, or if teaching methodology treatments are more effective for one age group than the other. In such an example, age and treatment would have been confounded.

**Consequential validity**   The rationale and evidence for evaluating the anticipated and unintended consequences of data interpretation and use.

**Construct**   An abstract theoretical concept that is not directly observable or measurable (e.g., motivation, language-learning aptitude) but that is considered to exist on theoretical grounds.

**Construct validity**   Construct validity describes the extent to which a particular instrument measures accurately constructs of interest that have been obtained theoretically.

**Content validity**   Content validity considers formally the extent to which a particular instrument measures accurately what it is claimed to measure. A group of experts would normally decide on this, focussing on the instrument's representativeness and com-prehensiveness.

**Continuous data measurement**   Continuous data show us how much of a variable is present in the set of data. It would be possible to score any value, within the limits to which the variable extends. You can count, order, and measure continuous data. For example, the variable "Amount of time needed to complete a test of reading comprehension" is a continuous data measurement/variable as it could take 30 minutes, 35 minutes, etc.

to finish. There is no set time limit. However, the variable "Number of correct responses on a reading comprehension test (Total score possible 50 points)" would not be a continuous data measurement/variable, as it would not be possible to get 32.15 on such a test. A variable that is non-continuous is also called "discrete".

**Control group**   Sometimes termed the "Comparison" group in a quasi-experimental study with no random assignment to groups, this refers to the group in a quasi- or pure experimental study that does not receive the treatment, later to be compared to the experimental or treatment group. In a pure experimental study, participants are allocated randomly to the treatment and control groups.

**Control variable**   The effects of a particular variable may be isolated by controlling its presence or its consequences. This is done by controlling its potential effect on the dependent variable. However, controlling in this way also places inevitable limits on generalisation of outcomes, since the researcher will not be able to generalise beyond the controlled situation in the study (see also Independent variable; Dependent variable; Moderator variable; Intervening variable).

**Correlation**   The correlation between two variables represents the degree to which variables are related. Typically, the linear relationship is measured with either Pearson's correlation or Spearman's rho. It is important to keep in mind that correlation does not necessarily mean causation. For example, there may be a high positive relationship between the number of ambulances attending a major car accident and the number of people injured. Does this therefore mean that the ambulances cause the injured?

It is more probable that the larger the accident, the more ambulances attend. Thus, the variable "seriousness of car accident" is the causal variable, correlating with the number of ambulances attending the scene (see also Negative correlation; Pearson correlation coefficient; Spearman correlation coefficient; Linearity; Scatterplot).

**Correlation coefficient**   A correlation coefficient is a number between -1 and 1 measuring the extent to which two variables have a linear relationship. A correlation coefficient of 1 is obtained if there is a perfect linear relationship with a positive slope between the two variables. In the case of a positive correlation, whenever one variable has a high (or low) value, so does the other. A coefficient of -1 is obtained if there is a perfect linear relationship with negative slope between the two variables. In this case, whenever one variable has a high (or low) value, the other has a low (or high) value. There are a number of different correlation coefficients appropriate to the different kinds of variables being studied (see Correlation; Negative correlation).

**Covariate**   A variable can be applied in an analysis to correct, adjust, or modify the data on a dependent variable before these data are related to one or more independent variables. For example, if a researcher was looking at the relationship between student age and L2 examination success, the researcher might first want to remove any effects due to the amount of time spent studying the L2. This latter would then be the covariate used.

**Crit(ical) values**   A critical value is used in significance testing. In most procedures, it is the value that a test statistic must exceed in order for the null hypothesis to be rejected.

For example, if you look at the statistical tables for the *t*-test distribution, the critical value of t (with 5 degrees of freedom using the .01 significance level (two-tailed hypothesis)) is 4.03. This means that for the probability value to be less than or equal to .01, the value of the t statistic obtained from the calculation must be 4.03 or greater. The critical value for any hypothesis test depends on the significance level at which the test is carried out, and whether the test is one- or two-tailed.

**Cultural validity**   Cultural validity assesses the extent to which an instrument of measurement or procedural element in a study satisfactorily appreciates the cultural and sociocultural values of those being studied.

**Curvilinear**   (see Linearity)

**Data**   Information collected in a research study is referred to as data. Data are often considered to be statistical or quantitative. Data can, however, also be found in many other forms, including transcripts of interviews and videotapes. Different kinds of data require different approaches to statistical analysis (see Nominal data measurement, Ordinal data measurement, Interval data measurement).

**Degrees of freedom (*df*)**   This value is frequently referred to in the organisation of tables of statistical distributions used in carrying out tests of statistical significance.

**Dependent variable**   A variable in a study, whose values are "dependent on" other variables for their outcomes. The researcher would try to explain these outcomes in terms of one or more independent variables. The distinction between dependent and independent variables is typically made on theoretical grounds to test a particular model of cause-effect or a specific hypothesis. You may also come across the term "criterion variable" to describe this variable (see also Independent variable; Control variable; Moderator variable; Intervening variable).

**Descriptive statistics**    A basic use of descriptive statistics is to summarise a mass of data in a clear and understandable way, both numerically and graphically. In numerical presentations, we might typically look out for measures of central tendency and variability, such as the mean and standard deviation. These statistics convey information about the most typical values obtained and how these are spread out across the data sample (see also Inferential statistics).

**Directional hypothesis**    When the researcher wishes to assess or compute the probability of differences in both directions of the distribution, this is referred to as a "two-tailed" hypothesis. However, other situations (for example, as a result of previous studies with these variables) may suggest to the researcher that he or she need only look in one direction for the probability of these differences. When only one direction is of concern to the researcher, a "one-tailed" test can be performed. When consulting statistical tables yourself, be sure to confirm whether these correspond to one-tailed or two-tailed hypotheses (see also Hypothesis testing).

**Dispersion**    The dispersion (variability or spread) of scores from a variable is the degree to which these differ from each other. If every score on the variable were about equal, there would be very little

dispersion noted. When the dispersion is large, the values are more widely scattered (bottom diagram); when it is small, they are more bunched around one point (top diagram). There are several measures of dispersion, two of the most common being the "standard deviation" and "range" (see below).

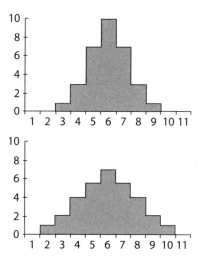

**Effect size**    An effect size is a standardised measure of the strength of a relationship. Its great advantage to the researcher is that the measure is independent of sample size and estimates the extent to which the phenomenon takes place. A number of different measures are used to test the effect size. The larger the effect size, the easier it is to detect (and, therefore, the fewer cases needed to do so). (See also Power)

**Eta$^2$**    A correlation coefficient that can be used to determine strength of association or effect size. It is interpreted as the proportion of the total variability of the dependent variable which is explained by the variation in the independent variable (cf., Omega$^2$).

**Expected frequencies**   In contingency tables (as presented in a chi-square test), the expected frequencies are the frequencies that you would predict (or expect) in each cell of the table, if you knew only the row and column totals, and if everything were equal as it would be if there were no relationship at all between the variables (see also Chi-square-test; Observed frequencies).

**Ex post facto designs**   A design in which the researcher – rather than creating the treatment to be tested – examines the effect of a naturally-occurring "treatment" after that treatment should have taken place (i.e., "after-the-fact"). This "treatment" is then related to some result or dependent measure. If a predicted relationship is confirmed statistically, this will not necessarily be an indication that the independent and dependent variables are causally related (cf., Pure experimental designs; Pre-experimental designs; Quasi-experimental designs).

**External validity**   A study would have external validity if the findings could be applied in the real world (i.e., outside the current experimental situation) and to similar events as in the present study. The extent to which threats to such validity are met affects our ability to credit the results with generalisable outcomes. External validity is of little value unless it has been preceded by adequate address of internal validity concerns, which give us confidence in the basic descriptive conclusions drawn from the data themselves.

**Face validity**   Face validity relates to content validity, but assesses informally and/or intuitively whether the instrument appears to measure what it purports to measure.

**Factorial ANOVA**   Two Way Analysis of Variance (ANOVA) is a way of studying the effects of two factors separately (their main effects) and, sometimes, together (their interaction effect). A factorial ANOVA can be designed with many different factors, but by adding more and more independent variables, the potentially numerous interactions can make interpretation difficult.

**Factorial design**   When a researcher wants to study the effects of two or more independent variables simultaneously, it makes more sense to manipulate these variables in one experiment than to run a single experiment for each one (such as a $t$-test). The treatments are combinations of levels of the factors. Moreover, such experiments involving more than one independent variable allow the researcher to test for interactions among variables.

**F Distribution**   The F distribution is the distribution of the ratio of two estimates of variance and is used to compute probability values in the analysis of variance. The F distribution has two parameters: degrees of freedom numerator and degrees of freedom denominator. In the tables provided, the vertical *df* corresponds to the within-group measure and the horizontal line across the top to the between-group measure.

**F ratio**   The F-ratio is the ratio of the between-group variance to the within-group variance in an analysis of variance.

**Frequency (data)**   Frequency measures how often something occurs, or tallies how many objects, people, or participants have a particular attribute.

**Frequency distribution**   Frequency distributions are portrayed in tables, histograms, or polygons. They can show either the actual number of observations falling in each range or the percentage of observations. In the latter instance, the distribution is called a relative frequency distribution (see also Bar graph (chart); Histogram).

**Generalisation**   Generalisation refers to the extent to which conclusions can be drawn about a PARAMETER or relationship in a population from data obtained from a sample of that population. Generalisation is biased or constrained when the population from which the sample is drawn is narrow.

**Hawthorne effect**   The Hawthorne effect refers to the tendency of participants to improve their performance under observation, simply because they are aware that they are being studied or are involved in an experiment.

**Homoscedasticity**   This assumption means that the error variance around the regression line is the same for all values of the predictor variable. In multivariate analysis, it is undesirable for the criterion/dependent variable to have variances which are considerably different for the same values of the predictor variable, in the different populations which have been sampled. The incidence of markedly different variances in the different populations is referred to as heteroscedasticity.

**Histogram**   A histogram is constructed from a frequency table (cf. Bar graph (chart)). The intervals are shown on the X-axis and the number of scores in each interval is represented by the height of a rectangle located above that interval. It is generally used when dealing with large data sets. A histogram can also help detect any unusual observations (see Outlier), or any gaps in the data.

**Hypothesis**   A hypothesis is a statement about the relationship between two or more

variables that are being studied (see also Directional hypothesis).

**Hypothesis testing**   Hypothesis testing consists of estimating the probability that certain, hypothesised effects are observed and calculating these against the null and the alternative hypotheses (see Null hypothesis). Data obtained are compared with theoretical expected data, and a calculation made of the probability that the observed outcome could have been due to chance. If the data are very different from what would be expected under the assumption that the null hypothesis is true, then the null hypothesis is rejected. If the data are not so different from those expected under the assumption that the null hypothesis is true, then the null hypothesis is not rejected. If the researcher does not reject the null hypothesis, this does not mean the null hypothesis is true; it only suggests there is not enough evidence against the null hypothesis in favour of the alternative hypothesis. Rejecting the null hypothesis suggests that the alternative hypothesis *may* be true (see also Research question).

**Independent variable**   An independent variable is one that can be used to predict or explain another variable, usually referred to as a dependent (or criterion) variable (see also Dependent variable; Control variable; Moderator variable; Intervening variable).

**Inferential statistics**   Inferential statistics are used to draw inferences about a population from a sample (cf., Descriptive statistics).

**Intact groups/classes**   Much of the research in L2 learning involves the use of groups or classes into which participants have been previously placed according to some criterion. Such groups or classes are referred to as "intact". In such research it is impossible randomly to select participants at the outset (cf., Random selection).

**Interaction (effect)**   An interaction occurs when two or more predictor variables not only have separate direct effects, but also a combined effect formed by the product of the two or more variables, which influences the dependent variable.

**Internal validity**   Internal validity is the extent to which the results of the study can be put down to the treatment applied rather than to the design of the study. It also reflects on the degree to which sound conclusions can be drawn about the results of the study.

**Inter-rater reliability**   The inter-rater reliability of an instrument measures the degree of agreement between two or more raters, and indicates the extent to which the raters assess by using the instrument in the same way (see also Reliability; Kuder-Richardson formulae).

**Interval data measurement**   On an interval scale the distance between any two positions is of known size. One unit on the scale represents the same magnitude on the trait or characteristic being measured across the whole range of that scale (cf., Ordinal data measurement and Nominal data measurement). For example, if language proficiency is measured on an interval scale, a difference between a score of 50 and 51 would be considered to be the same difference as that between 23 and 24.

**Intervening variable**   The intervening variable is thought to be a predictor of one or more dependent variables. It is a factor that theoretically affects these variables but cannot be seen, measured, or manipulated.

Therefore, its effect has to be interpreted from the effects of the independent and moderator variables on the observed phenomenon. Unlike the moderator variable (see below), the intervening variable could not previously have been identified precisely for inclusion in the research (see also Independent variable; Dependent variable; Control variable; Moderator variable).

**Kuder-Richardson formulae**   These formulae are measures of the internal consistency or reliability of tests that have dichotomous response categories (e.g. "yes/no", "right/wrong" items). (See also Inter-rater reliability and Split-half reliability)

**Kurtosis**   Kurtosis indicates the extent to which a distribution is more peaked or flat-topped than a normal distribution. The index of kurtosis measures the extent to which the distribution differs from the normal or bellshaped curve (see also Normal distribution).

**Levels (of a variable)**   The number of levels of a factor or independent variable is equal to the number of variations of that factor that were used in the experiment. If a researcher were interested in studying the variable "Native language" and obtained data from "L1 German", "L1 French" and "L1 Russian" students, there would be three levels of the variable.

**Likert scale**   A Likert type scale is a widely-used questionnaire format in which a series of statements is used to measure a particular characteristic by asking for a response. This usually involves choosing from among two or more possible cues, typically intended to gauge this response, perhaps in terms of the agreement or disagreement with each statement.

**Linearity**    When two variables are perfectly linearly related, the points of a scatterplot fall on a straight line. The more the points tend to fall along a straight line, the stronger the linear relationship. Curvilinearity might occur when the points plotted form a curve rather than a straight line (e.g., the correlation begins highly positive but finishes highly negative). The Pearson correlation coefficient is not suitable when the relationship is curvilinear (see also Correlation; Scatterplot).

**Linear regression**    Linear regression involves the prediction of one variable from another variable when the relationship between the variables is assumed to be linear (cf., Multiple regression).

**Longitudinal studies**    A longitudinal study involves the investigation over time of individuals or groups of individuals. A cross-sectional study is conducted at one single point in time. Most often, the study is of a sample drawn from a population at a particular time, but it may involve the investigation of the total population.

**Main effect**    The main effect of an independent variable is the effect of the variable alone averaged across the levels of other variables in the experiment. Analysis of variance provides a significance test for the main effect of each variable in the design (cf., Interaction (effect)).

**Matched participants/subjects (group)**    Two (or more) samples selected in such a way that each case (e.g., person) in one sample is matched on one or more preselected characteristics with a corresponding case in the other sample. Examples often found include two samples in which the members are clearly paired, or are matched explicitly by the researcher, or samples in which the same attribute, or variable, is measured twice for each participant, under different circumstances, commonly referred to as "Repeated-measures" designs.

**Mean**    The arithmetic mean is what is often referred to as the "average". The mean is the sum of all the scores divided by the number of scores (see also Central tendency; Median; Mode).

**Median**    Once placed in order, the median is the value halfway through the set of data, below and above which we find an equal number of data values. The median is less sensitive to extreme scores than the mean and this makes it a better measure than the mean for highly skewed distributions (see also Central tendency; Mean; Mode).

**Mixed (group) designs**    Also known as "split-plot" designs, these include both comparisons of independent groups (between-groups) and repeated-measures (within-group) of the same group of participants.

**Mode**    The mode is the most frequently occurring score in a distribution and is another measure of central tendency. It is the only measure of central tendency that can be used with nominal data. A disadvantage of this measure is that there can be more than one mode if two or more values are equally common (see also Central tendency; Mean; Median).

**Moderator variable**    A moderator variable is a variable in a cause-effect situation that interacts with a prior variable to modify its effect on a dependent variable (see also Independent variable; Dependent variable; Control variable; Intervening variable).

**Multicolinearity**   This occurs when two or more predicting variables are highly correlated in multivariate analyses, and the joint outcome is that they prevent the accurate estimation of the effects of the variables.

**Multiple regression**   The general purpose of multiple regression is to learn more about the relationship between several independent or predictor variables and a dependent or criterion variable. It is often used when the researcher wants to see the degree to which scores on a dependent variable can be predicted from those of two or more independent variables (cf., Linear regression).

**Multivariate analysis**   This is a blanket term referring to the family of procedures that involve the simultaneous study of two or more dependent variables in a study. One advantage of such analyses is that they allow the researcher to manipulate the variables and check if any specific group affects the dependent variable more than another.

**Negative correlation**   A relation in which the values of one variable increase as the values of the other variable decrease (see also Correlation; Correlation coefficient).

**Nominal data measurement**   Nominal measurement allocates items to groups or categories. Any numbers allocated are merely labels; there is no quantitative information provided. While you can count such outcomes, no ordering of the items is implied. "University degree studied", "place of residence", and "sex" would all be examples of nominal scales (cf., Ordinal data measurement and Interval data measurement).

**Non-continuous measurement**   (see Continuous data measurement)

**Non-parametric tests**   Non-parametric tests are often used in place of their parametric corresponding procedures when certain key assumptions about the underlying population are in doubt. In the case of a comparison, for example, between two independent groups, the Mann-Whitney U test does not have the basic assumptions that the data are strongly interval-based, or that the mean is the best measure of central tendency; its parametric alternative, the independent *t*-test does (cf., Parametric tests).

**Normal distribution**   The normal distribution is a theoretical concept and suggests a particular form for the distribution of the variable which, when plotted on a graph, produces a bell-shaped curve (see below and Skew(ed) distribution), rising smoothly from a small number of results at both extremes (the tails) to a large number of cases in the middle. The distribution has certain useful characteristics which lead to its widespread use in statistical tests. Most of these tests work well even if the distribution deviates slightly from normality:

**Null hypothesis**   The null hypothesis, often written H0, represents a theory or hunch the researcher has, either because it is believed to be true and/or because it is to be used as a basis for argument, but has not been tested. The null hypothesis suggests an effect does not differ significantly from zero or another set value. The alternative hypothesis (often written H1) postulates that an effect differs significantly from zero or another set value. Depending on the data submitted to the hypothesis test (see Hypothesis testing), the null hypothesis either will or will not be rejected as acceptable. The way in which the null hypothesis is communicated is often the opposite of what the researcher actually expects; it is postulated to allow the data to contradict it (e.g., "There is no difference between the test scores obtained from the experimental and the control groups"). (See also Type 1 and Type 2 errors)

**Observed frequencies**    In contingency table problems, the observed frequencies are those actually obtained in each cell of the table. Observed frequencies are compared with the expected frequencies and any significant differences between them used to suggest that the example expressed by the expected frequencies does not describe the data well (see also Chi-square test; Expected frequencies).

**Omega²**    A strength of association/effect size measure applied in certain statistical tests where the design is balanced (cf., Eta²).

**One-way ANOVA**    The one-way analysis of variance allows for comparison of several groups of observations, all of which are independent but possibly with a different mean for each group. In a one-way design, there is only *one* dependent variable and *one* independent variable with three or more levels. The comparisons (within-groups or repeated measures) of the means on the dependent variable are made across these levels (see also ANOVA).

**Operational definition**    An unambiguous definition based on the observable characteristics of what is being defined. The precision of this definition affects the nature and quality of the observations upon which the operational definition is based, as well as how they are obtained and subsequently measured.

**Ordinal data measurement**    Measurements with ordinal scales are ordered in the sense that higher numbers represent higher values. You can count and rank these data, but not measure them. It is important to remember that the intervals between neighbouring points on the scale are not necessarily equal (cf., Interval data measurement and Nominal data measurement). For example, on a five-point rating scale measuring motivation to learn L2 German, the difference between a rating of 2 and that of 3 may not represent the same difference as that between a rating of 4 and a rating of 5.

**Outlier**    An outlier is an observation in a set of results which is far removed in value from the others in the data – an unusually large or small value when compared to these. The existence of such cases can have important repercussions on certain statistical tests and distort the interpretation of the data. If an outlier is a genuine result, it is important because it might indicate an extreme of behaviour in the process under study. For this reason, outliers are best examined carefully before embarking on any formal analysis. Outliers should not simply be removed without further explanation or justification.

**Parametric tests**    A group of statistical techniques that – unlike non-parametric tests – make strong assumptions about the distribution of data from the dependent variable (e.g., that they are normally distributed). Strictly speaking, these tests assume that dependent variables are scored with interval data or data which are strongly continuous (cf., Non-parametric tests).

**Parameters**    A parameter is a numerical quantity measuring some aspect of a population of scores. When researchers make calculations to describe a sample, these are called statistics. If these same calculations were made for the population of interest in the study, these would be referred to as parameters. Parameters are rarely known and are usually estimated by statistics computed in samples. Greek letters often symbolise such parameters (e.g., $\mu$ = the population mean).

**Pearson correlation coefficient ($r$)**   When computed in a sample, it is designated by the letter $r$ and is sometimes called "Pearson's $r$". Pearson's correlation reflects the degree of linear relationship between two variables that have been measured on interval or ratio scales. The resulting coefficient ranges from +1 to -1. A correlation of +1 means there is a perfect positive linear relationship between variables. However, $r$ can be misleadingly small when there is a relationship between the variables, but it is a non-linear one. There are procedures, based on $r$, for making inferences about the correlation coefficient. However, these make the implicit assumption that the two variables are jointly normally distributed. When this assumption is not met, a non-parametric measure such as the Spearman correlation coefficient (see below) might be more suitable (see also Correlation).

**Phi correlation coefficient ($\Phi$)**   Phi is a correlation coefficient calculated between two dichotomous nominal variables.

**Point biserial correlation ($r_{pbi}$)**   A point biserial correlation is a correlation coefficient calculated between a dichotomous nominal variable and a continuous (interval) variable.

**Polygon**   This refers to the visual shape of the distribution of a set of data shown by the (curved) line connecting the plotted points.

**Population**   A population consists of an entire set of objects, observations, or scores that have something in common. It is the entire group the researcher is interested in, which he or she wishes to describe or draw conclusions about. For example, a population might be defined as all L2 language learners between the ages of 15 and 18. It is important that the investigator carefully and completely defines the population before collecting the sample, including a description of the members to be included. In many cases, such a population is hypothetical. If a researcher in France were testing a new method of learning L2 English vocabulary, for example, he or she might define a population that would be obtained if all teenage L2 learners in France received this new method. Such a population does not exist; the population suggested consists of the scores that would be obtained if they *were* taught with this method (see Parameters).

**Pre-test/Post-test**   These do not need to be "tests" as such before and/or after a particular intervention or treatment. These can also take the form of some kind of observation or measurement of the dependent variable.

**Power**   The power of a statistical test is its ability to detect a significant relationship with a specified number of cases. In other words, the power of a statistical hypothesis test measures that test's ability to reject the null hypothesis when it is actually false – that is, to make a correct decision. It is important to consider power in the design of a quasi-experimental or true experimental study. If the power of an experiment is low, there is then a good chance that the experiment will be inconclusive. There are methods for estimating the power of an experiment before the experiment is conducted. If the power *is* too low, the experiment can be redesigned by changing one of the factors that determine power (see also Effect size).

**Pre-experimental designs**    These designs are simple and inexpensive to implement and exploratory in nature, but lack control groups to compare with the experimental group. They are often used in preliminary research to provide direction and focus for further research using experimental designs, or when circumstances exclude more controlled research design. (See also Ex post facto designs; Pure (true) experimental designs; Quasi-experimental designs)

**Predictive validity**    Validity can be established relating a test to some real-life task behavior that test is supposed to predict. Thus, a test such as the IELTS which is supposed to predict student performance and success on a university course might be validated by measuring this in some other way once students have been working on that course for some time. The higher the predictive validity, the more useful the test.

**Predictor variable**    A predictor variable is one used only in correlational relationships for prediction. It can be likened to the independent variable in experimental research.

**Probability**    A probability provides a quantitative description of the likely occurrence of a particular event. In research, when an hypothesis is offered for testing, an educated guess is being made about what is or is not probable. An hypothesis is tested by finding out the probability of the result. Probability, once calculated, is the proportion of times a particular outcome would happen if the research were repeated ad infinitum.

**Probability value/level (*p*)**    The probability value (*p*) of a statistical hypothesis test is the probability of wrongly rejecting the null hypothesis if it is, in fact, true. In the majority of tests, the *p*-value is compared with the actual significance level of our test and, if it is smaller, the result is significant. That is, if the null hypothesis were to be rejected at the 0.05 significance level, this would be reported as "$p < 0.05$". Small *p*-values suggest that the null hypothesis is unlikely to be true. The smaller it is, the more convincing is the rejection of the null hypothesis (see also Statistical significance).

**Pure (True) experimental designs**    Criteria for a true experiment are (a) that participants should be randomly allocated to treatment and control groups, (b) that the treatment and control conditions should be randomly assigned to the groups so formed; and (c) the participants should be drawn randomly from an identifiable population. The reason for using random selection or random allocation is to exercise control over the identified and unidentified elements that might influence the outcome of the experiment, and to ensure that the results of the experiment can be generalised to an identifiable population. (See also Ex post facto designs; Pre-experimental designs; Quasi-experimental designs)

**Quasi-experimental designs**    In quasi-experimental designs, both control and experimental groups are used in the study, but participants have not normally been randomly selected nor randomly assigned to these groups (see also Ex post facto designs; Pure (true) experimental designs; Pre-experimental designs).

**Random selection**    In random sampling, each item or element of the population is chosen entirely by chance and has an equal chance of being chosen during the selection process. By using random sampling, the likelihood of bias is reduced (cf., Intact groups/classes).

**Range**   The range of a sample (or a set of data) is a measure of the spread or the dispersion of the observations. It is calculated from the difference between the largest and the smallest observed value of some quantitative characteristic. However, a great deal of information is ignored when computing the range, since only the largest and the smallest data values are considered. It also follows that the range will be greatly influenced by the presence of just one unusually large or small value in the sample (see Outlier; Standard deviation; Dispersion; Variance).

**Rank order**   (see Ordinal data measurement)

**Rate**   This is calculated to show how often something occurs in large sets of data. No standard unit is used, as this depends on the nature of the data; however, many studies provide rates such as "per 100 occurrences", "per 1000 words used", etc.

**Ratio**   Ratio scales are like interval scales except they have true zero values, that is, a point on the scale that represents the complete absence of the characteristic measured.

**Raw scores**   Raw scores are data or values that have not been subjected to statistical manipulation. They may or may not have been adjusted by having any abnormal values removed or corrected.

**Regression line**   A regression line is an imaginary line drawn through a scatterplot of two variables, around which most of the plotted points cluster. When it slopes down (from top left to bottom right), there is evidence for a negative or inverse relationship

between the variables; when it slopes up, a positive or direct relationship is indicated (see also Scatterplot).

**Reliability (coefficient)**   A measure of how consistent repeated measurements are when performed under comparable conditions. The reliability of an instrument can be discovered in a number of ways and is an index of the consistency or stability with which the instrument makes measurements. Before drawing any conclusions from an experiment, the reliability of the test instruments used in the experiment should have been assessed. However, such reliability can only be judged by administration of the instrument to a sample of participants. Thus, the coefficient is dependent on the characteristics of the sample, as well as the characteristics of the instrument (see also Inter-rater reliability; Kuder-Richardson formulae).

**Repeated measures designs**   (see Within-group designs)

**Research question**   A research question is a specific question asked in the course of investigation to which a specific answer or set of answers is sought (see also Hypothesis testing).

**Sample**   A sample is a group of units selected from a larger group (the population) to represent it, because the population is too large to study in its entirety. By studying the sample, the researcher might hope to draw valid conclusions about the larger group. The sample should, therefore, be representative of the general population. Since it is usually impractical to test every member of a population, a sample from the population is typically the best approach available. Before collecting the sample, it is important that the researcher accurately and completely defines the population, including a description of the members to be included (cf., Stratified randomisation).

**Sampling**    Refers to the process of obtaining a sample.

**Scatterplot**    A scatterplot shows the scores on one variable plotted against scores on a second variable. Each value computed contributes one point to the scatterplot, on which points are plotted but not joined. The resulting pattern indicates the type and strength of the relationship between the two variables. A scatterplot is a useful summary of a set of data from two variables, gives a good visual picture of the relationship, and aids the interpretation of the correlation coefficient or regression model. Scatterplots should be presented when the relationship between two variables is of interest. Statistical summaries are no substitute for a full plot of the data. The plot below shows a very strong, but certainly not perfect, relationship between two variables (see also Linearity; Correlation).

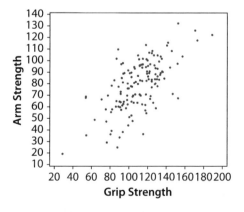

**Scheffé's test**    An example of a post-hoc test which is used to make unplanned comparisons among the means in an experiment. The Scheffé is one of the most powerful of such tests; for example, the combination of a one-way ANOVA and a Scheffé test will help the researcher identify whether there are significant differences in the means of different groups and pinpoint where those differences are really located.

**Scores**    Scores are the values given to participants which then signify the position in which they lie along a scale associated with a specified characteristic.

**SEE**    The standard error of the estimate is a measure of the accuracy of predictions made with a regression line.

**Skew(ed) distribution**    A distribution is said to be skewed when data plotted reveal that one of its tails is longer than the other. Positively-skewed data are graphically described in the first distribution below; there is a longer tail in the positive direction. In the middle graphic there is a longer tail described in the negative direction. Finally, the third distribution is symmetric and has no skew. It represents the familiar bell-shaped curve of the normal distribution (cf., Normal distribution).

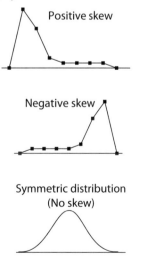

**Slope**   The slope of a regression line refers to its angle or steepness. Graphically, it is measured as the change in Y-axis values associated with a change of one unit on X-axis values. Lines with positive slopes are slanted up toward the right (small values on the X-axis align with small values on the Y-axis; large values on the X-axis align with large values on the Y-axis), while negative value slopes are slanted up toward the left (see also Regression line).

**Spearman correlation coefficient (ρ)**
Commonly used procedures for making inferences about the population correlation coefficient, based on the "Pearson correlation coefficient", make the implicit assumption that the two variables are jointly normally distributed. When this assumption is not justified, a non-parametric measure such as the Spearman rank correlation coefficient might be more appropriate. Spearman's rho (ρ) may also be a better indicator that a relationship exists between two variables when that relationship is non-linear (cf., Pearson correlation coefficient).

**Split-half reliability**   Split-half reliability statistics are simple measures of the internal consistency of a test obtained by dividing the test into two equal parts and calculating the correlation between scores on one half of the test with scores on the other half of the test (see also Kuder-Richardson formulae).

**Standard deviation (s or s.d.)**   Standard deviation is the most-commonly used measure of the spread or dispersion of a set of data in inferential statistical procedures. It is calculated by taking the square root of the variance and is symbolised by "s.d.", or "s". The more widely the values are spread out,

the larger the standard deviation. In a normal distribution, about 68% of the scores are within one standard deviation (either side) of the mean and about 95% of the scores are within two standard deviations (cf., Range; Dispersion; Variance).

**Statistic(s)**   The word "statistics" is used in several different senses. In the broadest sense, it refers to a range of techniques and procedures for analyzing, interpreting, and displaying data, and making decisions based on data. In a second usage, a "statistic" is defined as a numerical quantity (such as the mean) calculated in a sample. Such statistics are used to estimate parameters.

**Statistical significance (level)**   In hypothesis testing, the significance level is the criterion used for rejecting the null hypothesis. First, the difference between the results of the experiment and the null hypothesis is determined. Then, proceeding with the assumption that the null hypothesis is true, the probability ($p$) of a difference that large or larger is computed. Finally, this probability is compared to the significance level. If this probability is sufficiently low (i.e., less than or equal to the significance level), then the null hypothesis is rejected and the outcome is said to be statistically significant. The researcher would want to make the significance level as small as possible in order to protect the null hypothesis and to avoid – as far as possible – inadvertently making false claims. The Greek letter alpha (α) is often used to indicate the significance level chosen (see also Probability value/level). An "alpha" of .01 (compared with .05 or .10) means the researcher is being relatively careful. He or she is only willing to risk being wrong 1 in a 100 times in rejecting the null hypothesis when it is true (i.e., saying there is an effect or relationship when there really is not).

**Stratified randomisation**   There may often be factors that divide up the population into sub-populations (groups / strata), and we may expect the data we are interested in to vary among these different sub-populations. This has to be accounted for when we select a sample from the population so that we obtain one that is representative of that population. Stratified sampling helps us achieve such an aim by taking samples from each stratum or sub-group of a population. The first step in such random sampling is to identify the stratification parameters of interest (e.g., only female L2 learning students between the ages of 18-21). Each stratification parameter represents a control variable. The study would then restrict the population to L2 learning students between these ages as that is the specified control variable and then sample across only female students as this is the independent variable used. Any other strata would be similarly treated. Together with random selection within each stratum, stratification increases the chance that the sample will be representative of the population to whom we want to generalise any outcomes (see also Sample).

**Strength of association/relationship**   (see Effect size; Omega²; Eta²).

***t*-test**   A *t*-test is any of a number of tests based on the *t* distribution. The most common *t*-test is a test for a difference between two means.

**Type 1 and Type 2 errors**   There are two kinds of errors that can be made in statistical significance testing: (1) a null hypothesis which is actually true can be incorrectly

rejected, and (2) a false null hypothesis can fail to be rejected. The former error is called a Type 1 error and the latter a Type 2 error. A Type 2 error is only an error in the sense that an opportunity to reject the null hypothesis correctly was lost. More serious, however, is the case of a Type 1 error, since here a conclusion is drawn that the null hypothesis is false when, in fact, it is true. If a researcher sets up a test requiring strong evidence (i.e., setting the alpha level at .01 or .001) to reject the null hypothesis, it makes it unlikely that a true null hypothesis will be rejected (see also Null hypothesis).

**Variable**   a property or quality of a person, piece of text, or object which is able, or seen, to differ or vary across these people, texts, or objects (see also Independent variable; Dependent variable; Control variable; Moderator variable; Intervening variable).

**Variability** (see Dispersion)

**Variance**   The variance is a measure of how spread out about its average value a distribution is. The larger the variance, the more scattered are the observations on average. It is calculated from the average squared deviation of each number from its mean (see also Standard deviation; Range).

**Within-group designs**   Within-group/ participant designs are those in which one or more of the independent variables are within-participant variables. These are often called repeated-measures designs since within-participants variables always involve taking repeated measurements from each participant. It is normal that participants differ greatly in life. In between-groups designs, these differences among participants are uncontrolled and are treated as error. In within-group designs, the same participants are tested in each condition. Therefore, differences among participants can be measured and separated from error.

The distinction between within-group and between-groups designs will determine in part the choice of an appropriate statistical procedure for analysing the data (cf., Between-groups designs; Mixed designs).

# Appendices

## Appendix I    Flow chart

Reprinted from from Hatch, E., and Lazaraton, A. 1991, *The research manual.* New York: Newbury House Publishers, pp. 544–545.

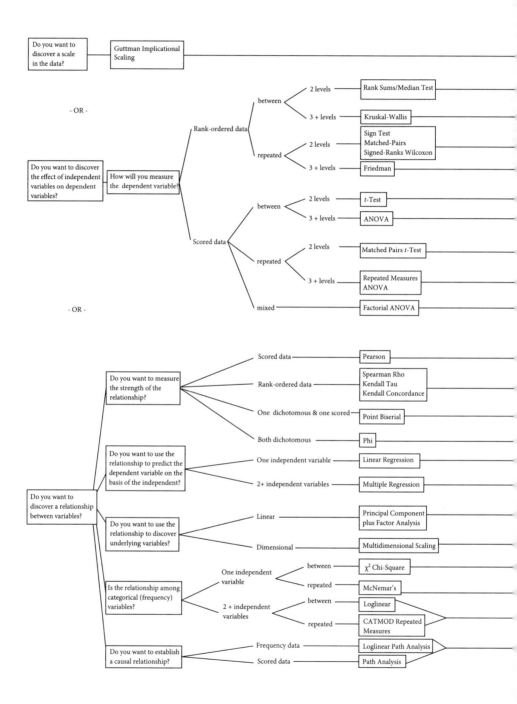

## How will you interpret the results?

| | Check that the coefficient of scalability is over .60 | Interpret scale in light of reasonableness of the cutoff point, number of instances required, missing values, and context used to elicit forms. |

Check that the coefficient of scalability is over .60 — Interpret scale in light of reasonableness of the cutoff point, number of instances required, missing values, and context used to elicit forms.

Compare the groups
Check $z$ value — If the $z$ score is significant, then one group has more $Ss$ in higher ranks than the other. Use eta$^2$ for strength of association.

Compare the groups
Check $H$ value — If $H$ is significant, the groups differ; use Ryan's procedure to locate which groups differ. Use eta$^2$ for strength of association.

Compare the groups
Check $R$ or $z$ value — If the Sign test $R$ or Wilcoxon $z$ is significant, there is a change from time 1 to time 2. Use eta$^2$ for strength of association forWilcoxon.

Compare the groups
Check $\chi^2$ — If $\chi^2$ is significant, there is a change over several time points (or msrs.) To locate the difference more precisely report the results of the Nemenyi's procedure. Use eta$^2$ for strength of association.

Compare the two means
Check $t$ value — If the $t$ value is significant, the two groups differ. Use eta$^2$ for strength of association.

Compare 3+ means
Check $F$ ratio — If the $F$ ratio is significant, the groups differ. To locate the differences more precisely, interpret the multiple-range test (Scheffé, Tukey, or Newman-Keuls). Use omega$^2$ or eta$^2$ for strength of association.

Compare the two means
Check $t$ value — If the $t$ value is significant, there is a difference in the means for the two times or measures. Use eta$^2$ for strength of association.

Compare 3+ means
Check $F$ ratio — If the $F$ ratio is significant, the same (or matched) $Ss$ perform differently on repeated measures. Use a multiple-range test to locate precise differences. Use eta$^2$ for strength ofassociation.

Compare the means
Check $F$ ratios — Step 1. If the <u>interaction</u> is significant, chart the means to show the interaction and interpret it. Interpret main effects in light of the interaction.
Step 2. If the interaction is not significant, interpret the difference in the main effects. Use a multiple-range test to locate precise differences. Use eta$^2$ toshow the strength ofassociation.

Check the strength of each correlation — $r^2$ shows the amount of overlap between each pair of variables. Be sure to correct for attenuation if measures are not of equel reliability.

Check the probability of the correlation — If the correlation is significant, it shows that the $H$ of no relation can be rejected. Interpret the value "sensibly" in terms of strength of relationship.

Check the value ofthe correlation — Explain the correlation in a "sensible" way.

Check $\chi^2$ for significance — Explain the correlation in a "sensible" way.

Report predicted scores
Check the SEE — The stronger the correlation and the smaller the SEE, the better the prediction will be.

Check each added variable — Identify the first independent variable, then the overlap ofthe second with the first to see how much each contributes (as well as their joint contribution) to explain variance in the dependent variable. Explain how much additional information is given by each succeeding independent variable.

Check each factor loading — If possible, once the <u>number</u> off actors has been determined, <u>label</u> each factor by consulting variables with high loadings vs. variables with low loadings on each. Else, label them as factorA, B, C, etc.

Check solutions and stress — Once a solution (about number of dimensions) has been identified or selected, label each dimension by consulting items in the cluster and those distant from cluster. Else, label them as dimension A, B, C, etc.

Check $\chi^2$ value & $(O-E)^2/E$ — If $\chi^2$ is significant, the distribution differs from the expected distribution. Show which cells differ most from expected cell frequency or do a Ryan's procedure to locate the difference more precisely. Use Phi or Cramers V for strength of association.

Check z value
values — If $z$ is significant, conclude there is a change in proportion of $Ss$ from time 1 to time 2.

Check parameter estimates to reduce model, compare models — The parameter estimates show which interactions and main effects are significant. To pare the model, compare various models with the saturated model. Decisions should be based on statistical and substantive arguments.

Check the paths to see which can be trimmed from the model — Use the analysis to trim paths from the model. Interpret the findings on both statistical and substantive grounds.

## Appendix II    Table of assumptions for popular statistical tests

Adapted from Brown, J.D. (1992), Statistics as a foreign language: part 2, *Tesol Quarterly, 26(4)*, 629-664.

| Statistical procedure/ Assumptions | Independence of groups | Independence of observations | Normality | Equal variances | Linearity | Non-multicolinearity | Homoscedasticity | Other assumptions |
|---|---|---|---|---|---|---|---|---|
| **Correlation** | | | | | | | | |
| *Pearson r* | | • | • | | • | | • | |
| *Spearman rho* | | • | | | | | | |
| *Kendall tau* | | • | | | | | | |
| *Kendall W* | | • | | | | | | |
| *Point-biserial correlation* | | • | | | • | | | |
| *Phi coefficient* | | • | • | | • | | | |
| **Correlation/prediction** | | | | | | | | |
| *Simple regression* | | • | • | | • | | • | |
| *Multiple regression* | | • | • | | • | • | • | |
| *Loglinear analysis* | | • | | | | | | No more than 20% of expected frequencies less than or equal to 5 |
| **Group differences** | | | | | | | | |
| *z statistic (large samples)* | • | • | • | • | | | | |
| *t test (any samples)* | • | • | • | • | | | | |
| *One-way ANOVA* | • | • | • | • | | | | |
| *One-way ANCOVA* | • | • | • | • | • | • | | |
| *Matched pairs t-test* | | • | • | • | | | | |
| *Repeated measures ANOVA* | | | • | • | | | | |
| *Repeated measures ANCOVA* | | | • | • | • | • | | |
| *n-way ANOVA* | • | • | • | • | | | | |
| *n-way ANCOVA* | • | • | • | • | • | • | | |
| *n-way repeated measures ANOVA* | | | • | • | | | | |
| *n-way repeated measures ANCOVA* | | | • | • | • | • | | |

| Statistical procedure/ Assumptions | Independence of groups | Independence of observations | Normality | Equal variances | Linearity | Non-multicolinearity | Homoscedasticity | Other assumptions |
|---|---|---|---|---|---|---|---|---|
| *Multivariate ANOVA* | • | • | • | • | • | | | |
| *Multivariate ANCOVA* | • | • | • | • | • | • | | |
| *Multivariate n-way ANOVA* | • | • | • | • | • | | | |
| *Multivariate n-way ANCOVA* | • | • | • | • | • | • | | |
| *Median test* | • | • | | | | | | |
| *Mann U/Wilcoxon* | • | • | | | | | | |
| *Kruskal-Wallis* | • | • | | | | | | |
| *Sign text* | • | • | | | | | | |
| *Friedman One-way ANOVA* | • | • | | | | | | |
| **Frequencies** | | | | | | | | |
| *Chi-square* | • | • | | | | | | Expected frequencies greater or equal to 5 if the df is greater or equal to 2; greater than or equal to 10 if the df equals 1. |
| *McNemar test* | | | | | | | | Differences all in same direction (same sign) |
| *Fisher's exact test* | • | • | | | | | | |
| *n-way chi-square* | • | • | | | | | | |
| **Exploratory statistics** | | | | | | | | |
| *Principal component analysis* | | | • | | • | | | • Factorability of R |
| *Factor analysis* | | | • | | • | • | | • Factorability of R |
| *Multidimensional scaling* | | | • | | • | • | | |
| *Cluster analysis* | | | • | | • | • | | |
| *One-way discriminant analysis* | | | • | | • | • | | Homogeneity of variance-covariance matrices |
| *n-way discriminant analysis* | | | • | | • | • | | Homogeneity of variance-covariance matrices |
| *Guttman scaling* | | | | | | | | Scalable and reproducible |
| *Path analysis* | | | • | | • | • | | All relevant variables • included; variables are causal |

## Appendix III   Useful statistical tables

The distribution of the $F$-statistic (.05)

| df | 1 | 2 | 3 | 4 | 5 | 6 | 8 | 10 | 15 | 25 | 50 | 100 |
|---|---|---|---|---|---|---|---|---|---|---|---|---|
| | | | | | | *df* for greater mean square | | | | | | |
| 1 | 161.5 | 199.5 | 215.8 | 224.6 | 230.2 | 234.0 | 238.9 | 241.9 | 246.0 | 249.3 | 251.8 | 253.1 |
| 2 | 18.51 | 19.00 | 19.16 | 19.25 | 19.30 | 19.31 | 19.37 | 19.40 | 19.43 | 19.456 | 19.476 | 19.49 |
| 3 | 10.1280 | 9.5521 | 9.2766 | 9.1172 | 9.0134 | 8.9407 | 8.8452 | 8.7855 | 8.7028 | 8.6341 | 8.5810 | 8.5539 |
| 4 | 7.7086 | 6.9443 | 6.5914 | 6.3882 | 6.2561 | 6.1631 | 6.0410 | 5.9644 | 5.8578 | 5.7687 | 5.6995 | 5.6640 |
| 5 | 6.6079 | 5.7861 | 5.4094 | 5.1922 | 5.0503 | 4.9503 | 4.8183 | 4.7351 | 4.6188 | 4.5209 | 4.4444 | 4.4051 |
| 6 | 5.9874 | 5.1432 | 4.7571 | 4.5337 | 4.3874 | 4.2839 | 4.1468 | 4.0600 | 3.9381 | 3.8348 | 3.7537 | 3.7117 |
| 7 | 5.5915 | 4.7374 | 4.3468 | 4.1203 | 3.9715 | 3.8660 | 3.7257 | 3.6365 | 3.5107 | 3.4036 | 3.3189 | 3.2749 |
| 8 | 5.3176 | 4.4590 | 4.0662 | 3.8379 | 3.6875 | 3.5806 | 3.4381 | 3.3472 | 3.2184 | 3.1081 | 3.0204 | 2.9747 |
| 9 | 5.1174 | 4.2565 | 3.8625 | 3.6331 | 3.4817 | 3.3738 | 3.2296 | 3.1373 | 3.0061 | 2.8932 | 2.8028 | 2.7556 |
| 10 | 4.9646 | 4.1028 | 3.7083 | 3.4780 | 3.3258 | 3.2172 | 3.0717 | 2.9782 | 2.8450 | 2.7298 | 2.6371 | 2.5884 |
| 11 | 4.8443 | 3.9823 | 3.5874 | 3.3567 | 3.2039 | 3.0946 | 2.9480 | 2.8536 | 2.7186 | 2.6014 | 2.5066 | 2.4566 |
| 12 | 4.7472 | 3.8853 | 3.4903 | 3.2592 | 3.1059 | 2.9961 | 2.8486 | 2.7534 | 2.6169 | 2.4977 | 2.4010 | 2.3498 |
| 13 | 4.6672 | 3.8056 | 3.4105 | 3.1791 | 3.0254 | 2.9153 | 2.7669 | 2.6710 | 2.5331 | 2.4123 | 2.3138 | 2.2614 |
| 14 | 4.6001 | 3.7389 | 3.3439 | 3.1122 | 2.9582 | 2.8477 | 2.6987 | 2.6022 | 2.4630 | 2.3407 | 2.2405 | 2.1870 |
| 15 | 4.5431 | 3.6823 | 3.2874 | 3.0556 | 2.9013 | 2.7905 | 2.6408 | 2.5437 | 2.4034 | 2.2797 | 2.1780 | 2.1234 |
| 16 | 4.4940 | 3.6337 | 3.2389 | 3.0069 | 2.8524 | 2.7413 | 2.5911 | 2.4935 | 2.3522 | 2.2272 | 2.1240 | 2.0685 |
| 17 | 4.4513 | 3.5915 | 3.1968 | 2.9647 | 2.8100 | 2.6987 | 2.5480 | 2.4499 | 2.3077 | 2.1815 | 2.0769 | 2.0204 |
| 18 | 4.4139 | 3.5546 | 3.1599 | 2.9277 | 2.7729 | 2.6613 | 2.5102 | 2.4117 | 2.2686 | 2.1413 | 2.0354 | 1.9780 |
| 19 | 4.3808 | 3.5219 | 3.1274 | 2.8951 | 2.7401 | 2.6283 | 2.4768 | 2.3779 | 2.2341 | 2.1057 | 1.9986 | 1.9403 |
| 20 | 4.3513 | 3.4928 | 3.0984 | 2.8661 | 2.7109 | 2.5990 | 2.4471 | 2.3479 | 2.2033 | 2.0739 | 1.9656 | 1.9066 |
| 21 | 4.3248 | 3.4668 | 3.0725 | 2.8401 | 2.6848 | 2.5727 | 2.4205 | 2.3210 | 2.1757 | 2.0454 | 1.9360 | 1.8761 |
| 22 | 4.3009 | 3.4434 | 3.0491 | 2.8167 | 2.6613 | 2.5491 | 2.3965 | 2.2967 | 2.1508 | 2.0196 | 1.9092 | 1.8486 |
| 23 | 4.2793 | 3.4221 | 3.0280 | 2.7955 | 2.6400 | 2.5277 | 2.3748 | 2.2747 | 2.1282 | 1.9963 | 1.8848 | 1.8234 |
| 24 | 4.2597 | 3.4028 | 3.0088 | 2.7763 | 2.6207 | 2.5082 | 2.3551 | 2.2547 | 2.1077 | 1.9750 | 1.8625 | 1.8005 |
| 25 | 4.2417 | 3.3852 | 2.9912 | 2.7587 | 2.6030 | 2.4904 | 2.3371 | 2.2365 | 2.0889 | 1.9554 | 1.8421 | 1.7794 |
| 26 | 4.2252 | 3.3690 | 2.9752 | 2.7426 | 2.5868 | 2.4741 | 2.3205 | 2.2197 | 2.0716 | 1.9375 | 1.8233 | 1.7599 |
| 27 | 4.2100 | 3.3541 | 2.9603 | 2.7278 | 2.5719 | 2.4591 | 2.3053 | 2.2043 | 2.0558 | 1.9210 | 1.8059 | 1.7419 |
| 28 | 4.1960 | 3.3404 | 2.9467 | 2.7141 | 2.5581 | 2.4453 | 2.2913 | 2.1900 | 2.0411 | 1.9057 | 1.7898 | 1.7251 |
| 29 | 4.1830 | 3.3277 | 2.9340 | 2.7014 | 2.5454 | 2.4324 | 2.2782 | 2.1768 | 2.0275 | 1.8915 | 1.7748 | 1.7096 |
| 30 | 4.1709 | 3.3158 | 2.9223 | 2.6896 | 2.5336 | 2.4205 | 2.2662 | 2.1646 | 2.0148 | 1.8782 | 1.7609 | 1.6950 |
| 40 | 4.0847 | 3.2317 | 2.8387 | 2.6060 | 2.4495 | 2.3359 | 2.1802 | 2.0773 | 1.9245 | 1.7835 | 1.6600 | 1.5892 |
| 60 | 4.0012 | 3.1504 | 2.7581 | 2.5252 | 2.3683 | 2.2541 | 2.0970 | 1.9926 | 1.8364 | 1.6902 | 1.5590 | 1.4814 |
| 120 | 3.9201 | 3.0718 | 2.6802 | 2.4472 | 2.2899 | 2.1750 | 2.0164 | 1.9105 | 1.7505 | 1.5980 | 1.4565 | 1.3685 |
| 1000 | 3.8508 | 3.0047 | 2.6138 | 2.3808 | 2.2231 | 2.1076 | 1.9476 | 1.8402 | 1.6764 | 1.5171 | 1.3632 | 1.2596 |

# Distribution of the F-statistic (.01)

| | df for greater mean square | | | | | | | | | | | |
|---|---|---|---|---|---|---|---|---|---|---|---|---|
| df | 1 | 2 | 3 | 4 | 5 | 6 | 8 | 10 | 15 | 25 | 50 | 100 |
| 1 | 4052.2 | 4999.3 | 5403.5 | 5624.3 | 5764.0 | 5859.0 | 5981.0 | 6055.9 | 6157.0 | 6239.9 | 6302.3 | 6333.9 |
| 2 | 98.5019 | 99.0003 | 99.1640 | 99.2513 | 99.3023 | 99.3314 | 99.3750 | 99.3969 | 99.4332 | 99.4587 | 99.4769 | 99.4914 |
| 3 | 34.1161 | 30.8164 | 29.4567 | 28.7100 | 28.2371 | 27.9106 | 27.4895 | 27.2285 | 26.8719 | 26.5791 | 26.3544 | 26.2407 |
| 4 | 21.1976 | 17.9998 | 16.6942 | 15.9771 | 15.5219 | 15.2068 | 14.7988 | 14.5460 | 14.1981 | 13.9107 | 13.6897 | 13.5769 |
| 5 | 16.2581 | 13.2741 | 12.0599 | 11.3919 | 10.9671 | 10.6722 | 10.2893 | 10.0511 | 9.7223 | 9.4492 | 9.2377 | 9.1300 |
| 6 | 13.7452 | 10.9249 | 9.7796 | 9.1484 | 8.7459 | 8.4660 | 8.1017 | 7.8742 | 7.5590 | 7.2960 | 7.0914 | 6.9867 |
| 7 | 12.2463 | 9.5465 | 8.4513 | 7.8467 | 7.4604 | 7.1914 | 6.8401 | 6.6201 | 6.3144 | 6.0579 | 5.8577 | 5.7546 |
| 8 | 11.2586 | 8.6491 | 7.5910 | 7.0061 | 6.6318 | 6.3707 | 6.0288 | 5.8143 | 5.5152 | 5.2631 | 5.0654 | 4.9633 |
| 9 | 10.5615 | 8.0215 | 6.9920 | 6.4221 | 6.0569 | 5.8018 | 5.4671 | 5.2565 | 4.9621 | 4.7130 | 4.5167 | 4.4150 |
| 10 | 10.0442 | 7.5595 | 6.5523 | 5.9944 | 5.6364 | 5.3858 | 5.0567 | 4.8491 | 4.5582 | 4.3111 | 4.1155 | 4.0137 |
| 11 | 9.6461 | 7.2057 | 6.2167 | 5.6683 | 5.3160 | 5.0692 | 4.7445 | 4.5393 | 4.2509 | 4.0051 | 3.8097 | 3.7077 |
| 12 | 9.3303 | 6.9266 | 5.9525 | 5.4119 | 5.0644 | 4.8205 | 4.4994 | 4.2961 | 4.0096 | 3.7647 | 3.5692 | 3.4668 |
| 13 | 9.0738 | 6.7009 | 5.7394 | 5.2053 | 4.8616 | 4.6203 | 4.3021 | 4.1003 | 3.8154 | 3.5710 | 3.3752 | 3.2723 |
| 14 | 8.8617 | 6.5149 | 5.5639 | 5.0354 | 4.6950 | 4.4558 | 4.1400 | 3.9394 | 3.6557 | 3.4116 | 3.2153 | 3.1118 |
| 15 | 8.6832 | 6.3588 | 5.4170 | 4.8932 | 4.5556 | 4.3183 | 4.0044 | 3.8049 | 3.5222 | 3.2782 | 3.0814 | 2.9772 |
| 16 | 8.5309 | 6.2263 | 5.2922 | 4.7726 | 4.4374 | 4.2016 | 3.8896 | 3.6909 | 3.4090 | 3.1650 | 2.9675 | 2.8627 |
| 17 | 8.3998 | 6.1121 | 5.1850 | 4.6689 | 4.3360 | 4.1015 | 3.7909 | 3.5931 | 3.3117 | 3.0676 | 2.8694 | 2.7639 |
| 18 | 8.2855 | 6.0129 | 5.0919 | 4.5790 | 4.2479 | 4.0146 | 3.7054 | 3.5081 | 3.2273 | 2.9831 | 2.7841 | 2.6779 |
| 19 | 8.1850 | 5.9259 | 5.0103 | 4.5002 | 4.1708 | 3.9386 | 3.6305 | 3.4338 | 3.1533 | 2.9089 | 2.7092 | 2.6023 |
| 20 | 8.0960 | 5.8490 | 4.9382 | 4.4307 | 4.1027 | 3.8714 | 3.5644 | 3.3682 | 3.0880 | 2.8434 | 2.6430 | 2.5353 |
| 21 | 8.0166 | 5.7804 | 4.8740 | 4.3688 | 4.0421 | 3.8117 | 3.5056 | 3.3098 | 3.0300 | 2.7850 | 2.5838 | 2.4755 |
| 22 | 7.9453 | 5.7190 | 4.8166 | 4.3134 | 3.9880 | 3.7583 | 3.4530 | 3.2576 | 2.9779 | 2.7328 | 2.5308 | 2.4218 |
| 23 | 7.8811 | 5.6637 | 4.7648 | 4.2635 | 3.9392 | 3.7102 | 3.4057 | 3.2106 | 2.9311 | 2.6857 | 2.4829 | 2.3732 |
| 24 | 7.8229 | 5.6136 | 4.7181 | 4.2185 | 3.8951 | 3.6667 | 3.3629 | 3.1681 | 2.8887 | 2.6430 | 2.4395 | 2.3291 |
| 25 | 7.7698 | 5.5680 | 4.6755 | 4.1774 | 3.8550 | 3.6272 | 3.3239 | 3.1294 | 2.8502 | 2.6041 | 2.3999 | 2.2888 |
| 26 | 7.7213 | 5.5263 | 4.6365 | 4.1400 | 3.8183 | 3.5911 | 3.2884 | 3.0941 | 2.8150 | 2.5686 | 2.3637 | 2.2519 |
| 27 | 7.6767 | 5.4881 | 4.6009 | 4.1056 | 3.7847 | 3.5580 | 3.2558 | 3.0618 | 2.7827 | 2.5360 | 2.3304 | 2.2180 |
| 28 | 7.6357 | 5.4529 | 4.5681 | 4.0740 | 3.7539 | 3.5276 | 3.2259 | 3.0320 | 2.7530 | 2.5060 | 2.2997 | 2.1867 |
| 29 | 7.5977 | 5.4205 | 4.5378 | 4.0449 | 3.7254 | 3.4995 | 3.1982 | 3.0045 | 2.7256 | 2.4783 | 2.2713 | 2.1577 |
| 30 | 7.5624 | 5.3903 | 4.5097 | 4.0179 | 3.6990 | 3.4735 | 3.1726 | 2.9791 | 2.7002 | 2.4526 | 2.2450 | 2.1307 |
| 40 | 7.3142 | 5.1785 | 4.3126 | 3.8283 | 3.5138 | 3.2910 | 2.9930 | 2.8005 | 2.5216 | 2.2714 | 2.0581 | 1.9383 |
| 60 | 7.0771 | 4.9774 | 4.1259 | 3.6491 | 3.3389 | 3.1187 | 2.8233 | 2.6318 | 2.3523 | 2.0984 | 1.8772 | 1.7493 |
| 120 | 6.8509 | 4.7865 | 3.9491 | 3.4795 | 3.1735 | 2.9559 | 2.6629 | 2.4721 | 2.1915 | 1.9325 | 1.7000 | 1.5592 |
| 1000 | 6.6603 | 4.6264 | 3.8012 | 3.3380 | 3.0356 | 2.8200 | 2.5290 | 2.3386 | 2.0565 | 1.7915 | 1.5445 | 1.3835 |

## Distribution of the *t*-statistic

| | Level of significance for one-tailed tests | | | | | |
|---|---|---|---|---|---|---|
| | 0.100 | 0.050 | 0.025 | 0.010 | 0.005 | 0.0005 |
| | Level of significance for two-tailed tests | | | | | |
| df | 0.200 | 0.100 | 0.050 | 0.020 | 0.010 | 0.001 |
| 1 | 3.0777 | 6.3138 | 12.7061 | 31.8202 | 63.6568 | 636.6409 |
| 2 | 1.8856 | 2.9200 | 4.3026 | 6.9646 | 9.9248 | 31.5971 |
| 3 | 1.6377 | 2.3534 | 3.1824 | 4.5407 | 5.8409 | 12.9250 |
| 4 | 1.5332 | 2.1318 | 2.7764 | 3.7470 | 4.6041 | 8.6097 |
| 5 | 1.4759 | 2.0150 | 2.5706 | 3.3649 | 4.0321 | 6.8686 |
| 6 | 1.4398 | 1.9432 | 2.4469 | 3.1427 | 3.7075 | 5.9587 |
| 7 | 1.4149 | 1.8946 | 2.3646 | 2.9980 | 3.4995 | 5.4079 |
| 8 | 1.3968 | 1.8595 | 2.3060 | 2.8965 | 3.3554 | 5.0413 |
| 9 | 1.3830 | 1.8331 | 2.2622 | 2.8214 | 3.2498 | 4.7809 |
| 10 | 1.3722 | 1.8125 | 2.2281 | 2.7638 | 3.1693 | 4.5868 |
| 11 | 1.3634 | 1.7959 | 2.2010 | 2.7181 | 3.1058 | 4.4370 |
| 12 | 1.3562 | 1.7823 | 2.1788 | 2.6810 | 3.0546 | 4.3179 |
| 13 | 1.3502 | 1.7709 | 2.1604 | 2.6503 | 3.0123 | 4.2208 |
| 14 | 1.3450 | 1.7613 | 2.1448 | 2.6245 | 2.9769 | 4.1403 |
| 15 | 1.3406 | 1.7530 | 2.1314 | 2.6025 | 2.9467 | 4.0728 |
| 16 | 1.3368 | 1.7459 | 2.1199 | 2.5835 | 2.9208 | 4.0150 |
| 17 | 1.3334 | 1.7396 | 2.1098 | 2.5669 | 2.8982 | 3.9650 |
| 18 | 1.3304 | 1.7341 | 2.1009 | 2.5524 | 2.8785 | 3.9217 |
| 19 | 1.3277 | 1.7291 | 2.0930 | 2.5395 | 2.8609 | 3.8835 |
| 20 | 1.3253 | 1.7247 | 2.0860 | 2.5280 | 2.8453 | 3.8496 |
| 21 | 1.3232 | 1.7207 | 2.0796 | 2.5176 | 2.8314 | 3.8192 |
| 22 | 1.3212 | 1.7171 | 2.0739 | 2.5083 | 2.8187 | 3.7922 |
| 23 | 1.3195 | 1.7139 | 2.0687 | 2.4999 | 2.8073 | 3.7677 |
| 24 | 1.3178 | 1.7109 | 2.0639 | 2.4922 | 2.7969 | 3.7454 |
| 25 | 1.3163 | 1.7081 | 2.0595 | 2.4851 | 2.7874 | 3.7252 |
| 26 | 1.3150 | 1.7056 | 2.0555 | 2.4786 | 2.7787 | 3.7066 |
| 27 | 1.3137 | 1.7033 | 2.0518 | 2.4727 | 2.7707 | 3.6896 |
| 28 | 1.3125 | 1.7011 | 2.0484 | 2.4671 | 2.7633 | 3.6738 |
| 29 | 1.3114 | 1.6991 | 2.0452 | 2.4620 | 2.7564 | 3.6594 |
| 30 | 1.3104 | 1.6973 | 2.0423 | 2.4573 | 2.7500 | 3.6460 |
| 40 | 1.3031 | 1.6838 | 2.0211 | 2.4233 | 2.7045 | 3.5509 |
| 60 | 1.2958 | 1.6706 | 2.0003 | 2.3901 | 2.6603 | 3.4601 |
| 120 | 1.2886 | 1.6577 | 1.9799 | 2.3578 | 2.6174 | 3.3734 |
| 1000 | 1.2824 | 1.6464 | 1.9623 | 2.3301 | 2.5808 | 3.3003 |

*To determine if your calculated value of t is statistically significant: (1) Determine if you are working with a one-tailed or two-tailed t-test, (2) find the appropriate probability level column, (3) find appropriate df (generally n-1), and then (4) find the critical value in the body of the table. Now, (5) compare your calculated value with the table value above. Your calculated value must be equal to or greater than the table value to be considered statistically significant at the significance level noted above.*

## Critical values of $U$ for the Mann-Whitney test

$p$-value = 0.01 for one-tailed test, 0.02 for two-tailed test

| N1\N2 | 9 | 10 | 11 | 12 | 13 | 14 | 15 | 16 | 17 | 18 | 19 | 20 |
|---|---|---|---|---|---|---|---|---|---|---|---|---|
| 3 | 1 | 1 | 1 | 2 | 2 | 2 | 3 | 3 | 4 | 4 | 4 | 5 |
| 4 | 3 | 3 | 4 | 5 | 5 | 6 | 7 | 7 | 8 | 9 | 9 | 10 |
| 5 | 5 | 6 | 7 | 8 | 9 | 10 | 11 | 12 | 13 | 14 | 15 | 16 |
| 6 | 7 | 8 | 9 | 11 | 12 | 13 | 15 | 16 | 18 | 19 | 20 | 22 |
| 7 | 9 | 11 | 12 | 14 | 16 | 17 | 19 | 21 | 23 | 24 | 26 | 28 |
| 8 | 11 | 13 | 15 | 17 | 20 | 22 | 24 | 26 | 28 | 30 | 32 | 34 |
| 9 | 14 | 16 | 18 | 21 | 23 | 26 | 28 | 31 | 33 | 36 | 38 | 40 |
| 10 | 16 | 19 | 22 | 24 | 27 | 30 | 33 | 36 | 38 | 41 | 44 | 47 |
| 11 | 18 | 22 | 25 | 28 | 31 | 34 | 37 | 41 | 44 | 47 | 50 | 53 |
| 12 | 21 | 24 | 28 | 31 | 35 | 38 | 42 | 46 | 49 | 53 | 56 | 60 |
| 13 | 23 | 27 | 31 | 35 | 39 | 43 | 47 | 51 | 55 | 59 | 63 | 67 |
| 14 | 26 | 30 | 34 | 38 | 43 | 47 | 51 | 56 | 60 | 65 | 69 | 73 |
| 15 | 28 | 33 | 37 | 42 | 47 | 51 | 56 | 61 | 66 | 70 | 75 | 80 |

$p$-value = 0.05 for the one-tailed test, 0.1 for the two-tailed test

| N1 \ N2 | 9 | 10 | 11 | 12 | 13 | 14 | 15 | 16 | 17 | 18 | 19 | 20 |
|---|---|---|---|---|---|---|---|---|---|---|---|---|
| 3 | 3 | 4 | 5 | 5 | 6 | 7 | 7 | 8 | 9 | 9 | 10 | 11 |
| 4 | 6 | 7 | 8 | 9 | 10 | 11 | 12 | 14 | 15 | 16 | 17 | 18 |
| 5 | 9 | 11 | 12 | 13 | 15 | 16 | 18 | 19 | 20 | 22 | 23 | 25 |
| 6 | 12 | 14 | 16 | 17 | 19 | 21 | 23 | 25 | 26 | 28 | 30 | 32 |
| 7 | 15 | 17 | 19 | 21 | 24 | 26 | 28 | 30 | 33 | 35 | 37 | 39 |
| 8 | 18 | 20 | 23 | 26 | 28 | 31 | 33 | 36 | 39 | 41 | 44 | 47 |
| 9 | 21 | 24 | 27 | 30 | 33 | 36 | 39 | 42 | 45 | 48 | 51 | 54 |
| 10 | 24 | 27 | 31 | 34 | 37 | 41 | 44 | 48 | 51 | 55 | 58 | 62 |
| 11 | 27 | 31 | 34 | 38 | 42 | 46 | 50 | 54 | 57 | 61 | 65 | 69 |
| 12 | 30 | 34 | 38 | 42 | 47 | 51 | 55 | 60 | 64 | 68 | 72 | 77 |
| 13 | 33 | 37 | 42 | 47 | 51 | 56 | 61 | 65 | 70 | 75 | 80 | 84 |
| 14 | 36 | 41 | 46 | 51 | 56 | 61 | 66 | 71 | 77 | 82 | 87 | 92 |
| 15 | 39 | 44 | 50 | 55 | 61 | 66 | 72 | 77 | 83 | 88 | 94 | 100 |

*For any N1 and N2 the observed value of U is significant if it is equal to or less than the critical values shown.*

## Distribution of chi square

| | | | | | | | Significance | | | | | | | |
|---|---|---|---|---|---|---|---|---|---|---|---|---|---|---|
| df | 0.99 | 0.98 | 0.95 | 0.9 | 0.8 | 0.7 | 0.5 | 30 | 0.2 | 0.1 | 0.05 | 0.02 | 0.01 | 0.001 |
| 1 | .000 | .001 | .004 | .016 | .064 | .148 | .455 | 1.074 | 1.642 | 2.706 | 3.841 | 5.412 | 6.635 | 10.828 |
| 2 | .020 | .040 | .103 | .211 | .446 | .713 | 1.386 | 2.408 | 3.219 | 4.605 | 5.991 | 7.824 | 9.210 | 13.816 |
| 3 | .115 | .185 | .352 | .584 | 1.005 | 1.424 | 2.366 | 3.665 | 4.642 | 6.251 | 7.815 | 9.837 | 11.345 | 16.266 |
| 4 | .297 | .429 | .711 | 1.064 | 1.649 | 2.195 | 3.357 | 4.878 | 5.989 | 7.779 | 9.488 | 11.668 | 13.277 | 18.467 |
| 5 | .554 | .752 | 1.145 | 1.610 | 2.343 | 3.000 | 4.351 | 6.064 | 7.289 | 9.236 | 11.070 | 13.388 | 15.086 | 20.515 |
| 6 | .872 | 1.134 | 1.635 | 2.204 | 3.070 | 3.828 | 5.348 | 7.231 | 8.558 | 10.645 | 12.592 | 15.033 | 16.812 | 22.458 |
| 7 | 1.239 | 1.564 | 2.167 | 2.833 | 3.822 | 4.671 | 6.346 | 8.383 | 9.803 | 12.017 | 14.067 | 16.622 | 18.475 | 24.322 |
| 8 | 1.646 | 2.032 | 2.733 | 3.490 | 4.594 | 5.527 | 7.344 | 9.524 | 11.030 | 13.362 | 15.507 | 18.168 | 20.090 | 26.124 |
| 9 | 2.088 | 2.532 | 3.325 | 4.168 | 5.380 | 6.393 | 8.343 | 10.656 | 12.242 | 14.684 | 16.919 | 19.679 | 21.666 | 27.877 |
| 10 | 2.558 | 3.059 | 3.940 | 4.865 | 6.179 | 7.267 | 9.342 | 11.781 | 13.442 | 15.987 | 18.307 | 21.161 | 23.209 | 29.588 |
| 11 | 3.053 | 3.609 | 4.575 | 5.578 | 6.989 | 8.148 | 10.341 | 12.899 | 14.631 | 17.275 | 19.675 | 22.618 | 24.725 | 31.264 |
| 12 | 3.571 | 4.178 | 5.226 | 6.304 | 7.807 | 9.034 | 11.340 | 14.011 | 15.812 | 18.549 | 21.026 | 24.054 | 26.217 | 32.909 |
| 13 | 4.107 | 4.765 | 5.892 | 7.042 | 8.634 | 9.926 | 12.340 | 15.119 | 16.985 | 19.812 | 22.362 | 25.472 | 27.688 | 34.528 |
| 14 | 4.660 | 5.368 | 6.571 | 7.790 | 9.467 | 10.821 | 13.339 | 16.222 | 18.151 | 21.064 | 23.685 | 26.873 | 29.141 | 36.123 |
| 15 | 5.229 | 5.985 | 7.261 | 8.547 | 10.307 | 11.721 | 14.339 | 17.322 | 19.311 | 22.307 | 24.996 | 28.259 | 30.578 | 37.697 |
| 16 | 5.812 | 6.614 | 7.962 | 9.312 | 11.152 | 12.624 | 15.338 | 18.418 | 20.465 | 23.542 | 26.296 | 29.633 | 32.000 | 39.252 |
| 17 | 6.408 | 7.255 | 8.672 | 10.085 | 12.002 | 13.531 | 16.338 | 19.511 | 21.615 | 24.769 | 27.587 | 30.995 | 33.409 | 40.790 |
| 18 | 7.015 | 7.906 | 9.390 | 10.865 | 12.857 | 14.440 | 17.338 | 20.601 | 22.760 | 25.989 | 28.869 | 32.346 | 34.805 | 42.312 |
| 19 | 7.633 | 8.567 | 10.117 | 11.651 | 13.716 | 15.352 | 18.338 | 21.689 | 23.900 | 27.204 | 30.144 | 33.687 | 36.191 | 43.820 |
| 20 | 8.260 | 9.237 | 10.851 | 12.443 | 14.578 | 16.266 | 19.337 | 22.775 | 25.038 | 28.412 | 31.410 | 35.020 | 37.566 | 45.315 |
| 21 | 8.897 | 9.915 | 11.591 | 13.240 | 15.445 | 17.182 | 20.337 | 23.858 | 26.171 | 29.615 | 32.671 | 36.343 | 38.932 | 46.797 |
| 22 | 9.542 | 10.600 | 12.338 | 14.041 | 16.314 | 18.101 | 21.337 | 24.939 | 27.301 | 30.813 | 33.924 | 37.659 | 40.289 | 48.268 |
| 23 | 10.196 | 11.293 | 13.091 | 14.848 | 17.187 | 19.021 | 22.337 | 26.018 | 28.429 | 32.007 | 35.172 | 38.968 | 41.638 | 49.728 |
| 24 | 10.856 | 11.992 | 13.848 | 15.659 | 18.062 | 19.943 | 23.337 | 27.096 | 29.553 | 33.196 | 36.415 | 40.270 | 42.980 | 51.179 |
| 25 | 11.524 | 12.697 | 14.611 | 16.473 | 18.940 | 20.867 | 24.337 | 28.172 | 30.675 | 34.382 | 37.652 | 41.566 | 44.314 | 52.620 |
| 26 | 12.198 | 13.409 | 15.379 | 17.292 | 19.820 | 21.792 | 25.336 | 29.246 | 31.795 | 35.563 | 38.885 | 42.856 | 45.642 | 54.052 |
| 27 | 12.879 | 14.125 | 16.151 | 18.114 | 20.703 | 22.719 | 26.336 | 30.319 | 32.912 | 36.741 | 40.113 | 44.140 | 46.963 | 55.476 |
| 28 | 13.565 | 14.847 | 16.928 | 18.939 | 21.588 | 23.647 | 27.336 | 31.391 | 34.027 | 37.916 | 41.337 | 45.419 | 48.278 | 56.892 |
| 29 | 14.256 | 15.574 | 17.708 | 19.768 | 22.475 | 24.577 | 28.336 | 32.461 | 35.139 | 39.087 | 42.557 | 46.693 | 49.588 | 58.301 |
| 30 | 14.953 | 16.306 | 18.493 | 20.599 | 23.364 | 25.508 | 29.336 | 33.530 | 36.250 | 40.256 | 43.773 | 47.962 | 50.892 | 59.703 |

*To determine if your calculated value of chi-square is statistically significant: (1) find the appropriate probability level column, (2) find appropriate df, and then (3) find the critical value in the body of the table. Now, (4) compare your calculated value with the table value above. Your calculated value must be equal to or greater than the table value to be considered statistically significant at the significance level noted above.*

## Critical values of the Pearson product-moment correlation

*If the observed value of r is greater than or equal to the tabled value for the desired level of significance and degrees of freedom (number of pairs of scores minus 2), we conclude that a statistically significant relationship between the variables does exist in the population sampled.*

| df N – 2 | \_Level of significance for a nondirectional (two-tailed) test\_ | | | | |
|---|---|---|---|---|---|
| | 0.10 | 0.05 | 0.02 | 0.01 | 0.001 |
| 1 | 0.9877 | 0.9969 | 0.9995 | 0.9999 | 1.0000 |
| 2 | 0.9000 | 0.9500 | 0.9800 | 0.9900 | 0.9990 |
| 3 | 0.8054 | 0.8783 | 0.9343 | 0.9587 | 0.9912 |
| 4 | 0.7293 | 0.8114 | 0.8822 | 0.9172 | 0.9741 |
| 5 | 0.6694 | 0.7545 | 0.8329 | 0.8745 | 0.9507 |
| 6 | 0.6215 | 0.7067 | 0.7887 | 0.8343 | 0.9249 |
| 7 | 0.5822 | 0.6664 | 0.7498 | 0.7977 | 0.8982 |
| 8 | 0.5494 | 0.6319 | 0.7155 | 0.7646 | 0.8721 |
| 9 | 0.5214 | 0.6021 | 0.6851 | 0.7348 | 0.8471 |
| 10 | 0.4973 | 0.5760 | 0.6581 | 0.7079 | 0.8233 |
| 11 | 0.4762 | 0.5529 | 0.6339 | 0.6835 | 0.8010 |
| 12 | 0.4575 | 0.5324 | 0.6120 | 0.6614 | 0.7800 |
| 13 | 0.4409 | 0.5139 | 0.5923 | 0.6411 | 0.7603 |
| 14 | 0.4259 | 0.4973 | 0.5742 | 0.6226 | 0.7420 |
| 15 | 0.4124 | 0.4821 | 0.5577 | 0.6055 | 0.7246 |
| 16 | 0.4000 | 0.4683 | 0.5425 | 0.5897 | 0.7084 |
| 17 | 0.3887 | 0.4555 | 0.5285 | 0.5751 | 0.6932 |
| 18 | 0.3783 | 0.4438 | 0.5155 | 0.5614 | 0.6787 |
| 19 | 0.3687 | 0.4329 | 0.5034 | 0.5487 | 0.6652 |
| 20 | 0.3598 | 0.4227 | 0.4921 | 0.5368 | 0.6524 |
| 25 | 0.3233 | 0.3809 | 0.4451 | 0.4869 | 0.5974 |
| 30 | 0.2960 | 0.3494 | 0.4093 | 0.4487 | 0.5541 |
| 35 | 0.2746 | 0.3246 | 0.3810 | 0.4182 | 0.5189 |
| 40 | 0.2573 | 0.3044 | 0.3578 | 0.3932 | 0.4896 |
| 45 | 0.2428 | 0.2875 | 0.3384 | 0.3721 | 0.4648 |
| 50 | 0.2306 | 0.2732 | 0.3218 | 0.3541 | 0.4433 |
| 60 | 0.2108 | 0.2500 | 0.2948 | 0.3248 | 0.4078 |
| 70 | 0.1954 | 0.2319 | 0.2737 | 0.3017 | 0.3799 |
| 80 | 0.1829 | 0.2172 | 0.2565 | 0.2830 | 0.3568 |
| 90 | 0.1726 | 0.2050 | 0.2422 | 0.2673 | 0.3375 |
| 100 | 0.1638 | 0.1946 | 0.2301 | 0.2540 | 0.3211 |

## Critical values of the Spearman rank-order correlation

*If the observed value of r is greater than or equal to the tabled value for the desired level of significance and number of pairs, we conclude that a statistically significant relationship between these variables does exist in the population sampled.*

| | Level of significance for two-tailed test | | | |
|---|---|---|---|---|
| N* | 0.10 | 0.05 | 0.02 | 0.01 |
| 5 | 0.900 | 1.000 | 1.000 | – |
| 6 | 0.829 | 0.886 | 0.943 | 1.000 |
| 7 | 0.714 | 0.786 | 0.893 | 0.929 |
| 8 | 0.643 | 0.738 | 0.833 | 0.881 |
| 9 | 0.600 | 0.683 | 0.783 | 0.833 |
| 10 | 0.564 | 0.648 | 0.746 | 0.794 |
| 12 | 0.506 | 0.591 | 0.712 | 0.777 |
| 14 | 0.456 | 0.544 | 0.645 | 0.715 |
| 16 | 0.425 | 0.506 | 0.601 | 0.665 |
| 18 | 0.399 | 0.475 | 0.564 | 0.625 |
| 20 | 0.377 | 0.450 | 0.534 | 0.591 |
| 22 | 0.359 | 0.428 | 0.508 | 0.562 |
| 24 | 0.343 | 0.409 | 0.485 | 0.537 |
| 26 | 0.329 | 0.392 | 0.465 | 0.515 |
| 28 | 0.317 | 0.377 | 0.448 | 0.496 |
| 30 | 0.306 | 0.364 | 0.432 | 0.478 |

*N = number of pairs

# Further reading

Aron, A., Aron, E., & Coups, E. (2008). *Statistics for psychology.* Upper Saddle River, NJ: Prentice Hall.

Baayen, H. (2008). *Analyzing linguistic data: A practical introduction to statistics using R.* Cambridge: Cambridge University Press.

Black, T. (1999). *Doing quantitative research in the social sciences: An integrated approach to research design, measurement and statistics.* Thousand Oaks: Sage Publications.

Blaxter, L., Hughes, C., & Tight, M. (2006). *How to research.* Buckingham: Open University Press.

Booth, W., Colomb, G., & Williams, J. (2008). *The craft of research.* Chicago: University of Chicago Press.

Borenstein, M., Hedges, L., Higgins, J., & Rothstein, H. (2009). *Introduction to meta-analysis.* New York: Wiley.

Borg, W., Gall, M., & Gall, J. (2006). *Educational research: An introduction.* New York: Allyn and Bacon.

Brown, J.D. (1991). *Understanding research in second language learning.* Cambridge: Cambridge University Press.

Brown, J.D. (1992). Statistics as a foreign language. Part 2: More things to look for in reading statistical language studies. *TESOL Quarterly, 26,* 629–664.

Brown, J.D., & Rodgers, T. S. (2003). *Oxford handbooks for language teachers: Doing second language research.* Oxford: Oxford University Press.

Campbell, D., & Stanley, J. (1966). *Experimental and quasi-experimental designs for research.* Chicago: Rand McNally.

Chapelle, C., & Duff, P. (2003). Some guidelines for conducting quantitative and qualitative research in TESOL. *TESOL Quarterly, 26,* 157–178.

Cohen, B. H. (2007). *Explaining psychological statistics.* New Jersey, USA: Wiley.

Cohen, L., Manion, L., & Morrison, K. (2007). *Research methods in education* (6th ed.). New York: Routledge.

Cresswell, J. (2008a). *Research design: Qualitative, quantitative and mixed method approaches.* Thousand Oaks: Sage Publications.

Cresswell, J. (2008b). *Educational research: Planning, conducting, and evaluating quantitative and qualitative research.* New Jersey, USA: Prentice Hall.

Dawson, C. (2009). *Introduction to research methods: A practical guide for anyone undertaking a research project.* Oxford: HowToBooks Ltd.

Dörnyei, Z. (2007). *Research methods in applied linguistics: Quantitative, qualitative, and mixed methodologies.* Oxford: Oxford University Press.

Duff, P. (2007). *Case study research in applied linguistics.* Mahwah, NJ: Lawrence Erlbaum Associates.

Fink, A. (1998). *Conducting research literature reviews: From paper to the internet.* Thousand Oaks: Sage Publications.

Gass, S., Sorace A., & Selinker, L. (1998). *Second language learning data analysis* (2nd ed.). Mahwah, NJ: Lawrence Erlbaum Associates.

Gass, S., & Mackey, A. (2007). *Data elicitation for second and foreign language research.* Mahwah, NJ: Lawrence Erlbaum Associates.

Greene, J., & D'Oliveira, M. (2005). *Learning to use statistical tests in psychology.* Milton Keynes: Open University Press.

Hopkins, D. (2008). *A teacher's guide to classroom research.* Buckingham: Open University Press.

Johnson, K. (2008). *Quantitative methods in linguistics.* Oxford: Blackwell.

Kelly, A. (2008). *Handbook of design research methods in education.* New York: Routledge.

Larson-Hall, J. (2009). *A guide to doing statistical analysis in second language research using SPSS.* New York: Routledge.

Leong, F., & Austin, J. (Eds.). (2005). *The psychology research handbook.* Thousand Oaks: Sage Publications.

Mackey, A., & Gass, S. (2005). *Second language research: Methodology and design.* Mahwah, NJ: Lawrence Erlbaum Associates.

Menn, L., & Ratner, N. B. (2000). *Methods for studying language production.* Mahwah, NJ: Lawrence Erlbaum Associates.

Mitchell, M., & Jolley, J. (2009). *Research design explained (International edition).* Belmont, CA: Wadsworth.

Norris, J. M., & Ortega, L. (2003). Defining and measuring SLA. In C. Doughty, & M.H. Long, (Eds.). *Handbook of second language acquisition* (pp. 716–761). London: Blackwell.

Norris, J. M., & Ortega, L. (Eds.). (2006). *Synthesizing research on language learning and teaching.* Amsterdam: John Benjamins.

Paltridge, B., & Phakiti, A. (2010).*The Continuum companion to research methods in applied linguistics.* London: Continuum.

Perry, F. L. (2005). *Research in applied linguistics: Becoming a discerning consumer.* Mahwah, NJ: Lawrence Erlbaum Associates.

Rasinger, S.M. (1999). *Methods for studying language production.* Mahwah, NJ: Lawrence Erlbaum Associates.

Ridley, D. (2008). *The literature review: A step by step guide for students.* London: SAGE Publication.

Richards, K. (2003). *Qualitative inquiry in TESOL.* London: Palgrave Macmillan.

Rietveld, T., & van Hout, R. (2005). *Statistics in language research: Analysis of variance.* Berlin: Mouton de Gruyter.

Sapsford, R., & Jupp, V. (Eds.). (2006). *Data collection and analysis.* Thousand Oaks: Sage Publications.

Seliger, H., & Shohamy, E. (1989). *Second language research methods.* Oxford: Oxford University Press.

Shaughnessy, J. J. (2008). *Research methods in psychology.* New York: McGraw Hill.

Sheskin, D. (2000). *Handbook of parametric and nonparametric statistical procedures.* Florida: CRC Press.

Silverman, D. (2004). *Doing qualitative research: A practical handbook* (2nd ed.). Thousand Oaks, CA: Sage.

*TESOL Quarterly research guidelines.* (2003). *TESOL Quarterly, 37,* 157–178.

Urdan, T. C. (2001). *Statistics in plain English.* Mahwah, NJ: LEA Publishers.

Wallace, M. (1998). *Action research for language teachers.* Cambridge: Cambridge University Press.

Willis, J. (2007). *Foundations of qualitative research.* Thousand Oaks: Sage Publications.

# Index of main subject entries in textbook

Page numbers with n represent note numbers.

**A**

Abstract (section of paper)
3–8, 12
Alpha (level) 165, 177
see also Probability
Analysis (section of paper)
136–147
Analysis of variance
(ANOVA) 183–194
ANCOVA 193–194
factorial ANOVA 189
interaction effect 110, 127
main effect 127, 187–192
MANOVA 193
one-way ANOVA 51, 183
APA Guidelines 3 N6, 64,
136–138, 154, 157, 210, 213
Assumptions (of statistical
tests) 14, 78, 140–145,
173–174, 193–194, 221
Attenuation, see Correlation
Attrition, see Mortality factors

**B**

Bar graph, see Graphs
Bell-shaped curve, see Normal
distribution
Between-groups designs 70,
110, 139, 141
Bi-modal distribution 159

**C**

Central tendency, see Mean;
Median; Mode
Chi-square test 137, 194–198
cells 198
loglinear analysis 198–199
marginals 196
Yates' correction factor 195
see also Fisher's Exact test
Conclusions (section of
paper) 206–229
Confidence level, see
Significance level
Confounded design 51–52, 114
Construct validity 81–82

Constructs 23, 52–55, 220
Content validity 81
Contingency table 195, 198
Continuous data
measurement 157–159
see also Non-continuous data
measurement
Control (Comparison)
group 70, 73, 98, 110,
112–113, 118–124, 174
Control variable 14
Conversion (of data) 14, 49,
157–158
Correlation
attenuation 169, 171
coefficient 81, 164, 166–171
curvilinear 167
negative 143–144
Pearson 165–168
phi coefficient 197
point biserial 164
positive 168
scatterplot 143–144,
166–167
Spearman 168
Covariate 193
Cramer's V 197
Criterion group 126
Critical value 166, 191
Cultural validity 83

**D**

Degrees of freedom (df)
166, 175
Dependent variable 12, 27,
45–47, 50–51, 111–122,
170–173, 187, 193
Descriptive statistics 138,
157–162, 190–191
see also Inferential statistics
Discussion (section of
paper) 206–229
Dispersion 155, 167, 170
see also Range; Standard
deviation; Variance
"Double-blind" technique 106

**E**

Effect size 164–165, 177, 179–183,
192–193
Eta$^2$ 181, 183 N44
see also Omega$^2$; Strength
of association
Ethical standards in
research 25, 83, 99–104
Experimental designs, see
Ex post facto designs;
Factorial designs;
Pre-experimental designs;
Quasi-experimental
designs; True experimental
designs
Ex post facto designs 110,
125–127
External validity 66, 74–76, 108,
123–125, 216
see also Generalisation;
Internal validity
Extraneous variable 118, 120

**F**

F Distribution 185
F ratio 183–186, 189–190,
183 N44, 197
Face validity 80
Factorial ANOVA 189
Factorial designs 110, 127
see also Factorial ANOVA
Feasibility (of a study) 43
Figures 155, 159, 176
Fisher's Exact test 186–187
see also Chi-square test
Frequency (data) 48, 138,
157–159, 194

**G**

Generalisation 55, 75
Graphs 155, 157

**H**

Hawthorne effect 103
Histogram, see Graphs
History factors 73, 119–123

Hypothesis
    alternative 40
    directional 38–41
    null 39, 40–41 N8, 166, 174,
        164 N37, 179, 186, 195 N46
    positive 39
    testing 38, 168, 178, 195 N46

I

Independent variable 13–14,
    45–47, 51, 111–117, 125,
    127, 170–173, 179–181, 187,
    189–193, 198
Inferential statistics 138–139, 160
    see also Descriptive statistics
Instrumentation factors 122
Intact group 66, 70–71, 103,
    117–118, 142, 145, 159,
    176–177, 211
Internal validity 66, 72–75,
    97–108, 123
    factors affecting 107
    see also External validity;
        History factors;
        Instrumentation
        factors; Maturation
        factors; Mortality factors;
        Selection factors
Interval scale 49–50, 124, 139,
    144, 159, 168
Intervening variable 46 N9,
    50–51
Interview 65, 83, 101–102, 142
Introduction (section of
    paper) 3–61

K

Kendall's tau 168
Kruskal-Wallis test 203
Kuder-Richardson tests 79
Kurtosis 162

L

Level (of a variable) 14,
    46–47, 51, 85, 110–111,
    113–114, 127, 139–140, 187,
    189, 191–192, 195
Likert scale 79
Linearity 143, 155, 169
Literature review, see Review of
    literature
Longitudinal studies 72–73,
    98, 121

M

Matching participants/
    groups 75, 120–121, 124
Materials (section of paper)
    62–93
Maturation factors 72–74,
    119–120, 122–123
Mean 51, 70–71, 120, 138,
    142–143, 159–162, 174
    see also Median; Mode
Meaningfulness 176, 197,
    199–200
Median 71, 138, 159–160
    see also Mean; Mode
Meta-analysis 15, 23, 37, 67,
    181–183
Method (section of paper)
    62–147
Mixed designs 116
Mode 138, 159
    see also Mean; Median
Moderator variable 46 N9, 47,
    50, 127, 187, 193, 197
Mortality factors 72
Multicolinearity 143–144,
    170–171, 173

N

Naturally-occurring
    variable 107
Nominal scale 14, 48, 139,
    157, 168
Non-continuous data
    measurement 157
Non-parametric statistical
    tests 71, 144, 160, 164, 168,
    174, 181
    see also Parametric statistical
        tests
Normal distribution 142, 144,
    159–160, 162, 173–174

O

Observer/scorer bias 65, 103,
    104–106, 141
Omega$^2$ 192, 183 N44
    see also Eta$^2$; Strength of
        association
Operational definitions 39,
    48, 52–55, 66, 81, 83,
    158, 182
Ordinal scale 14, 48–49
Outlier 159, 173, 174

P

Parametric statistical tests 71,
    142, 144, 157, 159, 164, 181
    see also Non-parametric
        statistical tests
Participants (section of
    paper) 62–93
Participant expectancies 103
Participant selection 69, 71, 76,
    165, 182
Percentage 14, 49, 55,
    157–158, 161, 167, 194
Polygon 155, 161
Population 71, 75, 76, 101, 138,
    142, 145
Post-hoc comparison tests 186,
    191, 197
Post-test 70, 96, 98, 119,
    122, 125, 177, 188–189,
    200, 211
Power 71, 144, 171, 181,
    192, 199
Pre-experimental designs 110,
    118–120, 122
Pre-test 70, 96, 98, 117, 119,
    122–125
Prediction 51, 81, 167, 170–171
Predictive validity 81
Probability 124, 165, 172,
    177–178, 196
Probability level, see
    Significance level
Procedures (section of
    paper) 94–135

Q

Quasi-experimental designs 28,
    37, 40, 64, 66, 74, 110,
    116–117, 119–124, 126,
    138, 142

R

Randomisation 75, 120, 122
Range 160
Rank order 49, 160
Rate (data measurement) 47, 81,
    123, 158, 186
Regression
    linear 170, 172
    logistic regression 172–173
    multiple 170–173, 187
Regression line 167–168, 170
Regression to the mean 70, 120

Reliability
  coefficient  79–80, 169
  inter-rater  79
  split-half/
    Kuder-Richardson  79
  test-retest  79
Repeated measures designs  98,
  110, 112–113, 139, 141, 164,
  185–186, 192
Replication (research)  15, 22,
  25, 37, 40, 42, 53, 64–68, 76,
  96, 99, 107, 115, 118, 126, 158,
  177–178, 214
Research question
  (section of paper)  36–61
Results (section of paper)
  148–205
Review of literature (section of
  paper)  20–35

**S**
Sampling  69 N14, 75, 165, 179
Scheffé's test  187
Significance of a study, *see*
  Meaningfulness
Significance level  145, 163,
  165–166, 171, 173, 177, 179,
  185, 198, 221

Skewness (distribution)
  143, 159
Slope  167, 170
Split-half reliability  79
Standard deviation (s.d.)  51,
  71, 138, 142, 160–162, 174,
  179, 188
Standard error of estimate
  (SEE)  167
Stratified sampling  75
Strength of association  179,
  181, 192
  *see also* Eta$^2$; Omega$^2$

**T**
Tables  51, 154, 165–166, 171
Test/practice effect  97–98
Test reliability, *see*
  Kuder-Richardson tests;
  Split-half reliability;
  Test-retest reliability
Test-retest reliability  79
Time-series designs  121
True experimental designs  66,
  75, 117–118, 123–125
*t*-test  14, 140, 173–177,
  180–181
Tukey test  186–187

Type 1 error  113, 174, 180, 183,
  186–187, 193
Type 2 error  113, 174, 180

**V**
Validity, *see* Content validity;
  Construct validity, Cultural
  validity; External validity;
  Face validity; Internal
  validity; Predictive validity
Variables, *see* Control variable;
  Dependent variable;
  Extraneous variable;
  Independent variable;
  Intervening variable;
  Moderator variable;
  Naturally-occurring
  variable
Variability  71, 138, 142, 144,
  157–158, 160–162, 181,
  183, 191
Variance *see also* Analysis
  of variance  71, 138, 143,
  160, 166–167, 171–173

**W**
Within-group designs, *see*
  Repeated measures designs

In the series *Language Learning & Language Teaching* the following titles have been published thus far or are scheduled for publication:

29   VERSPOOR, Marjolijn H., Kees de BOT and Wander LOWIE (eds.): A Dynamic Approach to Second Language Development. Methods and techniques. *Expected January 2011*

28   PORTE, Graeme Keith: Appraising Research in Second Language Learning. A practical approach to critical analysis of quantitative research. **Second edition.** 2010. xxv, 307 pp.

27   BLOM, Elma and Sharon UNSWORTH (eds.): Experimental Methods in Language Acquisition Research. vii, 292 pp. *Expected October 2010*

26   MARTÍNEZ-FLOR, Alicia and Esther USÓ-JUAN (eds.): Speech Act Performance. Theoretical, empirical and methodological issues. 2010. xiv, 277 pp.

25   ABRAHAM, Lee B. and Lawrence WILLIAMS (eds.): Electronic Discourse in Language Learning and Language Teaching. 2009. x, 346 pp.

24   MEARA, Paul: Connected Words. Word associations and second language vocabulary acquisition. 2009. xvii, 174 pp.

23   PHILP, Jenefer, Rhonda OLIVER and Alison MACKEY (eds.): Second Language Acquisition and the Younger Learner. Child's play? 2008. viii, 334 pp.

22   EAST, Martin: Dictionary Use in Foreign Language Writing Exams. Impact and implications. 2008. xiii, 228 pp.

21   AYOUN, Dalila (ed.): Studies in French Applied Linguistics. 2008. xiii, 400 pp.

20   DALTON-PUFFER, Christiane: Discourse in *Content and Language Integrated Learning* (CLIL) Classrooms. 2007. xii, 330 pp.

19   RANDALL, Mick: Memory, Psychology and Second Language Learning. 2007. x, 220 pp.

18   LYSTER, Roy: Learning and Teaching Languages Through Content. A counterbalanced approach. 2007. xii, 173 pp.

17   BOHN, Ocke-Schwen and Murray J. MUNRO (eds.): Language Experience in Second Language Speech Learning. In honor of James Emil Flege. 2007. xvii, 406 pp.

16   AYOUN, Dalila (ed.): French Applied Linguistics. 2007. xvi, 560 pp.

15   CUMMING, Alister (ed.): Goals for Academic Writing. ESL students and their instructors. 2006. xii, 204 pp.

14   HUBBARD, Philip and Mike LEVY (eds.): Teacher Education in CALL. 2006. xii, 354 pp.

13   NORRIS, John M. and Lourdes ORTEGA (eds.): Synthesizing Research on Language Learning and Teaching. 2006. xiv, 350 pp.

12   CHALHOUB-DEVILLE, Micheline, Carol A. CHAPELLE and Patricia A. DUFF (eds.): Inference and Generalizability in Applied Linguistics. Multiple perspectives. 2006. vi, 248 pp.

11   ELLIS, Rod (ed.): Planning and Task Performance in a Second Language. 2005. viii, 313 pp.

10   BOGAARDS, Paul and Batia LAUFER (eds.): Vocabulary in a Second Language. Selection, acquisition, and testing. 2004. xiv, 234 pp.

9    SCHMITT, Norbert (ed.): Formulaic Sequences. Acquisition, processing and use. 2004. x, 304 pp.

8    JORDAN, Geoff: Theory Construction in Second Language Acquisition. 2004. xviii, 295 pp.

7    CHAPELLE, Carol A.: English Language Learning and Technology. Lectures on applied linguistics in the age of information and communication technology. 2003. xvi, 213 pp.

6    GRANGER, Sylviane, Joseph HUNG and Stephanie PETCH-TYSON (eds.): Computer Learner Corpora, Second Language Acquisition and Foreign Language Teaching. 2002. x, 246 pp.

5    GASS, Susan M., Kathleen BARDOVI-HARLIG, Sally Sieloff MAGNAN and Joel WALZ (eds.): Pedagogical Norms for Second and Foreign Language Learning and Teaching. Studies in honour of Albert Valdman. 2002. vi, 305 pp.

4    TRAPPES-LOMAX, Hugh and Gibson FERGUSON (eds.): Language in Language Teacher Education. 2002. vi, 258 pp.

3 (1st) PORTE, Graeme Keith: Appraising Research in Second Language Learning. A practical approach to critical analysis of quantitative research. 2002. xx, 268 pp.

2    ROBINSON, Peter (ed.): Individual Differences and Instructed Language Learning. 2002. xii, 387 pp.

1    CHUN, Dorothy M.: Discourse Intonation in L2. From theory and research to practice. 2002. xviii, 285 pp. (incl. CD-rom).